SMOKE AND FIRE
The Chinese in Montreal

SMOKE AND FIRE
The Chinese in Montreal

Chan Kwok Bun

The Chinese University Press

© The Chinese University of Hong Kong, 1991

All Rights Reserved. No part of this publication may
be reproduced or transmitted in any form or by any
means, electronic or mechanical, including photocopy,
recording, or any information storage and retrieval
system, without permission in writing from
The Chinese University of Hong Kong

ISBN 962–201–461–5

THE CHINESE UNIVERSITY PRESS
The Chinese University of Hong Kong
SHATIN, N. T., HONG KONG

Printed in Hong Kong by Ko's Arts Printing Co., Ltd.

To Kate 淑懿, Nin 寧, and Yoan 融

Contents

Acknowledgements ix
Foreword by Professor Wang Gungwu xiii
Introduction 1
  1. The Chinese Are Coming 3
  2. Women without Men 21
  3. Ten Women 37
  4. A Private Man 83
  5. Uncle Jack, a Moral Entrepreneur 107
  6. Walking on Two Legs 153
  7. In Lieu of Family 175
  8. After the War 213
  9. Will You Provide for Me When I Am Old? 235
 10. Remembering the Mekong River 249
 11. Boat People Getting Organized and Keeping Distance .. 265
 12. A Sore on the Mouse's Tail 291
Conclusion 311
Bibliography 323
Index 331

Acknowledgements

MUCH of the fieldwork in Montreal's Chinese community undertaken for this study was funded by Shell Oil, Canada, through a block grant awarded to Concordia University's Oral History-Montreal Studies Program. This resulted in hundreds of pages of oral history interview transcripts with elderly women and men in Montreal Chinatown, which formed the basis of Chapters 3, 4, 5 and 9, as well as much of the inspiration for writing the rest of the book. In retrospect, intimate, personal accounts of life histories have proven exceptionally invaluable in my analysis and interpretation of ethnic social history. Copies of the transcripts titled *Oral History of the Montreal Chinese Community* are now with Concordia University Library's Non-Print Unit and The Public Archives of Canada in Ottawa.

Chapters 1, 2, 6, 7 and 8 were written as part of a series of ethnic minorities history reports commissioned by the Quebec government's Ministère des Communautés culturelles et de l'Immigration. The series was administered by the Institut Québécois de Recherche sur la Culture (IQRC). I would like to thank, specifically, Gilles Deschamps at the Ministry and Gary Caldwell, Pierre Anctil and Denise Helly at the Institut for making available various data for my analysis.

During the initial phases of my fieldwork in the Montreal Chinese community, I also received grants from the Canadian Federal Government's Multiculturalism Directorate (Montreal), as well as Canada Council (Explorations Program), much of which was used to hire photographers to produce a visual account and portrait of the community. A collection of over 100 photographs now deposited at the Montreal Chinese Community United Centre was displayed in several major exhibitions. The visual images in this book are works of well-known Quebec photographers Marik Boudreau, Gilbert Duclos, Suzanne Girard, Jack Goldsmith, and Claire Beaugrand-

Champagne. As friends, they stuck with me through many trying moments. As professionals, they strived to balance artistry and objectivity, a goal of immense importance in photojournalism. The Archival photographs are courtesy of the Notman Photographic Archives, McCord Museum, McGill University (Montreal, Canada).

My wife, Kate (王淑懿), helped in sharing part of the oral history interviews. Grace Wong joined the project mid-way as a research assistant, helping in transcribing and translating reels and reels of tapes (many interviews were conducted in Taishanese (台山話), then translated into English).

I should also thank IQRC and, in particular, Denise Helly, my long time intellectual friend and partner, for trusting and allowing me to use freely and translate her *Les Chinois à Montréal 1877–1951*, then in rough, manuscript form. Brenda MacDonald took on the unenviable and laborious task of translating the manuscript. She later doubled up, together with Agie Jacob, to edit parts of the transcripts. Brenda and I spent numerous hours in Montreal's many cosy cafes discussing and debating Helly's manuscript and the life histories of the Cantonese immigrants. Claire Zhang helped in re-organizing the older versions of Chapters 3, 4 and 5, contributed to the analysis and interpretation of some oral history materials, and graciously proofread the entire manuscript twice.

Parts of Chapters 9, 10 and 12 were originally published in *Canadian Ethnic Studies* (University of Calgary, Canada), Vol. XV: 3, (1983); Vol. XV: 1, (1983); and Vol. XVIII: 2, (1986) respectively. Chapter 11 is an updated version of Chapter 7 in *Ten Years Later: Indochinese Communities in Canada*, edited by Louis Jacques Dorais, Chan Kwok Bun and Doreen M. Indra (Montreal: Canadian Asian Studies Association, 1988). Part of the Conclusion Chapter was an adaptation of a paper entitled "Coping with Racism: A Century of the Chinese Experience in Canada." Denise Helly and I co-wrote the paper and published it as an introduction to *Coping with Racism: The Chinese Experience in Canada*, which was a special issue of the *Canadian Ethnic Studies* (Vol. XIX: 3, 1987). I would like to thank Professor James Frideres, Editor of the *Canadian Ethnic Studies* and the Canadian Asian Studies Association for allowing me to use their copyrighted materials in this book. On the basis of a review by a referee of The Chinese University Press, for whom I remain deeply indebted, I wrote the Conclusion and revised substantially Chapters 3, 4, 5 and 11 while I was a Visiting Scholar at the Centre of Asian Studies, University of Hong Kong,

Acknowledgements

in May–June 1989. In June 1990, I returned to the Centre to do fieldwork on Hong Kong's Vietnamese boat people. While there, I went through the entire set of galleys of this book. I would like to thank Professor Edward Chen (陳坤耀), the Centre's Director, and Dr. Coonoor Kripalani-Thadani for so kindly giving me access to the Centre's facilities and an office, thus the much needed quietness and tranquility to write.

I must also register my gratitude to Diane Moffat, who over the years typed the many drafts of this manuscript, and to Jorah Mohamed and Vanaja Thangaraju, both secretaries of the Department of Sociology, National University of Singapore, who took turns to word-process the manuscript during its final stages.

Lastly, I want to reserve my deepest gratitude to my very respectable elders in the Montreal Chinatown who have so kindly shared their life histories with me. Some even agreed to pose for my photographers! (I was once told by my Taishanese friend that some older Chinese dislike being photographed, fearing their spirit and soul being captured in the process. My father often told me while I was growing up as a kid not to allow strangers to take photographs of me for fear of being kidnapped and sold as a coolie or recruited into street gangs.) I cannot rightly call Messrs. Jack Huang, Jack Liang and Arthur Li, Mrs. Cai, Mrs. Fang, or any of the dozens of elderly women I spoke with, my informants or respondents in the way fieldworkers normally intend these words to be understood. They are the elders, the forebears of history, the "sacred" storytellers. For that, I remain grateful forever.

Jack Huang passed away in 1985, less than four years after I did the series of interviews with him at the headquarters of the Chinese Freemasons on St. Laurent Boulevard. Jack Liang was pale and frail at the time of the interviews in 1985; he passed away in 1988. The two dozens or so elderly women are quickly approaching their eighties and nineties: Mrs. Fang was 99 years old when she spoke with me; she passed away in 1985. At least two other women passed away since I left Quebec to take up my teaching appointment at the National University of Singapore in 1987.

Chan Kwok Bun
January 1991, Singapore

Foreword

THE growing interest in the study of the Chinese and the descendants of Chinese living outside China has unearthed new data and stimulated sophisticated research in all continents. This is particularly true of countries where Chinese have lived in small numbers for two generations or more without attracting any attention in the past. Today, the fascination with the achievements of the peoples of East Asia, especially after they migrated to North America, has led to dozens of new studies. Dr. Chan Kwok Bun's work on the Chinese in Montreal from the mid-nineteenth century to the present is a valuable addition to that list.

It is not a work of history. Much of that has already been done by Denise Helly in 1987, in her book *Les Chinois à Montréal 1877–1951*. What distinguished Dr. Chan's work is his success in collecting oral history materials through interviewing old residents of Montreal's Chinatown. As a well-trained sociologist, he has used a direct approach to the early migrants to this part of Canada. They were so small in number and so isolated compared to the larger communities of British Columbia and Ontario that they were neglected and, thus, suffered experiences unlike those of most Chinese migrants elsewhere. Letting them tell their own stories, however fragmented and imperfect, has provided us with new insights into the way ordinary men and women with little education, or none at all, survived and, in many cases, adapted to alien conditions not the least like the villages and towns they had come from. Their stories are somewhat thin and repetitive, but perhaps because they seem at times so threadbare, they are all the more moving.

Another distinctive feature of Dr. Chan's book is the way he has brought the memories of old Chinese who had mainly come direct from China together with descriptions of the new adjustment problems of recent refugees from Vietnam who are of Chinese descent. There are some similarities, but the differences are far more important. The settlement of Chinese-Vietnamese refugees, of course, is still too recent for anyone to offer close analysis or to make useful comparison with earlier patterns of settlements. Nevertheless, the juxtaposition of the two is refreshing and most interesting and should stimulate future research. And when more data have been gathered and organized about the Sino-Vietnamese migrants in Montreal in time to come, Dr. Chan's work will be recognized as the pioneer study that it is. Indeed, if the task of monitoring new refugees is done elsewhere together with the stories of older Chinese migrations, the comparative studies should be particularly valuable to all those concerned with Chinese and migration studies.

Wang Gungwu
December 1989, Hong Kong

Introduction

THIS book is intended to be a study of the experience of the Chinese with racism in Montreal, Quebec, Canada. It begins with the arrival of the first batch of largely illiterate Cantonese labourers in Victoria, British Columbia in the 1850s and continues on to the late 1970s and 1980s in Montreal which, like other major Canadian cities, saw the influx of two diametrically different groups of Chinese: refugees from Indo-China and economic migrants mainly from Hong Kong and other parts of Asia. As such, the study spans over more than a century, thus chronicling a series of disparate events and social phenomena: socio-economic and political circumstances surrounding the departure of Cantonese male migrants from Guangdong to North America; extended separation between husbands (in Canada) and wives (in China) and its implications and consequences for the people involved and for community organization dynamics; systemic institutional racism against the Chinese (imposition of head tax on the Chinese upon entry into Canada, the Chinese Exclusion Act, prohibition from voting and preclusion from electoral lists, prohibition from admission into professional schools, etc.); confinement of the Chinese labourers to two service trades: the laundry and restaurant business; the establishment of family and clan associations across Canada as "surrogate" or "substitute" families; demographic consequences (e.g., delay in birth of the second generation) of the state prohibiting entry of Chinese women into Canada and the unbalanced sex ratio in the Chinese communities. Sino-Indochinese refugees and economic investors from Hong Kong as two groups of newcomers to the Chinese community, the later being lured to Canada by federal and provincial government officials; urban encroachment by all three levels of governments on Montreal's Chinatown, thus plunging an ethnic urban space into a crisis threatening its survival.

On a personal and more intimate level, this study, using oral history and in-depth interview materials, probes the lives of Cantonese men and women, documenting the costs of racism and segregation for the individuals on one hand, and their strategies of adapting and coping on the other hand. As such, the study examines the intricate linkage between personal troubles and public issues,[1] while never for a moment forgetting the important fact that the burden, in the final analysis, rests on the individuals; the person must strive to make the best of the circumstances.

Any study of the Chinese experience in Canada and in Montreal is by necessity a study of racism. I intend to argue that the kind of racism the Chinese in Montreal have been subjected to is a systemic, institutional, collective one, a kind that has gone beyond the trivial fact of one person ill-treating another person. After documenting this phenomenon, the sociologist continues to be fascinated with how a Cantonese laundryman manages and negotiates his life. Or, in other words, how he and thousands of Cantonese men and women adapt and survive. Understood in that sense, the book simply intends to tell a story of human survival.

The Chinese used to say, "Where there is smoke and fire, there is a Chinese." For generations, the Cantonese in Montreal never for a moment forgot their ancestors: they burnt incense, joss-sticks and paper money to feed those in the other world. For decades, they were confined to only two ways of making a living: washing laundry and cooking Chinese food. In both situations, much wood or charcoal was burnt, evoking images of smoke and fire, steam and sweat, and, thus, the title of this book.

Note

1. C. Wright Mills, *The Sociological Imagination* (Oxford: Oxford University Press, 1959), p. 8.

1. The Chinese Are Coming

Archival portraits of the Chinese in Montreal, circa 1896–1913. Most probably of the merchant class. Only those who were well-off could bring their families along from China to Montreal.

Archival portraits of the Chinese in Montreal, circa 1896–1913.

1. The Chinese Are Coming

ANYONE taking a casual interest in the history of China is familiar with the famous Chinese expression "*nei-luan wai-huan*" 內亂外患, or domestic disorder and foreign invasion. This expression seems to sum up best the social, political and economic turmoil underlying the transition between dynasties from ancient times. The coincidence of foreign invasion and the inability of the dynasty to govern, the "simultaneous appearance of strong barbarians on the borders and domestic unrest," not only constitute the classic problem *par excellence* of the Chinese empire for centuries, but is also a particularly apt description of the currents of social change in China in the mid-eighteenth century. China was a country in turmoil, the crumbling Qing Dynasty (1644–1911) was not able to hold itself together, a nation was quickly disintegrating, the dynasty was on the verge of collapse.

The First Opium War in 1840–1842 第一次鴉片戰爭 between Great Britain and China marks the beginning of foreign invasion into old China as well as the unfolding of a new chapter of the history of modern China. A war was started by a European imperialist power that was intent on forcibly "opening up" China in an attempt to create trade markets in selected strategic Chinese sea ports and to harvest the hitherto untapped natural and economic resources of China. China was a feudal society before the Opium War. With the monopoly of the majority of arable land by a few landlords, the peasants, for generations after generations, laboured in small patches of leased land in village units using simple and primitive farming equipment as the only available means of production. Much of what was produced from such intensive "tilling of the soil" was paid back as land rental to their landlords in addition to various taxes paid to the government, thus forcing the peasantry into generations of seemingly endless debts. Such a peasant economy made the upgrading of farming technology and mass production of agricultural produce virtually impossible and resulted in a perpetual "scarcity" economy.

From the Ming Dynasty (1368–1644) to the Qing Dynasty before the eruption of the First Opium War, one witnessed the emergence of a small range of industries, notably iron refineries, the manufacturing of potteries, tea and textiles, an industrial development nevertheless considerably stifled by the cumbersome bureaucracy of the Chinese government. Consequently, the economy of pre-modern China was essentially a natural, scarcity economy made up of petty peasantry and home-based, manually operated industries. It was under these economic circumstances that foreign imperialism forced its entry into an industrially undeveloped nation.

With an economy founded on feudalism, the Qing government resorted exclusively to autocratic dictatorship and oppression in governing. The increasing political corruption of the governmental bureaucracy worsened the oppression and exploitation of the Chinese people, thus accelerating the growth of a glaring contradiction between the extravagance of those who governed and the hopelessness of the governed. It was this structural contradiction that was the background of a series of peasant-led rebellions and revolts.

When old China was still very much a traditional society operating out of a feudal economy, superpowers in Europe and America were coming out of industrial revolution. With the mechanization of the means of production and the resultant economic goods, industrial entrepreneurs in England, France and the United States were quickly commanding strategically advantageous and influential positions in the political machineries of their respective governments. China, with its huge population and largely untapped natural resources, became an easy prey to expansionist imperialism. Frustrated by persistent attempts on the part of the Qing government to prohibit the importation of consumer goods into China, the British brought in opium. Between 1801 and 1839, the enormity of the opium trade resulted in a severe outflow of silver from China as exchange goods. The simultaneous doubling of the value of silver and the drastic depreciation of the Chinese currency drove the peasants to the brink of abject poverty. Agricultural produce was sold below cost. Sons and daughters were sold to pay back debts and taxes. Land was mortgaged to landlords. With the eventual infiltration of opium into the poor masses, the rate of agricultural production shrunk, thus heralding the collapse of the Chinese economy and Chinese society.

When Lin Zexu 林則徐 (1785–1850), appointed by the Qing emperor to investigate and prohibit opium trade in Guangzhou 廣州, ordered the confiscation, and later, the burning in public of opium for twenty-four days on the beach of Hu Men 虎門 in 1839, the British troops decided the time was right to retaliate by military force. The Chinese were quickly defeated in this war, and, on 29 August 1842, on board a British warship off Nanking 南京, the Qing government signed the first "unequal treaty" 不平等條約 in the modern history of China—The Nanking Treaty 南京條約 (29 August 1842).

China's defeat in the First Opium War and the resultant Nanking Treaty severely undermined the autonomy of the Qing government. More opium was brought into the country, shaking the foundation of a self-sufficient economy. China was on the verge of being colonized by the Europeans and the Americans. The burden of indemnities to foreign military powers was quickly shifted by the Qing government to its people in the form of increased taxes, driving millions of peasants below the subsistence level of existence. It was this background of social and economic hardships and suffering that gave rise to about one hundred local uprisings and revolts among the peasants between 1843 and 1850, culminating in the Tai Ping Rebellion 太平天國之亂 (1851–1864), a massive, anti-feudal, anti-imperialist, peasant-led movement of the largest scale in the history of China. Led by Hong Xiuquan 洪秀全 (1814–1864), who established the Tai Ping Heavenly Kingdom in 1851, the Tai Ping Rebellion spanned fourteen years affecting more than half of the entire territory of China. With its members mainly consisting of secret party workers, miners, peasants, transportation workers, and the unemployed who were recruits from the lower echelon of a rapidly disintegrating society, the Rebellion was a threat to the dictatorial and feudalist regime of the Qing government.

In 1856, the British troops joined forces with the French in their invasion of China in the Second Opium War, which left the Qing government with no choice but to sign the Tianjin Treaty 天津條約 (26 June 1858) and Peking Treaty 北京條約 (24 October 1860). By this time, the entire territory of China was opened up for trade; the trading of opium was legalized; Chinese indentured workers were bought and sold for labour overseas; local government-imposed taxes on consumer goods were abolished; foreign ambassadors were allowed to set up their offices and quarters in Beijing; and Catholic missionaries were free to reach inland to set up their evangelical network. China continued to be subjected to colonization and, in the meantime, quickly abdicated its political, military, cultural and economic rights to self-government. One witnessed the immediate proliferation of "nations within a nation".

With the financial and military assistance of the British, French and the Americans who were handicapped in their trade with a nation in turmoil with revolts and riots, the Qing government upgraded its suppression of the Rebellion. The death of Hong Xiuquan in 1864 was quickly followed by the complete defeat of the Tai Ping troops, and subsequently, the collapse of the Tai Ping Heavenly Kingdom.

While the Western powers continued their political, military and economic invasion of China, Japan, after years of industrial and economic growth, was emerging as a major military force in the East. For the Japanese, an expansionist foreign policy and an imperialist military strategy made their invasion of neighbouring countries like Korea and China inevitable. In 1894, the Japanese initiated the Sino-Japanese War (甲午戰爭, 1894–1895), a war preceded by a series of military attacks on Korea. The Chinese lost the war and the Qing government was coerced into signing the Ma Guan Treaty 馬關條約 (17 April 1895) in which the Japanese, among others, acquired rights of ownership of the Liao Dong Peninsula 遼東半島, Taiwan and its many affiliated islands as well as permission to set up factories in inland China, along with receipt of heavy indemnities from the Chinese government. The signing of the Ma Guan Treaty had, thus, hastened the process of foreign invasion and ushered China into a new era: foreign superpowers rivalled each other for spheres of ownership and authority in China. By 1898, agreement was reached between the Chinese Government and the foreign military powers that the territory north of the Great Wall belonged to the Soviets while the British ruled over the Yangzi River Valley 揚子江; the Germans, the province of Shandong 山東; the French and the British, the provinces of Yunnan 雲南, Guangdong 廣東 and Guangxi 廣西; and the Japanese, Fujian province 福建省. China was sliced up "like a melon", an imagery once again evoking strong sentiments of anti-imperialism. The contradiction between the discontent of the Chinese people and the forces of imperialism and economic invasion was further intensified, thus bringing the spirit of revolt to another apex.

Since the Sino-Japanese War in 1894, the Western military forces stationed in China competed among one another in the construction of railroads, the taking over of major mines, farmland and houses, and in the destruction of waterways. Tens of thousands of peasants were driven away from their families and villages and became bandits and vagabonds. Imported foreign goods continued to flood local markets, causing the total bankruptcy of the villages as basic production units. Those who made their living by working in, or owning, family-based, manual manufacturing fared no better. Many closed shops and lost their ability to subsist. The Qing government continued to levy heavy taxes on its people to generate additional revenues to pay back foreign loans and indemnities. The inability of the Qing government to govern was further evidenced by its lack of diligence in doing repairs and preventive work along the banks of the Huanghe 黃河. From 1898, Shandong province was inundated by major floods almost every other year, causing the deaths of tens of thousands. It was reported that the peasants began eating "skin of trees and roots of grass"

1. The Chinese Are Coming

while children were bought and sold as cheap child labour or serfs.

The eruption of the Boxers Uprising (義和團之亂) in 1900 signified an outburst of the increasingly heightened and intensified sentiment of the people in reaction to a corrupt and helpless Qing government and, perhaps more significantly, to the seemingly endless infiltration of foreign imperialism. There was also an added religious dimension to the Uprising. Between the latter half of the nineteenth century and the turn of the twentieth century, missionaries had their network of religious institutions well established throughout China, thus ushering in a new era of religious oppression and exploitation. Missionaries forcibly took over the ownership of farmland and other properties, resulting in numerous litigation cases which were oftentimes solved by the partial backing of the missionaries by the Qing government. To a large extent, the Boxer Uprising was a struggle of the Chinese people against religious oppression.

In July 1900, the allied forces of eight foreign powers (British, French, American, German, Russian, Japanese, Italian and Austrian) began its attack of Beijing (八國聯軍入京). In August, the conquest of Beijing by the allied forces resulted in the massive slaughtering of thousands of people, the burning of houses, and the pirating or destruction of cultural treasures and artifacts. In 1901, the Qing government signed the Xin Chou Treaty 辛丑條約 (7 September) with eleven countries (the original eight countries of the allied forces along with Belgium, Spain and Holland), resulting in yet more indemnities and the stationing of more foreign troops and embassies in China. China became a half-colonized country, a "nation of nations" who were free to establish and impose their own laws and policies on China. By 1911, Taiwan, Hong Kong and the northeast territory of China were already conceded to the foreigners while Macao and Kowloon were forcibly loaned out. Eighty-two trading ports were opened up and "special territories" were set up in sixteen Chinese cities. With increasing foreign investment, about 80–90% of heavy industries, transportation and communications, as well as consumer goods markets in China, were monopolized by foreign investors. While desperately clinging to the external façade of a kingdom, China was helpless in fighting the inevitable fate of colonization.

The miseries of nineteenth-century China were perhaps as much a consequence of misgovernment as of an increasing disproportion between population and economic resources. The intense discontent of the common people underlying the many revolts and disorders culminating in the Tai Ping Rebellion, the greatest civil war in human history, was partly caused by the emergence of a demographic crisis besieging a country with increasing population pressure on the one hand, and rapid depletion of resources on the other. It was reported that many local histories of Henan 河南 and Jiangxi 江西 provinces at the time suggested that "by the first half of the nineteenth century, the urgent problem was no longer how to maintain customary living standards, but how to maintain bare subsistence."[1] Reports of soil erosion, major local floods and diminishing agricultural returns in the areas of Yangzi highlands and the Han River 漢水 were bountiful. Highly vulnerable economically as a nation, China relied, ironically, on natural disasters, man-made disorders and revolts in readjusting population and resources. By 1850, the demographic effects of population pressure were so debilitating that even the successive Tai Ping Rebellion and Nien wars (捻與天地會之亂) were not able to counteract them, other than providing a temporary relief. Throughout modern times, the absence of a major technological change to stimulate a hitherto stagnant land economy resulted in a population reaching about 400 million in 1850 and an increasingly impoverished nation. A modern Chinese historian, Ho Ping-ti 何炳棣, made the following conclusive observation:

> All in all, therefore, the combined economic and political condition in post-1850 China was such that the nation seems to have barely managed to feed more mouths at the expense of further deterioration of its living standard...The great social upheavals of the third quarter of the nineteenth century gave China a breathing spell to make some regional economic readjustments, but the basic population-land relation in the country as a whole remained little changed.[2]

With the somewhat more rapid growth of population in the South of China, writers of local histories, testifying to the ill-effects of overpopulation and impoverishment, were themselves southerners giving personal, first-hand accounts of a demographic crisis that left the southern provinces of China particularly hard hit. With the exhaustion of the "resources of Heaven and Earth", there was not enough for everybody. Extensive inter-regional migrations in search of subsistence living were of no avail. In the words of Gong Zizhen 龔自珍 (1792–1841) in 1820, "the provinces are at the threshold of a convulsion which is not a matter of years but a matter of days and months."[3]

While rural impoverishment caused massive inter-regional migrations and population displacement, poor harvests and increased taxes, regular occurrences during the fading years of the Qing monarchy, forced small landowners to sell their plots, often at low prices, in order to pay debts and

1. The Chinese Are Coming

to survive, thus ushering in the emergence of absentee landlordism, a decrease in land price during the early twentieth century and the rise of agricultural prices. These changes brought in a novel rural oligarchy in various regions, as well as a category of tenant-farmers who themselves owned little or no land at all.

The gradual impoverishment of a majority of peasants dispossessed of their lands, constrained to cultivating insufficient plots by the caprices of partitioning, burned by increases in rent and taxes, and no longer allowed to make up for deficits with their own handicrafts, seemed to have been almost universally the case.[4]

The forty years between foreign invasion, popular uprisings and the fall of the Qing Dynasty witnessed a period of social upheaval and intense transformation within the Chinese society. In a transition from the old to the new, China before the turn of the century was a disjointed and disintegrated society "slowly bereft of its soul and its spirit". Labelled by some novelists as a "man eat man" society (「人吃人」的社會), the old regime of China was too incapacitated by an assortment of political, economic and social conditions to help its people to cope with the three heavy pillars of exploitation: feudalism, imperialism and capitalism. While the northerners continued their almost century-long inter-regional migrations, the commoners of the southern provinces, in defiance of fierce laws prohibiting emigrations, took to the seas to seek better fortune. For many of these rural people, who still accounted for some 95% of the Chinese population, emigration overseas was the only viable way to enable themselves, and in some cases, their children and grandchildren, to escape from the poverty and debts that seemed endless and eternal.

One of the enduring and far-reaching principles of social organization in old China was one's responsibility to others, particularly to members of the family, the elders, parents and ancestors. Born here, growing up here and dying here, the Chinese peasants, for generation after generation, were bonded to the earth, toiling and tilling the soil, irrevocably responsible to ensuring the well-being of their ancestors, a task best done when one was close to the ancestors' tombstones in the village. The living and the dead communicated with each other. The living offspring made periodic sacrificial offerings to ensure the continued prosperity of the deceased and to insure them against hunger in their after-lives. The deceased, in turn, reciprocated by giving the living blessing, as well as protection from the influence of evil spirits and bad luck. In wandering off from one's village, one was liable to forego such responsibility. Inter-regional migrations and emigrations, while leaving the individual unprotected and uprooted, often elicited intense feelings of guilt and shame. For centuries, the sentiment against migration and emigration among the Chinese was strong. The pressure of public opinion was against leaving, against parting company with one's "native village and well", against the evasion of responsibility for the motive of self-preservation.

This overall sentiment against the "emigratory tendency" was institutionalized by Chinese laws and government policies. In further reinforcing the laws of the Ming Dynasty, the position of the emperors of the Qing Dynasty in regard to the emigration of their subjects was clear and explicit. Emigrants and their accomplices, when caught, could be punished by death.

> All officers of government, soldiers and citizens, who clandestinely proceed to sea to trade, or who remove to foreign islands for the purpose of inhabiting and cultivating the same, shall be punished according to the law against communicating with rebels and enemies, and consequently, suffer death by being beheaded. The governors of cities of the second and third orders shall likewise be beheaded, when found guilty of combining with, or artfully conniving at the conduct of such persons.[5]

At the outset of the eighteenth century, the Emperors Kang Xi 康熙 (r. 1662–1720) and Yong Zheng 雍正 (r. 1723–1735) still continued the official prohibition attitude, though both had made attempts to appeal to those then residing in foreign countries to return home. The official view, shared to a considerable extent by ordinary citizens, was that China remained a self-sufficient country and the loss of its subjects through emigration to foreign places could not be compensated by profits from commercial and trade exchanges.

The two Opium Wars and the largely unilateral Treaties of Nanking and Tianjin forced China open, resulting in the conversion of Chinese cities one after another into trading ports and points of external diplomatic contacts. In 1870, China signed the Burlingame Treaty 蒲安臣條約[6] with America by which the Chinese government "cordially" recognized the inherent and inalienable right of man to change his home and allegiance, and also the mutual advantage of the free migration of aliens and subjects respectively from one country to another for the purpose of curiosity, trade, or permanent residence. The official proclamation of the right to free migration and its advantages was embodied in subsequent agreements China signed with the British and the French. From the Ming to the Qing Dynasty, the Chinese emperors were unequivocal in their feelings and attitudes towards contact with the "aliens" and the "barbarians". As a nation very much embraced by an almost xenophobic attitude, China, by and large, was not particularly desirous of benefitting from free trade and free migration, and had never granted rights to its subjects to change residence and citizenship in foreign lands. It was the West that desired contact with China and wanted it badly enough to use military force.

But China, now, it seems, as in the past, asks little of that outer world except that it leave her unmolested so that she can pursue her own affairs in her own way.[7]

At the level of the common people, the familial and filial obligations were strong in both emotional and moral terms. The weight of tradition and the principle of responsibility dictated staying, not leaving and certainly not emigrating to "barbaric places" outside the confines of the Middle Kingdom. To the foreigner, acquainted with experience of other lands in modern times, the simple, obvious, indispensable recipe for the relief of many of the ills to which the Chinese are subject, is emigration. But this is an expedient which the Chinese themselves will not readily adopt, for the reason that it will take them away from the graves of their ancestors, to which, according to Confucianism, they are inexorably linked. Generally speaking, no Chinese will leave his home to seek his fortune at a distance unless he is in some way driven to do so. His ideal in life is to be "fixed like a plant on his peculiar spot, to draw nutrition, propagate and rot". And, no Chinese leaves his home not intending to return. His hope is always to come back rich; to die and be buried where his ancestors are buried.[8]

While one might be led to believe that those few who, in fact, had travelled beyond the confines of China were the "scum", criminals and refugees, social outcasts and vagabonds, in their native country, there were others who took to the seas because of dire necessity. The southerners from the "emigrant communities" of Guangdong and Fujian would find the overall public opinion against emigration more relaxed there because of the geographic contiguity of the two provinces to Southeast Asia, or literally, the "Nanyang" 南洋, the South Seas, as the pioneering Chinese emigrants put it.

The overseas Chinese came almost exclusively from the southeast provinces of Guangdong, Fujian and Guangxi, a fact at least partially attributable to their geographic locations in terms of their adjacency to contacts with the external world. While contacts with Europeans had always been one of the forces encouraging Chinese emigration, the first European attempts, mainly by the Portuguese, to trade with China made their initial entry into the Middle Kingdom through the ports of Guangdong. Macao was founded as a trading post in 1557 and remained as the chief port for Western trade in China in the eighteenth century. The English made their first unsuccessful attempt to join the trade in 1596. The setting up by the British of the East India Company represented a repeated attempt to trade with Guangzhou (Canton), a city remaining as the principal trading entrepot and the centre of Western diplomatic contact for subsequent decades. The Americans first traded with Guangzhou in 1784. For centuries, the coastlines of China's southeast provinces saw the coming and going of foreign merchant ships. In a sense, the southerners had become relatively familiar with, if not entirely used to, the sight of foreigners engaged in the exchange of goods. These experiences with the foreigners, as well as other reasons, seemed to have engendered among the southerners an acute sense of political and racial consciousness, as well as a deep-seated sensitivity towards Western invasion and exploitation. Such consciousness and sensitivity, quite ironically, underlined a parallel desire to make economic gains overseas. More exposed to foreign contacts, sharing less of the overall sentiment against emigration, the southerners were keen on benefitting from the opening up of China. Within decades, the provinces of Guangdong and Fujian quickly became the main emigrant sources. The common people from these regions regarded themselves "as having a privileged entree to the good things that came from the Nanyang", and later, America.[9]

An old Chinese saying goes, "When there is a rabbit in the fields, hundreds chase after it. When there is a nugget of gold found in the fields, hundreds compete for it." In 1848, gold was discovered at John Sutter's mill along the Sacramento River in California. Inflated news and tales of gold diggers quickly striking rich in America reached South China and had already brought in some 25,000 Chinese from the Pearl River delta region in less than five years. Having saved money for a passage to cross the Pacific in "stinking, rat-infested clipper ships",[10] the Chinese came to America, then known to them as Gold Mountain 金山, a term symbolizing fortune, hope and prosperity. For these Chinese fortune-seekers, the Gold Mountain also seemed to promise an end to starvation and poverty. With the gradual digging out of gold fields, as well as increasingly intense racism against the Chinese in California, some Chinese began drifting to Eastern

1. The Chinese Are Coming

United States looking for job opportunities.

As early as 1856, it was reported that there were a handful of Chinese from California following white adventurers into the southern part of British Columbia to look for gold.[11] In 1858, news of discovery of gold along the Fraser River and the Thompson River spread in California. The Chinese started travelling by ship from San Francisco to Victoria. Others arrived in the British Columbia gold fields on foot! Within two years between 1858 and 1859, about two thousand Chinese left the United States for Canada. By 1860, Chinese from Hong Kong, Macao and Hawaii started coming to British Columbia as part of the "Gold Fever" 尋金熱.

With the rapid over-crowding of gold mines within less than five years after the discovery of gold in 1858, thousands of Chinese found employment with the government in building roads and in municipal water works. Others became merchants, farmers, carpenters, construction labourers, laundrymen or housemaids.

Soon after the federal government decided in 1872 to build an intercontinental railroad from coast to coast to enable the exploitation of resources in the West, it was quickly realized that the timely completion of a project of this size required considerably more manual labour than could be provided by the native recruits. The western segment of railroad construction proved particularly difficult: the Rockies presented seemingly insurmountable natural barriers challenging human ingenuity and causing construction delays. In 1880, an American contractor, Andrew Onderdonk, whose railroad construction assignments in the United States included the Northern Pacific Railroad in Oregon and the Southern Pacific in California, brought in from Portland 1,500 Chinese.[12] They were mainly former skilled employees of the Northern Pacific Railroad Company looking for employment. In 1881, Onderdonk recruited two shiploads of some two thousand contracted Chinese labourers from Hong Kong, who were then quickly organized into work units for the building of workers' living quarters, hospitals and clinics, and factories. By 1882, ten shiploads of Chinese, a total of about six thousand, were contracted from Hong Kong and California into British Columbia, only a fraction of whom were actually hired as railroad workers while the rest drifted in and out of a wide variety of service jobs including peddling, and working in restaurants, cafes and laundries. By 1882, among the nine thousand workers hired by the Canadian Pacific, about six thousand five hundred were Chinese.[13]

When Onderdonk first arrived in British Columbia in 1880, there was a general fear in the province that he would be recruiting and employing Chinese labourers from overseas. The fear was fuelled by the belief on the part of the white workers that the Chinese were willing to work longer hours, for lower wages and under more adverse conditions than they were. Onderdonk's arrival in Victoria in April 1880 was, in fact, met by a representation from the Anti-Chinese association.[14] He assured them that first preference would always be given to white labour. He would fall back on the French Canadians of Eastern Canada by necessity, and would with reluctance use the service of Indians and Chinese, but only with the exhaustion of white labour.[15] When the Chinese were indeed hired out of necessity, they were all paid the same wage, $1 per day, regardless of the work performed, while the white labourers were paid $1.50 to $1.75 a day, and the skilled workers got between $2 and $2.50 a day, cooks and cooks' helpers and other amenities provided.[16] The wages paid to the Chinese railroad workers compared well with the years around the end of 1860 when a Chinese worker in a coal mine received $1 a day whereas the minimum wage of a white worker was $2.5 a day. By 1883, a Chinese miner would get $1.25 as compared to $2 to $3.75 for a white worker.[17]

As early as 1879, before the construction of the Canadian Pacific Railway (CPR), Amor de Cosmos, the founder of the *British Colonist* and one-time premier of British Columbia, supported in the House of Commons a petition signed by 1,500 residents of British Columbia demanding the banning of the Chinese in railway work.[18] In a cartoon published in that same year in the *British Colonist* titled, "The Heathen Chinese in British Columbia", the readers saw a tall, bearded and suited white man, left hand in his pocket and right hand grapping the queue (or, colloquially, the pig-tail) of an almond-eyed Chinese worker from behind, apparently deporting him off to the docks from his Chee Lung "washing and ironing" shop. Underneath the cartoon, the following dialogue was printed:

> Amor de Cosmos, i.e.: The love of the World or the Lover of Mankind.
> HEATHEN CHINESE: Why you sendee me offee?
> Amor de Cosmos: Because you can't or won't assimilate with us.
> HEATHEN CHINESE: What is datee?
> Amor de Cosmos: You won't drink whiskey and talk politics and vote like us.

The cartoonist, signed S. Westox, was particularly meticulous in alerting the readers' attention to the fact that the Chinese in question was very differently attired and spoke bad English. More importantly, the message of the non-assimilation of the Chinese into the white society, both in terms of ability and intent, was clearly delivered through the written word and the visuals.

This non-assimilation argument pertaining to the Chinese was echoed years later by Prime Minister John A. MacDonald, who agreed that the Chinese were "an alien race in every sense that would not and could not be expected to assimilate with our Aryan population". Nevertheless, in 1882, he put the Chinese question pragmatically to the Parliament: "It is simply a question of alternatives: either you must have this labour or you can't have the railway".

When the construction of the railroad was nearing completion in 1884, the first batch of Chinese workers was being disbanded. Onderdonk refused to honour his pledge to finance his Chinese workers' passage back to China.[19] Unemployed, a large portion of the Chinese congregated in Victoria and New Westminster at loose ends and looking for jobs. When the railroad was finally completed in the winter of 1885, all Chinese work units were disbanded creating an unprecedented crisis of joblessness among the Chinese. Some 400 Chinese responded to recruiting calls in Mexico to build railroads. The newly established Chinese Benevolent Association in Victoria rallied to send the Chinese back home. Out of the then Chinese population of seventeen thousand in Canada, no more than three thousand were sent back to China under such an arrangement.[20] Others went to Cariboo to work in the mines, or moved on along the CPR route to the Prairies and Eastern Canada taking up the only jobs left to them: in laundries and cafes.[21] A few became peddlers, grocers, cooks, gardeners and house servants for white families. This eastward migration of the Chinese ex-rail hands was partly due to the non-availability of jobs, any job, in the West coast with the abrupt dismantling of railroad work camps in 1885; it also represented a collective attempt on the part of the Chinese to escape the increasing feelings of racism against Orientals in general, and the Chinese in particular, in B.C. In the beginning of their long search for a niche in the Prairies and Eastern Canada, the Chinese ventured into small towns and cities along the CPR route finding work, providing services or setting up small businesses. In the midst of all this, they began setting up their own institutions for mutual protection against a hostile and discriminatory white society. By the turn of this century, one witnessed the springing up of a string of Chinatowns in cities and towns across Canada. While the CPR route had become the pulse line of Canada, it also, not at all accidentally, strung together a strip of Chinatowns which, a century later, still represent a permanent, visible part of the Canadian urban landscape.

Notes

1. Ho Ping-ti, "The Population of China in Ming–Ch'ing Times," in *The Making of China*, edited by Chun-shu Chang (Englewood Cliffs, New Jersey: Prentice Hall,1985), p. 341.
2. Ibid., pp. 344–45.
3. Ibid., p. 341.
4. Marianne Bastid-Brugiere, "Currents of Social Change," in *The Cambridge History of China*, edited by Denis Twitchett and John K. Fairbank, Volume II, *Late Ch'ing, 1800–1911*, Part 2 (Cambridge: Cambridge University Press, 1980), p. 580.
5. Victor Purcell, *The Chinese in Southeast Asia*, second edition (Kuala Lumpur: Oxford University Press, reprinted in Oxford in Asia Paperbacks, 1980), p. 26. Purcell took the quote from Sir George Thomas Staunton, *Ta Tsing Len Lee; Being the Fundamental Laws of the Penal Code of China* (London, 1810).
6. K. Biggerstagg, "The Burlingame Mission," in *The Criticism in American History*, Vol. 14 (July 1936), pp. 652–82.
7. L. Carrington Goodrich and Nigel Cameron, *The Face of China as Seen by Photographers and Travellers, 1860–1912* (New York: Aperture, 1978), p. 148.
8. Purcell, p. 30.
9. Ibid., p. 30.
10. Anthony B. Chan, *Gold Mountain: The Chinese in the New World* (Vancouver: New Star Books, 1983), p. 32.
11. David T.H. Lee 李東海, *Jianada Huaqiao shi* 加拿大華僑史 (A History of the Chinese in Canada) (British Columbia: Ziyou chubanshe 自由出版社, 1967), p. 36. (Text in Chinese.)
12. Pierre Berton, *The National Dream: The Great Railway* (Toronto: McClelland and Stewart, 1970), p. 204.
13. David T.H. Lee, p. 129.
14. Berton, p. 202.
15. Ibid., p. 202.
16. Anthony B. Chan, pp. 60–61.
17. Denise Helly, *Les Chinois à Montréal 1877–1951* (Quebec: Institut québécois de recherche sur la culture, 1987), p. 1. Helly's manuscript was condensed and translated by us into English in 1986 (before publication), resulting in a free translation document of 173 pages. In writing this book, I refer to Helly (e.g. page reference, citations, etc.) on the basis of this translated document.
18. Berton, p. 202.
19. Joseph F. Krauter and Morris David, *Minority Canadians: Ethnic Groups* (Toronto: Methuen, 1978), p. 61.

20. David T.H. Lee, p. 135.
21. Anthony B. Chan, p. 68.

2. Women without Men

Young Chinese women, 1917.

A rare portrait of husband and wife. (Source and date of photograph unknown.)

2. Women without Men

STUDENTS of Chinese culture and history have often underscored the subordination of the individual to collectivities and social institutions in the traditional Chinese society. As a person, a Chinese is cast in a complex web of socio-economic affiliations and relationships with their attendant obligations, expectations and roles which often, at first glance, offer the individual very little alternative. A Chinese is, thus, perhaps more appropriately viewed as a social, rather than autonomous, being. A Chinese is by nature a "synthetic"[1] person, a product of social-cultural synthesis. Unlike the Americans who adulate change and embrace the future, a future that is always viewed as "bigger and better," one integral core value of the Chinese is their orientation to the past.[2] The attitude of historical China was that nothing new ever happened in the present or would happen in the future; it had all happened before in the far distant past. In 1961, anthropologists Florence Kluckhohn and Fred Strodtbeck wrote, "The proud American who once thought he was showing some Chinese a steamboat for the first time was quickly put in his place by the remark, 'Our ancestors had such a boat two thousand years ago'."[3]

Such leanings to a past orientation may well have to do with some deep feelings of nostalgia about a Chinese culture and civilization in the ancient past that was once highly advanced. Accordingly, Confucius (551–479 B.C.) advocated in his teachings a preference for following customs, philosophies and behavioural practices that were once there in the distant past. These Confucian teachings have been cast into such concepts well known to the Chinese: following the ancient past (從古), admiring and emulating the ancient past (仿古), recovering and returning to the ancient past (復古). One might want to suggest that such adherence to the past is, in turn, the essence of a Chinese outlook that the best way of life is lived by the old people and rooted in tradition, a way of life that preserves the past, minimizes change, or even brings people back to the past, the further back, the better.

In a Chinese society that gives first order value preference to the past, there is a strong tendency to bring up and train children in accordance with the traditions of the past or the ways of the old people. The Chinese believe that the old ways are the best, and it is when children do not follow them things begin to go wrong. Ancestor worship and a strong family tradition are both expressions of this pre-eminent value preference to the past among the Chinese.

The Chinese have long been concerned with four major natural and inevitable phenomena in the human life-cycle: birth, old age, illness and death. In answering the pressing question, "What after death?", the Confucians introduce a "philosophy of eternity," which suggests that one would ensure the extension and continuity of one's life and that of the ancestors by leaving behind one's own children. Such an outlook and belief would help lessen one's melancholy towards dying and death.

When at an appropriate age, a Chinese must get married, and then bear and rear children. The bearing and rearing of children serves two purposes: first, to ensure the continuity of one's life and of the ancestors; and second, to commemorate all dead members of the family and to cater to their materialist and emotional needs in after life. Tasks such as marriage, child birth and child training, commemoration of the ancestors and providing for their needs, all need to be undertaken within the family and are often looked upon by the Chinese as the essential functions of the family.

To a Chinese, there is scarcely anything more important than getting married and raising a family. From ancient times onward, much energy of the Chinese has been expended on ensuring the continued existence and growth of the family, thus guaranteeing the persistence of the family lineage.[4]

From the standpoint of social organization, ancestor worship is a spiritual and psychological foundation on which the Chinese family and kinship systems are erected. Through a range of ritualistic worshipful activities within the households or in temples, the "shadow" of the ancestors symbolizes family continuity and kin solidarity. The ancestors need to be "fed" and provided for in order to continue their existence. To the offspring, the blessings and protection of their ancestors help ensure their own well-being in this life. As such, the attitudes and feelings of offspring towards their ancestors are often a mixture of veneration and fear, a phenomenon exceedingly familiar to those who are born and raised in a Chinese society.

Chinese parents often label the wrongdoing and misconduct of their children by accusing them of being "lacking in filial piety" in the treatment of parents. Traditional familism among the Chinese is closely associated with filial piety, a much emphasized priority for the Confucians. In a society dominated by traditional familism, every Chinese speaks of, as well as implements, filial piety. To a Chinese, filial piety is not only a virtue; rather, it is a matter-of-fact behaviour, a duty, an obligatory role within the family.

What functions then does filial piety serve? On one level, filial piety ensures the continuity of the biological life of parents and ancestors.[5] From this point of view, to put filial piety into practice is, again, to get married, to establish and raise a family by giving birth to children, thus fulfilling the most elementary and fundamental obligations of filial piety. Such a belief has been cast into the all-familiar Chinese saying, "Of the three ways to be lacking in filial piety, not having children is the worst" (不孝有三，無後爲大).

On the second and deeper level, putting filial piety into practice also means bringing up and training children in such a way that they internalize all the desirable and positive traits of the culture of the family. In this sense, Chinese raise children to ensure both the biological and cultural continuity of themselves and of the family image and tradition.

On the third and deepest level, filial piety extends itself to an obligation on the part of the children to realize unfulfilled dreams or desires of their parents and ancestors, as well as to redress their past wrongdoings or misgivings. The traditional Chinese folklore is filled with stories of parents expecting their children to one day excel in local and national examinations and to make it into the civil service elite, thus "bringing glory and honour to the ancestors" (光宗耀祖).

With the virtually uninterrupted domination of Confucianism in Chinese society for over two thousand years, tradition to a Chinese is almost synonymous with Confucianism. Authority, in the way the Chinese have understood it, is Confucian both in ideals and in practices. A Confucian conception of authority is hierarchical in nature in that: first, in politics, the emperor (the son of heaven) governs the bureaucrats who in turn govern the mass, the ordinary people; second, in the social sphere, the sages rule the intellectual elite who in turn rule the mass; and, third, in the family and kin system, the chief of the kin network holds authority over the heads of the household (father-husband) and other family members.

In intimate interpersonal relations, the family is an absolute value by itself; as a collective entity, it holds precedence over and above the individual family members.[6] On the basis of this spirit of collectivism, the lifestyles of an individual must accord with the direction of the collective, or be judged as deviant, calling for criticism and censorship. The older members of the kin network as well as the family heads are given, by society and tradition, the authority and obligation to train and discipline youth. Chinese society often blames parents and holds them responsible for the mistakes of their children. To the children, following the directives of their parents and other older members of the family is a natural and benevolent behaviour.

The authority structure in a Chinese society is thus highly stratified, vertical, hierarchical, pyramidal, and increasingly leaning and aspiring to the distant past. Underlying such a structure are features as respect for past knowledge and experience, conformity to existing social norms, as well as the pre-eminence of the collective over the individual. It is precisely these values that define, legitimize and regulate relations between husband and wife, the governor and the governed, parents and children, teacher and student. To the Chinese, such a hierarchical structure of authority is fundamental to harmony and order in society and in human relationships.

At least three central traits of the national character of the Chinese can be deduced from the value orientations discussed above: first, filial piety; second, love of peace and harmony; and third, diligence and frugality.[7] Like filial piety, the love of peace and harmony, the opposite of which being conflict, confrontation, war and destruction, is more likely to be motivated by a strong need to preserve and protect the family and kin system, than by a diffuse feeling of humanism. A Chinese peasant would tolerate a civil war as long as it does not endanger his family and kin. Numerous incidents in Chinese history indicate that the Chinese often choose to avoid war, conflict and confrontation by resorting to toleration and accommodation. A quick look at modern Chinese history reveals that the Chinese government, during wars with foreign powers, has to point to the likelihood of the destruction of the families and their ancestral tradition in order to recruit the peasants into the army.

In times of normal social discourse as well, the Chinese often strive for harmony instead of conflict, compromise instead of confrontation, equilibrium instead of unrest, sometimes at the expense of considerable personal suffering. While grounded in Confucianism, such an outlook towards social relations among the Chinese is consistent with the teachings of Buddhists and Taoists.

To be diligent and frugal is also directly and closely related to the strong sense of the family and familism. For thousands of years, the economy of the Chinese society has been founded on simple agriculture, limited manual industry, and small-scale commerce and trade, all of which operate on the basis of, and within, the families. Due to an underdeveloped technology and lack of capital, the process and outcome of production as well as the eventual profit tend to be limited, thus giving rise to an overall deficient and scarcity economy.[8] In order to ensure the continuation of production, the Chinese must be diligent. They must consume a lot of human labour to compensate for the lack of capital and deficiency in natural resources. While one must consume, the Chinese must also be frugal to reduce consumption to an absolute minimum. It is only by being frugal that the Chinese can ensure against starvation and guarantee surplus of materials. In a deficient economy, production must be extra laborious in order to produce sufficient commodity, and this is diligence. Consumption must be exceedingly cautious in order to guarantee surplus, and this is frugality.

A deficient economy has characterized traditional Chinese society over thousands of years; over time, the older generations have taught their younger ones both by moral precepts and by example the importance of diligence and frugality. In such an economy, diligence and frugality have gradually become part and parcel of family values transmitted from one generation to another irrespective of needs and circumstances. So even children in wealthy families are trained to be diligent and frugal, not only to save for the "rainy days," but also to protect their spirit from being corrupted by wealth and materialism. Diligence and frugality have thus become part of the national character of the Chinese, rich and poor.

The world economy at the turn of the twentieth century can be best visualized in terms of a world-wide search for cash-money. For the Chinese, the motive for migration across national boundaries was nothing more than an economic one. The all-pervasive and powerful imagery of gold nuggets paving the streets of America was at the very heart of the motive for emigration. To many Chinese, emigration promised the only opportunity to enhance his own, and more importantly, his family's status in the eyes of his fellow countrymen. Nevertheless, the decision to leave China was rarely made by the emigrant himself; it was often threshed out within the nuclear family as well as the larger kin networks, sometimes years before the emigrant himself knew about it. Chances are that the participation of members of the immediate kin network was a pre-requisite condition to emigration in view of the fact that the emigrant often depended on kin for passage money to come to Canada or America. The money was invariably assembled through loans, then given, not to the person in question, but to the family. The fact that the loans were made to the family, not the person himself, in order to upgrade family status as well as to enhance family honour, was not without psychological costs for the emigrant. He must make it. He must pay back his debts to his uncles and aunts. He has his whole kin and fellow countrymen on his back. He was put on an immense, physically taxing guilt trip months before he set foot on Canadian soil.

Besides, he began his venture indebted to his creditors, labour contractors, and his family and kin.

Contrary to what has been maintained in writings on early Chinese immigrants in Canada, they came not as "coolies" in the classic sense of the term, but as voluntary indentured workers, contracted, but not sold, to labour contractors or brokers,[9] who often arranged for the emigrant passage money to be paid back by the debtor by completing a work contract. Such a contractual arrangement with the creditors cast the Chinese immigrants in restrictive and sometimes exploitative labour relations with their employers, a relationship that often meant the almost total subordination of the fundamental rights of the workers under contract. To a large extent, this contractual relation often degenerated into some form of bondage and subordination.

The Canadian census of 1825 established the presence of a Chinese man in the district of St. Joseph in Montreal, while the 1881 census recorded 7 Chinese in the city.[10] The *Montreal Star* on 1 July 1888 reported that the early "Chinese colony" had about 30 residents, while *The Gazette* recorded the numbers of Chinese at 500 in 1894, 700 in 1902 and 800 in 1904.[11] The Canadian census recorded the numbers of Chinese in Montreal to be 1,608 in 1921, 1,705 in 1931, 1,884 in 1941, 1,272 in 1951, 3,998 in 1961 and 10,655 in 1971.

The Chinese Immigration Act of 1885 levied a head tax of $50 on almost every Chinese entering Canada; this was increased to $100 in 1900, and $500 in 1903. The Chinese Immigration Act of 1923 excluded almost all Chinese from entering Canada and was not repealed until 1947. In actual fact, therefore, the head tax paid out to the Canadian government by the Chinese immigrants upon entry into the country remained the major source of debts along with the borrowed passage money.

The completion of the Canadian Pacific Railway meant the abrupt disbanding of railroad work camps, as well as the termination of jobs for thousands of Chinese railroad labourers. The Chinese began to migrate eastward, mainly along the spine of the CPR, to look for jobs and to escape from intense overt racism against Orientals in British Columbia. Travelling along the Canadian Pacific Railway, the Chinese made stops in the Prairies, occasionally finding manual work there or, sometimes creating jobs for themselves by setting up small stores, grocery shops, cafes, restaurants and hand laundry shops through joint business partnership. The folding of these businesses almost as soon as they were begun seemed to be more the rule than the exception. It was also at this time when one began to witness the beginnings of the frequent shift and shuffle of business partners among the early Chinese immigrants in Canada. In the 1870s, a handful of former Chinese railroad workers found work at low wages with local industrial manufacturers in major Canadian urban centres, a line of work that co-existed with production in smaller local workshops.[12]

The early Chinese community in Quebec around the 1900s was primarily made up of those who had already worked for years in the United States, British Columbia and the Prairies before settling in Eastern Canada. As a matter of fact, as early as 1880, a few Chinese men left British Columbia to try their luck in Montreal. They were quickly followed by some 3,000 Chinese directly from Guangzhou who constituted the first influx of Chinese immigrants in Quebec. Having heard of escalating racial hostility toward them upon the abrupt depletion of job opportunities in British Columbia, these Cantonese came directly to Quebec to join their predecessors, thus adding considerable numerical strength to the slowly emerging Chinese community in Montreal. In 1891, there were 219 Chinese immigrants outside of British Columbia. By 1901, the number was increased to 2,420 and this population included those Chinese who opened small stores or took employment as agricultural labourers in Alberta and Manitoba.[13] Between 1891 and 1901, larger numbers of Chinese headed towards Ontario and Quebec. Montreal and Toronto became increasingly more attractive to the Cantonese than any other Eastern Canada cities, particularly those who were intent on avoiding employment with the whites, or becoming small merchants.

The early Chinese emigrants from Guangzhou and the larger Pearl River Delta area were quite homogeneous as an emigrant population. They were young, strong males, typically in their early twenties, had a rural, or rather, peasant's background, little educated, largely illiterate and had neither work skills nor experience pertinent to the needs of the Canadian economy at the time. There was little evidence of these Cantonese immigrants displaying any degree of proficiency in the written Chinese language either, let alone English or French. A considerable portion of them could have been married and had children shortly before departure from China, thus ensuring the continuation of the family lineage in their native villages before their sojourn in a foreign land.

There is evidence from oral history interviews[14] indicating that many of the 3,000 Cantonese who came en route to Quebec in the early 1900s seemed to have a good idea of the socio-economic realities they were about to face in Quebec. They came to the province to join their predecessors; they knew they were going to replace the life-long, poverty-stricken peasant life in an old, crumbling Chinese economy with that of an equally back-breaking destiny of a hand laundryman in a young, thriving Canadian economy. For many, the promises of this continental shift did not hold out for long.

The Chinese men came to Quebec without their women, nor their children. The costs of passage money and the head taxes imposed by the federal government were too exorbitant. Family intactness at the point of migration was a luxury the Cantonese peasants could hardly afford. Separated from their women and, in some cases, their children, these Chinese men went on a work trip overseas with a project in mind.

A student of ethnic migration to North America once described this trip overseas as a "suspended animation", with the migrant having little sense of the time dimension.[15] When a Cantonese man was making preparations for his trip abroad, he had very little idea of the length of time required of him for his sojourn in Canada to complete his project. Nevertheless, on the basis of the average number of years it had taken his uncles and older brothers in the village to return home, the young migrant, as well as his family and kin, were able to construct a norm, an expectation all migrants must strive to meet. To be a dutiful son, a loving husband and a caring father, he was expected to come home rich within a folk-based norm of a certain number of years. Failing that, he was expected to send back remittances periodically to justify his postponement of coming home. The young migrants were sent to Quebec to work for his relatives or countrymen who had settled there earlier. As soon as they arrived in Quebec, they were immediately put under the close watchful eyes of their elder kinsmen. A kin-based system of social control within the Chinese community overseas began to replace parental control at home. It was not unusual for parents to write long letters to the elders overseas asking for their assistance in monitoring the moral conduct of their children, and, under other circumstances, in punishing them for delinquencies and misdeeds. One such misdeed was failure on the part of the young migrant to send remittances home. Parents in China were often quick in prompting elders overseas to remind the young migrants of the importance of such old Chinese values as filial piety, obligations to ancestors, parental authority and the primacy of the family over the individual. Tens of thousands of miles away, the young migrants found themselves still

2. Women without Men

under the eternal grip of tradition and heritage, activated and reinforced by parents through remote control.

Men went abroad in a worldwide search for cash-money. Women were left behind. Oftentimes, men and women were united in matrimony only weeks or even days before the men took their trips overseas. As wives, they had little idea of what would become of their husbands whom they hardly knew. Chances were they did not even ask how long it would take their men to return home. Even when they asked, their men would not know. The women, however, knew how long it took the other migrants from the village and the neighbouring villages to come home, and in a large number of cases, these men simply never managed the return trip. The women did not ask about the details of overseas work conditions awaiting their husbands, though they seemed to vaguely know the work was going to be back-breaking, the hours will be long, wages will be low, and the Chinese were not well treated by the white society.[16] The women also seemed to know their men will be washing white men's dirty shirts and white women's soiled underwear. Their husbands will do what women in China have been doing for centuries—washing clothes. Many Cantonese migrants were destined to be a hand laundryman throughout their sojourn in Canada.

Chinese culture and tradition dictated that women "follow" their husbands. In the case of women left behind in China by their men, to "follow" had never been meant in its physical sense. The women did not come to America with their men. But they were expected to follow their men and the mores of the Chinese society in every other sense of the word: to follow orders of parents before marriage, of husband while married and of sons having reached maturity and in husband's absence (在家從父，出嫁從夫，老來從子). The Confucians have a term for this code of ethics for women, namely, "the trinity (three ways) of following" (三從). Expressed in marital terms, this conduct of following on the part of the women has been captured in Chinese colloquial sayings, "Married to a rooster, you follow the rooster for life. Married to a dog, you follow the dog for life."(嫁雞隨雞，嫁狗隨狗) Or, "Stick with the same man you have married till you die"(從一而終).

The men went overseas with one single duty to perform for the family: to bring home enough money to "buy a house, farming land and property." The women stayed home in China to perform their duties: to look after their husbands' parents and the children, to run the household. When women asked letter writers back home to send messages to their husbands in the "Gold Mountain", they reminded their men how difficult it had been for them to perform the duties of a wife and daughter-in-law without the foreign remittances. Women in China continued to talk in terms of duties and obligations to their husbands and their families; women worked and toiled to look after their husbands' children, not their own children; their husbands' parents, not their own parents. Women talked in terms of the sufferings of their husbands' families, but never of themselves.[17]

If it was a hard life for men trying to make it in a foreign land, it was a lot harder life for women at home, waiting and waiting, never assured of when their men would return. In some emigrant communities of Southern China, where sometimes more than half of their male population, young and old, had gone overseas, one often heard women chanting folk songs (the Chinese call them "hill songs" (山歌) dealing with themes of marital separation, the agony of waiting without knowing, longing, suffering and mourning over lost or dead husbands:

> Flowers shall be my head-dress once again,
> For my dear husband shall soon return.
> Ten long years did I wait,
> Trying hard to remember his face.

Recorded and printed in their entirety in little booklets, these "hill songs" were chanted by women in solitude, often as a lyrical vehicle of expression and release of pent-up emotions, or as a means of reinforcing their psychic and moral bondage with their men thousands of miles and many years away. While chanting, the singers say they can feel the presence of their men, to the point of almost touching their faces.[18]

The Cantonese men in Quebec would write home five or six times a year, usually when they had money to send along. Men sent back remittances to give women at home something to look for, to show they still cared a great deal about their women, to alleviate the guilt of not returning, of not being able to tell their women when they might return, of seemingly forever postponing homecoming plans.[19] The money sent home was quickly divided among immediate family members as well as among close or distant relatives. This way, the migrants managed to maintain or enhance his own reputation and his family's status in the eyes of his fellow countrymen back home. His preoccupation was, thus, more centered on his social position back home, than on where he was socio-economically situated in the host society. Over time, the act of sending home remittances was ritualized and institutionalized within the overseas Chinese communities.

2. Women without Men

One judged (and was judged by others) his moral conduct in terms of how much and how often money was sent. Psychologically, the sending home of remittances was often a psychically cleansing experience. It purified the soul, relieved guilt, and reaffirmed one's sense of responsibility to his woman, children and parents, and, therefore, one's ethnicity and continuity with tradition and the past. There were instances of overseas Chinese men continuing to send letters and money home knowing fully all their close family members had long passed away. The money was literally sent to ghosts. The Cantonese men, who were illiterate and therefore could not write, continued to ask their peers to write and send ghost letters home.[20]

While the men worked in the hand laundries in Montreal, the women laboured in the paddy fields, striving to maintain production in a subsistence-level rural economy aided by primitive farming technology. Life as a petty peasant tilling borrowed soil from landholders in nineteenth century Southern China was hard. It was particularly hard for women in the absence of men. In the village, there was practically little else to do but to farm on a few patches of meagre land.

Sons are the permanent part of the Chinese family. When female children are married, they are married "out" and "away" from their families of origin. They become somebody else's wives, mothers, daughters-in-law. When male children get married, they bring a woman into the household and she is expected to immediately transfer her loyalties and obligations from her parents to her husband and his parents. While sojourning in Quebec, the Cantonese men were still in every way an inseparable part of the community they had left behind. The emigrant village, as a community, did not see the Cantonese man as a lost member, but as someone who was sojourning overseas with a project to complete. During meals, a seat and a set of eating utensils at the dining table were known to be set aside for the absent emigrant. Children were instructed to remember that their fathers were abroad, but only temporarily; they also needed to verbally acknowledge the "presence" of their fathers before proceeding to eat. The child will face directly the seat designated by the absentee father, and say, "Father, please eat rice", and then begin his meal. There were incidents of the continuation of these practices years after the death of fathers in the foreign land.[21]

Mothers would send long, moralistic letters to their sons in Canada, reminding them of their filial obligations, their responsibility to wives and children, to their ancestors, their reputation in the village-community. Mothers would remind their sons of the importance of being frugal and thrifty, that they must work hard and save, they must not forget people back home, they must accomplish their project in the shortest possible time, they should never even think of staying permanently in a foreign land. They must return home. There were also letters from mothers or fathers to sons telling stories of bandits robbing and stealing, of hunger, starvation and natural disasters; of daughters, land and cattle, and ancestors' houses being sold to survive; of civil wars and a dying Chinese economy, of human beings eating roots and the bark of trees to stay alive, of birds, insects and game all caught and slaughtered for food.

The project the Cantonese man took on had a beginning from the moment his family decided he made a good "target emigrant." Money was borrowed from kin and neighbours. The family to the left side of his house furnished a loan. Another family three streets away also pitched in. In order for the family to survive, he must leave. Everybody in the village wanted to go to the Gold Mountain. Those who could not go were quite happy to loan out money to those "target migrants." In those days, loans were hard to come by. However, people were more than happy to finance the migrants' trip to America. Those who were going to America were considered "good risks" for loans. They would be able to pay back quickly. Those who stayed in the village would never be in any position to pay back the debts since the village economy was such that no surplus capital of any size would be generated.

For the Cantonese emigrant, his project overseas had no seeming end. For many, emigration and sojourn quickly became permanent exile. In the meantime, they continued to receive letters from women back home. Mothers and grandmothers asked letter writers to summon their sons home as if by sending enough letters the men would one day indeed return. The emigrants also continued to send letters and remittances home. By writing, by mailing letters, they were almost home. The project they began ten, twenty, thirty years ago became a project suspended in time and space, in morals and emotions.

Notes

1. Robert F. Harney, "Men without Women: Italian Migrants in Canada, 1885–1930," in *Canadian Ethnic Studies*, Vol. XI:1 (1979), pp. 29–47.
2. Wei Chengtung 韋政通. "Chuantong Zhongguo lixiang renge de fenxi" 傳統中國

2. Women without Men

理想人格的分析 (The Ideal Character of the Traditional Chinese), in *Zhongguo ren de xingge: Keji zhonghe xing de taolun* 中國人的性格：科際綜合性的討論 (The Character of the Chinese: An Interdisciplinary Approach), edited by Li Yi-yuan 李亦園 and Yang Kuo-shu 楊國樞, Zhongyang yanjiuyan minzuxue yanjiuso zhuankan erzhong 中央研究院民族學研究所專刊 (Institute of Ethnology, Academia Sinica, Monograph Series B), No. 4 (1971), pp. 1–36.

3. F.R. Kluckohn and F.L. Strodtbeck, *Variations in Value Orientations* (Illinois: Row, Peterson and Evanston, 1961), p. 14.
4. Martin M.C. Yang 楊懋春, "Zhongguo de jiating zhuyi yu guomin xingge" 中國的家庭主義與國民性格 (Familism and Chinese National Character), in Li and Yang, pp. 127–62.
5. Ibid., pp. 139–42.
6. Wen Chung I 文崇一, "Zong jiazhi quxiang tan Zhongguo guomin xing" 從價值取向談中國國民性 (Chinese National Character as Revealed in Value Orientation), in Li and Yang, pp. 47–78.
7. Martin M.C. Yang, p. 138.
8. Ibid., pp. 139–42.
9. Anthony B. Chan, *Gold Mountain: The Chinese in the New World* (Vancouver: New Star Books, 1983) pp. 37–46.
10. Denise Helly, *Les Chinois à Montréal 1877–1951* (Quebec: Institut québécois de recherche sur la culture, 1987), p. 22.
11. Hoe Ban-seng, "Folktales and Social Structure: The Case of the Chinese in Montreal", in *Canadian Folklore Canadien*, Vol. 1:1–2 (1979), pp. 25–35.
12. Denise Helly, p. 16.
13. Denise Helly, p. 17.
14. Kwok B. Chan, *Oral History of the Montreal Chinese Community*, 1983. Oral History–Montreal Studies Program, Shell Oil Canada. Copies of audio-tapes (mainly in Chinese), transcripts in English (450 pages) and slides based on in-depth oral history interviews with 15 elderly Chinese men and women in Montreal are deposited with Concordia University Library's Non-Print Unit, as well as Public Archives of Canada in Ottawa.
15. Robert F. Harney, p. 38.
16. Kwok B. Chan, *Oral History of the Montreal Chinese Community*, 1983.
17. Oral history interview with Mrs. Cai, at 1099 Clark Street, Montreal, Quebec, by Kwok B. Chan on 28 November 1982.
18. Ibid.
19. Ibid.
20. Ibid.
21. Ibid.

3. Ten Women

St. Laurent Boulevard. Widows having a chit-chat on a sunny afternoon.

Mrs. Cai in her room above a shophouse in Chinatown, 1981. The framed photograph on the left is her husband, long passed away, and the one on the right is herself, probably taken in China. Mrs. Cai came to join her husband in Canada at the age of 59.

3. Ten Women

ONE question the Chinese elderly widows often asked themselves is: which is harder, life in China or in Canada? For a long time, there seemed to be no straight, clear-cut answers to the question. The women gave personal accounts of life without men in China. They would tell you poverty in the Chinese village forced many men to go overseas to seek better fortune. Life as a peasant back in the native village in China was hard; a woman would toil in the rice fields from dawn to dark, while catering to the needs of her in-laws, her children, and, sometimes, her own parents. Life as a peasant in poverty-stricken, nineteenth century China was hard for a woman. Life as a Chinese woman in Montreal was no easier. Contrary to the myth that many women stayed home, a large majority of them, in the day time, washed dishes, made egg rolls or cleaned bean sprouts in Chinese restaurants. Not speaking English or French, they involuntarily subjected themselves to exploitation by the Chinese restaurant proprietors. During the evenings, some would find themselves helping out in their husbands' hand laundries till very late hours. In addition to the role of a wife and a mother, the Chinese women were in fact the heroic bearers of a triple role. One woman described her work in Canada as one "with no rest and no break", suggesting that even a poor peasant in China would have her time off in a year.

One of the many values transplanted from mainland China by these Cantonese men and women was their work ethic, their deep sense of devotion and dedication to work. Accentuated by a harsh economy and occupational segregation, this work ethic was, in fact, further enhanced and took an extreme form. Life of a Cantonese immigrant in Montreal was mostly hard and dirty work. What little time left for leisure and relaxation, and play, came in the form of a rare day off on Sundays, or occasionally watching shows put up by some travelling opera or musical troupes from China or Hong Kong. Once transplanted, the immigrants' accentuated work ethic became in fact an adaptation to a harsh work environment where one must work extra hard and long in order to remain minimally competitive. Survival was made possible through the exploitation of intensive labour.

Along with exploitation by Chinese restaurant owners, a fact recalled by these women with rage and frustration, there was racism. While children at schools often chanted, "Ching, Ching, Ching" to the Chinese, Chinese boys were tormented and bullied at school with teachers refusing to intervene. White children would throw mud at clean laundry hung at the backyards of the laundry stores or break windows with stones. The police would not answer to the complaints. The women described laundry business as degrading, dirty work. They would wash women's underwear or sanitary pads with blood and period stains on them. One woman recalled receiving laundry with human excrement on them. Her husband had to burn incense to get rid of the bad odour in the air. Another woman recalled her husband being asked, while going door-to-door to solicit laundry, by a white woman to climb under her bed to collect dirty clothing. Mrs. Fang Zhoushi 方周氏, then 99 years old, still recalled very vividly incidents of racism against the Chinese by the French; the latter ridiculed Chinese as rats, and praised the Japanese as bulldogs during the Sino-Japanese conflict.

Workers in the laundry would work and eat and sleep in the store; they would all sleep on the ironing boards after work. With few Chinese women in the community, the men would squander all their money gambling, visiting prostitutes, drinking or smoking opium; many of them never managed to save enough money to return to China, while others died of the guilt of not having sent remittances back to their wives and children.

Like the men, the women were completely shut out from any job available in the city at a time of quick industrial and commercial expansion. The Chinese often attributed this fact to their personal deficiency: lack of language skills. For more than a century, they remained in the Chinese community's ethnic labour market, thus finding themselves an easy prey to exploitation by the Chinese merchant class. With nowhere to go outside Chinatown, the class conflict within the Chinese community has never really surfaced.

Much of the Chinese women's life was one of frugality and thriftiness. There was very little leisure the way the modern society understands it. Meals were kept simple and expenditures kept low. Their men were old, fragile and sick; many of them quickly passed away. The women were left behind, seemingly growing stronger and happier day after day. Now rid of their many previous roles as helper (wife, daughter-in-law and mother) and labourer (day and night), these women, perhaps for the first time ever in their lives, found freedom, autonomy and independence for themselves. Living in the comfort and protection of their peers within the ethnic neighbourhood of the rooming houses, these women now feel relaxed, free and unburdened. Many apparently are enjoying themselves. Life is mahjong, shopping, watching video movies, participating in community events and social visits. It is a life of leisure, something unknown to them for much of their lives. Their money saved is still being sent back to kinsmen in

China from time to time. Their bondage with China has never been weakened. Yet Montreal is their place. There is no desire to go back to their birth place.

So, which life is harder, in Canada or in China? Clearly, now, these women know the answers.

FANG ZHOUSHI

Mrs. Fang Zhoushi 方周氏 was 99 years old at the time of our interview; she was living on her own in Montreal's Chinatown. She made Canada her home for over sixty years since she emigrated from Guangdong, China in 1921. Mrs. Fang was married at the age of 16. Living conditions in China were poor and only four short years after the couple were wed, Mr. Fang left China for North America in search of work. Sixteen years passed before Mrs. Fang and her daughter were able to make the journey to Canada. They landed in Vancouver and from there, they travelled to meet her husband, who was living in Edmonton. They rented a room for a few dollars a month. Mr. Fang earned a living by working in a Chinese restaurant. They moved to Montreal several years later when he developed a kidney infection and needed medical attention. Mrs. Fang recalled a sparsely-populated Chinatown inhabited by only five or six Chinese families.

In spite of her age, Mrs. Fang's memory at the interview remained extraordinarily accurate as she described the lifestyle of the typical Chinese immigrant at a time when steaks were 50 cents and a sandwich was a dime.

My home is Kai Ping 開平, in the province of Guangdong. I was married there at 16. My husband was one year older than me. He came to Canada four years later, when he was 21. When he first came to Canada, he arrived in Victoria, British Columbia. He worked as a dishwasher. My brother-in-law went along with him to Quebec. Eventually they both opened up a laundry. Later on, my husband's older brother went back to China and they changed it into a restaurant. He went back to China and when he returned to Canada he went to Edmonton. I came to Montreal during the Second World War. I have been in Montreal for forty years or so. My husband died in the Chinese hospital during that time. The hospital is no longer there now, it has been replaced by the Kum Ying Trading Company. The hospital took up both floors. The upstairs was much better, the left hand side of the building housed the Chinese Benevolent

Society. I took my husband to Montreal in 1940. I have been in Canada since 1921. My husband came over here when he was 21. At the age of 29 he returned to China. He stayed for nine years and then returned. At that time it was during the war. He stayed for less than a year. It was on 13 January when he went back to China. At the end of September he came back to Canada. He never returned to China again. I came here when I was 36 years old. When my husband was in China, we had a daughter. I came with her. She was 6 years old. In China, I lived with my mother-in-law. I did not work in the rice fields, but, when my husband came back to China, he bought a piece of land to grow all kinds of fruit trees. We bought that piece of land right in the village. We grew some bamboo trees to make it look like a fence. The bamboo surrounded all the fruit trees. He came back to China on 13 January. On the 19th he bought the land. We used all the bamboo to make a fence. However, we were afraid of outlaws so we moved to a small town called Chi Kan 赤坎 . We lived there until the end of September. It was in the beginning of September when he returned to Canada. On 11 October, my daughter was born. I came with her when she was 6 years old. I never went to school. I do not know how to write any Chinese words. That is why I have such a miserable life. When I came over here, my daughter went to school.

I came to Canada by ship. I took the *Queen Asian* for nineteen days. I was seasick all the time. I was seasick for nineteen days. I paid tax to come. It was $500 each person, in Canadian currency. At that time I had to pay Inter-Canada tax in 1921. In 1923, the Canada government completely cut off Chinese immigration. In 1922, there were just a few that were allowed in. In 1923 they completely stopped Chinese immigration to this country. I was very fortunate. My husband paid for everything. He looked after all that. He handled all the application forms.

I lived in Edmonton for over twenty years. The war broke out after that. That was when we came to Montreal. His kidney was failing him. When the war broke out, all the salesmen told him where and in which particular city to open a restaurant. We moved to four different cities before we finally settled in Montreal. When we first came to Edmonton, there were no Chinese. No Chinese at all. When I came to Montreal, I met a few Chinese ladies. There were no more than ten. When I first came to Montreal, there was the Leong Jung Grocery store and the Sue Shing Wholesale Company. We rented a house on Dorchester Boulevard. We came down to Lagauchetière since it was close to the station. The living room was not as big as it is here. It was $6 a month. At that time it was very cheap. People were still poor and had no money. We came over here and rented the house. It was $60 a month. It was not so cheap anymore. But $6 a month was cheap. The living room was so big. In the back of the room, you could put a bed and then cover it up. You could also put a chair and sofa in the front for a living room arrangement. It was only one room. It was not a flat, only one room. At that time the Canadian and the Chinese clothes were bright and quite nice. I made my own clothes. It looked half Chinese and half Caucasian. In Montreal there were only about ten families or so. There were some Huangs, Lis, Chens, Hans. I knew them. The Chinese had mostly grocery stores like Sue Shing, and some laundries and restaurants.

My husband was in the restaurant business. Since I arrived here, he had always been in the restaurant business. He worked 7 days a week with no rest. Everything at that time was cheap. Pork chops were 50 cents, steak was 50 cents, chop suey was 50 cents. If you put a little chicken in the chop suey, it was 75 cents. Potatoes and such things were a nickel, pies were 5 cents each. An order of toast and tea was 10 or 5 cents. In a small town, there was only one Chinese restaurant. After the war broke out, business became very slow. That was why we left. At that time, when you hired a waitress, it was for $3 a week. Now, you earn a couple of hundred dollars a week. Before you could work a whole year, you would not earn that much. It was $10 a week for a head chef. The salary was low, but things were cheap. You did not make much money. Salaries were low. It was just enough for us to live on.

In 1940 to 1941, we left Edmonton with my two sons. One was 17 years old. My other son died at the age of 18. He joined the Canadian army. The youngest son worked in Edmonton with him. My second son will be 59 years old. My oldest daughter is 57, and my youngest daughter is 55. The oldest daughter is in Toronto.

When you live in Chinatown for a long time, you get used to it. It is very convenient. Here, there are lots of Chinese ladies I can talk to. I buy Chinese groceries. Since I have been in Montreal, I have never gone to Eaton's (a large departmental store) by myself. I always have a companion with me. When I go to places like Eaton's, I always ask one of the ladies to come with me. I never go by myself. We visit each other all the time. One of the ladies, Mrs. Fang, lives on St. Urbain Street. The building was demolished and they now have a new building there. She lived there before. I lived on Clark Street. There is a church near there. Quite often, after supper, around seven, eight o'clock, I will go and visit them. I go to visit them on St. Urbain Street and make it home by eleven o'clock. Sometimes I play mah-jong 麻將 (a popular game of chance among the Cantonese). Mrs. Fang and I sit down sometimes and play for fun.

She has a mah-jong set. We take it out and teach ourselves how to play. The mah-jong set is made of bamboo. On one side it is white and on the other side it is made of bamboo. The set is original. This is a real mah-jong set. It is made in Hong Kong. You use a special kind of bamboo on the front side.

I also go to church and attend the church picnics with the ladies. We all used to see Reverend Paul Chen (陳保羅牧師). My husband and all our children attended the Catholic church. On one side would be all the ladies, on the other side, the men. All the men were baptized as Catholics. Most of the people were Catholics. I go on the church tours quite a lot. I went to the States, Washington, Boston and New York a couple of times. We go by bus. A lot of people attend these trips. It is usually packed. We went to Toronto a few times. I have not gone recently. This was only when I first arrived in Montreal that I went. Now that I am old, I have not participated in these trips for a couple of years. The last time I went on a trip, I was 90 years old. I have not gone since then. In the past, I loved to go to the movies at the church. They showed films there every Saturday and Monday. I would attend them. I also attend the Cantonese Opera if they have a good show.

When I first came to Canada, the Chinese were discriminated against. The meanest ones were the French, the French men. After the Second World War, the Chinese were better treated. Before the war, there was a lot of prejudice against the Chinese. These people, …the French …When my children, my son and daughter were small, they would laugh at them and yell, "Ching, Ching, Ching." They would yell, "Maudit Chinois." I would yell back, "Maudit Français. Tu es fou?" ("Are you crazy?") They shut up after that. I know some French, bonjour, midi, things like that. He said Maudit Chinois, I said Maudit Français. The French always fought. They were prejudiced and fought with the Chinese. They are afraid now, so they do not fight anymore. It is just like the time when the Chinese were at war against the Japanese. In the newspapers, when we lived in Edmonton, they printed that the Chinese people were like rats while the Japanese were like bulldogs. Everyone was laughing and joking about it. I told my children to go back and tell them that the Chinese people may be rats but they can go through any hole and they are more intelligent. The bulldogs cannot do anything about that. I told them that. The next day the Germans took over Paris. I said that the bulldogs cannot do anything to the Chinese people. The rats are the most intelligent. It made me laugh.

Since I have been in Canada, I send money back to China. Chinese people always think about the other people back in China. Now, I send money about two times a year, while before it was three times a year. Before, I sent money three times a year but now it is twice a year. I send it to my nephew and his wife. Also, I send money back to other relatives. I never went back to visit my hometown, but I did go to Hong Kong and to Guangdong. I stayed in Guangdong for about twenty days. I went with Mrs. Qian Qishi. She has passed away since then. She died just a couple of days ago. She went back to visit with her daughter in Hong Kong. We went to Guangdong to visit my nephew. He called me Auntie.

XU XIUHUA

Xu Xiuhua 許秀華 is an 83-year-old resident of the Senior Citizen's housing unit in Montreal. She was married in Tai Shan 台山, China, to her husband who was introduced to her by matchmakers. They were separated for a period of ten years when he left China for the United States. Their reunion was complicated by his illegal immigration to America. However, changes in legislation made their reunion possible after many years and Mrs. He joined her husband in Canada in 1935. She came to her new home and was immediately put to work in her husband's hand laundry business. Together they kept the store open 6 days a week, working 12 to 15 hour shifts every day with no break during the year except for New Year's Day.

For Xu Xiuhua, life in a foreign country presented many hardships and sacrifices. Alone and widowed, she now enjoys the serenity of retirement, but is embittered by the great sacrifices that she had to make and the alienation she had suffered.

I am from Tai Shan. People can tell where I am from, from the way I pronounce my words. People like listening to the way I speak. I was married when I was 19 years old. In China, it was common to get married at an early age, 16, 17, 18. If you were married at 19 or 20, you were considered an old maid. I was married in Tai Shan. I left for Hong Kong, and I was there for ten years. My son was in the United States for less than ten years before he came back to China to bring his family, but they were not allowed to go back with him because he had not stayed for the full 10-year period. He was granted permission to leave so he went to the States with his wife, but he had to leave his son in my care. I took care of him from the time he was 13 months old till he was five years old. I was living in Hong Kong at that time.

My husband was in the United States. He did not have his working papers, so he was not able to work. There was not any work to do so he went into the laundry business. He was here for five years and saved up his money to bring his sons over. Working as an employee in someone else's business you made $6 to $8 a week. Working for yourself as a boss in the laundry was only a little more than $10 a week. You could only save a few cents at a time. It was not like it is now, when one can earn as much as a couple of hundred dollars a week. What you earn in a week now, you would have to save for months then. My husband applied for his sons to come over here. He bought papers for all of them. After his sons came over, he applied for his uncle. In five years, he paid for taxes and travelling papers for his sons and uncle. He then bought papers for me, a visa to the States. He wanted me to come so he bought a visa for me. He had to borrow the money. My papers were over a thousand dollars! I came here over thirty years ago. Before, my husband lived in New York; that is where he brought my sons. My youngest son passed away.

My husband was 20 years old when we were married. We were introduced by matchmakers. We had to write on a paper the year, month and day of my birth. We wrote it on a piece of red paper and it was given to the matchmakers. They would give it to a family with a son. That is how we did it at home then. He was 20 years old when we were married and I was 19. He was 27 years old when he came here. He never went back to China. We saw each other again when I came here, ten years later. When he first came to North America, my husband had no close relatives here. There were some distant cousins from the same village who were here, but no one was a close relative. He had their address and he hid with them for a while. He had to hide with them because he got into the country illegally. He hid there till it was alright to come out and work, because the law was changed. When it was alright to come out of hiding, he bought a laundry and started out slowly and gradually. Later, he was able to bring his sons over. Then, when his sons were able to save some money, my husband sent them home to get married. The second son had a boy, but he had to be here for ten years before he was allowed to bring his family over. So, now the family is over here. I had a daughter in China, but she died when she was 14 years old. I brought my two sons over from China.

When my husband came here, he said it could be ten, twenty years before he came back. It was just talk. Then, making money was the most important thing. You had to consider how many people he had to support. He had to support his four brothers, his parents, that is six, his own family; that made two, three more. There were over ten people to feed. He always had to send money back. If he did not, how were we going to eat? His brothers were going to school at the time. He wrote whenever he sent money home. Whenever he had the money, he would send it. I was farming at home. The money he sent, we used for farming equipment, expenses, and paid for his brothers' education. I really had to work hard at farming. I had a lot of work to do. I had to plant, harvest and dry the plants. It was a lot of work. I did everything myself. I did not have any help from my mother-in-law. I had to work very hard. I alone did the work of several people! That is how hard I had to work every day. I had to do everything myself. I never went to school. The way it was then, girls did not go to school. Schools were for boys. Girls were not allowed to go to school. Later, my niece and my brother's daughter had some schooling. She was able to study with the boys. I do not know how to write. I never held a pencil. How would I know? To sign my name, I have learned to copy my signature in English, I have to print though. Let me show you...That is how I write it. To obtain Canadian status, they told me if I did not know how to write my signature, I should make an X.

I came here when I was 46, 48 and I have been here since then. Now, I am 83. I came to help my husband with the laundry. We had to wash socks, pyjamas and shirts. I had to be careful because if we damaged any of the garments, we had to pay for them. I washed everything myself, huge baskets full of clothes. I washed as many as 50 shirts. We just worked in the laundry ourselves. I did the washing, my husband did the ironing. I used to wash a large basket filled with socks in one night. Our laundry was at the end of Sherbrooke Street. It was all "*law-fan*" 老番 (a term the Chinese use to refer to non-Chinese people, especially Caucasians) business. Sometimes we had as much as $1,000 to $1,200 of business. We later sent some of our business out to someone else to do some of the washing. They sent it back to us for ironing. Dry cleaning is much better, we did not need anything for that. There were many laundries then, 30, 40 laundries. Now we do not have any at all. Now, the law-fan have taken over the business and there are automatic machines that people use. There are also clothes now that do not need ironing. Then, shirts needed starch in their collars and they needed to be pressed. The nurses' uniforms needed a lot of work, we charged about a $1 for nurses' uniforms. It was very hard money to make. There were no set working hours. When there was more work, we had to stay up and do it. We would work late at night sometimes till ten, eleven o'clock at night. We had to get up early so that customers could come and get their clothes. I did not work on Sundays. Customers did not bring their clothes, nor did they pick them up on that day. We were usually busiest on Saturdays. They would come and pick up their clothes and bed sheets. Bed sheets were sent out to get washed and pressed. We only made a few pennies on bed sheets. Clothes we did ourselves. We could not manage sheets.

My husband knew a little English. There was a lot he did not know. Law-fan collars were usually as dark as socks when they were brought in for us to wash. The *law-fan* harassed us all the time. They used to scream, "Chinitown, Chinitown!" whenever we would say anything. After a while, my husband knew a few English words, he spoke to those who chanted. He said to them, "How would you like it if I called you names?" They would shout these names everywhere, even those who came to our laundry. We did not get into any fights. Where we worked, there were children who were very bad. When they were coming home from school, they would throw snow at our clothes lines, where the clothes were hung to dry. There was one customer who came in to pick up his laundry one day, and my husband told him about the kids. He was a very nice gentleman, he went and told the teacher about what was going on. After that, they did not throw any more snow. Sometimes they threw it right indoors, or they would wet something in some water before they threw it in. They were bad!

I came down to Chinatown every Sunday with my husband to do some shopping. That was our day off, so we came into Chinatown to buy some groceries. The Chinese who did not work in laundries worked in restaurants. There were quite a few restaurants. It is not as difficult as the laundry business. You can hire people to help you out. So, you do not have to work as hard doing everything yourself. You can hire a cook to help you prepare food, a cashier to look after the money. You do not have to do everything yourself. You can get help.

There are many old women who live here, in Chinatown, alone. Their children come and visit them sometimes. Some come maybe once a month. The good ones may come two or three times a month, maybe even eight or ten times. People work, they do not have the time to come and sit with you. When you are collecting money from the government, your children are not going to offer you money. You are in bad shape if you have to ask them for money. Some good ones will ask their mothers if they have enough money to spend and offer them some money to help pay for expenses. If the mothers have enough, why take their money? All you need is enough to eat and find a shelter. Money is not good anyway, you will just end up giving it back to them. If the sons call once in a while and ask the mother if she needs anything and they buy some groceries for her, that is considered very good.

I like to play mah-jong, and my husband liked to play too. When we came down to Chinatown on Sundays, we would play mah-jong. We would play separately and we would not go home together. We would come home on our own. I used to play all the time. I would play with the men. I used to be a big number in Chinatown when it came to mah-jong. I was the number one player around here! I have played since I have been here! Do you know how I got started playing mah-jong? When there were not enough players, they would always ask my husband to bring me along to take someone's place. That is how I got started. The men were missing a player so I would go along and fill in.

I do not send money back to China any more. My husband used to send money back. He sent money home to all our relatives. We sent a lot of money back, twice a year to our close relatives and once a year to our distant relatives. We would send several hundred dollars and everyone would get something. We never went back because of the revolution. I mean, who knows what has happened there? Our children are here. There is really no point. Maybe they would ask for money but I have not got that much to give. If I do go anywhere, I would go to Hong Kong. I have no worries about going there. I can stay as long as I want and I could come home whenever I like. If people there ask me for money, I would not have that kind of money to give them.

YU CUIZHU

Yu Cuizhu 余翠珠 is a 66-year-old resident of Montreal's Chinatown. She was married in China but was separated from her husband shortly after their marriage when he returned to Canada. They stayed apart for a period of sixteen years until 1952 when she emigrated to Montreal to join her husband in his hand laundry business. Yu Cuizhu gave a vivid description of the arduous work involved in operating a hand laundry. It was a trade that demanded six days a week of 12 to 15 hour shifts without a break during the year except for a day off on Chinese New Year. She also described the typical lifestyle of the Chinese of that time and discussed some of the changes that have taken place over the last few decades.

I came from Tai Shan, Guangdong. I was married there when I was 19. Now I am 66 years old. My husband came to Canada when he was 12 or 13 years old. After he came here, they did not permit any more people to emigrate here. He had bought his student papers and soon after they closed off entry into the country. He came to Canada and returned to China to get married when he was 29 years old. He stayed almost a year after we were married, then he went back to Canada. He worked in a hand laundry with my relatives. He was quite anxious about coming back here in Canada. When you consider the long distance he had to travel to get here, he had reason to be a little anxious about it. He really was in a rush to get back. He did not really set a date as to when he would return. It was less than a year after we were married that he came back to Canada. I was married in November and he left in July. There was also the fear of the Japanese invasion to think about, that hastened his decision to return to Canada. After that he never came back to China. He wrote to me and sent me money. In China, I had a close relative who was quite wealthy. I spent a lot of time with her. When I came to Canada I was about 35 years old, that was in the year of 1952. I turned 66 this year. I came by ship. My husband sent me the money for the fare.

I came to Montreal and worked in my husband's laundry business. We did business with *law-fan*, washing and ironing laundry. I could not speak with the customers, so I did the ironing. My husband knew how to speak English. It was just the two of us working in the laundry. There were many laundries then. Our laundry was worth about $3,600 dollars and that amount was considered quite a lot and it was old but we managed to operate out of it. Then, people had to work very hard. We had to wash the clothes, dry them with a small heater and iron them. I used to get blisters on my hands from all the heavy ironing. It demanded a lot of strength. My husband was more used to it. Women had a lot of work to do then; I did a lot of ironing. We had about $300 worth of business, that was considered very good, but we had to work very hard. We used to wake up at six o'clock in the morning every day and walked to work. Work was only a short distance away. We would work till eleven o'clock at night, even on weekends. We did the ironing on weekends.

Since I have been here, I send money home every month to support my mother. I sent $50 every month. I have a mother and a younger brother in Hong Kong. I have my aunt in China to whom I used to send money also.

The Chinese never took any time off. If you had a restaurant, you could close it and people would not come in and eat, but with a laundry that could not be done. When people brought their laundry in, work had to be done. Laundry had to be washed. You had to go through it, sort it and wash it. Socks were smelly. In this kind of business, money was hard to make but it was worth something. Now, a few hundred dollars does not mean much. Later on, our laundry did not do so well, so in 1964 we went back to Hong Kong. We stayed there for a year. We hired someone else to operate the laundry till 1969. Around 1970, my son got married, after which I went out to work. I worked on 3510 St. Laurent for another Chinese. I worked there for about eleven years. I cut thread off garments and sewed buttons. I did not have to work at all in China, but I had to work when I came here. After working in the factory, I had to come back to the laundry on Prince Arthur and help with the ironing. I had to wake up at seven o'clock in the morning, go to work in the factory and when I finished work there at six o'clock in the evening, help out in the laundry. That is the kind of hard labour we had to live with. When I finished at the factory, my husband waited for me at the laundry. We were very much responsible for our own households then. Gradually people left the laundry business. There were automatic machines where you would deposit a quarter for some detergent and it would wash your clothes for you. We did the kind of business that catered to bachelors. Shirts, socks, handkerchiefs, towels, that is the kind of laundry we did. It was bachelor laundry. The people who had families had their own machines to take care of that for them.

People had to work very hard then, they really had to suffer. I did not like it at all. I did not like it one bit. I did not realize how hard it would be before I came. It was hard! Those in Tai Shan have always thought things in *"Gim-san"* 金山 ("Gold Mountain") were great. How were we to know how difficult it would be? Always carrying an iron and hard at work, that is what we were like then. There were no machines. If you were Chinese, what are you going to do? If it was not laundry, it was restaurant work. Laundries were more popular because one did not have to hire outside help. If there was a lot of business, there was good money there. Once all the expenses were paid, the rest was profit. The Chinese really worked hard then. They would make some money, but they never spent any of it. They did not decorate their homes, or anything like that. They were concerned with saving. Now, people are concerned with doing what is good for themselves, not like it was then. They were always saving money to go back to China. If you were working in a restaurant, you had to know how to speak the language. Most of the Chinese immigrants during my time were laundry workers, not so many were restaurant workers. They would make their money, and as hard as it was, they would go back to China and buy land to farm on. My great grandfather went back to China. He did not like it here. In China, there was the farming to do, but there were two times every year where you could take a break. Here, there was no time to take a break, we had to work all the time. To top it off, we did not know how to speak the language and there was not much of anything to eat. I have been here for so long and my son has not come but I do not see any point. Here, it is easier to save money and the society is more stable. If you do not want to save money, then there is no point coming here, it is so cold.

Then, there were still some Chinese who wore braids. We could even see it in the movies then. They wore braids, but they got them pulled. Then, the immigrants who used to come over were not even able to afford a good meal. They would have a simple bowl of rice with a few sticks of lettuce. They were very frugal. They wanted to save up their money so that they could go back to China. Sometimes they would even work when they were ill. Even if you were sick, you still worked. Now, things are much better. The government gives some support, there is old age pension.

The laundries were everywhere, but they were mainly grouped in Chinese neighbourhoods. Restaurants had heavy expenses but with laundries, a little soap, string, some paper, bleach that is all it took. It was an easy operation. I never went out, my husband always went out for everything. I just stayed home and did the ironing. It was only after my mother's arrival here that I went anywhere. It was she who took me to the department stores like Simpson's and Eaton's. I am the kind of person who is very quiet and not very adventurous. If it was not for my mother, I would not have ventured out at all. I would rather stay home and watch some television or listen to music. As a result I do not know too many places. The most I have done is go to Hong Kong a few times.

Working in the factory cutting thread was not very hard labour. You developed a rhythm after a while. I worked there for eleven years, until I collected pension; then, I kept on working until I wanted to leave of my own accord. My husband worked as a waiter in a restaurant before I came. We bought the laundry when I came over from China. We finished our operation in 1974. We closed it when business became slow. When I came here, the Chinese did not wear the Western-style pants. When my mother came, we were wearing the Chinese fashion in clothing, even to greet the customers. We had to wear dress suits. Now, we can wear Canadian styles, which are more convenient.

In the past, there were fights from time to time between the Chinese and the *law-fan*. I heard about them, but I did not really know too much about what was going on. Fights broke out in restaurants during meals. Clients would fight with waiters. A woman told me a story about how a client tried to burn a waiter with a cigarette. The waiter asked, "Why did you try to burn me?" The client responded, "Because I hate you." The waiter could not take that, so they fought. The fight broke out in the restaurant and ended up in the street. Some of the friends of the client held the waiter down while the guy beat him. They almost beat him to death. Everyone was asking, "How come he has been gone so long?" They did not realize he was lying on the street.

LI DEFANG

Li Defang 李德芳 is a 92-year-old resident of Montreal's Chinatown. She emigrated to Canada from Hong Kong in 1953, to join her husband in his hand laundry business. Together, they kept their operation going 6 days a week, working long shifts of 12 to 15 hours a day, everyday without a break during the year except for New Year's. They maintained a frugal existence in order to save their money to send home to their children in Hong Kong and their relatives in China.

Mrs. Li described the rigours of working in a hand laundry and her part in the operation of her husband's business. She also described the typical frugal lifestyle the Chinese immigrants had to maintain for the benefit of their families. Mrs. Li now enjoys the serenity of retirement and, despite her age, remains active and energetic within the Chinese community.

I am from Tai Shan. I was 21 years old when I was married. I am 92 years old now. My husband came here first, I came later. When he came to Canada, he started work in a hand laundry. It was on his return trip to China after he arrived here, that we had a daughter. When my husband came to Canada, he had an uncle here. When he first came, he said he would return within four years, but after his arrival here, he returned to China in five years. He just said he would return in four or five years. He was 19 years old then. He came to Canada first, before he returned to China to marry me. He was four years older than I was. When he was first here, he was 19. He returned to get married when he was 25. He wrote me often, every month. I received 14 or 15 letters from him a year. He sent money every month.

He came back to China about five times. Each time he stayed one year. I was staying with a relative, an aunt. We had a large farm. We had to hire people to help us work on the farm. I had many brothers-in-law. My husband was of eight brothers. His father had re-married and the second wife had a few sons as well, so the family became quite large; there were ten children in that family. I farmed but I did not have to do much hard labour. I had about three years of school. I also had one year of schooling when I was a little girl, so that is four years in all. When I was a young girl, I was very fortunate. My father was well-off, so we lived quite comfortably. I can write Chinese. I used to write letters quite often, but I do not write now, I am too old. I came to Canada in 1953. I have been here for exactly thirty years now. I came by plane. My husband sent the fare. He took care of everything. My youngest son could not come here, so he went to the United States. The others are all in Hong Kong. I have six grandsons and one granddaughter. They are all in Hong Kong too. I have always lived in Montreal and I visit my son in the United States as often as I like. I have always lived in Chinatown.

When I came here, all the Chinese wore nice clothes, they did not wear cheap clothes. It was the food that we skimped on. We did not want to spend the money on food. We had to make sacrifices. When I first came, I did not eat any chicken. Now, I eat plenty of chicken. Then, meals were very simple and plain. We usually had meals of salted shrimps or fish, spiced bean cake and a few potatoes occasionally. Some Chinese worked in restaurants, some worked in laundries, some worked for others, some women went out and found jobs as dish-washers. Almost everyone worked for other Chinese; we could not work for Canadian people because we could not communicate in their language.

Our laundry did not do any business with Canadians. Most of us kept the business within the Chinese community. We did not have much business. Just a little. There were a few Chinese that were self-employed working out of laundries. The majority went to work for others. We did not hire anyone in our laundry. My husband and I did the work ourselves, we only had twenty dollars or so worth of business a week. That was not much. We had to pay taxes, rent and expenses. We barely broke even. Those were hard times. There were some larger laundries that hired people to work for them. At that time we had to rub clothes by hand, then we would hang the clothes in a room. The room was heated with charcoal. The clothes were hung indoors in any season. It was very hard work. We had to do all the ironing and washing ourselves, and the clothes that had to be laundered were very dirty. Most laundries were in Chinatown. Chinese businesses usually had Chinese clients. There were also a few Chinese restaurants, mostly small ones. The restaurants attracted many Canadians as well as Chinese. In our business, we had to work everyday—we did not get weekends off. We had to start work first thing in the morning at six o'clock. We had to go and collect the clothes for various shop-keepers. I had to deliver them to rooming houses. We worked till about nine or ten o'clock at night, we would work till the work was finished. If there was more work, we would get up earlier. If there was less work, we would get up later. When the clothes were washed, I delivered them regularly on Sunday. I collected others at the same

3. Ten Women

time. Sometimes clients would bring their own clothes, and we would give them a ticket. I spent ten to fifteen years doing laundry. We always hand-washed the laundry. We gave it up when we reached our elderly years. The laundries where the men worked usually had machines, but the laundries which were operated by women did not have any. They usually did their laundry washing by hand. Near the end, we did buy a small machine. We sold it when we gave up the business.

People are old now, they are too old to keep up with the rigours of the business so they have all shut down. I guess that is why people are bringing their laundry to businesses outside the Chinese community. *Law-fan* laundries are more expensive; the Chinese do not charge much. They give cheap rates so they can get more work. *Law-fan* businesses charge more. Most of our children do not want to do that kind of work anymore. Some of them have gone into the restaurant business. When we came here, there was not much else we could do; we did not have any skills. If you did not know how to cook or speak the language, there was not too much other work available other than working in a hand laundry.

When my husband retired, so did I. We just spent less money. We could not work and we did not know any other trade. So, we did not do anything else. Some others, with more initiative, found work in restaurants as dishwashers. We just worked in our laundry and that was it and when we sold it, we did not do anything else. While we worked, we sent our earnings back to China to help our children and grandchildren. We used to spend all day at the laundry. I made supper for the two of us and we ate there. We worked 7 days a week. Sometimes we would go out and buy some roasted chicken; we would be very happy with that, roasted chicken, stewed beef and carrots. We would buy that in a restaurant in Chinatown. If we were lucky, we would go out and buy a piece of chicken to eat with rice, but then we never ate a whole chicken. My husband always did laundry work since he was 19 years old. He retired in his 70s. He died when he was 83 years old. When he first came here, he was employed by someone else. Later he bought a small laundry.

When I first came here in 1953, I guess there were a few hundred Chinese in Chinatown. The men played mah-jong. There was not any entertainment for the women. The women did not even have time to sit together and chat. Now, there is time for it, but then we were out to try to make money. We did not do anything, we sat at home, we did not go out. We read a little, we sang, that is it. It has been over ten years since I have been baptized. My husband played cards. He played every week at the association. We sent money home to our children and grandchildren in Tai Shan about four, five times a year. We sent about $1,000 a year. We sent about $200 at one time. It was divided up amongst the family. We also sent money to our nephews. We sent $1,000 not too long ago, and it was all divided up amongst them. It was just the other day.

FANG YULAN

Fang Yulan 方玉蘭 is an 81-year-old resident of Montreal's Chinatown. She was married in Tai Shan, China when she was 18 years old. Her husband left China to emigrate to North America less than a year after they were married. Mr. Fang travelled from Canada to China three or four times over the span of thirty-five years while he worked in restaurants struggling to support his family in China and save up enough money to pay the passage fare for his wife and children. Eventually, Mrs. Fang was able to join him in Trois-Rivières, Quebec in 1953.

Mrs. Fang learned the difficulties of having to adapt to the lifestyle and customs of a new world. She found the problems of language particularly difficult to overcome. She described the unethical practices of her boss at the sewing factory where she was employed and the frustration she felt over her inability to communicate.

I came from Tai Shan. I was 18 years old when I was married. Now I am 81. I was married in 1929. My husband came to Canada first. He came when he was 17 years old. He was here for seven years, then he went back to get married and was back here before the year was over. When he came here, there were all kinds of things for him to do. He learned to cook. He was a cook, working for someone else and later he opened his own restaurant. He went to Vancouver first and worked there for a few years. Later on, he went to Winnipeg. After we were married, when he came over here, we never talked about when he was going to come back. Then he was only making $20 or $30 dollars a month. It was very difficult. I had to work and I was only making $25 dollars a week washing dishes. I have lived in Montreal for over ten years. It has been quite a few years. I have always lived in Chinatown, on Clark Street.

After my husband came here, he always sent a few letters and money. If he had not sent money, how would I be able to eat? When my children were older, I did some farming. Not while they were young. I have a girl and a boy. When I came to Canada, they were still at home. My daughter was married at the time. My daughter is in the United States now. My son is in China. While I was still in China, my husband went back to see me three or four times.

When I came to Canada, I worked for Chinese people. I did not speak any English. I worked for five or six years. I made $20 a week. They did not have raises during that time. They used to give as little as $3 a month. That was much earlier, when they were still building streets, $3 a month for washing laundry; it was only a few pennies a wash for a garment. Then, a dozen eggs cost 10 cents, it was very cheap. It was cheap then, but you had to work for your money. Workers got together and shared meals. My husband always worked as a cook. When I worked washing dishes, there was one day off a week. I worked over 15 to 20 hours a day. Now the working day is much shorter.

I came to Canada by ship. My husband sent the fare home for me. I got off the ship in Vancouver. I took a bus here, and then I went into a small town. It was very pretty there. Business was not good there because it is such a small town. My husband had a restaurant there, but he later closed it. It was hard to make any money from it. We had to work every day. It is so much easier today. Today people go to school, they have better jobs, they can work as professionals. It gets better as time passes. Chinese people are doing good business with the *law-fan*. Generally, *law-fan* like to eat Chinese food. We had both Chinese and Canadian cuisine. When I first came, there were not many Chinese in a small town. There are many Chinese now. The Chinese came here to escape the revolution. There are several thousands here in Montreal, perhaps 30,000 to 40,000.

I like living in Chinatown. It is very convenient for me. I have been here over ten years. When I was working in a factory, my boss reported my income to the government, but he reported less than what I was earning. I did not know how to speak for myself, so there was not much I could do about it. I did not know better. I received $15 a week. He gave me a $5 raise every year. He was a real money hoarder. He was very bad. My husband worked for 30 to 40 years but he did not collect any pension. He did not know how to apply. He worked in a few places. He paid income tax. I remember sticking stamps. We did not know how to do anything. We had problems with language. It would have been good if we had someone, a *law-fan*, to teach us these things. My boss at the restaurant was fairly good. I got a raise of about $5 a year. I had one day off a week. I did not know anyone. I did not go out anywhere. Now I go to Church and I get to meet people. I have not been baptized yet, but I still go. I have been going to mass for over ten years. From time to time I will go. Before, I would attend more diligently. Since my husband died, I have not been there as often. He passed away this year.

Thirty years ago, when I first came, there were *law-fan* who tried to harass the Chinese. They would always say, "Ching, Ching, Ching." They do not say it anymore. Sometimes there were fights. I heard of one man who was beaten to death. They were fighting over a girl. I forgot the exact details. He was brought to the hospital after the fight was over. He went after the girlfriend of a *law-fan* and the *law-fan* beat him to death. Later, the *law-fan* was killed in the United States. The fight was one against one. People were watching it happen. It was near the Yen-Gin Restaurant, near that building. People are better now. China has become a much stronger country. The revolution has made her stronger. It is better at home now. You have your farm and cattle, and after you pay your taxes, you still have enough to eat. Sometimes I send a few dollars back to China. I send whatever I make from work. I send money to my son and also to my nieces and nephews. I was there when they were born, I have watched them grow up. I went back in 1967. I stayed for a few months. It costs money to travel and on top of that I like to shop. So spending money comes easy when you are travelling.

ZHANG LINGJIAO

Zhang Lingjiao 張玲嬌 emigrated to Canada in 1957 when she was 50 years old. She married at the age of 30 and worked on a farm; her husband left China to find work in North America. It was ten years before she saw her husband again, when he returned for a visit. She saw him three or four times over a span of twenty years, until they were finally reunited in Canada. She joined him in his efforts to operate a hand laundry and worked 7 days a week, 15 hours a day to make a living. She was accustomed to hard labour, having spent most of her life toiling over rice crops in China. Work in the laundry demanded even more from her. At least in China there was a rest from farming two seasons out of the year.

Mrs. Zhang encountered the typical problems of adapting to life in a foreign country. She never learned to read or write and could not speak any other language but Chinese. There was no communication with Caucasians and she found them hostile and cruel. She recalled that their antagonism was particularly difficult on their young son who was the only Chinese boy in his school. The other boys tormented and bullied him relentlessly.

She is 76 years old and at present lives in Chinatown. She prefers the

3. Ten Women

convenience of living in an environment where she can be independent and self-sufficient.

I am from the Kai Ping region. I was 30 years old when I married. I am 76 years old now. My husband came here when he was 15. His wife died and then he re-married. I became his second wife. In Canada, he was in the laundry business. He was an employee. He had an older brother here. He had to pay an entrance fee in order to come to Canada. He went back to China four times. When he came back to China, we were married and then he returned to Canada. The Second World War broke out and Japan invaded China. It was ten years before he came back when we were first married. He wrote me four, five times a year. He would send money when he wrote. The money he sent was enough. We had a lot of rice fields in China, a number of acres. We rented them out to people. My husband used to come back to visit every three years. Sometimes, he stayed a little more than a year, sometimes it would be for two years or so. He helped out in the rice fields. I had to work as well. I had to work very hard. I never went to school. I do not know how to write. I learned how to write my signature but just in English. I print the letters only. When I was working in the laundry, I picked up a few sentences in English.

I came to Canada when I was 50 years old. I came in 1957, on 23 October. I came by plane. My husband sent the fare for the plane. We came over together, my son and I. We lived in a small town, named Belanger. My husband worked in a laundry there. We lived there for about three years. Then, we moved to another place, around St. Hubert. I moved to Chinatown last year. When I first came to Montreal, it would cost 25 cents for three bus tickets, now it is 75 cents for one ticket. Before, it used to cost 18 cents for a loaf of bread, while now it costs about $1. That is quite expensive. At that time, most of us were poor. Sometimes at the laundry, customers would bring clothes in to get cleaned and they would leave them behind and never come back to pick them up again. We would take them and use them. There were some Chinese who wore expensive clothes and there were some who were more conscious of money. I wore what I could and dressed simply.

When my husband first arrived, he worked for someone else. He worked there as an employee ironing clothes. He never went to school. I helped him out in the laundry. It was seven days a week. We worked on Sundays too. Everyday we got up at five o'clock in the morning and worked until midnight. We only slept a few hours. Enough sleep or not, it was the same. Even if it was not enough, it amounted to the same thing. When you had to use the hand iron, it was difficult. The work was very hard, harder than farming. Farming was two seasons a year, from February to July or August. When the season was over, you only began work again in October. There was a break in between; this way I think the work in China was a little bit easier. It still was not easy work. Rain or shine, you had to be in the field, you had to work.

Three years after I arrived here, my husband passed away. The customers were all Caucasians. When customers came over to pick up their laundry, my husband helped me out. I did not understand the language. In the Belanger area, there were some other Chinese laundry shops as well. They were not far away from where we were. There were quite a few others in the area. There were some in Chinatown. They were everywhere. If the shops were big, there were hired hands to take on the extra work. Most of the laundries were small operations, run by couples or individuals. After my husband passed away, I did not know how to run the business, so I hired someone to help me. I paid him $40 a week. The business earned about $100 a week. The man who operated the presser was paid $18, the one who worked at the wet laundry was paid about $20, so in the end there was not much left to take in. As time went on we could not break even, and I could not stand on my feet anymore. Subsequently, I left to work elsewhere, but was laid off. At that time, my son had not graduated from the university yet. He was telling me not to work. One day, he left a note on the door saying that we would not be collecting any more laundry. The Caucasians came around and asked, "Why are you not working, you will have nothing to eat." I replied, "Look at my feet." They in turn said, "Oh Madam, you better take it easy and rest."

My son started to work at the age of 14 at the Foo Chow Restaurant. He cleaned the utensils for them. Later on, he was hired to chop the spare-ribs and help with fried foods. He had to cut hundreds of pounds of spare-ribs. When he came home at night, he was very tired. When I asked him about it, he said it was very painful. He worked over the weekends and during holidays. He worked his way right through school. After I closed the laundry shop, I went to work around the Jean Talon area. It is around the underpass, the bridge area. My job was to cut away the understitching from garments. This was around 1963. I was paid 90 cents an hour. The Chinese laundries disappeared due to the fact that you just cannot earn much money at it. Also, the work was dirty and people had to work very hard. There was dirt and excrement to wash off. After putting all the clothes into proper order, you would then have to burn incense to get rid of the odour in the air. The work was filthy and there was not much money involved. The Chinese went into the laundry business because

3. Ten Women

there was no other work for them. My husband went door to door to customers' homes to pick up laundry. The Caucasians would tell him to go under the bed and pull out the pads. It was very different from now, when sanitary napkins are used. He would have to bring the pads back, use salt, soak in water to clean them, iron them, and deliver them. It was a degrading job!

The younger generation eventually went into other lines of work. The older generation did not go through too many transitions because they did not speak English. Things were very different in those days. There were no snow blowers to remove snow, one had to use a shovel to clear the streets. In the winter time, my husband's moustache would be frozen like icicles and he had no snow boots. He would be dressed in Chinese attire, and the Caucasians would throw snowballs at him, trying to hit him until he dropped dead. It is a lot better these days. When I arrived in Canada, I still heard people say, "Jambé, jambé, macaroni." They were mostly kids around the age of 14 or so. They disliked the Chinese.

When my son went to school, they would always chase after him and try to beat him up. He was the only Chinese boy in the school. He wanted to tell on them but he could not speak any English. One boy who had the same name as him told him that there was someone trying to beat him up. He would help him and accompany him back home. At school, some boys would try to put thumb tacks on his chair without him knowing. The Caucasian boys were very bad. In the past, when my son came down to Chinatown, they would chase him and ask him for 5 cents. If he did not have any money, they would try to beat him up. Now, things like that do not happen as often. The Caucasians are much nicer and have a better attitude toward us. They did not treat us too well in the past. Before, they would hate us. When my son was little, the Caucasians would always try to beat him up and make him suffer. Now, the Caucasian friends he met in school get along with him quite well because he can speak English now. When you know how to speak the language, there is no problem.

My son visits me every week. Sometimes he takes me out to the tea house. He does not like to eat at the tea house. He is thrifty. When he was younger he was taught to be thrifty like his father. If you spend too much, you do not save. I still have a son and a daughter in China. My husband's first wife passed away, leaving behind the children, so I have to look after them. I still send money once in a while. The children are from my husband's first marriage. They are all married and now have children of their own. It is usually once a year, during Chinese New Year, when I send money. These past few years, I have been getting old and cannot work. My son has his own family and so do the children in China. There is a better standard of living, so I can send them less money. I used to send money three times a year. Not too much, perhaps $70 or $80. Over the Chinese New Year, it would be more. The two sons would each receive about $100. My younger sister would receive another $100 and my other relatives would receive $40 or $50. Altogether I sent a few hundred dollars.

I like living in Chinatown. It is much more convenient. If I lived with my son, I would just sit around all day. Over here, you can visit with the neighbours and walk around the neighbourhood. I live at the Catholic Mission Old Age building. I have a close friend who lives on the fifth floor with whom I visit, Mrs. Zheng. Sometimes I go down to the fourth floor. They have a videotape machine there. A lot of people have that nowadays. If I do not like to watch one thing, I can move around and watch another show.

ZHU ZHENAI

Originally from China, Zhu Zhenai 朱珍愛 emigrated to North America from Hong Kong in 1959. Her trip was made possible through the hard work and dedication of her husband. On a salary of only a few dollars a week, he eventually saved over three thousand dollars to pay for his wife's passage to Canada and her immigration tax. She knew very little about Canada before she came, only that one had to "work very hard ironing". She was referring to the hard labour that was involved in the hand laundry business which thrived in Chinatown during the height of Chinese immigration to North America. When she arrived, she opted to work in a Chinese restaurant washing dishes. She soon discovered that this work was not any less demanding than working in the rice fields of China. Her six and half days work a week consisted of 15 hour shifts, with few breaks during the year.

Mrs. Zhu found that adapting to life in a foreign country presented many difficulties. There were many problems of communication and racial discrimination which she had to learn to cope with. Moreover, being a woman in the Chinese community in a foreign country at the time presented another set of problems. Women were confined to their homes and could not venture out without fear of harassment from the men in the community.

She at present lives on her own in Chinatown. She prefers the convenience of living in an area in which she can communicate and live independently.

3. Ten Women

I went to Hong Kong in 1955, from Tai Shan. Tai Shan was my hometown in China. I left mainland China in 1955. If I had not left, I do not know how I would have been able to survive since the work was so hard. There was planting in the rice fields, harvesting. My back was killing me all the time. It is hard work. In China, I had to do that kind of work. On top of this they would hold meetings until eleven o'clock at night and assign work to be done and you had to report what you did that day. I heard someone say that it is better now.

I married at the age of 19. I am 69 years old now. My husband was going to university and I went to teacher college back then. My husband was at a university in Guangzhou. I was in an all girl's college. I did not graduate. I was in that school for just one year. After I passed my entrance examination, I went to school and then I became engaged. I was married soon afterwards. My husband told me to return to school, but I became pregnant and eventually quit altogether. My father was very open-minded. He had two businesses. All my brothers, sisters and everyone in the family went to school. My older sister-in-law was very intelligent. She taught school. My mother-in-law did not allow me to teach. I had to look after the children. I have three children. One of them left China ahead of me and the younger one, along with the third, came after me. They did not let us go all at once.

My husband came to Canada first. He came back again to China before I went to Hong Kong. He just paid money to purchase a visa and came to Canada. Most of the Taishanese, who were not allowed to go to the United States, came to Canada. If you purchased a visa to come to Canada, there was a possibility that you would eventually go to the United States. Some people did that and some did not. Over here in Canada, it is very nice. This is especially so with the security benefits. I do not want to go back. I like it here.

The visa cost a few thousand dollars. It was more than three thousand dollars. It was at the time when the Japanese invaded China. You had to work a long time to earn that amount. The wages were low back then. It was just a few dollars a week. When we were over here at that time, it was $30 or $40. At that time you could buy a lot with a small amount, 19 cents for a loaf of bread. Milk was the same price. Now it is eight times that amount or more.

When we came here, both my husband and I worked. Everybody worked. Everyone came to try to make some money. Everyone knew that if you came to Canada, you would have to do the ironing. In the old times, there were not many people in the restaurant business. While I was here, I washed dishes. Also, at that time, there were not many ladies doing these chores. In addition to this, there were not many people in the sewing business either. I did not speak the English language so I did not have the guts to go to the clothing manufacturers to work. Some people went to pack the bean sprouts and make egg rolls. When I first arrived, a person talked to me about getting a job. It was to wash dishes. I took that job and made egg rolls as well.

In the beginning, my husband worked at a laundry. Afterwards he worked in a restaurant as a cook. No matter how educated you were in China, when you arrived here, you had to do hard labour. When my husband came to Canada, he wrote me all the time. If you do not write to your wife, who else are you going to write to? He also sent me money, even when I was in Hong Kong. I wanted to earn extra money so I went to work in a clothing manufacturer cutting thread. I lived in Hong Kong four, five years. In Hong Kong, when you lived close to the Taishanese people, you would all speak that language. If you did not, then you would have to speak Cantonese.

In China, I worked in the rice fields. At night it was not as bright as over here. They would call meetings at night. The roads were very bad at night. It was bumpy and muddy. There were snakes right along the road sides. It was scary. The meetings would finish around eleven o'clock. The grass and wheat were so high that you would not know if there were any snakes hidden in them. My youngest son nearly died from a snake bite once. The snake had a black and white stripe. The rice fields were just a little way down from someone's doorstep. It is true that the rice fields were divided equally.

I came to Canada by steamship. I did not have the money to come by plane. Fortunately, I was not seasick. I took meals to the individuals who were. I was travelling alone. My husband sent me the fare. One lady said to me, "You are lucky, Madam, when you arrive in Canada, you are going to become fat." I told her that I was not sure if I was going to survive there or not.

When I first came to Montreal, I lived on St. Laurent Boulevard, near the Metro. I do not know my way around the city very well; the location then was very convenient. Most of the Chinese lived there. I would say practically all of them. A lot of people lived in small towns. On Sunday, the people from small towns would drive down to Chinatown. I think there were about 10,000 to 20,000. The younger Caucasians would threaten the older Chinese. They would laugh and call, "Ching, Ching, Ching." I would stop and say, "I am going to hit you." Then, they would leave, but as soon as I started to walk, they would follow and taunt me again. When I was walking out from Warsaw Market one time, they were laughing and harassing me. I grabbed a mop handle and they disappeared. They were children about 10 years old.

Once, there was an old man, he was walking down the street and was pushed down by some guys. He was carrying his money in his hands. They pushed him down and both of his hands went into the snowbank. One guy went through his pockets and could not find the money. He had fallen and the money went into the snowbank. Later on, he went back and the money was still there. This happened to me once. It was a purse-snatching incident though. It was about eighteen years ago. They also took my eyeglasses. I had to get a new prescription. It was inside my purse. There was nothing else in it. I had no money in the purse, the cash and the keys were in my pocket.

When I was working at the restaurant as a dishwasher, I worked only six and half days a week. We had a half day off. It was Wednesday. On Wednesdays, I would go in the morning and leave in the afternoon. First, I had to clean up everything before the night shift would come in. I worked 12 hours a day. In the past, it was 12 times six and half days, equalling 80 hours a week. It was not so fortunate for us then. Where I worked, it was damp. They said that the conditions were good but in reality, they were bad. They trimmed all the fat from the meat and steamed it with black beans. A lot of the employees, the males, went home for supper. Later on, I went to another restaurant where the conditions were a lot better. The meals were bad and the salary was low too. When I first started, I asked them if I could work a little longer. If you did your work properly, then, eventually your salary would increase. However, as time went on, I received no increase. So, I asked the owner about it, "Sir, I have been working for quite a while, what do you think of my work so far?" "It is good," he said. Then I asked him about my salary. He said, "Okay," he would add an increase which would start next week. If you did not ask for it, they would not give you a raise. If they made any money, they would pocket it.

There were not that many Chinese restaurants around then. It was mainly laundry shops. It was because you did not have to speak English. When customers brought in the laundry, you just had to mark down how much for how many. It was simple work. Also, there were no washing machines at that time, so they had to do it themselves. If you are in the laundry business now, you would not make a living. There is not much demand for it anymore. Everyone has an automatic washer to do their washing for them. It was mainly old people who went to work in the laundries. The younger generation did not want to work in laundries. So, a lot of them went to work in the restaurant business. The older people do not work now since they have their pensions. The younger people did not want to work in the laundry business. There were dirty diapers and some of the ladies had their period on the clothes which you had to wash. I knew some people who said that I made a lot of money. It is a degrading task. One of the older men, when he finished washing the clothes, he would take them to the backyard where he would hang them on a line to dry. However, there were some Caucasians who threatened to throw mud on his clothes and dirty them all up again. He started to scream at them and they left. But when you started to hang the clothes back on again, they would do the same thing. They really bothered the Chinese. It was a degrading life, but now it has improved. There is a big difference.

Over the last couple of years, I changed jobs. I went to a Jewish store to wrap meat. It was very good. The pay was by the hour. However, if there was not enough work, you would then have to go home. In the beginning, when I first started, I put in a lot of hours. When I was working at the restaurant, they paid me $80 a week. The wages did not increase. However, when I quit that job and went to work over here, I made $120 a week. In the beginning, at the restaurant, the pay was $35 a week. They gradually increased it, but very slowly. I then changed to another restaurant. At the Jewish store, each year we had a five week holiday with pay included in it. When I was on vacation, I would go out with the ladies and take walks.

In 1959, all the Chinese people did not live in Chinatown. Most people lived outside of Chinatown. There were only a few people living at the Four Seas Hotel. This was upstairs of the Lung Fung Restaurant. People did not like the air in Chinatown because it was polluted. Everyone rented a home on the city outskirts. They would go to work, and when they closed up shop they would then go home and sleep. Most of the residents of Chinatown were single men.

I sent money to China three times a year. My granddaughter is working a little now. She was born in 1967. Now she is in the United States working at the immigration office in Boston. She works on the night shift. She started right after school. When she told me, "Oh Grandma, I have started work." I told her to work and make money. When she makes money, she would then have to send some money to me so that I could buy food. My daughter works in electronics. She works as a foreman. Her job pays $7 an hour. My son-in-law works in a restaurant. He makes "*dim-sum*". My other son who is in Montreal is in the restaurant business too. My son visits me all the time. He just came down to see me yesterday. Whenever he comes down to Chinatown or downtown, he always comes and visits me. They live near the Warsaw supermarket. This week he did not go to work because he injured his hand. He cut his hand and had to go to the hospital for stitches. He started work again today. It has been exactly one week. Whenever he offers to give me money, I refuse. Sometimes I will go out and buy things myself since I live so close to Chinatown.

CAI JINE

Cai Jine 蔡金鶯 is an 81-year-old resident of Montreal's Chinatown. For many years she was separated from her husband when he left China to make a living in North America. Their reunion was further delayed by strict government legislation over immigration and the desperate lack of funds. Over the span of thirty long years, he went back to visit his wife only three or four times until she finally emigrated to Canada in 1960 at the age of 59. She joined her husband in St. Jean, Quebec, where he operated a restaurant business with his brother and son. Shortly after her arrival, they gave up the business in favour of moving to Montreal.

Mrs. Cai has been widowed for twelve years and now lives alone surrounded by close friends. She lives simply and remains in good health. She has in recent years learned how to play mah-jong. She ventures out occasionally to socialize with friends and enjoys visits from her children from time to time.

In the past, they did not permit women to come to Canada. There were very few women here. When my husband came here, he never said anything to me about when he would be returning to China. Some of the men who came here were like nomads who ran around for eighteen years, or a lifetime. Some of them would come back to visit within four or five years after they settled here. You never could predict what they were going to do. My husband came back to China once. He was married for ten years when he returned to China. He was a gambler. If he had any money, he would gamble it away. He gambled whether it was a small or large amount, it did not make any difference. In the past, people gambled every day, all the time. The police raided and arrested a few of the gamblers. They stopped it for a while, but eventually they started again, playing in secret little rooms that were locked. They played for a couple of days here and there. They changed their locations around frequently to avoid detection by the authorities. The government put a stop to it, but that did not stop the people who still had a strong desire to play.

My husband was in Vancouver first, then he went to Winnipeg. He was a cook. He did not do anything else other than being a cook. He left Winnipeg to come to Montreal. When I came to Canada, I stopped off in St. Jean, where my husband was. I came to Canada in 1960. I was 59 years old. My son, my nephew and my brother-in-law were in St. Jean. My husband's uncle moved to Montreal because he could not find a job in St. Jean. When he was a cook in St. Jean, he was making about $30 to $40 a week. When he came here, it was about $50 a week. He had to work about 12 hours a day. Now, the kitchens are more modern. Before, they were very poorly equipped. In the past, they burned wood in their stoves. The wood was quite long and you had to throw it into the burner, or you used coal. It was like a table, there was one hole in the centre and a grill on both sides. They did not have woks then like they do now. The restaurant in St. Jean was very small. When I came here, they closed it and opened up a new one. They made pork chops and steaks. Now everyone cooks chop suey and Chinese lettuce. They did not have a wok to fry the chop suey in, they would boil it, cool it and then refrigerate the food. When the Caucasians came in and ordered that, they would boil it again, and add some corn starch to make the sauce. The Chinese would fool the Caucasians into thinking they were eating food that was freshly prepared. If it was busy, they would have more cooks. If there was less business, they would have less cooks. There were many partners involved.

When I came to St. Jean, the restaurant went out of business. The one that was closed down was owned by two of my husband's brothers and a nephew. My oldest son repaired television sets, he was in electronics. He came here in 1951. I have a son and a daughter. My son later went into the restaurant business. He is still in it now. My daughter came to Canada around the year 1969 to 1970. She came from Hong Kong. She was married there.

When my husband came to Canada, there was a $500 fee to enter Canada. His fourth uncle paid it. When my husband entered Canada, he went to work and paid back what he owed. It took him quite a few years to pay it back. Those kinds of debts take forever to pay back. It took eight to ten years before he was able to pay it all back. When I came, I did not have to pay tax because at that time I was a landed immigrant. There was a war with the Japanese following the World War. It was during this period that the Chinese were allowed to become Canadian citizen. The ones who had courage became citizens earlier. The ones who were less brave took a longer time before they applied for their Canadian citizenship. They became landed immigrants. In the past, when you first arrived in Canada, you had a business visa. Everyone came over here with a business visa. Subsequently, if your business was not good enough, then you

3. Ten Women

could not apply for too many people to come over. After the Second World War, the Canadian government allowed the Chinese to become Canadian citizens. You had to report how many people were in your family and how many children you had, then your children and spouse could enter Canada. When you became a Canadian citizen, you were allowed to bring your wife and children into the country.

I did not like living in St. Jean. It is only now that there are some Chinese people in that area; before there were not many at all. It was lonely, there was no one for me to talk to. There was not much for me to do up there and there were not any jobs. So, I came here to find a job washing dishes. I washed dishes for about seven years. It was hard labour. I worked in several places. I have worked in Chinatown, Sun Kwok Ming, Sun Ah, Silver Moon, China Garden, Wing Wah and Sun Sun. I worked in all those places. I worked six days a week, or sometimes seven days a week, 12 hours a day. You can figure out then how many hours a week I worked. I stopped working in April of 1968. I went to visit Hong Kong. I stopped working in April and in the month of June I left for Hong Kong. In 1969, in September, I came back to St. Jean. After a couple of months of living there, I came out here. In 1967, I became a Canadian citizen. They did not ask me to answer any questions. If they had asked me to say anything, I would not have been able to. It was when they were celebrating the centennial year and people were allowed to obtain their Canadian citizenship without any formal testing. A lot of people from all areas applied to get their citizenship then. A lot of people. It was a good opportunity, especially for those who could not speak any English. It was a lucky break for us. In 1967, I became a Canadian citizen and in the following year, 1968, I went to Hong Kong. I would not have been able to apply for it otherwise. I cannot speak any English.

My son and daughter come to visit me once a week. They come on Tuesday because that is their day off. Some of the grandchildren do not come, they have school. The old age pension I get from the government is enough for me to live on. If you save your money, you have enough for all the expenses, like food, rent and the essentials. I pay $85 a month for rent. I do not really know how much I spend on food. I make my own clothes. I buy the material in stores. They have shops like that all over the place. When I have the time, I do a little sewing. I do a little at a time. I have lived here nine years. It is very spacious and roomy. This room, I do not know what you would call it, a living room, a bedroom, whatever, this is where I put my things.

In the past, there were fights between the Caucasians and the Chinese. You might not always have heard about it, but it did happen. There were some men who came from China and knew how to defend themselves with kung fu. I do not have a good memory so I have forgotten all about that. Before, there were men who knew kung fu. There was one man—he was short. I forget his name now. I think it was Hong or something. He was very short and he knew kung fu. He was very good in fighting against the Caucasians. The people who emigrate over here now do not have to suffer the discrimination like we used to.

In Chinatown, there was a Chinese hospital. It was here for quite a few years before they moved it to St. Denis. The government said that the Montreal Chinese Hospital would not be as sanitary if it was located in Chinatown. The air was not as clean here, so they moved it. It was supposed to belong to the Chinese people, but those who had money did not want to donate it for the hospital. So the hospital was built from the funds the government lent out. It took over a million dollars to build the hospital. There are more Caucasians than Chinese in the Chinese Hospital. It is not just for the Chinese. The government loaned us the money to develop the hospital so there is an equal share in it for the Caucasians. This year, they added on a few more rooms at the Montreal Chinese Hospital. I have been there. My health is good. However, sometimes I suffer from arthritis. When there is a change in weather, I can feel it. Besides, I have high blood pressure as well.

In Chinatown, I am close to everyone. I cannot count how many people I know. I am close to everyone here, since I have been here for so long. However, I also greet those I am not that close to. Those I have known for twenty years I am closest to. I ask the people who live here to accompany me when I do my shopping. On this floor, there are over ten people. They are all females. The second floor is inhabited by women, and third floor by men. There are over ten men on the third floor. I think I am the oldest person in the building. One woman is only 50 years old. Everyone goes up and down here. You get to know everyone. Everyone greets each other. I rarely go for visits though.

In the past, there were a lot of laundry shops. Now laundry businesses have machines, so there are very few hand laundry shops the way we used to know them. Then, they only had a board with a roll. You would insert the clothes through the roll and roll out the clothes that way. In a room, they would hang wet clothes and make the room hot by heating it with hot coal in the stove. They cleaned, dried and ironed the clothes by hand. In those days, everyone used coal, they did not have electricity then. They used coal to heat the irons. Now, everything is more convenient. The laundry men and women were very dirty and sloppy. Some of them even slept on their ironing board or the folding table. Some of them slept upstairs and some of them slept on the steps as though it were a shelf. They would use the ironing table to sleep on. The laundry shop was used for sleeping, working, washing, cleaning and ironing. Everything took place in that one area. It was open 7 days a week. If there was work to be done, they would keep the operation open all week. Before, it was not permitted for shops to be open on Sunday, but there were some men who would work secretly in the basement with the door closed. It usually started out with one man and when he got his wife over here, they would work together. If the children came, they would also work. They would help with anything that needed attention. I remember there was a Cai family who had a laundry shop on Park Avenue. There was another one next to the bank, but that has since closed.

My husband knew how to write Chinese. He wrote me two, maybe three, letters a year when I was in China. It was only when he had money that he would send a letter. Sometimes he would send one or two hundred dollars. It was enough. Things were inexpensive then back in China. Two or three times a year was enough. In China, there was no rent to pay. My husband came to Canada by ship, directly from Hong Kong. For people who were going overseas, they would take this ship to go to Canada. The ship ride was a month long. Sometimes it was exactly thirty days. Later on, with the express ship, it took eighteen days. When he came, the fare was over $100. I came by plane. My son arrived here by plane as well. It was only the older generation that arrived here by ship.

My husband did not work for a number of years before he died. There was no money, I went to work instead. I worked and my son worked. I also had to work to send money home to my relatives. I will be sending money over for the New Year. I send money once a year. If I have more money, I send more. If I have less, then I send less. I do not write letters. I do not know how to write. If I have money, I will write a few words along with it. If I do not have any money to send home, I do not write. I went to Hong Kong once, but I did not go back to China. I do not want to go back to Hong Kong. I do not have the strength to go. I cannot walk very far without tiring quickly. It is only with relatives when I can go anywhere, otherwise I cannot venture out. I do not have enough money. Even if I had the money, I lack the strength and the energy to travel.

When I first arrived, there were no Chinese operas. Two years later, there were a few. They had Cantonese operas, but not from Hong Kong. That was about twenty years ago around 1963 to 1964. I think it was in 1964 when they started a Cantonese music society called "Xian Yuan" 閒園. They played musical instruments. This was beside the Sun Kwok Min Restaurant. So whoever had any talent would go there and learn, I forgot the names. It was about 20 people. Whenever they played, I must see it. I always went. It was about $10 for admission. The least expensive tickets were about $5. The last time they played here, the company was from Guangzhou, China and the show starred Hong Xiannü 紅線女. I went on a Saturday. My daughter-in-law went with me. She bought the tickets. Every year, when the Cantonese opera comes, I go to see it. Once in that year I saw it all. They played on five occasions, I saw all five shows. Sometimes if they have six shows, I will try to see them all.

TAN WUSHI

Mrs. Tan Wushi 譚吳氏 emigrated to North America from Hong Kong in 1966. She joined her son in Canada and helped support herself and his family by working in Chinese restaurants as kitchen helper. She found restaurant work arduous and retired after ten years to help her son raise his family. Mrs. Tan is one of the few women who emigrated to North America before her husband. Immigration authorities did not permit her husband entry into Canada; therefore, they stayed apart for a period of sixteen years. He lived in Hong Kong while she struggled to make a living in the new world. Over the years, Mrs. Tan made frequent visits to Hong Kong to see her husband and only recently have they been reunited in Canada when he emigrated to Montreal in 1982.

In her interview, Mrs. Tan recalled how immigration procedures were complicated and disrupted by the Cultural Revolution 文化大革命 which stormed China. She discussed some of the changes that have taken place in Chinatown over the past few decades and adjustments to life in the Canadian society.

I am from Kai Ping. I was married there when I was 16 years old. I was quite tall and very mature for my age. My husband came to Canada on 9 August of last year (1982). He was in his 70s already, he was 79 or 78.

He could not work. I collected pension. My son had applied for pension for him, and they gave him a lump sum of $529. I have been here a lot longer than my husband. My son came to "*Gim-san*". I said I was coming out, my son said that he was coming to Hong Kong to look after me, that is how I was able to get out to Hong Kong. I was in Hong Kong for ten years before my son brought me over here. He came here first. He had been gone from China for four, five years when I left for Hong Kong in 1956. I came here in 1966. He came here during the *"Gat-min"* (the Chinese term for the Cultural Revolution) at home. That was the time when people were being stripped of their power and possessions. He went to Hong Kong, then came to Canada. My great-grandfather sponsored him. He bought him his immigration papers. It cost about $1,000. You had to buy papers then. My son knew I could not come. It was during the revolution. He was here for eight, ten years before he got married. He had a bride sent here from Hong Kong. Soon after my daughter-in-law arrived, the Revolution started. My youngest son left Hong Kong one year earlier than I did. I left the following year.

I was working in Hong Kong. I made gloves. I did that for seven, eight years. As you get older, it gets more difficult to find a job there. I was 49 years old when I left. Those last few years before I left Hong Kong were difficult. They did not want to hire you because you were too old. They minded age even for work like cutting threads from garments.

My great-grandfather came when he was 10 or 12 years old. He came with his father. They came to Montreal. My great-grandfather did the ironing in a hand laundry. My father-in-law had a hand laundry and later he opened a restaurant. He did not have to work anymore when he was in his 60's. He rented a flat for elderly gentlemen. At that time, laundry work was tough work, even if you owned your own business. He went back to visit China. He had a pretty good life. After he was married and had a son, he came to *"Gim-san"*, then to Montreal. After eight years, he went home. He sent money back. My husband went back to study for three or four years, became a teacher and later a principal, and worked as a principal for a few years. He studied two years of secondary school. Earlier on, he wanted to continue his studies. He was with my father-in-law and his wife, and they said he spent too much money so they did not allow him to continue his studies. Therefore he went into teaching and eventually became a principal. He worked as a principal for four, five years and then went into business. His father did not want to bring him over because he felt that life here would be too harsh. So, he felt since he could not come he might as well stay and study. In those days, women followed their husbands. My mother came over to Canada to marry. My brother was in Toronto, and my father had travelled to Thailand. People travelled to have a better life. There was no money at home. If you went abroad, people could lend you money, but if you borrowed money at home, where would you get it to pay them back? My husband felt he would rather stay home and teach. He was an accountant until the revolution, after which there was not any work. We were lucky that there were no serious problems; they were arresting people then for stealing; people were sent to prison. They told him to leave and go to Hong Kong, but he did not go.

My husband and I have been separated for many years, until recently. I went back to visit him twice a year. I still have three sons in China. My son told me about the laundry and restaurant business. He said it was very hard work. That was partly the reason why he did not send for me even when my son asked him; he said, "Life is too harsh here. What is she going to do here? She is better off staying at home and looking after the family." I was not in very good health then. It was ten years after I came here when my son came. I started off working in a restaurant making egg rolls. I was working at King Wah. It was too difficult at King Wah. I could not keep up with the pace of making egg rolls. I was new at it and had never done that kind of work before. I could not keep up. King Wah does very good business. I switched over to Li's Garden Restaurant; they paid me $35, I thought that was cheap. I was paid $60 per week at King Wah. It was not by the hour. It was for as long as it took to get the job done.

I started at about half-past nine to ten in the morning every day and finished around ten or eleven at night. You had to finish your work before you could quit, and I could not keep up. On the weekend, my daughter-in-law had to come and help me. Tuesday was my day off. I did it for a month, and I quit. My son told me not to work because the Christmas season was coming up and it was going to get even busier. If it was busy, you had to work faster. My boss was Chinese. He was not a bad man. It was just too much work. Business was good, there were line-ups and take-out business. We had to prepare the vegetables and make egg rolls, we just could not keep up. Every day we had to go through two cases of carrots, two boxes of shallots and two boxes of celery. And on top of that, we had to skin the chicken. I just could not keep up. If it was just making egg rolls, I would be alright. I could manage. After that, I went to work at Asia Restaurant, on Henri Bourassa. I received $45. I only had to make egg rolls and skin chicken, that was all. So, I did not have any problems keeping up. Later, I went back to Hong Kong. After six months, I went to China for a visit and applied for my youngest son to come over. He has three children, two girls and a boy. My son asked me to look after them for him, that is why I quit my job, after five years. I worked for two years at the race track. When my son came over, I did not work anymore. I stayed home to look after his children. I was 60 years old when I came to Canada. I retired at 70. I worked for ten years. When my son came over, he asked me to quit my job and help him look after his children. He and his wife went to work. Three of my sons came to Montreal. The other two are in China. I write and send money to them. It is only fair for a mother to help her son. I send money about three times a year.

I spent six to seven years in school. I know how to read. I started to study when I was 7 years old. I was very bad-tempered and mischievous when I was small. My uncle taught me, he was a teacher. I was such a mischievous child, I was sent to school. But when I came to Canada, I did not learn any English. I did not have the time, we were too busy working. I came by plane. My son paid for my fare and my expenses. I came directly to Montreal, by myself.

Now I do not go to Chinatown too often. I go with my son on his day off, if he asks me to. If he does not ask me, I do not go. When I came, there were not too many people in Chinatown. There were only a few restaurants. We did not have teahouses then, we had noodles or rice. There were two grocery stores, Leoung-Jung and Sun Sing Long, that was about it. There was not much in the way of salted fish. It was only after that Mao Zedong 毛澤東 (1893–1976) allowed goods to come out. Until then, things would be coming from Hong Kong. Things were not too expensive.

When we were young, we were afraid to meet my grandfather. I was 16 or 22 when my great-grandfather came back to China. We were too shy to meet him or even talk to him. Then people were shy, they were not as open as they are today. We would be too shy to say hello when we met face-to-face. We would want to run away. When he came to Canada, he was writing to his wife and his brothers. My great-grandfather went back to Hong Kong. He did not want to bring his wife here to Canada, so he went back to Hong Kong. Later, when his sons went to Hong Kong, they applied for immigration status to come here. His wife was getting old so he returned to China. He did not apply for immigration status. When I came here, he was telling the children, "What is the use of bringing your mother over here? She should stay home and look after the household." Then, the revolution was taking place and they were forcing people out. I left three sons in China when I came out to Hong Kong. It is much better here than in Hong Kong. There is more money to be made here. It is more comfortable here. The living conditions are better. I can send money back to help my sons with expenses. They have households and the expenses add up. As a mother, I feel it is only fair that I work and send money back. I worked in a restaurant for over ten years. Apart from having one day off a week, there were two weeks of paid vacation a year. They would ask you to take two weeks off.

My children are over 50 years old now. I was married for thirteen years before I had my first child. I had two children every three years until I had five. The first one is a waiter. The youngest is a cook, the fourth is a dishwasher and does a variety of other kitchen work. My daughter-in-law is a sewing machine operator. Everyone works. Everyone has to work when they come here. She worked as a seamstress in Hong Kong, she was doing the same thing. The fourth daughter-in-law was a teacher in China, now she is a seamstress.

When I first came to Canada, I heard some stories about how the *law-fan* took advantage of the Chinese people. I do not know exactly what happened, we just went on with our own business. I used to hear from Mrs. Long that some children would throw snow. They would throw snow at Chinese people. But that did not happen too often when I came. Before, when I came here and was working weekends taking care of my grandchildren, there was an incident. There was one time when a *law-fan* chased after me. We were living on Mont-Royal and around the corner was our house; he chased me right around and up to the house. I managed to run in and climb up to the second floor. He did not follow me up there. He wanted my money. It was a Sunday. There were not too many people on the street at that time of day. Everyday there were buses that could take you around but not on Sundays. He chased me all the way to the second floor of the building; I did not even scream! He just stood there. I was ringing the bell, but they were afraid to answer the door. My daughter-in-law finally opened the door for me. My sons did not hear of any such stories. They were young when they came here, so they learned how to speak the language and even became friends with the *law-fan*. When we first stayed here we were with my great-grandfather. My son would come out and play with the *law-fan*, he learned how to speak their language. He is very intelligent.

My children live far. It is easier for me to live in Chinatown. I can go out and buy groceries on my own. Whenever there is something going on, my children invite me to join them. If I know the way, I like to go on my own. If I do not know the way to some place, they will come pick me up. My third son has a car, the other two do not. One is in Lasalle, one is in Longueuil, and the other son is on Park Avenue. I know the way to his place. Living in Chinatown makes it much easier for me. Now that my husband is here, it is much better. Even if he had not come, I would have planned to live in Chinatown. I was planning to move here when I started collecting my pension.

CHEN MEIYU

Chen Meiyu 陳美玉 is a 70-year-old resident of Montreal's Chinatown. She left her family's farm in China to emigrate to Canada where she was married to a man twenty years her senior. It was a "blind marriage" 盲婚, arranged by relatives.

Chen Meiyu soon discovered that life in a foreign country involved many restrictions and sacrifices. She learned that living conditions were harsh and that hard labour was the most dominant factor in the life of a Chinese immigrant. She described the isolation experienced by women who lived in this predominantly male-populated society and explained some of the attitudes and manners which prevailed at that time. She also spoke of the hardships encountered in having to deal with problems of language and custom in a new world and of the antagonism that existed between the Chinese and the Canadians.

I came from China, the Guangdong region. I was married when I was 21. I was married in Victoria, near the sea-port. I came to Canada by ship to get married. It was a "blind marriage", arranged by relatives. I am not fortunate like people nowadays. I was accompanied by some relatives, not my parents; they were still in China. I came here in the same year they closed off entries into the country. I was lucky, I did not have to pay a head tax. It was $500 then. Even with the head tax, a lot of people still wanted to come. There were many opportunities here. There were not too many Chinese families here then. There were mostly men. Of course, there are a lot more now. My husband came a long time ago. He was about 10 or 12 years old when he came. He is much older than me, about twenty years older. He was about 40 or so when we married. He came here to work.

Everyone came here to work, in a restaurant, laundry or shop. Shops were few. They came here to work, it was very difficult. Then, people were only paid a few dollars a month and they had to send money home to support their families. People rented rooms. Sometimes a few people would live in one room at a time. Brothers would live in the same room together or friends would live together. It was not as comfortable as it is now. Then, people used to sleep on wooden boards! Some even lived in washrooms. When I came, we rented a house. It was the bachelors who lived in washrooms. My husband came with his brothers. He never wrote letters from here. He did not know how and he did not have any family back in China. They were all killed in the war.

In China, I helped my parents on the farm, tended the cows. I came here by ship. It was a Japanese ship. My relatives here arranged for me to come and paid for the fare. In return, I helped babysit their children. Then, the ship fare was very cheap, maybe $200 to $300. It was a big thing then to travel by ship. I came to Victoria first and stayed there six or seven years. My husband rented a house. He had a business: a restaurant and a shop. He sponsored his brothers to come over here to work with him. It was a rented house. Then, not too many people bought houses.

People were more intent on making money and going back to China. They did not want to stay here, but the war in China forced many of them to stay. Then rent was quite cheap, the range was $10 to $20 a month. We rented a two-storey house. We used the downstairs for business purposes and we used the upstairs for our living quarters. A two-storey house with seven or eight bedrooms was about $25 a month to rent. I lived there for about twenty years before I had to move because they were reconstructing the streets. I would have stayed there if I could have, because the rent was so reasonable and the place was at a convenient location. I later moved in with my daughters and lived with them for a few years. There were many who made their money and went back home. Many of the men had families in China, and they wanted to go back and visit them. Of course, they came back. The fare was very cheap, a couple of hundred dollars. They would go back and visit from time to time, but only those who did not gamble and managed to save some of their money. They would go back and visit for a few months.

Many men gambled, but there were a few who did not and they would go back a couple of times to visit their homes. Then, if you could save a few hundred dollars, that meant a lot. They could buy a one-month or two-month visiting paper. If you had the money, you could afford to stay as long as you wanted. They went home because their families could not come here. That is why they had to go back. People were very frugal! The ones who gambled or chased women spent all their money. Times have changed now, people have a few hundred dollars a week in earnings. Then, one had to be very frugal to save up enough money to go back. People had to work very hard for the money they had. People would work in restaurants as cooks or be employed by *law-fan* or by Chinese grocery store owners.

The grocery store we owned was in Chinatown. It is still there, but it is owned by someone else now. I do not know the name of it, it is next to the Jade Garden. We used one side as a restaurant and the other side as a store. Now, the new owners have renovated it and it is all one restaurant. We gave up the business when my husband passed away. That was about thirty years ago or so. When he could not manage the business, he had my nephews help him out. I did not work. Then, women did not go out and work, it was unthinkable. People would start talking, the gossip would kill you. Women had to stay home and look after the household. Then, when there happened to be a special occasion, say a baby being born, or a baby turning a month old, or a women getting a daughter-in-law, no women had the courage to go out alone. You had to get together with a few other women before you dared to venture out. If you were ever caught alone, all the old men in the neighbourhood would come out and look you over and make comments like, "Oh so and so's wife is good looking, or whatever." It was terrible! Women did not go out with their husbands. Maybe we would go out once a year for a special occasion. It was not a big community, there was not too much going on. Now, you are free to come and go anywhere accompanied by your children. At that time, that was not acceptable. Women had to speak to each other on the telephone. Some of the households were very busy with as many as ten children! The women were too busy looking after the house and taking care of the children, no one had time to spend on the phone. There was always the cleaning, ironing and cooking to do. Domestic chores kept one occupied enough. The women had to cook lunch and supper for their husbands and children. Where could you go? I was afraid to go to Chinatown because people would laugh and talk about you. Chinatown was mainly inhabited by gamblers. There were very few women. Few families lived in Chinatown. The ones that had businesses were there. But families were few, perhaps 30 or 50. There were about 1000 to 2000 people. Many sponsored their siblings to come over from China.

A lot of people worked in the restaurant business because there was not much else to do. They had to work in the restaurants. People tend to work in a trade that they know well. The restaurants attracted many *law-fan*. They like to eat Chinese food. Our restaurant did very good business, there were line-ups. We had both English and French clients going to Chinese restaurants. Now women can go in with their children to eat in restaurants. Then we could not. Men did not take their children out. They would usually get up in the morning and go to their business as early as seven o'clock and work into the next morning, until four o'clock after midnight. My husband had his brothers helping him out. He would work till eleven o'clock or midnight. They worked 7 days a week. People did not take any time off during the year. Now, of course, people can take vacations. There are government regulations that allow you to take holidays. Now, the working day is 8 hours. Then, you had to work till the closing hour. Our employees were paid about $20 or $30 a week. If business were better, the salaries would get better.

In the restaurants, arguments arose over seating and they would become hostile fights. People would start arguing over seats, especially when it was busy and the place was full. People would fight with each other for seats. They were mostly *law-fan* clients. Sometimes, fights would erupt when an employee would try to say something to a client. What usually happened was that people would fight out of frustration. It happened that a client had been waiting for a table for quite a while and there were no tables available because other diners were sitting and chatting. Naturally, he would get frustrated and that is how fights would start. Well, I guess if you were a troublesome person, fights could break out anywhere, especially with drunks and French people, they were really bad. There was a lot of hatred against the Chinese by the *law-fan*. There were some people like that. There were some drunks who would express their hatred against the Chinese, but that did not happen all the time. The courteous ones did not do that. It was mostly drunks. Some of the young ones, the ones who did not work, were pretty malevolent as well. Now, there are some *law-fan* who save up their money and visit China. They have a better understanding of the Chinese now.

My oldest daughter is a dentist and my second daughter is in business and so is my son. He is not self-employed, he works for someone else. He graduated from McGill University. He does not have to give me money. I would not take his money. I have enough to live on. But sometimes he gives me money as a gift. I do not live with my children. If I move out to the *law-fan* neighbourhoods, I would not be able to speak to anyone. I do not speak English. At least here in Chinatown, you open the door to someone and you can communicate with them. I am familiar with this neighbourhood. I know the people here. My children live in *law-fan* areas, where everyone speaks English. I could not get along there as easily as I do here.

I do not send money back to China anymore. I have no money to send. Before, when we were working in the laundry, the pay was so little. For 15 cents a shirt, we had to make enough money to pay for detergent, bleach, electricity, rent and expenses. People did not realize how hard money was to come by. Some people even lost money in those operations, because they would damage a shirt or a garment with an iron, and they would have to pay for it. People should think more before they spend their money. Some of those who went back to China would get a pat on the back and people there would say, "Ah, *gim-san haq*" 金山客 (guest of the Gold Mountain); they would be so impressed. People at home did not know how hard making a few dollars was then. Now, things are different, money is not so hard to come by. I think this city has the best living conditions.

4. A Private Man

The survivor, now a retiree living in a small room above shophouses in Chinatown.

St. Urbain Street before widening, in a Chinatown quickly transformed into a tourist district.

4. A Private Man

UNLIKE his more fortunate village friends, Liang Wozuo 梁沃佐, "Jack", had an uncle in Canada who did not want to lend him money, nor assistance of any sort. First landed in Victoria after having "bought a visa," Jack worked in the railroad for the Canadian Pacific Railway, and after that, worked through a variety of manual, "typically Chinese" jobs (picking strawberries in Japanese-owned gardens, working in Chinese hand laundries, and live-in cooking for rich white families in Westmount, Montreal). In the meantime, Jack doubled up as a gambler, sometimes jointly owning a gambling house.

Jack gave a series of testimonies of the hard life of Chinese laundrymen and their personal experience with racism. White housewives would chase the laundrymen away with broomstick when they were making door-to-door calls to pick up laundry. White men would hit you, laugh at you, throw stones at you, pull your pigtail, and chant, "Ching, Ching, Chinamen." You would be afraid to hit back; you would hide in a corner, let things pass. You will not stand a chance fighting back, thus the phrase "Chinaman's chance".

Jack recalled the costs of racial discrimination and segregation: Chinese male bachelors, in the isolation of Chinatown, gambled away their hard earned money, some allegedly committing suicide out of shame and guilt; poverty-stricken French girls, some as young as 15, "crowding" Chinatown for sexual service for 25 or 50 cents, and spreading venereal diseases; white men's machine-run, large-sized laundries monopolizing rich, institutional clients; gambling places all over "Chinatown", bribing, corrupting the Mayor and the police, and attracting clients from the class of ethnic, immigrant workers.

Jack went back to China to get married in 1930, returned to Canada alone and, eight years later, his wife passed away. When his son was 21 years old, he joined him in Montreal. Throughout much of his working life, Jack was denied jobs in white men's factories and workshops. Though he had a mechanic's license, Jack did not get the opportunity to work in an aviation company. Chinese were occupationally stereotyped and, thus, confined to laundry and restaurant work. Totally separated and alienated from white society, Jack looked back with fond memories on his special relationship with Mr. Scott, a relationship (perhaps the only one with a white person), after all, between a master and a servant, a live-in cook.

Jack had a difficult relationship with his son and his daughter-in-law, finding it hard to live with them. The son, like his father years ago, gambled and often asked the father for money. Jack gave his son much of his life savings to buy him a house. Very much a private man throughout his life, Jack kept largely to himself, not bitter, not cynical about life, accepting life as it happened.

Living for years in one of the several rooms upstairs of the Chinese Young Men's Christian Institution, an old, deteriorating building amidst a quickly gentrified tourist district, Jack passed his days alone in the most simple way he knew. He took walks in the nearby park every morning, concerned about his diet and careful enough not to take too much alcohol. He was intent on nursing himself back to health, after a close shave with death a few years ago because of alcoholism. He and the building seemed odd and out of place in an area thriving on commercialism and tourism. Both struggled to hang on and survive.

His friends had all moved to Toronto. His only male friend in Montreal recently got married, and Jack reasoned it was best he not bother him too often since he had a family to look after. Jack had no close family ties left in China. He had no strong desire to go back there, yet all this did not seem to stop him from sending remittances back to kinsmen in his native village. Jack said, "I would like to bring them over to Canada, but I am not able to." He had inserted his roots in Montreal. He would not go anywhere. He was alone again, like, decades ago, when he had first arrived in Victoria, young, alone, unassisted. He passed away in 1988.

I was born in Tai Shan, China. I have an older brother and an older sister. I am the youngest one in my family. I did not do anything when I was in China, except to attend school. Living in China was very difficult then. I just had a mother. My father passed away a long time ago. We had a little bit of land which we inherited from my grandparents. My mother went to the countryside; she hoed, cut trees down for burning. She had an older brother in Havana, but he did not send any money home. She also had an older sister who was married. She gave us a hand when we needed help. My mother and her sister-in-law went to till the land. My brother would send money to enable me to go to school. I had to work as well. I was responsible for school, work and family. (Jack's sister married and left home.) She wanted to try to find a better way of life for herself. She was thinking of sending me to the Philippines or Cambodia since it would only cost a few hundred dollars. It was difficult to raise that kind of money. My mother said that the only way to go about it, since it was so hard to earn the amount, was to ask her aunt and her father-in-law. He was the person responsible for me coming here. He drew up all the necessary docu-

4. A Private Man

ments. At first, he refused to do it, but eventually he changed his mind and agreed to help me. It was my mother who suggested that I leave. I was not sure about it myself. When I was 14 or 15, we were very poor and my aunt's father-in-law arranged for all the legal papers to get me out of China. Even though he agreed to help me, there was not much I could do in terms of work. I did not have any skills. I did not learn any English or French. Never did, never had the opportunity. My mother said that the best skill to learn was carpentry, but to learn that trade you needed a $50 deposit and three years' training. Wow! I did not have that kind of time or money. What else could I learn? My mother suggested I become a banker and apprentice with someone. But that required $25 and three years of training. It was hard. My mother then thought she would buy me a car and teach me to become a farmer. I thought that was a good idea.

I bought the visa. I came on a student visa. I paid $500 to the man who charged the government tax for entry into Canada. It was $500 Canadian money. Altogether, it came to about $3,000.

Mr. Liao sold me the visa. He was the one I met when I came off the ship. He looked after me when I was in Victoria. (Jack was in Victoria about one month.) He was supposed to be my father. I pretended to be his son. His last name is Liao 廖 and my name is Liang 梁. Since he pretended to be my father, he had to be responsible for me and report to the immigration office with me. The visa was shown to me. Mr. Liao gave the visa to Mr. Huang 黃 and he in turn sold it to me. When I entered Canada my name was Liao, but later I took back my original name which is Liang. When I arrived in Victoria, Mr. Liao took me to a hotel. They asked me at the hotel what occupation I had. I had no money. It was difficult to find a job, so they told me to go to Vancouver. I departed for Vancouver. I went to Vancouver when I was 15 years old. People called me a guinea pig. I knew what they meant. Mr. Huang, my aunt and her father-in-law said they would accompany me to go to Cariboo, a small town. It was a gold mining district. He said, "I will go with you and everything will be alright." I thought over the situation. People said that I was a guinea pig, what did that mean under those circumstances? I asked my neighbour and three of the bosses at a neighbouring store. They told me that I would be treated like a slave. How could this be? I asked them why they thought this way. They said they would give me $20, while he (Mr. Huang) would give me $10. In addition to this, I would know no one, and could ask no one for help. I thought about this. The boss then offered me a place in the basement if I would help him out with his workload. I would help them by cooking and making deliveries. Later on, they would help me look for another job. I thought that was a fair deal. Mr.

Huang insisted that I go with him. He said, "No matter what, you have to go with me because you owe me money and you have to pay me back." That was when I ran away from him. He could not catch me. Eventually the Huang brotherhood advised him to let me do what I wanted to do. When you are young, you get the opportunity to meet other young people. As time went on, I did not stay in the basement. Instead I went to stay with the young people with whom I had become acquainted. The meals were plain, but no one seemed to mind. I would help them carry potatoes and vegetables. The potatoes were in hundred-pound bags. Mr. Huang Shengying liked me very much. He realized he could not force me to do anything I did not want to do, so he eventually left. Mr. Zheng Yen offered to help me look for a job and he found me one as a dishwasher. I worked in a restaurant that sold fish and chips. I washed dishes and peeled potatoes. Most of the Chinese (at that time) had jobs in farming—gardening and growing vegetables. Many worked in the lumber industry, cutting down trees, and there were others who picked fruit for a living. I also worked on the railroad for the CPR (Canadian Pacific Railway), but (before I worked there) I was a dishwasher and I peeled potatoes and cleaned fish at a Caucasian restaurant.

I did not know a word of English when I started to work at the fish and chips place. It was not Chinese, it was owned by a European. They paid me $5 a week. I paid for room and board myself. You worked from seven o'clock in the morning to seven o'clock at night. At that time I lived at the Tan Association 譚氏公所. The rent was $3 a month. The meal was included in the rent as well. I worked at the fish and chips place, but I did not eat their meals. I ate at the Association. When I finished work, I would go to the Association and we would all eat together. In one room, we would all huddle together. Rent was $3 a month. At that time, pork chops were 5 to 10 cents, and they would give you green onions free. The economy was bad, and it became hard to find work. This was around 1923 to 1924. During the winter, I asked some of the older people, who had been in Canada for a longer period of time, if they knew where I could find work. At first it was $5 a week but eventually it was increased to $7 a week (Jack worked for the Canadian Pacific Railway for three months.) Practically everyone was Chinese. The Chinese had a separate camp of their own. (There were about eight to ten of them in the camp.) Most of the Chinese did not have to speak English, except perhaps to the foreman, or to the other Caucasians, but they had their own foremen. It was like seeing my old comrades. I was the youngest one there, I was 16 or 17. We worked eight hours a day, from nine in the morning to four or five o'clock in the evening, so you could run around.

4. A Private Man

You worked six days, maybe five days a week. You did not have to pay room and board. The meals and the rooms you did not have to pay for. You slept in railcars so when you finished a section of the crossroads, you could then go and sleep on the train. When it was time for dinner, they would make a "kong, kong" noise.

The wages were $2.25 a day. You banged on the tracks. It was very hard. They did not want to hire me in the beginning because I was too young. I was 16 or 17. The foreman asked us to join them. He was a Caucasian and he said that I was better than some of the others. It was not dangerous. Some history books mentioned that a lot of Chinese who worked on the railroad died in accidents. The situation was different. They made the route through Alberta and British Columbia. The water and the weather did not agree with everyone. That is why a lot of Chinese had swollen feet. The water was contaminated. I went through a difficult period myself. The Chinese people would boil some ginger soup with turnip, ginger root, and mandarin orange peel. They would boil all this in a big pot every morning. It was medicine. Everyone would drink a bowl of this soup in the morning before they had their meal. Not everyone wanted to drink the soup, but it was better for you if you did. If you did not, your feet could swell up later. The water was from the hillside. It was fresh water, not tap water. The Indians drank this water and they did not die. (Jack left the CPR after three months because the wages were too low.)

You could earn a lot more money picking fruit. You could earn as much as $4 to $5. If you had fast hands, you could earn more. There were raspberries and strawberries to pick. These were Japanese gardens, but a lot of Chinese people worked there, around 300 to 500 people. The hillside was filled with these gardens. The Caucasians owned a place called Rock which was about 300 acres. There were blackberries, strawberries, raspberries, red corn, black corn and all kinds of fruit. Mason City had the most. Canadians did not know they could produce so much. The raspberries were the best fruit.

I earned $3.25 a day. If you worked part-time, they counted how many boxes you could fill. It was your choice. I picked by the box. By the box, I earned about $5. There were no foremen. Depending on how many boxes you filled—let's say, for example, 24 boxes, the owners would give you a piece of paper and they would turn it over to the Japanese owners. The Japanese were quite rich. Some people claimed that the Japanese government bought the land and grew the fruit. That is what a lot of people said. Some were privately owned. (Jack picked fruit for about two years. He saved money and paid back the debts he had incurred from his immigration taxes. He also sent a little money home to his mother every year.) My mother was happy. I had been overseas for about two years. My uncle was here, but I did not know where he was. I was still young and I did not know of these things.

Little Kin Support

I had relatives in Toronto. He was my uncle. He was no good, but my aunt was very nice. When I was in China, he said that if I came over he would help me, but as soon as I came here, he did not want to have anything to do with me. I asked him to lend me $50 and he refused. He said, "No, no money." He did not like to lend me money and I had none of my own. I did not even have a blanket, not even a blanket. His friend told him to lend me some money, so the least I could do was purchase a blanket. He gave me $25, that was it. He told me not to ask him for anything and that he did not care about me. I had to look after myself. I guess he was afraid that I would become dependent on him.

My brother in Havana knew I was here and wrote to my uncle. My uncle then wrote to Vancouver looking for me. He did not know my address so he sent a letter to Mr. Liang Wozuo. Fortunately, a young man from Vancouver came to Mason City to pick fruit. When he met me he asked me who I was. I told him my name was Liang Wozuo. He told me there was a letter waiting for me in Vancouver. It was really there, at the grocery store. It only cost 50 cents for it to come to Vancouver.

I was surprised to find out that I had an uncle in Montreal. So I tried to write a letter to him. He wrote back and told me to go over there. He told me it was better over there and that I should go over. (This was in 1925.) I asked some people for their opinion. I asked some people who were from Montreal. They told me that all the people in Montreal were laundrymen. There were a few restaurants but if I went there, there would be no turning back.

My uncle was a housecook in a private, Caucasian residence. There were a lot of cooks in homes then. All the Chinese worked as cooks in Westmount. Nine out of ten cooks there were Chinese. It was a popular occupation for the Chinese. Now, if you want such a position, it is much more difficult. The living standards were very good. You lived with the family you were cooking for. The pay and the living standards were very good. At that time, if you were a house cook, you would earn about $25 a week. Restaurants paid their cooks an average of $9 to $17 a week. The Paris Restaurant on St. Catherine paid the best wages to their cooks, they made $40 a week. If you were a house cook, you

4. A Private Man

would earn an average of $25 a week. That is a big difference. Some house cooks earned even more. The boss's wife would sometimes increase your salary by a dollar and on special occasions the increase could be more. If you were earning $25, it could be increased to $35. They were very happy as house cooks. Many of them made a lot of money and they were able to go back to China. In the past couple of years, there have been no such employment opportunities. Around 1925, there were about 600 to 700 Chinese working as house cooks.

There were a lot of Chinese in the laundry business also. It was hard work though and there was not much money involved. There were at least 200 shops and they were located all over Montreal. There were a few Chinese restaurants. Chinese meals were not as popular then. The restaurants were scattered around Chinatown, three or four of them. It was hard to make a living. For example, Welcome Cafe charged 5 cents for a cup of coffee and a biscuit. Nan King Cafe had a car to pick up their customers.

My uncle was married, but he lived alone. At that time, there were no Chinese families around. I do not think there were more than a dozen families living around here, out of the three to four thousand people here. Most of the men here were bachelors, they did not have families here. They lived alone. You could not really support a family. Work was hard to find. There were no women here. The men lived in the laundry shops and slept on ironing boards. They would work at whatever they could find.

Associations like the Li 李氏 , Ma 馬氏 and others were crowded with people. Most of them were unemployed. That is why they lived there. Other associations would rent a place. It was very cheap at that time, about $10 a month for a flat. (People did not have to go to the association bearing the same name as their family name. If they were accepted by the association, they could stay there.) I stayed at the Ma's association.

Working in a Laundry

When I first arrived in Montreal, I lived in the Hum Laundry. They wanted me to stay and work at the laundry shop. The laundry shops would use a big pot and boil their laundry in it. There was an oven room that was used to dry the clothes after they were washed. The big garments, the ones you could not wash by hand, were put in the steam machine. All the smaller pieces were washed by hand. It was very difficult work. The laundry business was very hard. There were times when you had to work 18 hours a day. You would get up five o'clock in the morning and wash and iron till midnight. Can you guess how many hours a week that was? They worked an average of 18 to 19 hours a day. Every day you would do the same thing until Saturday. It was only when you were finished with your work that you would get a chance to sit. Saturday was the one day during the week when you got a chance to relax. At the end of the day, your feet would be aching. It was very hard work, you had to stay up on your feet all day. There were no major illnesses, just swollen feet. The feet and the hands would become swollen. They did see some doctors, although it was very difficult. This was around the time of the early to mid 1930's. At that time in Chinatown, they had porridge. They were handouts. The church would give them out to everyone, Chinese and Caucasians. There was a line-up for the porridge and stew. Most of the people who went for these handouts were unemployed. There were many. The laundry shops did not offer work. There were too few of them. The prices were very low. For example, to clean about 200 shirts would cost about $2 or $1.50. And, there was overhead to pay. You could not earn much money working in laundry shops.

It was expensive to buy a laundry shop. Prices ranged between $300 to $2,000. Some of the most expensive ones would cost about $6,000. This meant that the shop earned very good business. These shops were usually located in Westmount, on Victoria Avenue. The Westmount area was the best. All the rich folks lived there and the prices were much better. Shops in that area would range between $4,000 and $6,000. The cheaper ones would cost a couple of hundred dollars. People earning such small incomes found it hard to send money back to China.

You had to kill yourself working for the money to buy a shop. There was the opportunity to borrow money from the Association. A little at a time, you could get a few hundred dollars together. You could also buy a business with partners. Two or three people could work together. If a laundry shop was selling for $1,000, then three people would get together and pay $300 each. If you had some money saved up, it was not hard to raise the rest of it if you went into a partnership. With three people operating the laundry, the work could be divided up. One could do the pick-ups and deliveries. The other two could work inside washing and ironing, day and night. The price of cleaning was very low.

You had to pick up and deliver. They made the deliveries on their backs. There were many cruel people. The worst ones were on Bishop Street. The laundry men usually went to places, rang the doorbell and asked whoever it was at the door if they had any laundry. There were a few places on Bishop Street, they were rooming houses. People who lived in those places were not

4. A Private Man

rich, they got room and board there. Anyway, four or five people would ring the doorbell, asking the occupants if they had any laundry for washing and the Madam would exclaim, "You Goddamn Chinaman!" And she would use the broom and beat you away with it. "Bang", she would slam the door shut. One guy I know finished high school and could not find a job, so he went to work for his father. He and his brother would carry a bag to go pick up laundry and ring the doorbell on every door.

There was a lot of suffering then. They would hit the Chinese all the time. They would hit you and sometimes they would throw rocks and laugh at you. When you do not speak English, you cannot report anything. They would laugh and make fun of you, screaming, "Ching, Chang, Chinaman, what a man, Ching, Chang ...". They would follow you and chant this. They pulled your pigtail and you could not get away. You suffered a lot. The Chinese were afraid to hit back. Besides, you did not stand a chance against them. They were around 16 to 17 years old. You would hide in a corner and let them pass. They were all nationalities. The blacks were the worst, along with the Italians. The French were not so bad. The blacks were wilder and had no class. They would hit too. That was not good.

Jobs—"Jack of All Trades"

I like to learn a little about all kinds of trades, for instance, like the automobile. I have some knowledge of automobiles and airplanes. If I like, I can still do it. Working at Canadair was a good job, but I did not like it too much. I was a mechanic. I did very well with drilling. This was from 1942 to 1948. I had tried to get a job at a plant. It was wartime, so everyone came over here for employment. I got a job with Mr. Fisher as a cook. He gave me $25 a week and I was satisfied with that. I worked for him for only two weeks. I wanted to work on airplanes at the time. I did not like to work in a kitchen. It was a private residence. There were about five people, three children and the parents. I cooked three meals a day. Sometimes they would go out for dinner. Most of the time they stayed home with the children and had simple meals. Rich people like R.E. Thorn had two or three servants. There were just the two of them in the family. Do you know how many servants they had? They had four servants. My God, they had somebody there every second day. A lot of loot, you know. They used to have parties there all the time. "Make me a party, make me a party." It cost a lot of money. It was a good job though. Sometimes you could get $28. The range was $20 to $30 a week. I had a beautiful room. It was a dressed up room, the linens were changed every day, just like all the other rooms. I did not eat with them. As a servant, you could not eat with the boss. You served the boss, then you cooked something for yourself. You could cook whatever you liked. Sometimes I ate with the servant, the cleaning woman. I worked in a private home a long time ago. I made money to go home by working in the laundry. I worked there for about ten years. I made a lot of money. That time I wanted to work in aviation, in a plant. I could not get into it, so I went to work for Mr. Fisher. I worked for them for only two weeks. Mr. Fisher said, "Hey Jack, all Chinamen like to work and cook in kitchens." I said, "No, not me." He said, "Why don't you come cook for me?" "I want to work on airplanes. I want to train myself for something. I'm young. I want to repair cars and stuff. I don't like to work in a kitchen. I could not get into anything else. I could not get into aviation, because I do not have the training." So he said he would give me the chance. He wrote me a letter and told me to go see someone in Cartierville, a Mr. Darwood or something. I said, "Okay." I packed up and went to see this guy and showed him the letter. He looked at me and said, "Come on in." Then, he asked me to go there tomorrow and I could get the job. I went back to see Mr. Fisher and said thank you very much. He appreciated the fact that I made up my mind on my own, and decided to get into aviation mechanics. He gave me an extra $25, altogether he gave me $50. I did not know anything about the job, I did not even know what a screwdriver was. Well, Mr. David, the foreman of the department, it was a French name. He gave me the job. He came to help me. He told me everything. He explained the names and the uses of all the tools. In two to three weeks, I got to know all the equipment. I picked it all up. I made about $80 to $100 a week.

A lot of Chinese worked in factories then. Some of them had learned to speak English for a long time by then. They would take you anyway if you did not know English. Maybe if you knew absolutely nothing they would not take you. In the laundries, men were getting old and they were giving up some of the business to others. They gave them piece-work. For example, if they charged a customer 17 cents, they would give me 8 cents a shirt for pressing it. He would wash, and I would press it and I got 8 cents for each shirt I pressed. I would go to the laundry after I finished work in the factory at five o'clock. I would have supper at the laundry shop and put in about four to five hours' work. I ironed about ten, eleven shirts an hour. Sometimes twelve shirts. I made a few dollars. I saved quite a bit of money. I worked like that for about seven, eight years. The laundryman wanted me to do even more work, but there were not enough hours in the day. I only have two hands!

A lot of Chinese lived at the Young Men's Christian Institution. At that

4. A Private Man

time, it was pretty cheap, about $16 a month for rent. After the war, there were no jobs. They laid the men off. I was laid off too. I decided to work in a car garage on St. Catherine Street, the St. Taylor Motor City. They have closed down now, about ten years ago. They made repairs on cars. I worked there but I saw that it was not good for me. Because I was Chinese, they did not like it. They kicked me around a lot. They were jealous. They said, "Why don't you get a cooking job?" They were jealous because I took their work, their share of the work. So, they laid me off. I worked there about one to two years. I was making a lot less there than what I was making as an airplane mechanic. They did not give you a high position. I had a mechanic's license. It was not difficult to get a license. No other Chinese was a mechanic. I was the only one. I knew about four or five other guys but they did not stay long. They could not get the job. I do not know if the people there did not like me because I was Chinese, but I think so. I left the garage, I went to work in a private home. I worked for a family. I advertised in a paper. I wrote, "Chinese cook wants to work in private home." I wrote down the number in the ad, and they called me. The last job I got there was not all that long ago. I worked for Mr. Scott, I worked for him for eight years. Mr. George Scott was Jewish. He was a widower. His wife had been dead for two or three years. He asked me to stay, look after him and work for him. I said I did not know at first. I had four to five job offers. He said, "How do you know the family with the children will like you?" I told him he did not pay the highest salary. He did not have anything to say to that. He told me that it would be an easy job. All I had to do was look after him and that half the time he would be away anyway, so I had the house to myself. No one would bother me. I would have it easy. I thought about it. Maybe he was right, maybe I would not be able to get along with them. One single man was much easier to look after. I thought it over and decided it was better to stay with him. So I took the job. I worked for him from 1970 to 1978. I left in 1978 because I became ill.

I have a problem with my lungs. I drink too much. There was this woman that he was very close to. I told him he should marry her. I did not want to work for him anymore because I did not want to be in the way in case he did marry her. I talked to his daughters. He has two daughters. His daughter told me it was better that I did not work for him, it was better for him to marry this woman. That woman was a widow. She lived in New York and she came down all the time. He had a lot of women coming down. He is living in the same house, same apartment. Last year, I went to see him. He used to call me all the time. Since I left his employment, he has given me $50 for a Christmas present every year. He has never missed a year. When I go to see him, I bring him some ginger. He likes ginger. He sometimes says, "Hey, why don't you come back and work for me?" I always say, "No, I am getting too old." He says, "Never mind, just work for me, I'll make it easier." He married that woman I mentioned. He has a house in New York, another house in Boston. That woman has a daughter and a son and they both have good jobs. They have a lot of money. They have cars too. I kid them and ask them to give me one.

I was head of a gambling house. I wanted to gamble. I gambled to my heart's content. I gambled every day, for ten years straight. Whenever I put money on fan-tan, I would win. When I walked into the gambling house, people would give me dirty looks. Some of them would throw coins and sand at my feet. I did not mind. I let them do it. I had a pocketful of money. I was loaded. I was partners with Mr. Ge, Mr. Li, Li Zhongyong, Ge Xin and Liao Yongjian in the lottery. I could go into a gambling house for a few days straight and win every time I played. This went on for two to three weeks. When they saw me coming, they would flee. Eventually I did not want to work at the lottery anymore. I decided to quit. I faced my partners and cleared my title from the partnership. "Don't call me and I won't call you." I did not take anything. I made $5,000 to $7,000 from the lottery and I just wanted to scrub my hands from it. I did not want anything else from them, I told them they could have it. They wanted me to take some back. I did not want anything in return, I told them to keep my share. They asked me where I was going. Employment was difficult to find. Whether it was easy or not, that was going to be my business. I was not with these people anymore. I went to my room. They let me take the bed. So I took it and drove it to my friend's place, the laundry shop.

I went to look for work and bumped into Mr. Xu Xiao. I asked Xu Xiao if he knew where I could find work. I asked him if he would hire me. He lived at the gambling house for so long he knew me well enough. A week went by, then on Bleury Street, where Mr. Xu's laundry shop was located, they needed someone as a helper. Working in a laundry was hard. I was with Uncle Xiao and together, we went over to the laundry shop and stayed there. I would help them out with the work. I was happy over there. I stayed and helped out a little. They would give me shirts to iron for $3 a week. I lived and ate there. What else could you get for $3 a week? I was having such a hard time, and I had to worry about how I was going to feed my family. What was I going to do? I will say this much though, things were very cheap then. God, the work was difficult. You had to wake up at five o'clock in the morning and work until eleven o'clock at night or midnight. You had about five hours sleep. On Sunday it was

4. A Private Man

nine hours. I washed and ironed. I averaged about twelve pieces of clothing in an hour. God, it was tough! You just do not know if you could take it anymore. But, you had to endure it. Your bones ache from fatigue. But, I stopped gambling. It was all Chinese. The Caucasians would not be able to endure the long hours. (They never hired Caucasians to work at these laundries.) There were very few Caucasian laundries, but they had the rich clientele. The rich ones collaborate with the rich. Rich people have class. They knew that the Chinese could not compete with them. They had a lot of advertisements. The Chinese's best location was on St. Catherine Street near Green Avenue. The Clawn Laundry. It does not exist anymore. It moved to Lachine and the business deteriorated. It was the biggest operation then. Clawn Laundry was number one. In 1936, there were a hundred or so Chinese laundries. There were not too many people in the restaurant business. They were mostly all in the laundries.

The boss made a lot of money. It was not only the boss though. Some workers made money since they had steady work. But, primarily, it was the boss. Most of them had three or four people partnerships.

Love and Marriage

There were a few inter-racial couples. In the end, they would split and get a divorce, no matter how long they were together. I went out with a Caucasian girl once. I was in Cornwall, Ontario at the time. I decided to leave town and she chased after me and tried to stop me. Honestly speaking, when I went out on walks with her, I did not touch her. The restaurant business in Cornwall amounted to $10,000 when I sold it. I left there to come to Montreal. She decided to follow me to Montreal. She wrote to me and told me that she loved me. I wrote to her and told her it was no use. I could not afford a family then. I went to work for Mr. Li as a waiter. I started as a cook. Then, I went to work for Mr. Li Rong at the Montreal Chop Suey Cafe. I started there as a cook. Mr. Li Rong suggested I come out of the kitchen and work on the floor as a waiter. Anyway, about this girl, I told her not to follow me. That is the truth. She sent me some handkerchiefs. She said that I was cruel. She wanted me to be her companion, and I just did not want to be. I told her that I had no right. I also told her that I thought she was a good girl and a nice person. I told her that we were not suitable for each other. That is the reason why I did not touch her. If I had, I would have been hooked. She would have gone after me even more vehemently.

In 1930, I went back to China to get married. It cost around $1,000. I stayed for one year. I was on holiday. I went on a tour. I went all over the place. (He came back to Canada alone and eight years later his wife died.) She was like everyone else in China. I sent money back there every now and then. (He did not know how she died.) It was during the war, the civil war. You did not know what kind of sickness it was, all you knew was that you died from it. I have one son. He is here in Canada. He was 21 years old when he came to Montreal. My son is a waiter. Now, he is over 50 years old and married to a Chinese. They have two children, one boy and one girl. My granddaughter is married. She has two daughters and one son. She is married to a Chinese. (Jack lived with his son and his daughter-in-law for a few months.) There is a generation gap between the old and the young. It is best to go our separate ways. No matter how good the relationship is, the differences are there and sometimes it just does not work.

Family Relations

I see my son about once a week. He is on his own now, he is very independent. He just comes to see me at Christmas time now, he wants me to go to his home. I do not go there much, because his wife does not like me very much. You know, little things—she just likes money, that is all. She just thinks of money all the time. His wife is from China. I do not get along with her. I do not even get along with my son. Because he likes to gamble. He gambles quite a bit. He does not do that now, he needs the money. He is getting smarter. He used to gamble away a lot of money. He used to work with his friend Li in Granby. They worked there for three years. Li bought his parents a house. He told his parents, "I bought this house for you, so if I marry or not, you don't bother me—you have a house. I bought you this house, so I can do whatever I like. You have your own home now, so don't bother me." My son always asked me for money. He still asks me, he asked me two years ago if he could have some money. I gave him $8,000 the last time. No more. He was still not satisfied. I do not really need the money because I get my old age pension cheques, but he went to talk to my friend. He encouraged my friend to persuade me to give him money because I was old and going to die. He talked to my friend and had him tell me that I was not going to stay long in this world, and whatever money I had I should give to my son. So I could avoid giving it all up to the government when I died. I had a fight with my son. I told him I did not have any money, my money was all gone. He did not have anything to say after that. He needed the money for a house. He bought a house two years ago in Greenfield Park and then he bought a house in Ottawa for his son. His children are in their early

4. A Private Man

thirties. His daughter is about 31 or 32. My grandson is an accountant in Ottawa. He went to university and studied accounting. My granddaughter married a boy with the surname of Li. He is in engineering, he makes about $12,000 a month, perhaps more now. I see them every now and then, a few of them anyway. I do not see much of one of my grandsons. My granddaughter just had a son in April of this year. My son was very happy about it, they were all happy. She had two daughters and she really wanted a boy. She wrote to me and told me she was hoping for a boy. I have not heard from her since then though.

Pastimes

As a pastime, we would go to Chinese movies. Sometimes the Chinese YMCI sponsored a modern opera. The Chinese performed in these shows. The shows were primarily to tell people to be good, to behave properly and they gave advice to correct misbehaviour, and on how to be better citizens.

In Chinatown, there were many gambling houses. There were fourteen "fan-tan" gambling houses. They were privately run. There were Huang Guangxu, Huang Dafa, Yuan Lang; these people were at the head of it. They would squeeze money from the poor and hurt them in the end. Gambling made a lot of people suffer. I used to work at a gambling house in 1932. It was a difficult time. When I came back here in 1931 from China, there were no jobs. I finally managed to get one, it paid about $40 a month. The Christian people helped us look for jobs. They helped me look for a job. One of them found a job for me, but I could not work for them. It was a good employer and the job was good too. It was just that if you worked over there, you had to stay and live there too. Jobs were hard to come by. I knew one person, a Mr. Ge, who sold Chinese lottery tickets. At that time, there were over ten lottery companies. The lotteries and the gambling houses boomed around the Second World War. There was gambling all over Chinatown. The Caucasians called it "singo", a Chinese dice game. St. Denis Street and Black Street had over three gambling houses on the same street. Every time I was there, the place was filled with people. I was one of the owners along with Mr. Ge.

A company usually had two people. Names of people were used to identify the company. For example, Shan He and Guang Da were the names of the two people in it. There were three draws. There was one in the afternoon at two o'clock and another one in the evening at eight o'clock, the last one at eleven o'clock at night. There were draws three times a day. Caucasians, Blacks, and Chinese were all involved in the lotteries. No one bothered you about them. You would not get arrested for it. There was so much gambling back then. I made a good living out of this, so I did not need to work. It was good. I made a lot.

The most popular games were "*pai-jiu*" 牌九 (a popular Chinese game of chance) and poker. I do not like that. People played a lot of blackjack too. Those three games were the most popular. The dice game cheated the Caucasians. Some of them cheated. The dice would be at a "clown angle", five to six square box. It was crowded in these places. There were gambling houses from Ontario Street to St. Antoine Street, from Dorchester Boulevard to St. Denis Street. Most of the gambling houses were on St. Denis Street and du Bullion Street. It was a poverty-stricken area. Most of the residents came from a European background. Some of the workers worked hard and gave to the Chinese. The city mayor was corrupted since he received pay from the gambling operations. The head of the house would give him money and, in turn, he would ignore the operations. The Chinese would offer him big gifts so that there would be no arrests. The head of police had a lot of money in his pockets. When they made a call, they knew it was a signal call because there would be no one on the line. The silence indicated the police were planning to raid the place. They would come in and arrest a few people. They would then have to appear in court. The judge would ask, "Were you gambling?" They would receive a fine of about $30. After the hearing, they were released. The fine was to pay for court fees. These kinds of gambling houses ended around 1941 to 1947. They were around for about six to seven years. Some of the Chinese made a lot of money from this. Mr. Huang Dafa was a rich man. Before this gambling stuff, he had nothing. He made over half a million dollars in gambling. He demolished the old Nan King restaurant and built a new one in its place. The government questioned this action. They wanted to know where all this money was coming from. He seemed to have so much of it. Mr. Huang Guangxu also built a new Lotus Restaurant. The Chinese who became rich from gambling have since all died. Some of them went back to China and died there. When they became rich, they went back to China. It was sad for the ordinary Chinese people. When the Chinese were not working, they did nothing much, just talk, walk, tell stories, go to the associations, play music, read the Bible and some went to the race track. Even women went. A lot of Chinese women went to the Blue Bonnets and gambled on the track.

Then, all of a sudden, all the gambling in Chinatown was stopped. Drapeau is the best mayor of this city regarding the Chinese. There was no one more effective at stopping the heads of the gambling houses. The first offence cost you anywhere from $100 to $200. They were later raised to $500. If you

4. A Private Man

did not pay the fines, you would be jailed. They gave you a warning to stop the operation or face charges. Since then, all the heads of the gambling houses stopped their operations, and eventually there was a complete stop to the gambling. As soon as Drapeau came to power, everything was cleaned up. He cleaned up the city's prostitution, gambling and drug rings. All along, not many places had opium. Just a couple of places perhaps. Not many people took opium. Perhaps a few did. They had a lot of opium in Vancouver. There were a lot of merchants who had businesses there. Montreal then was small and did not have as many businessmen. There were only about five. I mean men who had stores or grocery shops. Li and Qian dominated the grocery market. The richest Chinese people were Huang Dafa and Huang Guangxu. They were rich. After them, it had to be Li Rong and Frank Li. Frank Li was the real businessman. He owned the Montreal Chop Suey Company. That was where he made all his money.

Prostitution was rampant in Montreal. The Chinese went to these places a lot. This was the kind of thing that could end up killing you. At that time there were only about four or five doctors in Chinatown. A lot of the sicknesses that came up were the result of prostitution. There were so many Caucasian girls in the rooming houses. If the girls came down to see you, it would be around 25 to 50 cents, 75 cents to $1. The prices varied. Even for a dollar it was cheap. At that time, things were cheap. The girls were about 16 to 17 years old. Some were even younger, 15 years old. They were mostly French. Their parents did not care about them. The police did not seem to care about them either, they never got arrested. Chinatown was crowded with these girls. No matter what Association you were in, you would not be respected if people saw you with any of these girls. Everytime you go with any of these girls, you would get a sickness. Some have died from it. The disease looked like a cauliflower. It had a lot of veins, and there was so much poison in it. You had to use a towel. The germs were very infectious. You could get it all over the face and the mouth. You could get medication for it, but it was very expensive. If you had the money, you could get it, otherwise nothing could be done about it. The poison that would erupt from this disease was terrible. You had to be extremely careful. The disease could drive you insane. Zhou Xinlai, Li Rui, Ye Duozhu, we all worked together at the same restaurant. Whether the doorbell rang, they would get all excited. On a few occasions, they would ask me to join in. I participated some of the time. I did not have the energy. They would go two or three times a day. "Mr. Zhou," I would say, "I can see blood." The body could not take that. You cannot force that much endurance. "How many times?" I asked him. "Four times," he replied. He was a young man about 18 to 22 years of age. Very strong, but you cannot always do that kind of thing. Two or three years ago, I asked about what happened to them. They had all passed away. Then I looked for Mr. Ye, he died also. I asked people about Li Sew, they said he was at Mount Royal Park, the cemetery, resting on the hill top. Some people have asked me, "Since they are already there, what about you?" I reply to them, "I will eventually go, but not now."

Tragedies Due to Gambling

Many Chinese gambled away their life savings. Had it not been for their gambling, they would not have died. They just did not care about themselves anymore. One man was Li Wei, he asked me to shake hands since he thought our friendship would end. The matter is he had lost over ten thousand dollars. He had saved all that money, and he lost it all gambling. We were shaking hands. He said he could not live through it. They were not supposed to have taken it seriously. A few friends had gotten together and they wanted to try their luck. He lost about ten thousand dollars. He was thinking of suicide. I asked him, "Why?" He did not want to talk about it anymore and shook his head. There was another. Mr. Huang Shu gambled on *pai-jiu* and also lost all his money. He was left with a few pennies. The door to his room was closed. There was nothing in the room. The person was gone. There were no clues as to what happened to him. He must have died. The way he died no one ever knew for sure. People guessed he may have jumped into the river. How did we guess that he did this? The police searched all over for his body but they could not find a trace of it. There were people fishing on the banks and they hooked up his body. His body was marked up. His clothes, bones ... that was all that was left, his clothes and bones. He was wearing clothes, but when they hooked up the body, they could tell it was suicide. There was another man named Li Sheng. He was in his 40's. He was a young man. He was intelligent and very good looking. He was one of those people who made a living from gambling in Chinatown. He went over to Toronto and eventually made his way back here. He must have been involved with a drug ring or something. They gave him $3,000 or so to come here and set up business in this line of work. People were guessing this. When he came here, he lived at the Asia Hotel. It was owned by Pan Yenrong, Ye Wen and Qian Guang. They ran the hotel but they all have since died. He rented a room there. The $3,000 he was supposed to use to buy drugs, he played with at a gambling house. He played and lost the $3,000.

I do not know what happened after that. He lost the money and there was

4. A Private Man

no way out of it. He could not go this way or that. He went to a Jewish pharmacy. If you went there and spoke Chinese to them, they would understand you. They ran the business in Chinatown for so long, they understood Chinese. You did not have to speak English to them. Li bought two bottles of medicine. He locked the door to his room and drank it. He thought he would die from this. He drank two bottles of medicine, even though it was difficult to swallow. He had the strength to drink all two bottles. After he drank it, he suffered terribly. It was very painful. The bedspreads in the room were a chaotic mess. Everything was upside down. In each room there was a sink. He was thirsty after drinking the medicine. His hands went down to open the faucets for water, but he crushed his head in the process. That was how he died. He died, after lying there for two days or so in terrible pain. People were remarking, "Where is Li Cheng? He came to Montreal, and now we don't see him anywhere." They knocked on his door, but there was no answer. Where was he? After breaking the door down ... Oh, my God! he lost all that money gambling and this was what happened. The $3,000 he was to use buying drugs, he lost gambling. That was why he committed suicide.

Life as a Chinese in Canada

I do not want to go back to China. Of course not. What do you get when you go back to China? You do not get anything out of it unless you have a family back there. I do not have anything left in China. Why should I go back? I do not know anyone there anymore, maybe two or three old men in the village but the rest of them are all strangers. I do not have a home there. I have a home here. I am more comfortable here. The last time I went back was in 1930. I do not want to go back, not even to travel. It takes a lot of money to travel. You have to spend a lot, how much can I spend? I still have some relatives from my mother's side of the family, they ask me for money. I send money home. I send money to my niece. I have another niece from my sister's son. My sister is dead now, but she has a son. My sister's son has seven children. He has five sons, and two daughters. I sent about $8,000 to $10,000 over three years. This year alone, I sent back $3,000. Their home is very run down. They need a new building. They want to come to Canada. I would like to bring them, but I cannot.

I would like to stay in Montreal. I think it is the best thing for me. I am still able to send money home. I travel around a bit. I like to travel to the small towns, but I do not go like I used to. I used to have a friend whom I would travel with. We would keep each other company. I do not like to go by myself ...

When I first came to Montreal, when the older people died they were buried here. Before, they used to send them back to China after they were cremated. They used to send their ashes back to China. They would raise the money in Chinatown to have their ashes sent back. They do not do this anymore. Some of them are buried on Mount Royal, and some in the east end somewhere. I know quite a few people buried there. This year there were many old people who were buried on Mount Royal.

I sometimes go to Chinatown. I go there and do my banking. I take my cheques to the Royal Bank there. I spend a little time, chit-chatting over a cup of coffee. Sometimes a few of them will invite me to play mah-jong. That is why I do not really want to go. I just stay by myself. I like it that way. They call me often to go and play mah-jong with them. I know them, because I used to live with them. They all called me to go over. I always said that I was too tired. I am getting too old for the walk. They like the company, I guess, but you have to spend money though. I spend my time taking walks. I get up about five o'clock in the morning. I bend, I relax a little bit. I exercise a little. I have breakfast and I walk around. I do not have very much for lunch. I have breakfast and when I come back I will have a bottle of beer and a cookie or something. I will sit down, relax, and walk around again. I will walk to the Steinberg's (a food supermarket) on St. Catherine Street. There is a big building there. It is very nice and comfortable in there. During the summer, I like to go to the Mount Royal Park. Sometimes I go to the Lafontaine Park or Chinatown. I do not go there too often. Well, I go there to play mah-jong. They really nag you to go and play with them. I have a friend called Jimmy Huang. He came here a lot. Since his wife died, he has not come as often because he was married to a white woman. After his wife died, he tried to find a Chinese woman to marry, but he could not find one. Chinese women are demanding. We have been friends for a long time. We help each other quite a bit. Sometimes, if I am short of something, he will try to help me, or I will try to help him. He does not lend me money though, and I do not lend him money. He does not owe me anything and I do not owe him anything. I used to have a television but I do not have it anymore. Since the old television broke down, I have not bought a new one. I cannot watch television anymore, it is not so good for my eyes. I have a radio now. I do not want to buy a television. I do not have time for television anyway. It is all the same. I have watched television for thirty years. It is about time I stop. I get the Chinese paper and the *Gazette* (an English daily newspaper). I read them every day. I have them deliver it. I will go on living here for the rest of my life. I guess when I am sick I will have to go to the hospital. I want to stay in Montreal. I like Montreal best. I guess I would like Toronto next. I have a lot of friends in Toronto. People often invite me to go there, but I say, "Well, what about my pension?" I can go there, but what about my pension? I have three times more friends in Toronto than here in Montreal. A lot of them moved there. When I am sick, I will go to the Montreal General Hospital. I have not stayed there for fifty years. Oh, I go there for check-ups. I had an operation in 1978. I had a lung operation. I go there twice a year for check-ups. They give me medication. They tell me I drink too much. I drink a lot of whisky. About twenty ounces a day, for about twenty years. The doctor told me to stop. He suggested I stop or die. I drink beer now. I drink about six bottles a day. Two in the morning, two in the afternoon, two at night.

In Chinatown, once, long time ago, a lot of people died. They were very sick. I think it was because the air was not clean. People were living too close together, like in the Li's Building. There was not any fresh air. The air was dirty. Some doctors told me that. (There was a Chinese hospital, but people went to the Montreal General.) There was no ventilation, no windows. How many people lived in the Li's Building? Ten at least. There were no windows there. If you had a window, it was okay, but they had no windows. More Caucasians than Chinese suffered mental illness. It was mainly due to the influence of alcohol. There were not many Chinese who drank. I know only one Chinese that was a drunk, only one ...

5. Uncle Jack, a Moral Entrepreneur

The Montreal Chinese Hospital on 112 Lagauchetière Street in Chinatown before it was moved to St. Denis Street. Uncle Jack Huang (Huang Jinzhuo) was a pivotal figure in the beginnings of the Hospital. (Source of photograph unknown.)

108 Smoke and Fire

During celebration of the
Confucius Festival.

Head tax certificate issued by the Canadian federal government to Uncle Jack dated 29 September 1947.

5. Uncle Jack, a Moral Entrepreneur

The uncle of Huang Jinzhuo 黃金灼, "Jack", already in laundry business in Montreal for years, took him to Canada during one of his trips back to China. Jack never asked what life was like for a Chinese in Montreal. Perhaps what one needed to know was already known among those destined to go overseas: brutal, hard work as a hand laundryman, day in and day out. His uncle a laundryman, Jack "naturally" also became a laundryman, as Jack himself put it.

Jack gave a personal account of the hardworking life of the Chinese laundrymen in Montreal. He would sometimes work non-stop for two days with no sleep at all. During Sundays and New Year's Eve (supposedly rest time for the white men), he would simply pull down the drapes and work.

Jack quickly got himself out of the hand laundry business and involved in joint partnership in Chinese restaurants, thus operating as a successful proprietor, and, subsequently, establishing a reputation for himself. This facet of his work life might have paved the way to his public involvement in the affairs of the Chinese community. He is best remembered for his pioneering work with the Freemasons in Montreal and with the establishment of the Montreal Chinese Hospital, at the time, the only one of its kind in Canada. First elected in 1931 as the Freemasons' president, he remained in the post for an astonishing twenty consecutive terms. During the city-wide epidemic in 1918, Jack accompanied a Chinese doctor making rounds in the Chinese community to hand out the "Wong-lau-kit" tea 王老吉茶, a Chinese curative herbal drink. As a result, Jack claimed, only two Chinese did not survive.

Jack also helped form an organization to raise money for China to fight the Japanese; he organized security councils and trained *"Bow-on"* 保安 squads among the civilians to protect the city residents during the Second World War.

In an era when few Chinese dared to cross the racial boundaries, Jack, at the age of 40, married a 16-year-old French girl. Intermarriage was considered by the Chinese community as an act against the Chinese culture, a gesture of loss of love for the motherland. No Chinese came to attend Jack's own wedding, in spite of his public standing in the Chinese community. His elder son subsequently married a Francophone (eldest daughter of the former Mayor of Jacques Cartier), and his younger son, an Irish woman.

Following the death of his wife's brother in a parachuting accident and her mother's death (apparently from grief), Jack's wife lapsed into a nervous breakdown which she never seemed to recover from.

Jack cannot help recalling with some personal pride his ability to get work in factories and workshops owned by white men though, at the same time, he did not fail to report incidents of racism against the Chinese in Montreal. The press would be diligent in providing graphic portrayal of incidents of the Chinese having violated, and been punished by, the laws, thus perpetuating a range of derogatory stereotypes of the Chinese. Jack also recalled dozens of opium dens in the Montreal Chinatown area, selling opium at 25 cents, 50 cents or $1. There would be routine police raids levying light fines and collecting bribery money from the Chinese.

In spite of his French wife and the fact that his two sons married white women, Jack's contact with the white society was limited and superficial. Yet, at the same time, like Jack Liang, he has no desire to go back to China. As a matter of fact, on each and every trip back to China, he was very clear about wanting to return to Canada. He said, "China has nothing to offer me."

The two Jacks, along with the ten women, at least in the latter part of their lives, provide living evidence against white ideologues who accuse the Cantonese immigrants in Canada of being sojourners only, intent on making quick money in Canada before retiring to China. The "immigrant mentality" in terms of "a disinclination to assimilate" is by no means intrinsic or natural. The immigrants would very much like to enter the mainstream society; it is the latter that continually thwarts their desires and intentions. The sojourner argument has quickly found its way into the core of the ideology of racism against the Chinese.

For years, Uncle Jack continued to go back to the Freemasons every afternoon to chat, read newspapers, or catch up with community affairs. Over the years, his life became increasingly private. Yet, it was his intensive and persistent involvement in the public affairs of the Chinese community that seemed to have given him a personal and ethnic identity that, in the long run, was the unmistakable source of his personal strength. His life was a contrast to that of Jack Liang. Huang was extroverted, outgoing, sociable, charismatic, public-minded and involved. Liang was private and introverted, much of his life minding his own business and looking after his own needs. Both strived to adapt and survive in their own ways.

Uncle Jack died in 1985. Personal accounts by the ten women, Jack Liang and Jack Huang, taken together, allowed us a brief glimpse into the "immigrant economy" of Montreal's Chinese community. The overall economic structure was polarized into the merchant class on the one hand and the workers on the other. One may want to roughly divide immigrant institutions into two types. First, there are those family and class associations that are socio-legal-financial in functions, many of which have become an vital source of credit and finance for setting up various ethnic businesses. Second, there are the different types of ethnic businesses that themselves are the primary source of income for both merchants and workers: laundries, restaurants and a small number of grocery or variety stores. In strict economic terms, all are severely marginalized businesses and rely heavily on intensive, cheap, unskilled and considerably exploited immigrant labour in order to survive. All strive to fill a niche in an otherwise controlled and restrictive economy.

I started my schooling at the age of seven. This continued on until I was eight, nine, ten, eleven. When I turned 12, I started having private tutorial lessons. At the age of 13, I went up to another grade, a secondary level which included composition and a teacher accompanying us to explain matters. I finished at the age of 15 for one year. At the age of 16, I went to Hong Kong with my uncle.

I never learned any skill. In China, there was nothing like that for anybody. Many years ago in China, there was nothing. You could not learn anything. The only things available to learn were fishing, farming, woodcrafts, wood cutting and agriculture. I had never seen any industries during all my life in China. The situation was worse in the villages. Overall, it was not too bad but there was a great deal of hardship and suffering.

I have one older brother and one younger sister. Along with myself, there were three of us altogether. My older brother is still residing in China. He is working there as a teacher in a public school. When I first came to Canada, my sister was about eight to ten years of age. Eventually, when I returned to China, she got married.

I first came to Canada in 1913 at the age of 16. I was born in Du Jie 都解, Guangdong province, in the village of Nan Tang 南唐村.

My father was about 17 years old when he first arrived in the United States. He was in the United States for twenty to thirty years before he went back to China. When he went back, he married, at 50 years of age. He went back (to China) and never returned.

When my father first came here, it did not cost a lot of money. It just cost him the fare of the boat ride, about $30 or $40, given to him by my grandparents. He worked in a Chinese grocery store and also dealt with herbs. He knew a little about herbs and medicine. If someone had a cold or a common ailment, he could treat and deal with that person like a doctor.

My Uncle

My uncle and I were very close. He lived in Montreal and when he went back to China he asked me if I would like to come to Canada. I replied that I would, so he brought me here. My uncle was in the laundry business. When he first set up business, it was in Montreal. I really do not know why he picked Montreal. Maybe there were relatives on his side of the family who were there before. There were a few people from his village living here in this city too. By the time he returned to China he was about 60. He died there.

I did not fully comprehend what exactly went on in Canada. Neither did I know how to go about asking him. He just asked me if I would like to go to Gold Mountain and I said, "Of course." Therefore, he said that if I wanted to go, I could come. He also mentioned that the work would be very difficult. The money would be hard to come by along with bits of information like that. I knew nothing about the geographical regions of Canada, nor about the climate or people. At that time it did not dawn on me how significant these questions would be, nor how important it was to know how to ask them. One thing that he did tell me was that there was a lot of snow outside in the winter. I asked him, "How did they go outside then?" He replied that even with snow being there, you could get dressed up in winter clothes and be warm when you went out.

When I first arrived here with my uncle, he told me that since I was in good health, I could give him a hand instead of going to school. The Chinese people rarely went to school here in Canada. My uncle thought that, since he was in the laundry business, I should follow in his footsteps and be in that business as well. Eventually, I could open up my own business. If I helped him, he would give me room and board, clothes and spending money. When I grew up, I could earn even more. I listened to him with his point of view in mind and followed his advice. It was difficult, for I did not want to refuse or go against an elder. Not all the conditions were suitable to me, nevertheless, I accepted it. I worked for him for two to three years.

Everything was done by hand. It was real hard labour. Every week, the business earned about $60 to $70 for the owner. The workers, however, earned about $6 to $7 a week. This included room and board along with food. The most that you could earn was $8.

5. Uncle Jack, a Moral Entrepreneur

We all lived inside the laundry area. It was not too shabby, just fair. There were some customers who came to the locale and gave us the address to go and pick up the laundry. Once it was cleaned, we then had to go out and deliver it to them as well. However, there were others who came to give it to us and later returned to pick it up. There were both kinds.

I cannot really say how many hours we worked, but the minimum was 15 hours a day. In the mornings, you had to get up at six o'clock, and you finished by midnight. If there was more business, it could even last till two o'clock in the morning. If there was less work, then you worked shorter hours. But the workers did not mind not having a fixed time schedule. They worked around the clock at the regular rate. They were just happy to be employed.

On Sunday mornings, we worked for one to two hours, if there was work; but then we had the afternoons off. The laundry workers even worked during New Year's. We would pull down the blinds so passersby would not be able to look in. Then, we would start to work. It was a difficult and miserable life. We worked for about six days a week, even six and half days at times. There were times when we did not get any sleep for as much as two days. If the boss was nice, then we would get credit for the extra long hours. Then, he would add a dollar or two to the worker's pay.

My uncle and the workers got on relatively well. They were all treated well by my uncle for all of us were Chinese. My uncle married around the age of 20, but he came alone to Canada. Every five to six years, he would return to China at least once to see his wife and family. In his lifetime, he went back to China on numerous occasions. In the olden times, the Chinese who lived in Canada could go to China for a time period of one year. It was a one-year visa. After the period of one year, the authorities would take away your right to stay here.

Early Jobs

In 1914 the war began. In 1915, I was about 18 or 19 years of age. I came to Montreal. On the road from Montreal to Lachine, there was a factory named Dominion Bridge. Dominion Bridge was a steel factory specializing in building bridges. The government at that time contracted that company out to make ammunition, guns and bullets for the war. I had a chance at that time to work in that company. Working in the factory for one week was better than working in the laundry business for one month—the money was so much better! You made a few more cents an hour. I worked there for one year.

I earned about 60 cents an hour. I earned that rate for one year. The work was relatively easy. I checked the cartridges for any defectives. All the while, people were jealous as to why this Chinese had the chance to work at this kind of job. People thought he had no education. Then the foreman told me about the problems which were brewing. I understood and went to another kind of job. It really did not bother me. Later, I got another job in the machine-making department. It consisted of making shells out of copper. This was not a comfortable job because of the odour of the hot copper hitting the water. I just could not take it. So I quit. Fortunately, a friend of mine told me about a job opening in St. Catharines in Ontario. There, a lot of Chinese were making clay pipes.

Knowing this, I went down to St. Catherines and got myself a job. I earned about 50 to 60 cents an hour. I was there for one year. After that, I went on to Niagara Falls. I worked there on a machine burning a type of substance similar to lard. In those days, they used a type of substance to get rid of the smell from the dead soldiers on the battlefields. There was a factory there. It was difficult work but the pay was good, between $1 and $1.10 an hour. It was difficult, nevertheless, I still worked there, despite the fact that my friends told me not to. I worked there for about six to seven months.

In 1918, I went back to Montreal. My uncle was in St. Jean, Quebec, in the laundry business. At that time, he wanted to go back to China and did not plan on returning to Canada. He talked me into taking over his business and I did. Then, there were five people working for him. Including myself and the five employees, there were six altogether. The weekly salary at that time was about $10 for the employees. I managed to get about $20 net. I worked there for two years and after that I sold the business. I received about one thousand dollars for it. Who would buy it? Only a Chinese person would buy it, for it was too shabby. I sold it for about one thousand and five hundred dollars in cash. Within that time, I managed to save about three thousand to five thousand dollars. That was a lot of money back then. I saved it up and planned on going back to China. I was twenty-four at that time.

I returned to China only once. I was 24. I went back to China, but I did not get married there. Why did I go back to China and not get married? Because those who went overseas did not bring their families with them. While a few, with some savings, went back to China once every ten years, many others never returned. So, if I married, I had to leave my wife behind in China, this was my idea. At that time when I returned, my mother was still alive. My mother, my brother and my other relatives told me to get married. Besides, since my brother's wife and my mother did not get along well, I was afraid that if I got

5. Uncle Jack, a Moral Entrepreneur

married, the same thing would happen to me. My wife and my mother would then have arguments between them. Therefore, the idea of marriage did not appeal to me. I only went back to China for travelling purposes. I travelled for a few months to Hong Kong, Macau, the countryside and even had time to go and visit my brother at the school where he worked. My brother was very good in Chinese literature. He taught me and I was very eager to learn from him. I stayed in China for twenty months. There was nothing to do there. I just went there with some money and spent it all as if I was on a vacation. No matter what, I planned on returning to Canada. I was very much interested in coming back to Canada. My relatives and schoolmates told me not to go. But my desire was to go back. The people there had never been to Canada, so they really had no idea what it was like back there. To them, I remarked that I planned on returning to China in two to three years to see them all again. When I was about 25 or 26, I finally returned from China to Canada. Upon coming back to Canada, I got off in Winnipeg. In Winnipeg, there were a lot of people from my village, Nan Tang 南唐. I knew some. Some of them had gone to the same school as I. Others were friends of my father. The younger people hardly ever talked to the elderly ones. There was a generation gap between them. The younger and older people had nothing to talk about. With others, I just recognized them from the village. So when I was in Winnipeg, some of my friends asked me to stay there.

During my stay, I opened up a restaurant in Chinatown. It was named Hong Kong Restaurant. The building belonged to a Chinese person. The rent on the building was very low. Also, the proprietor was from the same village as I. He wished at that time that someone would open up a restaurant. I did not have much expertise in that area, but I had a friend who was a Chinese chef. So he helped me out. It did not cost me too much, about five thousand dollars overall. Everything was by hand, no machinery. How did I get all that money? My friends and relatives all helped me out. Some lent me five hundred dollars, and others, one thousand dollars.

They all offered to help. For example, uncle was opening up a new restaurant and needed some financial help. Some were willing to lend out some money. There was no interest on the loan. As I worked, I would repay the money to them. It took me a few years to pay back all my debts. Then I had a lot of trouble with the employees. In that city, there were no cooks. I had to hire help from Vancouver. As time went on, I did not feel good in that line of work. So, I sold the business.

I worked there for about four years. In the kitchen, there were about five to six people, plus the three waiters. I did not hire Caucasians since they could not do the work. It was a Chinese restaurant. Whenever I bought a chicken, I had to chop and clean it myself. The dishwasher also did the cleaning of the chicken. The Caucasians would not know how to do this.

In Winnipeg, overall, I would say there were two or three Chinese restaurants. My restaurant was the biggest in that area. I was there in Winnipeg for about eight years. My financial situation was not bad. I had a few thousand dollars, so I went back to Montreal. It was a lot better then. I had more friends and I went to visit them. Overnight, they all told me not to go back out west. This was around the year 1929 to 1930, a few days before New Year's day of 1930. Upon returning to Montreal, I had no work. I rented a room in Chinatown. It was very cheap. It was on Lagauchetière Street near St. Catherine Street. The rent was about $6 a month.

My friends told me to get involved with certain local Chinese clubs and organizations. I was very interested in this idea. In Winnipeg, I had wanted to join the Chinese Freemasons. However, I saw that in this organization there were two factions that fought all the time. Sometimes they even used firearms in the streets. The fights were very fierce and violent. The two groups were Zhigongtang 致公堂 (now known as the Chinese Freemasons) and the Guomintang 國民黨. They never got along. In Chinatown on King Street, there were some fights. They used firearms against each other, but fortunately no one was hurt. Some of the store windows were broken. I really did not enjoy being a part of these types of gangs, so I came to Montreal.

Early Community Work: The Chinese Hospital

In Montreal, I had a friend who warmly invited me to join Zhigongtang, of which he was a member. He mentioned my name to that organization and they all welcomed me. I arrived here in 1931. I became a member in 1932. At that time, there were only about one hundred to two hundred members. They were very happy together. Later on, through the years, they voted to elect the president of the organization. I was elected president.

When I was with that organization, there was a Chinese Hospital. There is a story about the Chinese Hospital. This was about 1918 while World War I was ending. The injured soldiers were coming home with infectious diseases. An epidemic started to spread. It was contagious and it spread throughout the city. Fortunately, I did not get it. Not too many Chinese fought in the war. Primarily, it was the Caucasians. The first few Chinese who went, worked in the kitchen. Those people who came back from the war spread the disease. I would say

5. Uncle Jack, a Moral Entrepreneur

about 80% of the population of Montreal got it. The Chinese laundries were even closed, about seven hundred of them. One establishment, a Chinese variety store, Van Lun, the biggest in Chinatown, now torn down, had a doctor, Mr. Xiang. Whenever the laundry shops had the need for a doctor, they would contact me. Mr. Xiang and I would go and see them. Mr. Xiang said that this type of sickness was not hard to cure. First of all, the best thing to do was to boil some "Wong-lau-kit" tea. You bought two packages of "Wong-lau-kit" tea which you boiled in a big pot. Then, you would drink it. The sickness should go away soon. If not, you would go and get some Chinese medicine. The Chinese people were very fortunate. In the whole city, only two Chinese people died in this epidemic. The Caucasians had a lot more deaths. Everyday, when you walked down the street, you would see a funeral car. In every street you would see one. There seemed to be a pall of darkness which had come over the city. There seemed to be no hope.

The reason why only two Chinese people died was mainly due to the things they had to eat, how they grew up in China, their digestive system, and so on. As well, the Chinese people had their kind of medicine which helped them. The Chinese doctors could not go and see the Caucasians, and the Caucasians did not know about them. But, there were some who found out about them and bought some "Wong-lau-kit" tea. This went on for some months. Everyday, Mr. Xiang and I would make the rounds of all the laundries. We would go out to buy herbs and teas, to deliver it to each shop and boil it for them to drink. We did this day and night. I was very lucky not to get this sickness. So the Chinese survived that period. The Chinese people were very scared when they had to enter the hospital. They could not communicate properly. They had a difficult time getting a hospital bed. The hospitals were always full.

There was so much racial discrimination that there was no need to mention it. Even though I myself had not experienced it, there was discrimination in Canada. There was rarely any in Montreal. The worst was out in British Columbia, Alberta and Saskatchewan, all further out west. The racial discrimination there towards us was very prevalent. The French people here were not as prejudiced against us. In this period, the older people who were sick had no place to go. There were no hospitals available for them. So, on Clark Street, we rented a house. We fixed up a few beds and made it into a clinic. If some Chinese people were sick, they would be able to come to the clinic. There was a Caucasian doctor—a French man. An order of nuns, from the Mother House, had become nurses of the clinic. There were only one or two nurses. You did not need so many for there were just a few beds. They worked full-time. In 1920 to 1921, or 1922, the Chinese people launched a massive fund-raising campaign to buy a building.

It involved a few thousand dollars. All those belonging to the hospital helped to organize. All the Chinese people got together and started to raise money. The building that was bought on 112 Lagauchetière West is now used as the Chinese Restaurant Association. We registered with the government, and it was officially known as the Chinese Hospital of Montreal. When the building was fixed up, it had fifteen beds. It was full all the time. The Chinese population in the city was more than three thousand. Of course this did not meet the demand.

In Canada, the Caucasians had different types of doctors. There were the general practitioners, head doctors and the specialists. The specialists would only come two days a week to visit the hospitals. The head doctor would only go if he was needed on call. The general doctor would go every week. There was an old doctor named Dr. Push. A very good one. He gave excellent treatment to the Chinese people and had a good attitude towards us. Another doctor was Dr. Lescal, a surgeon. He is very good and is still alive today. The head doctor was Dr. Ostiguy. When he died, his son took over his practice. He would only come if you phoned him and made an appointment.

Funding for the hospital came from raising money in the form of lotteries. If the lotteries were not all sold in Canada, they would be sold in the United States. We did this once a year. Let us not speak only of us being discriminated against by the white people; the Chinese themselves did not get along with one another, not even now. As a result, not all the tickets in Canada were sold. We sold more in the United States. In order to raise funds from the lottery, we had to get a permit from the government. So, once a year, with permission from the City Hall, there would be one day set aside to sell the lotteries. This was known as "Hat Day". The Chinese women would look after this occasion. The women sold lotteries for two days. It was similar to the way Canadians sold the lotteries. There were boxes deposited at the schools. There would be twenty to thirty boxes per school with one hundred to two hundred tickets ready to be sold. The results were quite good. The women collected a few thousand dollars. Everyone bought tickets, Caucasians and Chinese. We would sell tickets door to door, in front of the schools, and so on. At that time, the government did not help. Ours was not an accredited hospital yet. We did not belong to the union yet, so there was no real help in that direction.

In that period, I joined the Chinese Hospital as a committee worker, then

5. Uncle Jack, a Moral Entrepreneur

as a supervisor. I spent a lot of time working for the hospital. I worked there for almost twenty years as a volunteer for no money at all. I paid for everything myself. Whenever the doctor came to the hospital, I was there. I was there to translate and help the doctors communicate better with the Chinese patients. I knew that language better, so in that way I helped. I spoke a little of both French and English.

I was soon promoted to a higher level. In the third year, I was elected as the vice-president. In the fifth year, I became president. I remained as the president for twenty consecutive terms. I did not miss a single year. As soon as I became president, I made it clear to my members that I would not be as able as my predecessors to drive from city to city to pick up the donations. I could only try my best. Then there was a convention in the Mount Royal Hotel held by the medical doctors of Canada. Several sisters and I attended this convention. We applied to join the hospital union, but we were told that our hospital was too small. We had too few beds. Altogether we had to have ninety-nine beds to be eligible. Only then would we be allowed to join. The Chinese Benevolent Society took up the second floor of the building. I was with the society at that time. I thought we could move the Society to the third floor, making the second floor part of the hospital. We applied again. This time we had a bit more hope on our side. We got some help from several Caucasian priests: Father Breton, Father Lapointe and a few others. We applied again and were refused. We only had twenty-six beds, so the answer was still no. Later, due to our efforts and after having understood our needs and the fact that we were the only Chinese hospital in Canada, they allowed us to enter the union. The hospital beds for each patient cost $1.50 a day. This included all the other essentials. There were times when the hospital could not meet all the payments for the costs. The government would pitch in whenever we ran a bit short.

During the twenty years when I was there, the hospital did not have much of a crisis. In the year 1960 to 1961, we asked for a grant to build a new hospital. The old hospital was too dirty. This comment was made by health officials who visited the hospital. They said there were cockroaches there and that it was unhealthy, and so on. The inspector caused a lot of trouble. I do not believe at all that cockroaches existed in that place. The inspectors also said that the kitchen where Chinese food was prepared was not hygienic. Also, we had to hire a Chinese cook. Eventually a friend of mine who was a Caucasian told me to go to the head of the health department and work out something with them concerning the hospital. I was very angry at the health inspectors. I asked the head of the department if he would help me. I told him I needed about twenty beds to transfer the patients out of the Chinese hospital which had so often been the object of complaints and criticisms. I also stressed that I had no money to renovate and, due to complaints by the health inspectors, we would have no alternative but to close down. The head of the health department understood and sympathized with me and did not send any inspectors after that. Since then, the hospital came along smoothly; but we thought that it was not really a hospital overall. It was just too small.

From that point on, we set out to build a new hospital. We applied to the provincial government. Along with Father Lapointe, Chinatown's MNA (Member of National Assembly) and several sisters, we met with the government to discuss this matter. It was not a long process. We met two or three times in Quebec City. Eventually the government approved. First of all, we had to buy a new building. The government helped us out on this. We had been searching for quite a while for the right building. Finally, we found one on St. Denis and we discussed the matter of buying it. It was a church at that time. We bought it and had it torn down. We planned on building a new one in its place. How much did it cost us? It was approximately one million dollars. The place was not very good but it was suitable. We had fifty beds now. The provincial and the federal governments gave us a certain amount of money to spend on this project. Altogether it came to seventy thousand dollars. Along with the lottery, there were suggestions to raise funds within the Chinese community, but there were some people in the community who were against this idea.

For example, the Reverend Paul Chen did not have much esteem for me. He was saying, "How can he do such a thing? Will the government trust him and give him money for the new building? He is crazy if he plans on raising more money within the Chinese community." From that point on, I started to publicize this issue and wrote letters to all the Chinese organizations. This included an invitation to attend the Nan King Cafe for dinner. We managed to get representatives there. Those who came to dinner did not agree among themselves. Everyone had his own point of view. I did not favour one party over another. With me, what is public remains public and what is private remains private. I keep my opinions on certain matters very privately to myself for the sake of the public. In building the new hospital, it was to help the Chinese community. It was non-profit. I worked for the sake of the community, not for myself. In the end, I did not ask for any contributions from the community due to the problems which arose from the idea I had put forward.

It was the Chinese Nationalist League that was the most opposed to the idea. Back then, the Chinese Nationalist League was headed by Bill Li of Li's

5. Uncle Jack, a Moral Entrepreneur

Association. He was also at that time the owner of the Montreal Chop Suey Company, and had a lot of money. Also there was Mr. Huang Yatan who was the owner of the Nan King Cafe. Mr. Huang was a member of the Chinese Nationalist League, but between the two of us we talked like brothers. In the end he finally agreed to help. He tried his best to raise between three and five thousand dollars. Afterwards Li went to the Li's Family Association to call a meeting. He was the chairman at that time. He told the members not to give any money to me and that as a member of the Chinese Nationalist League, he would not help out in any way in fund raising. So I went to the Montreal Chop Suey Company to meet with Li. I said to him, "You yourself have no problems now. There is no hardship ahead of you since you are well off now. Your future will be very comfortable and easy. But, what about the next generation? When the next generation comes to the Chinese Hospital, they will ask, 'Why didn't Li contribute to this cause?' Your children would feel guilty. The parties in the Chinese community should not be divided all the time. It is not good." As we talked, he finally agreed to combine forces and work for the hospital's fund raising. Now, the Chinese Hospital has his name in memory of him.

The hospital cost one million dollars to build. The Chinese people came up with about eighteen hundred thousand dollars altogether. I was very poor, but nevertheless I still gave a few thousand. From the others, the Chinese Freemasons and Huang Jiang Xia Tang 黃江夏堂, each donated one thousand dollars or more. After the hospital was built, we had an opening day. The hospital operated just like a Canadian hospital. That day everything was working out well. Things were settled amongst the members and everyone was happy. That was my main ambition at that time—to see the hospital completed. Also I decided that perhaps at this time I needed a replacement since my goal had been accomplished. There was a general meeting held by Dr. David Lin (林達威) to which he had invited a group of people, both Caucasians and Chinese. It was at this meeting that I felt I lacked the ability to communicate my thoughts fluently to them as the chairman. Perhaps, a change was needed at this time in the leadership position. After that, an election was arranged at which time I stepped down. I resigned in 1965, when the goal was accomplished.

In 1964, what did the Chinese Hospital give me? They gave me a certificate. There were two flowers on top and written on it was, "Mr. Jack Huang, President of the Chinese Hospital for twenty years." There was a picture also. They gave me a certificate to take home and hang on my wall. There is another one in the hospital where everyone signed their name as a momento. Concerning the memorium, I was very satisfied with it, very happy. After I resigned, the hospital still sent me reports on the progress of meetings that went on. I worked very hard for that goal and to see it achieved. At present, the people have a better workplace than the ones in the past. It makes you happy.

Anti-Japanese Activities

Let me go back to the time when I came back from Winnipeg to Montreal; this was during the period when Japan invaded China on 7 July 1937. In Montreal, the Chinese people discussed amongst themselves the idea of forming an association, the Kiu Yen Association, to raise money for China from around the world. This would be an extremely hard task since organizations in the Montreal Chinese community never co-operated. Fortunately, two Chinese officials, Mai Yentong and Qian Xiangguo, natives of Si Yi 四邑 (En Ping 恩平, Kai Ping 開平, Xin Hui 新會 and Tai Shan 台山), came to Montreal. They arrived in Montreal around the second year of the Japanese invasion of China. During that time, members of the Chinese government continued to come. I personally took them out for dinner. It was not solely for the pleasure of the meal, but rather to explain to them the situation in Montreal. They were very understanding about the situation. These two individuals managed to get everyone together and forget about past differences. Everyone was united.

The Chinese people got all together to help China who was at war with Japan. Therefore, for the sake of saving our country, an association was born. The Chinese people in the whole city of Montreal united and combined forces. I was the chairman of that association during that time. I was very sorry for all the Chinese who were forced to pay in order to raise the funds. If they did not pay, they were arrested. If we asked them to pay and they refused, we had the military right to arrest and punish them. I would be like a soldier marching off to war to do anything for his beloved country. Everyone had to pay, somewhere around $50 or more. Well, if you did not pay, you would be put in a parade which showed others how cold-blooded you were not to care, that you did not think of your country, and that you were very disloyal. Chances are you would try and get your friends to help since you did not want to feel ashamed.

There were about three thousand Chinese living in Montreal and they each gave $50 or more. It was only the elderly and the honest people who would do the collection. Then, by telegram, they would wire the money overseas to China. It would be received by the Finance Minister, Quon Chung Hee. From that point onward, he would send back a certificate indicating to us that it had been received. This would be encased in a frame. It was hung up in Chinatown

5. Uncle Jack, a Moral Entrepreneur

for everyone to see. Everything was done correctly and legally. Then came the government debts which approximated hundreds of thousands of dollars. They were all sold here as government bonds in a matter of days. I still have some of those bonds even now, which were worth one thousand dollars each.

They were Chinese government bonds. After the Second World War, a Boy Scout Jamboree came over here from Taiwan. I personally received them. I asked some of them about the government bonds. One of them, a gentleman about 40 years of age named Mr. Qian, remarked that he had never heard of such a thing. I showed him some of the bonds. As well, I gave them some of the smaller bonds, worth about $50, to take back with them. Mr. Qian was also head of the organizers of the Jamboree. When they went back, the government declared that the bonds were worthless. In China, the representatives of the Chinese government were crooks. The overseas Chinese loved their country whole-heartedly. There were some people like myself who did not work for a few years just for the sole purpose of raising money. We suffered. In that time it was not only the Chinese who were against Japan; there were others who were allied with us.

The Chinese here formed a group named the Security Council. This Council dealt with matters of security, protection of persons and property, and many other things. If there was a war, we had to be prepared. We arranged the war shelter and the headquarters of the Council at the Sun Ya Restaurant. The Chinese people had to have their own safety precautions in case a war erupted. Overall, there were 83 security members consisting of young and old. In order to become part of the Security Council, one had to attend drills. I passed each exercise, and eventually I became the leader. I had an office where I could use the telephone to get in touch with the other members of the National Security Council. There were usually two girls who worked in the office as well. Every weekend we went to test out some of the guns at Ontario and Amherst streets. There was a very big market there. I led 50 men over there. I would assign my 50 men to an officer from one of the many security officers and I would take another fifty men and train them. We did this once a week.

The Security Council was set up for the war. If a bomb hit the city, these security officers would be ready to administer first aid and to see to it that lives were protected. These security officers were not only for the Chinese, but for everyone else in the city. If there was a fire, or a bomb, the officers would lead people to safety. The Canadians' Security Council was named CDC. In Chinese it was called "*Bow-on*", meaning to protect and keep safe. Each day we had to train and teach the people. Primarily the lessons dealt with first aid. I did this for six years. I was busy every day. There was no time to find food or earn any money.

I could not go to work. I was just too busy. Finding a meal was no problem. In Chinatown I had some good friends who were in the Chinese restaurant business and they would call me over to eat. Usually I had my two meals there.

Love, Marriage and Family Relations

At that time, 1937, I had a family to raise. I was about 40 years old. My wife is French. She was 16 at that time. Her father was a war veteran. I really cannot remember how I met her. I met her father first. I only knew her father at that time, and there were a lot of girls in that family. But she was the one who would always follow me around to go out with me and eat with me at the restaurants.

One day her father said to me, "Jack, you should not be doing this. Why don't you marry her?" In return, I said, "Well, I have no money to support her or to give her any type of security." He said, "You could marry her and live with us. Later on, after you started a family and worked yourself up to a better position, you could find a better place and be on your own."

There were very few people at my wedding. There was just the registration officer. We went to a Catholic church. My wife is a Catholic. It was sort of like a secret marriage. Her father and I talked, and the wedding proceeded from there. It was very simple. Just her family attended the wedding. I did not invite any of my Chinese friends. It was all her side of the family. Altogether there were between 10 and 20 people. We went home, drank some tea and had some pastries. It was like a tea party.

So I lived with her family after our marriage. We moved out after the second child was born. The first son was born in 1936 and the second was born in 1938. In 1939, we were looking for a house to rent and the possibility of opening up a restaurant. The first restaurant was the Kim Lun Restaurant, popularly known as the Cathay Restaurant. I worked with Qian Tai. It did not bring in a lot of money but we made a living.

In Montreal, there were very few inter-racial marriages at that time. Most probably not more than ten. The older generation of Chinese people felt that if you married a Caucasian, you would be going against the culture you were brought up in. You did not love the motherland anymore. If you married a Caucasian, you were useless. The elderly Chinese thought along these lines.

In my time, I did not hear much talk about our marriage. Perhaps they just did not talk to me about it in my face. My friends were very respectful of my decision. We did not have a banquet, but there was a wedding ceremony. I could not afford a banquet. There were Caucasians at our wedding, her family and relatives. I have two children. Two boys. The older one is 46 and the younger one is about 44.

My older son works with the bus company. He has been in that line of work for about twenty years. He goes to each bus shelter, measures and fixes the materials, and reports back to the company. My younger son works in the office of a shipping company. He has worked there for about twenty years also. He has been quite successful and has a very good position. He has been in charge of the payroll department.

They went to high school, but we could not afford to provide them with higher education. They loved to talk, "Daddy, I don't want to go to school and I would like to work. I may not be able to give you any money, but you do not have to give me any either. You do not have to buy me things to eat, clothes or anything else. I can look after myself, and be independent. I will look after you and help you out. However, if you want me to go to university, I am afraid I cannot oblige. There are a lot of other people who come out of university as lawyers but cannot get a job. The money spent on education like that is often a waste."

The elder son got married at about 21 to a Francophone. They went out together and that was how it happened. She is the eldest daughter of the former mayor of Jacques-Cartier. My younger son got married at 20. He and his wife went to school together. They dated and finally got married. My older son has six children, five girls and one boy. Last year they moved to St. Hubert from Montreal. Now he drives back and forth to work.

My younger son married an Irish girl. He lives near Verdun. I cannot recall ... yes, Ville Lasalle. They have four children—three girls and one boy. The oldest girl married two years ago, and so did the oldest boy. Most of my grandchildren are married now. They are very good. Every weekend they will either visit me or phone to see if everything is going well. They all speak English and French and a little Chinese. Before, they could speak Chinese fairly well, but as they moved away, they rarely spoke it anymore. Over time, they lost the ability to speak Chinese. Only once in a while would they come down to Chinatown for a bit of shopping or having dinner at a restaurant.

After the two children were born, my wife's brother died in a parachuting accident. She loved her brother a lot. My wife was very sad and suffered greatly from this event. Day by day, she got sicker. It was a psychological problem. She did not eat. Every day the doctor would come and see her, and as a result she started to get better. Then, one day, her mother died. My wife then had a nervous breakdown. She was 22 at that time. My father-in-law and I sent her to Long Pointe Hospital where there were a lot of people to look after her. The doctor said to me, "Don't worry. She should be alright in about six months' time."

He said, "Take her home, watch her carefully and report her progress to me from time to time. If things are not going well with her, bring her back here." So I took her home. For two to three weeks she was not doing well at all. There were times when she was not aware of anything going on, sort of like in an unconscious state. I brought her back to the doctor and my father-in-law accompanied me. My wife did not want to return to the hospital. The doctor told her she had to stay there for a few weeks and then I could come back to fetch her.

She was there for about three to four weeks. Every day she would phone home and say that she wanted to come home. I asked the doctor's advice, and he said that I could bring her home again. But the best thing to do according to him would be to take her to a remote place where she would see new faces and different sights. I did just that. We went out west and toured the whole area out there for about two months. We visited all the major western cities such as Vancouver, Victoria, Winnipeg, Calgary, Edmonton and Moncton.

We went straight down to all these places and toured them all. When we came back home, she was a lot better, just fine. She went back to work in a pastry shop for about three years. The work was very hard and her health started to decline. In the end, she did not work anymore. This was about two to three years ago. Her sister invited her to go up to her summer cottage in a small town. So she went up there for a few weeks. One day she was picking blueberries and fell, breaking her arm. She went to the hospital to get it fixed, but she still has pains in her arm to this very day. You cannot do too much at the age of 60 or so. The only thing to do is to let each day take its course.

At home, if we are preparing a Chinese meal, she will prepare the rice while I will cook the vegetables and meat. If it is a Canadian dish, then she will do all the cooking. She can do almost anything, the grocery shopping, and so on.

Even if I am sick, I still have to go out. I have to keep busy. Last year, I could not see anything. My son would come and pick me up to bring me to Chinatown on his way to work. Then, he would come to pick me up again after work. I have to exercise and keep fit. At this age, if I do not exercise, I will become run down. Usually these days the latest I arrive in Chinatown is about two o'clock in the afternoon, and I leave at four. At night, if the weather is fine, I leave at seven o'clock and arrive home by nine. I like to take the bus or just

5. Uncle Jack, a Moral Entrepreneur

walk. Even when I am sick, I still come here. I rarely visit any other place, just Chinatown. I just do not have the energy. Plus, my eyesight is not very good.

I read the newspaper, keep in touch with friends who correspond with me. Even if it is difficult, I try to write back ... chat with some of the old people and talk about international affairs; for example, the Falkland crisis—the British versus Argentina, basically whatever is in the news. I enjoy reading the newspaper. Even if it is difficult for me, I still read it. Sometimes, I read two to three newspapers to pass a day.

My wife does not do much. She rarely goes anywhere, mostly stays in the house. She does not like the movies. She enjoys smoking cigarettes. I tell her not to smoke, but she says to me that smoking is what she enjoys the most. She says, "I do not go to the movies, do not drink, there is nothing else for me to do. If you tell me to quit smoking, then it is like locking me up in a jail cell." She only smokes and walks around the neighbourhood. Usually once a week she will go out and see her sons. I tell her to go. She usually spends a few days there. Then in the next week, another son will phone her and ask her to go over to his place. It is very nice.

My wife has not worked in the past few years. She cannot work. She worked only for two or three years. She worked in a factory and then at a bakery shop for about two years. She has some family still in Montreal. Her parents have passed away along with her brother, but she has a few sisters. We get together when my wife or myself wants to go out or when they telephone and invite us over for a visit. They seldom come to our place.

On festive occasions, I am not allowed to be at home. During the Chinese New Year, we are usually over at my son's, like last year. During Christmas time I would be at one of my son's homes and at New Year's I would be at another son's.

In Chinatown we have Chinese videos. A lot of people watch these Chinese video programs, especially on Sunday. At about two o'clock, people come down to Chinatown to make payments to the credit unions set up at various family and clan associations. And they all sit around and watch the video programs, between one hundred and two hundred people. The parents come down to buy groceries so they will leave their kids at the associations to watch television. The mothers can then go shopping.

Chinese Restaurants—Entreprenurial Efforts

In Chinatown I opened up a restaurant, Kim Lun's, now known as Cathay. I worked with Zhu Gentang. I worked a few years there till 1950. In that year I got together with some other people, some of them members of the Freemasons, to open up another restaurant, Kim Lun, on Dorchester Boulevard near the YWCA Kim Lun was very busy and profitable. However, the city was starting to tear down certain buildings in order to widen the streets. Before the city did this, I knew that they had a layout of the plans for the neighbourhood. I went to the City Hall with a lawyer to see about the property. The commissioner who was in charge of real estate and property asked us how long we were planning to do business in that area. I asked if he would be satisfied with a period of ten to twenty years. The commissioner said that they were going to pay for the property but not the cost of the business. The government had no money. There was no road there. He asked me to take a chance and open the business anyway. I went ahead and started the restaurant. It was a very nice restaurant, making quite a bit of money. Also at that time, a hotel known as the Champlain opened nearby.

The business I had there was very profitable. It was extremely busy. Then the news came. They tore our buildings down in 1950 to make the streets wider. All the other buildings there were also torn down. The debt we owed for starting the enterprise was over ten thousand dollars. This was the starting cost, including the money we used to fix up the place. When it closed, everyone left. I was the one who went to the bank, signed the documents and generally looked after everything.

I was the only person responsible for it. The Caucasians were very considerate about the matter. They discussed things with me and gave me a chance to work things out. The maturity date was even extended for repayment of the outstanding amount. In the end, I could not meet the payments. So I went to the South Shore in the Jacques Cartier area. A Caucasian and I bought a restaurant together. He was a real estate expert. The restaurant was originally a snack bar. We converted it into a Chinese restaurant and eventually obtained a liquor license. We also added a few extra rooms. My Caucasian partner closed down the snack bar and also the billiard room. We sold all the pool tables and used that room as a night club, selling drinks. This worked out extremely well and it soon became a very profitable business. However, problems arose. Certain Caucasians were very jealous. Which ones? The ones in the Air Force. The air base was situated in St. Hubert, very close to the restaurant. If you drove, all you had to do was to take the highway and drive straight through St. Hubert to Jacques Cartier. The business was in Jacques Cartier, a very short distance away. At first there were no problems. But trouble arose when certain people came from British Columbia. Among them were people from the Air Force.

5. Uncle Jack, a Moral Entrepreneur

These people who came to the restaurant did not like the Chinese. They discriminated against us and caused a lot of trouble. They did this every day. Eventually we reported this to the head of the Air Force. But this did not help much. It was only when they were dressed in proper military attire when the Air Force had some control over their conduct. If they were dressed in civilian clothes, the Air Force had no power over them. I could also send for the police. A military police officer was sent over. However, they did not cause any trouble when he was there. It was only when he was not there they started the trouble. They caused trouble by irritating the customers, especially the ladies, and spilling the drinks all over the place such that you could not operate the business anymore. In the end I did not feel the effort was worth it. Eventually I talked with a group of members—similar to an underground syndicate, something of that sort. I asked them if they could do something about the situation. They knew how to deal with it. If you could not get them to stop, then the only alternative was to get a fight going. We had some Caucasians who helped us out. My oldest son knew some friends in the gambling houses and bars; the bouncers helped us out. The Air Force continued to ignore us. A fight started. We could tell who was in the Air Force, but they did not know who was going to fight them. The light was very dim. The ones who were on our side did not get injured. However, those in the Air Force, seventeen of them, were taken to the hospital, and one of them had his eyes ripped out and another had a broken rib. All the injured were from the Air Force.

Some of us used baseball bats and sticks that were not too strong, while others fought bare-fisted. The men from the Air Force were beaten up terribly. They lost the fight. The MP could not really do anything about it, nor would they inspect the situation, for they knew who the real trouble-makers were. The Air Force did not give up though. They still caused trouble. Once they drove a jeep and, in passing, they used a rifle to shoot into the restaurant. They even caused a fire once.

When the first time this happened, we managed to put the fire out. The second time the fire broke out from the roof. They poured gasoline on the roof and made a hole. It was a small town on a highway so there was no real possibility of finding out who the culprits were. The restaurant was burned to the ground. The insurance company did not want to renew the policy. So how were you supposed to conduct a business? The workers could not work either. So you had to end it there. Before, there were not a lot of Chinese people in the restaurant business as there are now.

In Montreal, I set up a restaurant named Quon Wah, now known as Lung

Fung. I worked in that restaurant for three years. Then I opened up Sun Ya, Sun Kou Min and Sun Kong Woo. This was not all done by myself, but with a group of friends. I just wanted to earn enough money for a bowl of rice. I drew no salary. For the last two years, everyone said that this was not fair. So they thought that I should get some money, at least to buy some cigarettes. Therefore I just drew a salary of about $100 a week. Trouble started again when some of the partners began arguing. This was about two to three years ago. In 1979, the business was finished and we all broke up. Since December 1979, I have not worked. I could not work due to health problems. At the age of 80, you cannot do much.

Montreal Chinatown: Memories

When I first came to Montreal, the conditions in Chinatown were very poor. On the north side, the houses were very old. On the other side, the homes were not too old, but old nevertheless. The main street in Chinatown was Lagauchetière Street, from St. Urbain to Clark Street.

On the north side, there was nothing. At the corner of Dorchester Boulevard and Clark Street, on the east side, there was a Chinese grocery store, Gin Hing. If you walked further down, about halfway, there was Gun Yake, run by Mr. Hong. This was a grocery store too. There were only two Chinese grocery stores. There was not much Chinese business in that sector, and there were no restaurants on Clark Street.

In those days, the biggest restaurant was House of Wah Ying. It is now the upstairs of the Jasmine Cafe. Long time ago, this restaurant was the most exclusive. On Sundays they had a tea brunch for the customers. There were three or four other restaurants, but they were a lot smaller. It was more like a snack bar. There were no big restaurants at that time.

The seating capacity at the House of Wah Ying was about eight hundred. If there was a convention or a banquet, the restaurant would make the food and deliver it to the association or organization. As for banquets in the restaurant, they were rare. During those days, the Chinese held neither wedding ceremonies nor banquets.

There was another grocery store, called the Hop Wah, not far from Chinatown. It was past Beaver Hall on the south side, and was owned by a native of the province of Xin Hui, Mr. Zhao. Besides Hop Wah, there was a Chinese Christian Church. Not too many people attended the church though. Every Sunday, the Reverend Qian Nanjing would accompany a group of Chinese to Chinatown. He would preach and pray outdoors at the corner of Lagauchetière

5. Uncle Jack, a Moral Entrepreneur

and St. Urbain Street. The whole service took about an hour. Very few people attended these public sessions. The reason for this was that the people in Chinatown were just not interested in the church.

On the other side of Chinatown, there were two grocery stores, Gune Sen and Chin Sen, both owned by Mr. Huang. On that side, that was about all. On another side down St. Urbain, there were Wing Wah Lun and Wing Hing, both small grocery stores also. The building that was recently torn down at the corner of the street was the biggest grocery store, Wing Lun. The other buildings were Li's Association and the Quon Yee Association which were very old. It was most likely around 1920 when they bought the building from a contractor, had it torn down and then rebuilt it. At the time, the Hum Quon Yee Association rebuilt the building; they also had a big tea house, Gin Quon Lau, inside it.

Across the street, there was a restaurant, Lung Fun. In its place before, it was Ling Nam Lau. It was the biggest restaurant then, around 1920. Every day they had a tea house with excellent and celebrated chefs. As well there were two waitresses from Vancouver. After that, from the Yee Fung Company down to the New Lotus Cafe, all the buildings were very old. It was then that the Chinese used them for restaurants and snack bars.

In 1920, the Chinese people formed a company, Ching Hing Company, which cost about $500 a share. They leased it from the city of Montreal. The contract was for fifty years. They tore down the buildings and planned on rebuilding new ones. The only building they did not tear down was Li Fung. All the restaurants, Cathay to the New Lotus Cafe, were torn down. No, the Lotus Cafe was not torn down. After the lease expired, the city would then repossess it. New Lotus Cafe used its upstairs as a restaurant while the downstairs was a gambling house. The buildings up to the Jade Garden were then all torn down. From that point onward, it went to the Pon Kai Restaurant and Cathay. All of these three buildings were being built by the Ching Hing Company. After they were built, they were leased back to Sun Kwok Wah. The Cathay Restaurant used to be a cafe shop. It was called the Moon Cafe Shop and the Quok Kou Fung used to be a gambling house.

In Chinatown, there used to be five or six gambling houses. There were different kinds of gambling: *fan-tan* 番攤 , *pai-jiu* 牌九 , *zi-hua* 字花 , *mah-jong* ... that was about all. All of them were operated by the Chinese. A few Caucasians played, some played because they had nothing much to do. Others knew some of the Chinese people, so they learned to play. The gambling houses were open usually from noon to midnight. Sometimes after midnight, there would be some small groups of people who would play till dawn. There was a law which made gambling illegal and there were no licenses given out either. There were some police raids. If they arrested you, it was not a serious offence. If they arrested you and you declared that you were innocent, you would get a lawyer. This happened rarely. Most of them admitted their guilt and were fined. The fine was about $5 or $10. The judges knew that the Chinese people had no family here. Aside from their work, they had no other pastime. They did not attend dances, committees or any other social functions. They would gamble. The fines were not heavy, about $5 or $10 per person.

Aside from gambling, there were some men who sold opium. There were three or four places that were known where opium changed hands. These were in basements and on the highest floor of buildings; for example, the Huang Yun Shan Association's highest floor. There were some old people who sold opium too. On Saturdays and Sundays, the laundry people would go out and have some opium. It was quite cheap back then. It sold for 25 cents, 50 cents, and at times, $1. They would buy the stuff and smoke it right there. The equipment would be ready to use. This was similar to the opium house back in China. The only exception was that it was not as nice. I have been in those areas. My friends asked me to go over there so I have seen these people selling the drugs. At that time, the police on occasion arrested those who were involved. Yet, the fines were not heavy. It was lighter for the ones who bought the drugs. It was only around $10 or $8 per person. However, for the ones who were selling the drugs, it was $50, $70 or $100 per person.

If the RCMP caught you in the act of smuggling, then they had evidence to put you into jail. You did not need to go to court. The RCMP would be very fair to you. If you were proven guilty, you would be sentenced to six months in jail. There were no fines levied. It was in 1930.

In the beginning, there were separate charges for those who possessed the drugs and those who were smuggling. Later on, very quickly, the law was changed and the two offences were combined into one. There were very few big drug rings. They were their own bosses. In Montreal, I do not think that there were any big drug rings. At the most the penalty was six months in jail. In any one year, there would be three to four people who were caught and sent to jail. After that, the government would then deport them. Not too many Chinese were deported. In Montreal, I would say altogether there were about thirty to forty people deported over the years. This was not in the same period though. In every period there have to be a few. Why? Because if one opium house was in trouble, a few people were arrested and found guilty at the same time.

5. Uncle Jack, a Moral Entrepreneur

The opium stopped during the Second World War. The young people were never interested in it. That is why today there is no more opium left. The law later became very strict, which was why no one touched it. However, there were some individuals who sold drugs to the Caucasians. That was a personal matter of making profit. Caucasians usually bought the opium from the Chinese. The opium was usually brought in by the sailors who were usually from the South of Asia. They bought it in pounds. When the sailors docked here in Canada, they would begin selling. It was a bit more expensive since there was a mark-up on the original price. The opium might have been brought over by the Chinese people, but I do not believe that it was grown in China. It was grown more in the area of the South East Asia. There might have been some from China but I am not sure. Most of the drugs were being supplied by the sailors.

I have never heard of any individuals who went broke and died due to the pressures of debts from gambling. Nor have I heard of people who ran into debts of hundreds of thousands of dollars because of gambling. Up until now, I have not seen or heard anything like that happening. Since some folks did not have any of their family here, they could gamble away their money and no one would know about it. It was a personal matter. At that time, people did not earn that much money. If the person gambled his money away, rather than send it back to China, the relatives would not know about it.

Aside from gambling, the older Chinese rarely went to see any movies. In my time, we all liked to go out and see movies, but the older generation seldom went. They did not spend much money, just saved it. Most of them sent the money back to China to buy land, farms and new houses. Also, there were others who planned on going back to China with some money, and some put money aside for their sons to be used when they got married.

I think that during that time practically all the people saved up their money. I would say about eight out of ten saved up their money to return to China. In that era, none of them were planning on living and staying in Canada. There was an overseas Chinese who was a member of our party, the Chinese Freemasons. He was very old and could not work. Everyone in the party tried to raise enough money to buy the fare to send him to China. He did not have to pay anything for the trip. It was free, for he had no money. His health was very bad and he could not work. Subsequently, all the members and the relatives donated the money to him. These were donations of $1, $2, $5 or $10 ... it all added up. So we had enough money for the train and ship fare. This sort of thing happened quite often and it happened in every city in Canada.

When I first came to Montreal, the Chinese population was about three thousand. There were not over twenty families from China. There were very few females, about twenty or thirty of them. The rest were all males.

In the past, if you were married in China and a Canadian citizen, you could bring your wife over. But you had to have some money in order to do that. There was a head tax you had to pay. Anyone had the right to bring their folks to Canada. You did not have to apply. It was a direct process. You just had to pay the $500 head tax.

Most of the Chinese population at that time were in the laundry business. There were about seven hundred laundry shops, and each laundry had about three workers. There were very few restaurants. In Chinatown, there were fewer than twenty restaurants. The restaurant workers did not live in Chinatown. Usually they would rent a place near their restaurant. At the most there were between one hundred and two hundred people working in the restaurants.

In Chinatown, there were some people who had no jobs. They were obliged to rent a room and live with two, three or four people, all crowded into one room. If you were lucky and had a friend or relative in the laundry business, you could ask to stay with them. You could give them a hand doing the laundry, and they would give you some spending money—about $2 to $3 per week. Usually there were three people doing the laundry, but on some occasions, there were five. Friends living in the store would help out. In the old times, the Chinese were more united than today. There was a camaraderie which the young people today lack.

The population of Chinatown was not over two hundred. At that time, there were no hotels or apartments in Chinatown. Later on, on St. Catherine Street, at the corner of a park, there was a hotel. That was the only hotel operated by the Chinese. If you wanted to rent a room then, that was where you would go. This hotel opened around 1920.

Later on, another one opened but it was very small. This was around 1920. The location of this is now the upstairs of the Welcome Cafe. In those days, the hotel was very old. There were about twenty rooms upstairs. The property did not belong to the Chinese; it was rented. They opened up a coffee shop and rented the rooms upstairs. The rooms cost about $1 a day. It was very expensive at that time. Most of the Chinese rented rooms in Chinatown for $5 to $6 a month. It was very cheap.

There were no laundry shops in Chinatown. For the laundry business, the location was very important. If the shop was in a residential area, then there

5. Uncle Jack, a Moral Entrepreneur

would be business. If it was not in a residential area, then there would be less business. There were no laundry shops in the business sector. They were all in the residential districts.

It is difficult to say which area had the most laundry shops—north, south, east or west. They were distributed equally. In the far north, which was a bit far, there were not many. The east was quite far also. Towards the west, it was as far as Westmount. Overall, on the island of Montreal, there were about seven hundred laundry shops. How do I know this? Because to operate a laundry shop you had to have a license. It cost about $50. If you knew how many licenses were given out, you knew how many laundry shops there were.

Some Chinese worked in households as servants or maids. Some worked in private homes as cooks. In those days, if you worked as a cook, you had to have some knowledge of the English language. The people who hired you were practically all English. There were no French people who hired cooks. Not that they discriminated against the Chinese, rather they did not have the same means as the English to enjoy their living. They could not afford it. Also, the Chinese did the housework as well. This included cleaning and watching the home against intruders. You had a room in the basement or around that area. You earned about $30 to $40 a month. It was not much. I do not know how many Chinese cooks there were working in households. There were not so many. I believe that in this city, there were about 30 to 40.

When I first came here, there was an organization named Zhigongtang, now known as the Chinese Freemasons. The other organization was the Chinese Reform Party (憲政黨). Later there was the Chinese Nationalist League (國民黨, Guomintang). The Chinese Nationalist League only began in the second year of the founding of the Republic of China. When this League was first organized, most of the members were originally those of Zhigontang. Why? This was due to Dr. Sun Yat Sen 孫逸仙 (1866–1925) who was the first president of the Republic of China. Also he was a member of the Chinese Freemasons which he said was not a political party. That is why Dr. Sun Yat Sen directed all the members to organize and form another party, but he also stood for the preservation of the tongs. Therefore, the members organized another party under the name of Guomintang. There were not many Chinese organizations then. The Chinese Reform Party existed to protect the Qing Dynasty (1644–1911). The Zhigongtang revolted against the Qing Dynasty. These two parties did not get along well. In the city of Montreal and across Canada there were these two political organizations. They seldom clashed, though. The Chinese Reform Party was not aggressive. Its members were all educated. Both groups had their ideas and respected each other. Aside from the Chinese Benevolent Society, founded around 1920, the Tan Guang Yu Tang 譚光裕堂, Li's Association and the Huang Jiang Xia Tang came into existence. These were the three family associations at that time.

Religion among the Chinese was here before I arrived in Montreal. I know that some religious ceremonies were held, but not a lot of people attended. This was due to the fact that a lot of people did not believe in the church. There was no established Protestant or Catholic church among the Chinese population. The ceremonies or sessions were held on Lagauchetière Street, past Beaver Hall and at Hop Wah. Mr. Zhou, the owner of Hop Wah, was a believer in God. Beside his grocery store, he rented a house. Perhaps that house was used as a church.

The Protestants were here first. The Catholics came many years later. It was around the 1920's. Services were held where the flower shop now stands. The father of that church was not a Chinese; he was a Frenchman. He was quite good. He liked the Chinese people, or otherwise he would not have preached there. A lot of people called him "head of the gang". If the Chinese people needed any help, they would go and see the "boss". He would help them solve some of their problems. He made a lot of money that way.

Some of the old people would get together and play mah-jong with others their age. A lot of them played this game. Now in the Chinese Catholic Church, they have an old people's club, with about a few hundred members. Every day they have a few tables there for them to play mah-jong. It is for small amounts, $5. This helps them pass the time.

In Chinatown, there was one big event that happened on 3 March 1952. There was a fire at the Lotus Cafe, now the site of the New Lotus Cafe's parking lot. The restaurant, which was very big, was extremely busy. During the two years it was open, it was the busiest of all the restaurants in Chinatown. There were two floors and the upstairs was used as rooms for rent. In 1952, a fire erupted and burned the building to the ground. Seven people died in it.

Five of them were Chinese—Cantonese, while the other two were Caucasian girls. One of the girls was the wife of one of the cooks, Mr. Zheng. She also had a younger sister who worked upstairs as the maid. The two of them were sleeping in the same room and in the same bed. Both of them were burned to death. They were natives of Alberta. I was the person who looked after matters as to where to send the bodies. The two girls' bodies were sent back to their home town in Alberta. The other five bodies were buried in the City of

5. Uncle Jack, a Moral Entrepreneur

Montreal. The Caucasians helped us out a lot in this mishap. I even went to the radio station and talked about it.

The Caucasians donated money and the department stores sent clothes. Some of the survivors did not have much clothing, so stores sent winter coats, underclothes, shoes, socks, etc. They sent a lot of things. They were all business people who helped. This was the worst disaster to ever occur in Chinatown. It started after the restaurant closed. I really do not know how. On top of the third floor, there was a chimney that started the fire. The fire department examined the chimney and said that it had too much grease. The grease was blocking the circulation and the installation was not properly done in the first place. The flames from the stove went up and ignited.

There were some photographs taken about twenty to thirty years ago, which concerned a Cantonese opera visiting Montreal's Chinatown. About 1910, or later, there was a group from Vancouver, the Kock Jong Heng Cantonese Opera that played the whole year round. There was also the Kock Mien Heng Cantonese Opera. There was this place near the bus garage that was used as a small theatre, seating about three hundred people. Sometimes they would play there for a few months, at other times, for a whole year. Due to the bad economic conditions, the company did not have enough money to pay their players. A few members of the group pulled out and went to China.

I never read the English newspapers. I could not understand them. Also, foreign newspapers rarely wrote about the Chinese people and when they did, it was usually not flattering. They rarely mentioned the good points of the Chinese, but they mentioned a lot about their bad points. Matters that were of little consequence were often magnified to considerable proportions. During that time the Chinese people did not have the resources or capabilities to speak out against these accusations and misrepresentations. What was wrongly reported or distorted was taken as the truth. Our country was weak, so we had no say in foreign affairs. Also, the people had limited education. Therefore, you were powerless to fight back. You had to endure the distortions and take them as reported. For example, if someone gambled, they would write that if you go to Chinatown, there will be someone there who will butcher you. It was all bad news. They never reported anything that was beneficial to our community. I think that racism does exist overall. It is always there. In my opinion, there is racism everywhere. However, it has never happened to me. In general, people from my country often experienced racism. The Caucasians discriminated against our country. Why? If the old people had the opportunities that the younger generation have, such as the chance to go to school and learn how to speak and write, they would have got along with the Caucasians. There would have been less stereotypes and biases toward us. In those days, only one in ten thousand was able to associate with the Caucasians.

There were no licensed doctors in Chinatown. The Chinese doctor did not have a license to practice. I will tell you about it. There was a Mr. Tang and another person, I forget his name now. They were in the Chinese grocery business. If you needed a doctor, you would go and see them. Subsequently, they would tell you where to get hold of one.

Even back in China, they had no licenses. The government in China had nothing to do with them. Chinese doctors learned the practice by following the teachings of the elder Chinese medical doctors and worked in a medicine store, like a drug store. In that way, they gradually knew which medicine was good for what specific symptom and things like that. What may be good for some diseases may not be good for others, they knew the difference. In that way, they became doctors. They could even check the pulse rate and then figure out what to prescribe. This was around 1913. When I first arrived, the Chinese doctors were already here. They stayed until about 1920, when most of them went back to China. After that, there were no more.

There were only two Chinese medicine stores. They had things for minor ailments, like the cold. One was Sun Kong Wo and before this there was Sue Shing. There was a twenty year difference between the two stores. Sue Shing was much earlier in time. Later, they also had a dentist. Whether he had a license or not, I do not know.

I went to him to have a lot of my teeth taken out. He was Mr. Ye Lansheng. He did not have a clinic. He saw his clients in a room, which used to be in the upstairs of Jade Gardens. He died about ten to fifteen years ago. Whether he had a license or not I really do not know. But I believe that he did not have one. A lot of people were scared to have their teeth pulled out. It cost about $1 or $2.

When the Chinese people were sick, they would go and see a Chinese doctor and take the prescribed medication. However, the old Chinese people considered going to the hospital a sign of bad luck. It is not true, but to some, it is an indication that they will die soon. They just refused to be admitted to the hospital. In that way, they had no more chance for survival, and no one could save them anymore. Even Dr. Hua Tuo 華佗 could not save you and make you live. They did not like to go to the hospital, but were usually coerced to go when they were dying. By then, their families were required bylaw to take them to the hospital.

5. Uncle Jack, a Moral Entrepreneur

The cost of seeing a Chinese doctor varied. They had no fixed price. You just paid what you could afford. If you gave $1 or $2, they would accept that as payment. You had to go to the drug store and pay for the medicine. The Chinese doctor wrote a prescription and you went over to the drug store to pay for it. The Chinese doctor would then tell you how to brew and cook the herbs and in how much water. The worst diseases were probably lung disease and internal ailments. Most Chinese had common ailments such as the cold and pneumonia. There was a special kind of disease you could get from prostitutes—venereal disease. For that you would have to see a Caucasian doctor.

If the patient had a serious disease like cancer, but was not in immediate danger, then he would consider returning to China. Since he was born in China, he wanted to die in China. Everyone thought that way. Everyone eventually wanted to go back to China, which is why that generation of Chinese did not own any property. If things back then were more like today, the Chinese people would have owned a lot of property. At that time, property was not expensive. Even if some had the money, they still would not invest. Most of them would take their money back to China. In that way, they would be happier in their native land. As they got older, they did not want to stay here, but wished to go back to China. About every ten or fifteen years in this city, the friends and relatives of the deceased, about eight to ten people, would go to the cemetery and take some bones back to China.

The Chinese Benevolent Society was one group that would take responsibility for sending bones back to China. So when you raised enough money, you would hire someone who knew about the bones and body structure. They would hire some Caucasians who had knowledge of the bones to go and pick up the remains. They would be picking up the bones. Some pieces might have been missing. They would pick up the pieces and clean them up. After this, they would put the bones in a wooden box—a box that was of a good size, and on the outside they would cover it with steel or metal and weld it. Then, after all this, the box would be sealed. The custom officials could not even open it. There would also be a government seal on it. From here, you could send it directly to Hong Kong to the Tung Wah Groups of Hospitals 東華三院. There would be someone there to write in the individual's province, country and all the other necessary details. Then it would be sent back to their place of birth. Their relatives in Canada would receive $10 Canadian money from the Society. This was for the purpose of picking out the bones. Why? If you could prove that you were related to the dead person, then you would get the money. The reason was that we were worried that poor families might not have the means to send remains of their dead family member back to China. We would also buy the urn and put the remains in it. This happened once every ten years.

There were no ceremonies, no temples. Whatever religion you belonged to, you would believe in it. But most of the Chinese people were Confucians. If I wanted to pray in the Chinese way as taught by Confucius, I could go down to Chinatown and buy the incense, paper money, etc. You would pray and the dead relatives would eventually go to heaven. In our headquarters, we have the statue of Wu Zu 五祖. If one of the members wanted to pray, he would only have to light up some incense in front of the statue.

I know that they write down the names of the deceased and pray for them. I believe that those who had family here worshipped on every possible occasion just like the way they did in China. During my years in Montreal, a lot of people did not have their families with them. There were less than twenty females here. Those who were married followed the tradition faithfully. Most of the people who were married would worship their ancestors. Only those with a family would have the images of their ancestors in the household.

It was mostly the women who worshipped and followed the tradition. They knew the occasions and the dates that were reserved for praying. All of them would pass this on to the next generation—by showing them what to do, bowing and so on. For those who did not have a family here, what could they do?

The Chinese women did not work. They could not speak or write English or French. They had difficulty in communicating with the Caucasians, so jobs were very hard to come by. They did the housework and looked after the children. That was all.

The Chinese women became organized and active in their community around the time of 1947 to 1948. The first Chinese women to work outside the home worked in the sewing factories. In Montreal, there were not many women's groups. Later, there were women from Hong Kong who were skilled in sewing and things like that. So they started to work in the factories. They introduced one another to work in the factories and everyone else followed. The Caucasians in the sewing industry were very satisfied with the Chinese women as employees. The Chinese were very honest and did not cheat. For the pay that they were getting, say, $3 a day, they gave their best. The Chinese ladies working in the Canadian companies could not be faulted. Even when business was bad, they were not laid off. The owners knew that the Chinese people were very responsible. I think that even now a lot of Chinese ladies in Montreal work in the sewing factories.

There was also the Wong Wing Egg Roll Company. They sold bean sprouts and things like that. They made egg rolls and frozen foods. Then there was the Montreal Chop Suey Company, and some others. These companies hired a lot of Chinese women. They made egg rolls, canned foods and other things. That was basically what they did.

Women started being employed outside the home in 1950. There was nothing like it before that time. There were not many Chinese ladies before, and there was nothing for them to do. Even now, there are not too many women's groups. In every Chinese organization, they had a department set up for the ladies to come out and give a hand. That is what they would do. At the Chinese Hospital, the women would sell things, set up sales and raise money. Also the Chinese Catholic Church, the Li's Association, Huang's...they all had a women's auxiliary. If there was a special occasion, they would all pitch in and give a hand, but they did not organize anything special.

In the past, all the old people celebrated the Chinese New Year. The younger generation now all celebrate the Christian New Year. At that time, no one knew how to celebrate Christmas. Now, the Father and the Reverend at the church will tell you how to celebrate Christmas...with the Christmas tree...

Qing Ming Festival 清明節 is celebrated annually within each organization. They go to the cemetery to pay their respect to the dead or "walk the mountain". In our Chinese Freemasons Society, we go to the cemetery to pay our respect on 30 May.

We follow the old customs with barbecued pork, flowers, fruit, chicken, and so on. Many years ago it was a lot more crowded. We had to rent a bus. Now, the people all have their own cars. They pick others up as well. So, when they all arrive, they pay their respects and eat. The Freemasons had this tradition even before I arrived in Canada. When they had the first Freemasons Party, this tradition already existed. When I organized this event, we had three buses. There were a lot of people. The seating capacity was for forty people. Now, the younger generation do not have the same ideas. They now go there to have fun. They do not reflect on the past, on how their ancestors and folks suffered, and how they became what they were. They think it is just a picnic.

There are three public cemeteries. At Mont-Royal, they have one for the Catholics and another one for the Protestants. The Chinese Benevolent Society bought some land in the cemetery on Sherbrooke Street East. I think that they had eight to nine hundred people buried there. Yes, nine hundred people buried there. At the Protestant cemeteries, the Chinese had about a hundred graves, while at the Catholic one there were two hundred graves. Why did we have so many graves? The reason was that no one organized anything. There was no one willing to go and pick up the bones to send back to China anymore. Now, the people who bought the graves would remain buried there forever. Before, you would be taken out again and sent away. Now, whether you are rich or poor, you have to pay for the grave. Before, if you died and had no money, the Chinese Benevolent Society would help pay for it. Now, you have to pay $100. Before, it was $20. When I bought it from the company for the Chinese Benevolent Society, it was the same price as you would pay to the Chinese Benevolent Society. Now, I hear that it is about $100.

About ten years ago, I was involved directly in nine out of ten funerals. Now, I may not have organized the meetings, but I still go to the cemeteries to pay my respects. Now, the new generation is very smart. They understand a lot of things and do not need me to explain things to them. I am very happy that they are more capable and intelligent. They will have more opportunities, and living conditions will be better; they will make money and be more creative in their ideas. Between the old and the young, the ideas are very different. But I do not have a problem. I accept your ideas and you would accept mine. We would combine forces. It makes no difference to me. It has to come from the heart. There are some who respect the old and there are those who kick them out and refuse to live with them. Their ideas and values are so different. The social climate and the century have changed and the Chinese people have become very different.

Concerning the community organizations, for example, the Chinese Freemasons, the Chinese Nationalist League and the Chinese Reform Party, they have done nothing which has been of special significance to the community. Primarily, as groups, they have tried to unite their own party members. They all help their members to keep in touch with one another. But, in terms of contributing to the welfare of the community, there has been very little of any significance. Let us take the Chinese Benevolent Society as an example. The Chinese Benevolent Society's first priority is to get all the Chinese people together. At the same time, they are supposed to protect Chinese property and life, help to solve problems and things like that. Yet, from my knowledge, they have not done much of consequence and significance. When I was part of the Chinese Benevolent Society before the immigration liberalization laws, a lot of people wanted their children to come to Canada. This was 1948 to 1949. During that time, I was Chairman of the Chinese Benevolent Society. I wanted the young folks to acquaint themselves with the society. So I organized and sponsored a picnic in the park. The park was very big. I cannot remember its name. It was specially reserved for the picnic by the Chinese Benevolent Society. The soft drink companies donated crates of Pepsi Cola and Coca Cola and delivered them to us. Even the banks helped us. They donated between $30 to $40. That day, expenses ran up to about a thousand dollars. The money to pay for these expenses came from Chinatown's gambling houses. The people there gave $200, $300 and some gave $100. The rest of the money came from donations. We never used one cent from the Chinese Benevolent Society.

There were four buses rented for one day. Overall, it cost us about eight hundred dollars. It was extremely busy in the park. There were all kinds of amusements for the children and there were numerous events. I had the honour of going to the stand and speaking in front of the loudspeaker for the whole day. I was very proud of this moment. I told them how fortunate the Chinese were in that the government was permitting the immigrants to come to Canada, where they have a chance of improving their living conditions. As they arrive here, they have to obey the laws, regulations and customs in order to become good citizens. If they break the law, they will be punished for it. They have to be aware of this. I also mentioned the Chinese Benevolent Society, while outlining to them the functions of this organization.

After the picnic, some people became dissatisfied with what had been done for the people. They thought that the money they sent had not been used properly. I believe that these people were from the Chinese Nationalist League. Afterward, during the Chinese Benevolent Society election, they used money to bribe the Chinese Benevolent Society to work for their cause. In the following term, I did not join, or get involved with, the Chinese Benevolent Society. I really did not care any more.

I think it was around the year 1948 to 1949. From that year on, I did not join the Society anymore. They asked me to join, but I was not interested. If you want to work for the community, then you go and work, not do something else. There is a Chinese saying: "Two persons can sleep in the same bed, but have different dreams." You should always work for the good of the public. I left my position and then let them do it all. If you have to fight and bribe your way into the top hierarchy of the Chinese Benevolent Society, then there is no honour in attaining that position. In order to be in that position, you must work for the people. If you become too high-class and snobbish, then the public will not like you. If you work for the people, people will like you. The Chinese Benevolent Society is backward. These past ten years there has never been an election. Those people who had the reins of power in the past still have control now. Even so, no one runs for the positions or shows any interest in them. They really have no one working for them. Nor does this Society reveal any type of information to the public.

Back then, Chinatown did not have any special days for festive celebrations. The biggest event would be V-J Day, after the Second World War was fought against the Japanese. That day, all the Chinese people got together and celebrated. The Chinese Freemasons donated a lot of money. They built a stage on Lagauchetière Street in front of Guang Yi Tang. From Toronto they invited the Gin Hong Sing Cantonese Opera to perform in the streets. There was a lion dance and many people gathered around to watch it. As the Chinese saying goes, it was so jam-packed that even water could not go through. The lion went down from Chinatown to the Sherbrooke Street area.

Communist China soon became the People's Republic of China. Then every year we had a National Day, like an anniversary from the first year, second year, third year, and so on. Sometimes, the Freemasons would have two lions parading down the streets. We rented one place to hold festivities to welcome all the Chinese to join. If you felt like it, you could join. If not, there was no pressure on you to join. It has been going on for about eight years now. The first Autumn Moon Festival (中秋節) was started by the McGill Students' Association. They did it the best. So, after that, other people continued the tradition and that is why we still have it today.

From about 1950 onwards, there was this monthly magazine printed by the East Wind Club. It was called the *East Wind Monthly* (東風月刊). The editors were Tan Zhuoping 譚卓屏 and Xie Wenbin 謝文彬. They were in the restaurant business. A few young men from China formed a group and rented a place on Clark Street. Together they formed a club, the East Wind Club. They would organize activities on Chinese National Day and during holidays. The magazine that they printed was not for sale. If the people liked the communists, then they would have something about them to read. If not, then they did not have to read it. The paper was small, about twelve to thirteen pages; it was hand-written and printed by a duplicating machine. There were maybe between one hundred and two hundred copies. It had little local news, a bit about China, and some international news. It was not too bad, but it was not all news either. Then the Chinese Nationalist League started a magazine of their own, but I do not know if they printed it or what the title was. The *East Wind Monthly* lasted about seven to eight years. Later on, people's lives and circumstances changed. Also, there was no profit to be made. You could not earn any income. The magazine was not for sale; it was a non-profit enterprise. The writers received no pay for their work. If you wanted, you could donate between $3 and $5.

5. Uncle Jack, a Moral Entrepreneur

If there were big fights in Chinatown between the Chinese and the Caucasians, it was usually over the matter of the customers not paying their bills for the meals. The first time this happened was in a restaurant now named Lung Fung, around the year 1920.

His last name was Huang. He worked in a restaurant, Yit Dong House, now known as Lung Fung. One night, when the customers came to eat, they started to argue and fight. I am not sure if Huang was murdered or whether it was an accident. They fell down the stairs to the street. That was the first incident. The second was in the Nan King Restaurant. This was around the period of 1947 to 1950 after V-J Day. The customers had finished their meal and I believe they were Jewish. The person who was killed was not an employee of the restaurant. He was a bystander. His name was Huang Yadong. He liked being a show-off. When one of the workers and the customer were arguing, he rushed over. I do not know if the person pushed him or what. Either he fell down the stairs to the street or was pushed by somebody. He was killed. After this occasion, the Huang Association asked everyone who was a Huang to contribute about $5 each in order to go to court over this matter. A lot of them paid and a lot did not. There was no proof of how he was killed; also he was not an employee of that restaurant. Therefore, it was officially declared an accident. The case went to court for three to four months, but they lost.

No one knew how the first Chinese got killed. No one saw what happened, until he was lying on the street. So, who are you going to charge? You would then call the police to check what happened. They would ask questions and that was about all. Both were Huangs.

If you called the police, they always came. Sometimes they were on the side of the Caucasian, but most of the time they were impartial. They thought over the matter and gave justice where it was due. If you eat, you have to pay. If not, then it is up to the owner whether to press charges against the customer or not. If charges were pressed, the police would escort the person to the station. If he wanted to get out, then bail would be granted. Usually, the matter was quickly resolved. It was very seldom that one would go to court. The police often treated the Chinese fairly.

Government laws look after everyone equally. Overall, everyone was treated equally. But the judges were a different matter. Some of the judges did not like the Chinese. On some occasions they judged unfairly. The judges who were fair gave no special treatment to the Chinese. The Chinese had Caucasian friends, but when it came to national or foreign affairs, contacts with the Caucasians were very few.

I did not have a lot of Canadian friends then, but now I have many. Today the young people are very open about it. Why? Because of problems in communication. The old-timers had to pay tax in order to come to Canada. For most of them, when they arrived in this country, they were farmers or peasants. Also, they were usually over 30 years of age when they came to this country. Therefore, when they arrived, they had to work in order to pay back what they owed. They also had to make a living to feed the family back in China, with the result that there were no real opportunities to learn English or French. That is why the Chinese lived together and worked together. If you are not fluent in English or French, how can you expect to communicate with the Canadians? You may want to mix with them, but you can communicate very little due to the language barrier. For myself, I was young with very little education, and I did not care if I knew the languages or not. I made some good Canadian friends nevertheless.

I cannot think of anyone who has ever become famous for his contribution to the Chinese community. I really cannot think of anyone or see anyone with outstanding qualities, or who has done something good for the community. Everyone wants to be rich and thinks only of himself. No one particularly wants to do anything for the good of the community. Overseas Chinese across Canada have this mentality. I have been to the big cities. I think the Chinese in Montreal are the worst, in terms of organization and cohesion. Each person holds a different point of view. I do not know why. Maybe this is because of the tradition. I think that maybe from a long, long time ago, the whole city was like that already.

The Chinese community in Vancouver is the best. I have never lived there, but I have often visited the city. Every second year I went there, because the head office of the Chinese Freemasons was located in Vancouver. The party members treated me with great respect and in turn I gave my best efforts when working for them. The party elected me to be a special representative for them. I was given the special duty of inspecting certain branch offices. In doing this, I inspected the American branch offices and I also went to Mexico, Cuba, Jamaica, Peru, Guatamala...about six or seven countries. I did not stay long in any one country. The visits were very brief. When I arrived at an airport, I would be greeted and taken to a hotel, and then to the party's head office. After that, there would be dinners, meetings, and perhaps a welcome party. Sometimes there would be activities going on concerning the party members. Everything was aimed at how to make the Chinese Freemasons Party bigger. In every place I visited, we had a report written up for the headquarters. Immediately

5. Uncle Jack, a Moral Entrepreneur

following the meeting I would leave for my next destination. As a result, I was never able to do any sightseeing.

The Canadian Chinese Freemasons Party holds a convention every two years. We have had a total twenty-five conventions to date. The twenty-sixth convention is coming soon. In all of America, the conventions used to be held every three years. Now, there has not been much happening. If something of significance happens, one can then ask to have a convention. At present, there is no fixed schedule for party conventions for the whole of North America. Before, it was every three years, while in Canada, it was every two years. If there was something to be done, then they would do it. If there was not anything to be done, then they would do nothing. There are times when something could come up and you have to call a meeting. If at any time during the meeting a decision was not made, then you have to call upon all the members to vote upon the issue. Also, the members cannot do anything that has political overtones. Everything has to be legal and done in a correct manner, no criminal activities. If a member of the party is having a bad time, then the party will help him through it. That is our function. There are one hundred and fifty members in the Freemasons Party in Montreal. At least sixty of them actually work for the Party.

In the past, though known to us as the "Gold Mountain", Canada was not booming, nor was it in economic expansion. At that time it was still quite a backward country. When I first came here, there were quite a lot of households without electricity. They had to use lanterns. Even if they had electricity, the power was not at all strong. It was very dim. The light bulbs were not bright and did not burn well. There were not any big buildings, even the Canadians themselves were very poor. Food, clothing and accommodation were not readily available. If the father did not have a job, the entire family would be in trouble. In the city of Rosemount, to be exact, near Pie IX Boulevard, there were few homes at that time. You would only see a house every few miles. There were no streets, no pavements, only mud. I considered Canada to be very backward when I first arrived here. It was not a thriving country. When did it start booming? After the Second World War, the whole of Canada started to develop. Before this, it moved very slowly. After the First World War, Canada moved a little. It still was not moving fast, but after the Second World War, it really started to expand. Skyscrapers and other buildings were all built after the Second World War.

I do not know much about the olden times; I do not know why they picked this place for Chinatown. I never studied that. You know how the

Chinese people were: if one person did well in a particular line of business, the others would follow and set up a similar business nearby. Then the third, and the fourth...As to why the first one came, I really do not know.

There is the question as to why the Chinese went into the laundry business. You see, when people first came from China, they did not have any specific trade. They had no training. So, when you came to Canada the relative who applied for you to come here would most likely be in the laundry business. Therefore, you would learn from that relative and work your way through life in that trade. You could not do any other type of work. You opened up a laundry and earned about $40 to $50 per week. In the residential districts, the rent was low. For $10 to $13, you could rent a house which was quite big. So you lived, slept and worked all in one place. It was like a compass. In the beginning, the first person made the trail and pointed the way, then there were others who followed. There were no other alternatives. For example, if you were a professor, you would tell me to go to school. On the other hand, if you were in the restaurant business, you would tell me to work in the restaurant. Since you did not go to school, and had no education, what could you do? Nothing. For any other type of work, you have to be trained and acquire skills. You could only be a labourer. You wanted to work for a Caucasian, but you lacked the knowledge and the abilities. If my relatives were in the restaurant business, I would have worked in the restaurant. If they were in the laundry business, I would have become a laundryman.

When I arrived in Canada, I really had no big ambitions. I just thought that if I could save eight thousand dollars, or ten thousand dollars, I would go back to China and remain there. Slowly, day by day, you realized that perhaps you could not attain your goals. Even if you did, the situation in China had changed and it was not the same anymore. This happens everywhere. When you go back to China, things are different and you realize it. I think life in Canada is better than in China, the old country. The government in power in China was the Nationalist League. People's lives were very difficult, full of hardships and very tough. So, why should I go back? China had nothing to offer, and life there had no real meaning. I thought it was useless for me to go back though I am Chinese and I should love my mother country. I devoted my life to working for the good of China. I love China and Canada too. China is the country where I was born and I love my motherland. Whether I spent my life there or not, it does not matter.

I have forgotten many things. Many things are not very clear to me. Those

5. Uncle Jack, a Moral Entrepreneur

things I remember, I have tried my best to relate to you. I am sorry for what I have forgotten. I have told you only the truth, nothing but the truth.

Jack Liang, the private man, was a forlorn, lonely émigré—a drifter—who "did not make it" in the economic sense. He did not develop any business—his skills, interpersonal ability and personality characteristics did not encourage any useful business orientations. He did not talk fondly or proudly of his wife, son and grandchildren or much about them at all. He was a bystander, an observer, a non-participant in mainstream public life. Yet, that was where his individualism was most significant—in a private, personalised manner, he shunned and warded off any possible conflict (including with his own family members) and entered into his little world, consisting mainly of visits to Chinatown, sessions of drinking and gambling with friends, and routine management of daily living. His strength was paradoxically expressed through the loneliness and aloneness that characterised his life—a strength that steeled his will before an unkind uncle, drummed up his early efforts to find employment, even though he did not speak a word of English, and empowered him to endure working at two hard jobs, a day job in a factory and a night job in a laundry, for eight years. Despite little social support, he still managed to find jobs that he enjoyed, such as being a cook. Despite all odds, he did not, in the end, over-indulge in self-destructive, obsessive gambling or sex, like some of his friends did. There was no trace of self-pity in this individualist, but a strong suggestion of his pragmatic acceptance of life as a "foreigner" who wished to hang on, in his quiet, dignified private way, to make the best of what he had in Canada. China remained a remote and unfamiliar land; his adaptation was complete.

On the other hand, Uncle Jack Huang, the community man, was a go-getter who exhibited many of the entrepreneurial qualities—vision, spirit, and organizational abilities that enabled him to succeed to some extent in his business and community activities. His introduction into a foreign land was certainly made easier by having a father and an uncle who had already been to Canada. He was psychologically more equipped to combat the world "out there" once his economic needs were met upon arrival by his uncle who offered him to work with him in the laundry business. Through chance, he met up in Winnipeg with friends from his village in China and began his restaurant operations. Through sheer hard effort, he made profits.

One is tempted to describe him as a "moral entrepreneur" in his incessant attempts to undertake projects to make life better for the Chinese community. But he was not a money-oriented entrepreneur (working in the hospital as a volunteer for twenty years for no money at all). He was motivated by his own conscience. There is something so significantly chauvinistic about this man, in his talks about doing good for the Chinese community, that one finds it rather puzzling that he married a Caucasian, and, in his wedding dinner, did not invite a single Chinese friend. Subsequently, his children all married Caucasians, the "Chineseness" in them being further diluted. Yet, Jack, in his old age, unable to go anywhere else, continued to visit Chinatown regularly. His memories of Chinatown, how it was and how it had changed, remained vivid and nostalgic.

Uncle Jack was a winner, in any socio-cultural context. His adaptation experience expressed a great degree of flexibility—a useful case material for analysing change and resilience in coping strategies. "I accept your ideas and you would accept mine. We would combine forces. It makes no difference to me. It has to come from the heart," he said. This is a man with a center, who knew his gut sentiments and cognitive orientations. His gut reactions propelled him to feel, think and act for the Chinese community on one hand, and, on the other hand, his cognitive understanding of a changing society and new values softened his chauvinism and allowed him to cope pragmatically in marriage and family relations.

One does not get a clear picture of any of the ten women portrayed—their accounts were brief and largely confined to their feelings about work conditions, theirs or husbands'. The accounts lacked strong personality characterisation so that one would find it difficult to empathise with any one of the ten women the way one easily could with both Jacks. Portrayed thus, one does not sense the individualism of these women. What stood out was their strong pragmatic acceptance of their separateness, as migrants and as women, in a foreign society. They would do all the odd jobs or take care of the nitty-gritty details in their husbands' business—toiling close to 14 to 16 hours a day in order to one day see that their children go to the university and make good for the family. They spoke with little nostalgia about China or their old days, reflecting a pragmatic approach that put the past behind them in order to move ahead without regrets. They were migrants who willingly chose to migrate. So, in facing even the most difficult times, the rationalisation most often used to gear themselves up for another hard day would be, "If everyone could do it, why not me?" There is indeed a better life to look forward to—they could observe and experience their improvement over time. "Now I eat plenty of chicken," one said. As women and as wives, they continued to do, and probably with less constraint, what they did back in their villages in China, looking after children, doing housework, going to the market, laundering and ironing, chatting and going to movies with women friends. "Life is more comfortable here," one said. Life in Canada is not only more comfortable, it is made easily acceptable because there are Chinatowns, the re-created social structure that enabled social, personal and commercial relations to flourish and consolidate. Chinatowns are places where Chinese migrants feel at home, secure and familiar. They buffer the impact of alien values on adapting individuals; they also nurture, through contact and information exchanges, new adaptive values and coping strategies.

All these individuals are governed by different sets of background and socio-economic factors, making each adaptation story essentially a unique one. Age, sex, marital, educational and previous village contexts all could have an impact on the feelings migrants have about migration. Nevertheless, there is a dominant spirit that marked these migrants of diverse origins. One is characterised by pragmatic acceptance and perseverance, which they expressed with such tenacity, integrity and courage. Pressured on the one hand by family economic needs and limited on the other by racism, inadequate skills and educational qualifications, these migrants learned to adapt to their situations. When they could not adapt to a particular work situation, they would find another job, and another, yet another (albeit mainly menial ones long disdained by white workers). Years of toiling and sheer hard labour taught them to accept with equanimity "the migrant way of life"—one characterised by easy flexibility, instrumental orientations, and family centredness. The remarkable feature in their work orientation is the belief that any decent person must strive to support himself and his family. Otherwise, he will be considered a "good-for-nothing". This compelling work ethic and its stress on diligence and frugality pushes Chinese migrants into doing jobs that are most degrading and back-breaking. Directly related to this work ethic is their familial orientations—migrants worked either to support their families in Canada or to send money home to their village family members—a form of familism that is both motivating and constraining in their economic pursuits. In a way, the endorsement and persevering support of these Confucian virtues helped shape the spirit of pragmatic acceptance in these migrants and provide the *raison d'être* for their very way of life in a foreign land.

6. Walking on Two Legs

Nanking Cafe at the corner of Clark and Lagauchetière streets.

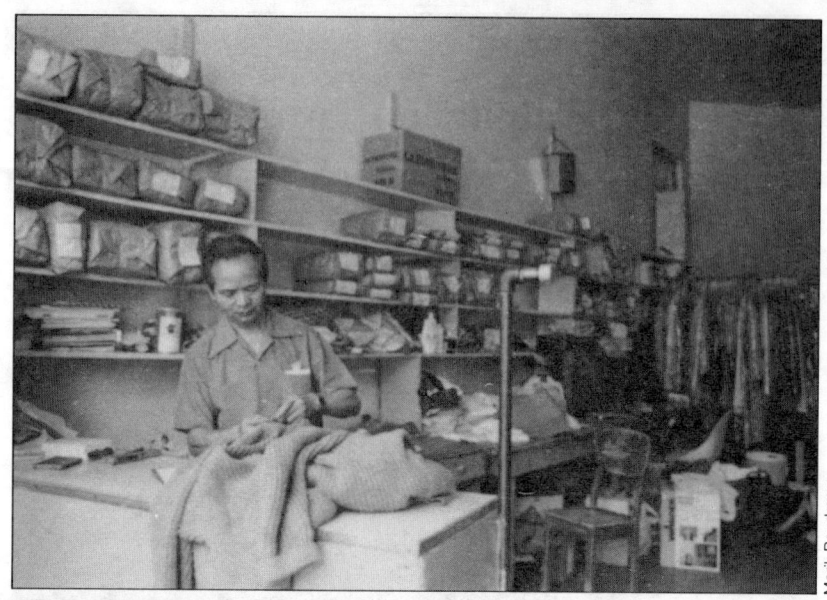

Inside a Chinese hand laundry at 1525 Van Horne.

Mr. and Mrs. Hing Dere, Harry's Laundry, Verdun, Quebec, 1956. (Collection of William Dere, son of Mr. and Mrs. Dere.)

6. Walking on Two Legs

IN a predominantly male, rugged frontier in the wild west, dirty linen and soiled shirts in San Francisco were cleaned and ironed by the Spanish-American and Indian women at Washerwomen's Lagoon, now the Marina.[1] It was reported that some laundry was sent by clipper ships to the Hawaiian Islands, or to as far as Guangzhou (Canton), China—a process that could take two to three months.[2] The price charged for washing just one shirt and the long waiting time made it more sensible to sometimes simply discard it and purchase a new one. In 1850, the *Alta California* stirred up quite a bit of excitement in San Francisco when the following item was printed:

> Much excitement was caused in the city last week by the reduction of washing prices from eight dollars to five dollars a dozen. There is now no excuse for citizens to wear soiled or colored shirts. The effect of the reduction is already manifest—tobacco-juice-bespattered bosoms are no longer the fashion.[3]

The prices were reduced because the first batch of Chinese began joining the "workforce" at Washerwomen's Lagoon, thus launching the first Chinese laundry business in the United States in 1850.[4] In the spring of 1851, Wah Lee is reputed to have been the first to set up "wash-house establishment" when he put out his store sign for business. Other Chinese were quick to grab the opportunity. Wash-houses sprang up all over the city, relying on recruits from cousins, brothers, or village kinsmen back home, for labour help.[5] Bancroft, in his 1890 book, *Essays and Miscellaneous, Mongolianism in America*, reported that the Chinese, in order to meet the high rents and save expenditures, shared space and facilities between two firms, worked in shifts round the clock, and alternated store signs day and night.[6]

By 1879, the bulk of the 2,000 laundrymen in San Francisco were Chinese and the city had some 300 Chinese laundries employing an average of five men each. One could hardly walk by a block in the city or pass through a town on the west coast without seeing a Chinese wash-house store sign in attractive red with bilingual characters, a symbol exerting its presence in the evolving western frontier. Eastward expansion of the Chinese laundrymen promptly began: Chicago and St. Louis in 1872, Baltimore in 1875, and New York in 1876. In American cities, east and west, one saw Chinese laundrymen on the streets making their pick-up and delivery with a bamboo pole over their shoulders, baskets suspended on each end, a familiar sight in the urban areas, which was later outlawed in 1870 by the pole ordinance. The

Chinese were ordered bylaw to switch from "jouncing with poles to using a blue laundry bag thrown over the shoulder."[7]

Back in Quebec, the 1825 census indicates the presence of a Chinese man in the district of St. Joseph in the city of Montreal. The census of 1881 claims seven Chinese in the city. In 1877, Jos Song Long, the first in a wave of 2,000 Cantonese to travel from Canton to Quebec, opened the first Chinese wash-house at 631 Craig Street East, an area which was predominantly English. His neighbours included workers of mainly English origin; French–Canadian owners of restaurants, furniture stores and groceries; and five Jewish brothers who were making a living as silversmiths. In 1880, a Chinese immigrant put out a Wah Lee store sign at 501 Craig Street East; the sign suggests that this laundry could have originated from California.[8]

Between 1877 and 1892, one could count the opening of 40 Chinese laundries in Montreal. By 1923, the number of Chinese laundries founded increased to 1,585, about half of which (609) closed their doors during the first year of operation, and 283 during the second year.[9]

Southern China saw the departure of their men for Canada at a very young age in the period from 1877 to 1892. The majority of these men would have left China at the ages of 19 to 25. The early Chinese community in Montreal would have been made up of Cantonese immigrants who had worked for a considerable number of years in the west coast of the United States, or in the mines or railroad work camps of British Columbia and the Prairies prior to settling in the French–Canadian metropolis. Their employees or business partners were more likely to be Chinese men later brought in from Southeastern China villages under the assistance or sponsorship of their families, relatives or kinsmen who already resided in Montreal.

The salaries earned by Chinese who worked in Western Canada between 1860 and 1885 varied quite a bit and depended on the sectors of occupation they found themselves in. The mine workers of the closing years of the 1860s made a daily salary of $1.25 to $2.50, thus yielding a monthly income of $30 to $60. Those who worked in the construction sector made a little less, receiving around $20 to $30 a month. The Cantonese launderers earned a monthly income of $10 to $40. Those few who were fortunate enough to find employment as cooks or servants with white families were about the only Chinese workers with a permanent, guaranteed monthly income.

With the completion of the transcontinental railroad line in 1885, the Chinese began to find work in coal mines, fisheries, farms, wood factories,

6. Walking on Two Legs   157

FIGURE 6.1

Chinese Hand Laundries in Chinatown Area
(1877–1916)*

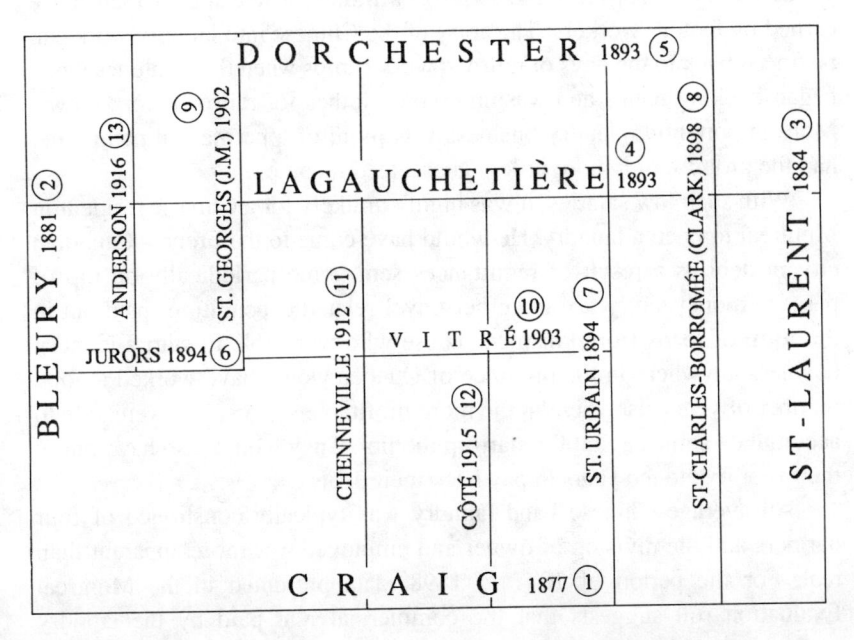

```
                    DORCHESTER  1893 ⑤
                ⑨                            ⑧
           ⑬                            ④
      ②                  LAGAUCHETIÈRE 1893                          ③
                                                                
                                   ⑪         ⑩   ⑦
                                         VITRÉ 1903
       JURORS 1894 ⑥              ⑫
                                                                
                    CRAIG  1877 ①
```

(Streets labeled: BLEURY 1881, ANDERSON 1916, ST. GEORGES (J.M.) 1902, CHENNEVILLE 1912, CÔTÉ 1915, ST. URBAIN 1894, ST-CHARLES-BORROMÉE (CLARK) 1898, ST-LAURENT 1884)

1. 1877: Craig

2. 1881: Bleury

3. 1884: St. Laurent

4. 1893: Lagauchetière

5. 1893: Dorchester

6. 1894: Jurors (E Vitré—1928)

7. 1894: St. Urbain

8. 1898: St-Charles-Borromée (Clark—1912)

9. 1902: St. Georges (Jeanne Mance—1928)

10. 1903: Vitré

11. 1912: Chenneville

12. 1915: Côté

13. 1916: Anderson

* The above map is based on Lovell's Montreal Directory

shoemaker's and carpenter's shops, earning monthly salaries between $20 to $40. Ironically, the most lucrative line of work for the Chinese during the period of 1886 and 1900 was in the laundry business, which in some cases yielded a salary between $40 to $100 a month, a rate higher than those earned by factory workers. The entry of the Chinese into laundry work can be traced back to the days of railroad work camps when the Cantonese men began cooking meals and washing work clothes for railroad work crews. More importantly, laundry business was more of a permanent nature and had the promise of a more or less guaranteed income.

With such low salaries, it was highly unlikely for a Chinese resident in Montreal to open a laundry. He would have come to the French–Canadian city in debt as a result of remittances sent home periodically on top of passage money, entry tax and other travel-related expenditures paid out in the form of loans from kinsmen. Those who were able to start a laundry business anywhere in the province of Quebec would have worked a good number of years elsewhere in the more profitable sectors, and were able to accumulate some capital for start-up monies. They would also have put in their first five to ten years to pay back their debts.

An average Chinese hand laundry was typically constituted of four partners and the division of owner and employee was more apparent than real. For the period of 1877 to 1898, data presented in the Montreal Evaluation roll suggests that the commercial rent paid by the laundry owners ranged between $100 and $200. Then there were costs involved in buying such work equipment items as boiler, stove, basins, irons, tables, washing products and fuel. Salaries needed to be paid to owner and partners during the first month of opening, thus putting the total amount of start-up money at about $500. In the 1890s, a four-person Chinese hand laundry business was required to make do with minimum annual expenses, as seen in Table 6.1.[10]

It was during the early period of the history of the formation of the Chinese community in Montreal that surplus funds for start-up capital were scarce, business loans from banks for the Chinese were an impossibility, and loans from within the Chinese community were few and far between, often with invariably prohibitive interests attached to them. The $500 required to start a laundry business would need to be pulled together in the form of three or four persons entering into business partnership, often called "cousin-partnerships", thus making the laundry's owners and employees virtually indistinguishable.

TABLE 6.1
Minimum Annual Expenses to Operate a Hand Laundry in Montreal in 1890s

Expense Items	Amount
1. Commercial rent	$150.00
2. Residential rent	$ 65.00
3. Business tax	$ 10.50
4. Water tax	$ 10.00
5. Fuel, lighting	$170.00
6. Washing products, starch, tools, etc.	$ 30.00
7. Food, clothes for four persons	$520.00
8. Religious practice expenses	$ 22.00
9. Medical expenses	$ 15.00
Total	$992.50

Other than borrowing money from friends and relatives, the amount of which rarely exceeded $200 to $300 at one time, prospective owners of laundries would try to obtain a loan-grant from the credit system within the Chinese community known as "*woi*" (供會).[11]

The *woi*, an immigrant institution, means "get together", or "put together", and was a sort of collective loan fund administered by a small group of people, usually affiliated with the clan or with a store in Chinatown. It was one of the ways, if not the main way, by which Chinese laundrymen obtained their financial resources to operate their laundry enterprise. One can secure a grant of *woi* either by his own right or by the right of a relative. In order to secure a grant, either one or both of them must be members of the "*woi*". The *woi* has two functions: one is to offer its members the opportunity of securing a sizeable sum of money to establish a laundry shop, and the other is to make profit for its members in a business proposition. Each individual put an equal amount of money into a pool, and made it available for the one in need of funds for business. The prospective loan-maker signed a petition for the sum. He may receive it, provided he offered the highest interest among the competitors. The interest offered by the *woi* loan-maker was sometimes as high as 20%, in case of urgent need. Ordinarily, the interest was about 5%. The higher the interest offered, the less the amount the members of the *woi* invested per month.

Though a widely used and popular practice among the Chinese immigrants in Southeast Asia, the spread and use of *woi* was probably rather limited within the early Montreal Chinese community due to the relatively small size of this Chinese population, thus making the simultaneous formation of several *woi*s unlikely. Besides, there simply were not a lot of surplus funds to make these "get-togethers" possible. The prospective owners of laundry business would, thus, have to turn to the few better-off Chinese merchants for short-term, high-interest, "high-risk" loans. The prospective Chinese owners of wash-houses, thus, found themselves in a business with a grim prospect. They had incurred considerable debts at the outset of the business adventure. It was also a business with meagre revenue, considerable annual minimum expenses, as well as a back-breaking, highly labour-intensive lifestyle. For many, it was a business doomed before it was even begun.

Towards the tail-end of the nineteenth century, urbanization, industrial growth, and commercial prosperity in the provinces of Quebec and Ontario were strong magnetic forces attracting rural migrant populations from Europe, as well as workers from Western Canada. Toronto and Montreal, the two quickly evolving metropolitan cities, were directly benefited by such a trend towards urban and industrial growth. With the springing up of small industrial towns in the French province, Quebec was steadily taking on an urban character and look.

In Montreal, the prosperity that had persisted since the 1880s came to an abrupt halt in 1913, and in the two subsequent years one witnessed an economic decline and a steady rise of unemployment in the city. While the resumption of industrial production in 1915 brought forward a temporary demand of manpower in the following year, as well as an increase in wages as high as 20% between 1915 and 1918, there was also a concurrent rise in prices of 40% which lowered the living standard considerably. This inflation persisted until 1920, affecting about two-thirds of the workers in Montreal. Management personnel and those in supervisory and administrative positions seemed to have escaped the effects of inflation, wage deterioration, and rising living standard. By the spring of 1921, unemployment was affecting more than a quarter of unionized workers in the province. The economic revival in 1923 and its continuation till 1928 brought forward growth in chemical products, in steel and iron industries, as well as in automobile parts and equipment. However, a significant number of wage earners in the province did not seem to be the beneficiaries of such an overall favourable economic climate. Many received enough wages only to

6. Walking on Two Legs

subsist. Poverty was a way of life for the bulk of working class people. When the prosperous decade of the 1920s peaked in 1928, more than 80% of male adult workers earned below the minimum wage, and these were the same persons who were to support a family of four or five people, thus making it almost imperative for some to send their wives and children to work to attain a sufficiently comfortable standard of living.[12]

Quebec remained essentially French and English throughout the entire duration of the nineteenth century. Persons of other ethnic origins never accounted for more than 2% of the Quebec population, a phenomenon that remained unchanged till the 20th century when Canada received its largest influx of immigrants in history.[13] The two largest groups of such immigrants who found their way into Montreal were the Eastern European Jews who soon made up 6% of the Quebec population (and saw the most significant social growth during the post-war years) and the Italians who first came to the French–Canadian metropolis as construction workers.

The deteriorating economic conditions in the years from 1913 to 1915 did not seem to dampen the spirit of Cantonese immigrants making their way into Montreal, nor their intent of finding themselves an occupational niche in the hand laundry business. The 737 Cantonese immigrants came to Quebec between 1911 and 1915 when economic conditions were less than favourable for newcomers in a foreign land. Jobs, any jobs, were hard to come by. Laundry businesses folded as soon as they were begun. Nevertheless, the Chinese continued to "pull resources together" in striving for a minimally viable economic life. The laundry business continued to remain as the principal line of work for the Chinese immigrants in the city of Montreal.

The increase in the sheer number of salaried workers during the decade of 1910, while creating an added and slowly growing clientele for the laundries, along with the merchants, businessmen and small shop owners, ironically did not contribute to the growth of the laundry business. Toward the end of the decade of 1910, one saw in fact the beginnings of a real stagnation in Chinese laundry business.

In British Columbia, racist groups, seeing the Chinese as a threat to a white province, were getting more and more intense in their anti-Oriental sentiment. Chinese were accused of being both unwilling and unable to assimilate into white society. Other times, they were portrayed in the mass media as a people of moral depravity and questionable character with inferior intelligence. With the Chinese representing 11% of the population of Victoria and 3.5% of the Vancouver population, the sheer physical presence of the Chinese was perceived of as a threat to the interests of the racist groups. This "oriental menace" culminated in the 1907 looting of the Chinese and Japanese areas in Vancouver. Alleging the unassimilability of the Chinese and their taking jobs away from the natives, racist groups tried in the same year to block entry of the Chinese into farming.

While British Columbia was working hard on "Educating the East" about the "Oriental Question",[14] feeling very much isolated from, and occasionally betrayed by, Ottawa and Eastern Canada, the Quebec government in 1915 imposed a tax of $50 a year on all Chinese laundry owners. The collective protests staged by a group of launderers along with the Catholic church (which was then preaching within the Chinese community) and the Chinese Council in Canada did not meet with any success. The $50 tax levied against the Chinese launderers in Quebec in 1915 took effect a little over ten years after Ottawa had brought up entry taxes levied on Chinese immigrants from $100 in 1900 to $500 a head in 1904, half of which was awarded to the provinces that took in the immigrants. Quebec received $22,500 entry tax from the Chinese in 1908. In 1923, the federal government passed the Chinese Immigration Act that effectively prohibited the entry of almost all Chinese into Canada except diplomatic personnel, children born in Canada, Chinese students and businessmen having invested $2,500 in Canada three years before arrival in the country.

The large number of closings of Chinese laundries within one or two years of their opening, along with the difficulties the Chinese had encountered in their "economic insertion" into the host society did not seem to prevent the laundry trade from being more heavily taxed by the municipal government than other more lucrative and profitable lines of work. A Chinese laundryman found himself paying the city higher license fees and more taxes proportional to their revenue than most of his neighbours, be they auctioneers, pawnbrokers, meat wholesalers, detectives or theatre owners. Thanks to the cumulative impact of provincial, municipal and federal measures, the hand-laundry business, the major lifeline for the Chinese, had, thus, become a most precarious, extremely vulnerable, high-taxed, high license-fee, but low-revenue trade.

While toiling through hard times to find an occupational niche for themselves in the hand laundry business, the Chinese were by no means the only launderers in the city. Operating from their homes, Francophone women offered to do their neighbours' laundry at a fee, and they were joined by the female staff of religious communities.[15] The Montreal Steam

Laundry, established at 21–25 St. Antoine Street in 1886, was equipped with steam presses and had contacts with hotels, restaurants, major institutions and maritime companies. The Cantonese men and Francophone women did all their work by hand. Between 1888 and 1891, large-scale Anglophone-owned laundry stores made their first entry into the business; promotional campaigns were launched by offering reduced rates in return for monthly commitments from their clients. This business strategy forced the Chinese launderers to survive on yet more reduced rates.

For the Chinese launderers, the stiffest competition did not come from the British steam-pressers, but from the Francophone women who, operating from their homes, paid no commercial rents nor taxes or license fees. With their stores located in the centre of the city with a dense concentration of working class people, the Chinese often encountered difficulty in accessing clients who themselves could ill-afford to regularly use laundry services, no matter how inexpensive they seemed. Yet the Chinese had to compete with the Francophone women in gaining access to this same clientele. At the turn of the century, the heavy Anglophone working class concentrations were along St. Antoine, St. Laurent and St. Anne. The 1881 Canada census ranked St. Antoine and St. James as the top two areas in population concentration with 33,845 and 25,398 residents, respectively. St. Anne and St. Laurent claimed 20,443 and 14,318 residents, respectively.[16] With the growth and expansion of leather and shoe manufacturing in St. Antoine, as well as a boom experienced by the textile and garment industries in St. Laurent and St. Louis, one saw the proliferation of successful Chinese laundries between 1877 and 1909 along such neighbouring streets as St. Catherine, Notre Dame, Dorchester, St. Antoine, St. Jacques and Lagauchetière. There were some laundries that somehow managed to bring in enough profit to survive the first or second year of operation. Their "successes in surviving" were, thus, very closely tied with their ability to "trail" in the direction of economic growth and expansion in the city. They made their living off the prosperity enjoyed by the immigrant working class populations in the western part of the city. Those Chinese launderers who set up their shops in Montreal east were less fortunate in that they must get their clients from a largely unskilled, poor French-Canadian working class.

There was yet another "naturalistic" source of competition for the Chinese hand launderers, as soon as their numbers began to increase, from among the Chinese themselves. While the entire economic history of Chinese laundry business in the city of Montreal was more one of constraints, failures, setbacks, false starts and premature closures, no more than a handful of Chinese launderers had actually experienced any measurable degree of economic success. Thomas Li Yuan used his savings upon arrival in Montreal to set up his laundry shop on McGill Street. Li Sheng appeared in 1889 on St. Antoine Street, which quickly multiplied into branch companies throughout the city. The success enjoyed by the two Lis in the laundry business foreshadowed the domination of the laundry trade by the Li clan, a trend persisting well through the thirties into the fifties. The same trend, along with other internal dynamics within the evolving Chinese community in Montreal, marked the beginnings of a class division among the Chinese that paralleled the dividing line of the well-to-do and the poor in Montreal society at large. The 1923 Chinese Immigration Act that put an abrupt halt to Chinese immigration into Canada, rather ironically, contributed to the consolidation of this class division. While the more successful Chinese launderers continued with their businesses, few new Chinese laundries were set up due to the non-availability of cheap and dependable labour from China. The rift between the successful and the failed, the rich and the poor, was opened up and widened further. For the Chinese in Montreal, their dependency on laundry business for their livelihood, whether they were owners or employees, continued well into the mid-1920s when the few better-established Chinese launderers began investing their revenues from the laundry business in restaurants. Between 1912 and 1915, one counted the increase of Chinese restaurants from 10 to 25, half of which opened and closed in the same two years. While the prevailing economic conditions were not favourable for setting up the restaurant business, this new economic activity was of considerable significance to the Chinese in that it opened up a new line of work and revenue for them.

Within a span of four years between 1924 and 1928, more and more Cantonese immigrants ventured into the restaurant business for the first time. The financial crash of 1929 and the prolongation of the subsequent depression till 1934 were followed by a period of stagnation that persisted well into 1939. Nevertheless, within this same decade, Montrealers were taking money out of stocks and bonds, and invested in small, local shops expecting better profit. The massive upsurge of entrepreneurial interest in small businesses and the retail sector, thus, gave birth to the proliferation of small shops. In Montreal, the multiplication of candle stores, tobacco shops, hair dressing salons and barber shops provided the necessary incentive as well as the demand for restaurants.

6. Walking on Two Legs

The economic prosperity Montreal knew in the 1930s did not benefit the Chinese to any appreciable degree. The number of Chinese restaurants in the city actually declined over these years: 66 in 1929, 55 in 1934, and 49 in 1939. The Chinese restaurateurs were facing stiff competition from the French who had the strongest hold in the business, as well as from the Greeks and the Russians. Most Chinese restaurants were concentrated in the Chinatown area, though the trend of spreading out in other areas of Montreal had already begun to emerge. Restaurants opened up in St. Paul and St. Henri were experiencing some initial success. Within the decade from 1931 to 1941, successful Chinese restaurant owners began divesting their profits in other types of business, such as tobacco store, fruits store, rooming house and grocery. The success of Chinese restaurant business both in terms of profit gained and in sheer number opened up a new demand for Chinese groceries and fruits, and, thus, another line of economic activity for the Chinese.

Lacking capital and traumatized by the 1923 discriminatory act that effectively cut off the supply of cheap labour so essential to the restaurant business, the Chinese restaurateurs never benefited from the prosperity and economic expansion Montreal experienced in the 1930s. Only a handful of the members of the Huang clan, through the gradual accumulation of capital and mutual aid within the clan, managed to open restaurants that were attractive to the white clientele.

Ever since the 1920s, the Chinese launderers were to face the challenge of the inevitable in a quickly mechanized and automated society: the introduction of specialized and mechanized methods of washing, ironing and dry cleaning into the laundry business. These machines and equipment were expensive, required a large space for installation and operation, and would prove cost-efficient only when the laundry owners had access to a large clientele, preferably those found in hotels, restaurants, institutions and companies. The Chinese hand laundrymen never managed to acquire a fair share of this clientele. Using telephone service and home delivery, these non-Chinese laundry companies, for the first time in the history of laundry business in Montreal, were directly applying pressure on the Chinese, forcing one after another to close shop. In 1932, these white laundry companies organized without success to lobby the municipal authorities to increase hand laundry permit fees from $50 to $200.[17] Nevertheless, the abandonment of hand laundries by the Chinese continued to multiply. Others coped by spreading out their laundry shops. Many became sub-contractors for white laundry companies by washing linen for them that required hand ironing. By 1941, the Chinese lost half of their laundries: the 150 laundries in 1931 were reduced to less than 70 in 1941. This downhill swing continued through the 1940s with the inevitable onset of home washing machines. Old Cantonese men retiring from the business were never replaced.

From 1923 through the thirties to the forties, the total Chinese population in Montreal did not grow to an appreciable degree. The total active Chinese work force was reduced by old age, illness, deaths, retirement and return to China. In 1951, 34.5% of the Chinese in Quebec were more than 55 years old. This aging and shrinking Chinese population of Quebec never managed to attract the attention of potential investors from China and Hong Kong. Montreal was bypassed, and the trend was not arrested until the latter half of the 1980s, when the Quebec government began to actively compete with other provinces for Chinese entrepreneurs or "economic immigrants" and investors from Hong Kong. In this endeavour, Quebec and Montreal faced strong competition from Toronto and Vancouver, especially the former.

The early Chinese population in Montreal consisted of all-male migrants from British Columbia when job opportunities in the western province began to exhaust themselves, when the transcontinental railway was completed and when work camps were closed one after the other. The Chinese took their eastbound trips, principally by train, making temporary stops at the many Prairie towns and cities before ending their wanderings in Toronto and Montreal, the two major metropolitan areas in Eastern Canada. When the handful of Chinese came to Montreal in the late 1880s, Montreal was already quite industrialized, capitalist and urban. Industrialization and urbanization had already begun in Montreal, thus giving the city that unmistakably urban look before the arrival of the Chinese. As a city known for its commercial prosperity and religious fervour, Montreal proved to be a city of irresistible charm and attraction to the jobless Chinese. Upon arrival in the city, they found themselves competing with a fantastic blending of other immigrants from Europe, a competition that was virtually doomed at the start: the competitors were already well "in place", in every way, particularly in occupational terms.

In 1921, Chinese males, as compared to all other gainfully employed males in Canada, were over-represented in laundry and restaurant businesses. Table 6.2 shows that the Chinese accounted for almost 90% of all laundry owners and managers (of all ethnic groups) in Canada, about 75% of all laundry workers, and 32% of all cooks, waiters and other restaurant-

6. Walking on Two Legs

related workers.[18] In 1931, there were slight increases in the percentage of Chinese males working as cooks, waiters or restaurant keepers as well as those working as laundry workers. The job segregation of the Chinese was more intense in Eastern Canada.

Table 6.3 shows that for the year of 1931, 91.5% of the Chinese males in Ontario, and 89.1% in Quebec, were in the personal service sector (laundering included) as contrasted with 25.6% in British Columbia.[19] Also in the same year, more than half of the Chinese males in Quebec were in the laundering business, as compared to about 16% for the whole of Canada, about 40% in Ontario, and only 3% in British Columbia. About 35% of the Chinese males in Quebec were in restaurant-related occupations in 1931.

Irrespective of their former occupations held in Southeastern China, and later in Western Canada, the bulk of the Chinese in Montreal were at first "funnelled" into one single job: the hand laundryman. Unlike the Chinese in British Columbia, those in Montreal were never employed to any significant degree in the primary sectors. In terms of sheer numbers, there were more Chinese laundries in Montreal than anywhere else in Canada over the years immediately before, and for decades after, the turn of the century. Proportionately, there were more Chinese involved in the hand laundry business in Montreal than any other Canadian city. For about half of the century, the domination of hand laundry business was total. The Chinese as well as non-Chinese old-timers recall "hundreds and hundreds" of Chinese-operated wash-houses on every other block in the city. One elderly woman remembered "as many churches as Chinese laundries" in the core of the city.[20] Hundreds of Chinese over the decades found themselves entering into the personal service sector, mainly, or almost exclusively, in laundry and later restaurants. The Chinese were literally "shut out" from any other way of making a living in a massive, significant way. The Chinese went into, and stayed in, the laundry business. They never managed to get out of it. They were stuck for half a century until the transition of a few successful launderers into the restaurant business. They carried on their lives in the midst of hundreds and thousands of European immigrants in the St. Laurent area who were making it as pawnbrokers, barbers, butchers, shoe repairmen, cigarette store owners, leather manufacturers, electricians and plumbers.

In traditional Chinese society, pathways to honour and prestige were limited to education for the imperial examinations that led to becoming gov-

TABLE 6.2
Major Occupations of Chinese Males in Canada, 1921 and 1931

Occupation	1921 %	1931 %	% of Chinese male in selected occupation[b] 1921 %	1931 %
Personal service				
i. cooks, waiters and restaurant keepers	24.0[a]	30.6	31.6[b]	31.5
ii. others[c]	8.3 50.9	5.5 51.9	6.1	2.9
Laundering				
i. laundry owners	9.6	2.2	89.2	48.9
ii. laundry workers	9.0	13.6	75.5	46.3
Labourers and unskilled workers[d]	4.8	21.5	1.8	1.6
Agriculture	9.7	11.8	0.3	0.5
Trade	7.8	6.7	1.1	2.0
Others	26.8	8.0	0.7	1.1
Total percentage	100.0	100.0		
N	(33,922)	(40,004)		

a: restaurant keepers are listed as hotel-restaurant keepers in 1921 census.
b: calculated as % of Chinese males employed in an occupation out of 100% males of all races in that occupation.
c: laundry not included.
d: not agricultural, mining or logging.
Source: *Census of Canada*, 1931, Vol. VII, Tables 49 and 69, in Laura Pao-Mercier, "Immigration, Ethnicity and the Labour Market: The Chinese in Montreal" (M.A. Thesis, Department of Sociology, McGill University, Montreal, Quebec, Canada, November 1981), p. 15.

ernment officials or mandarins, or investment in, and accumulation of, land. The traditional social hierarchy was, from top to bottom: the gentry (intellectual, scholar, official); teachers; farmers; artisans and workers; merchants; and the "outcasts" made up of soldiers, beggars, actors, musicians, prostitutes, eunuchs and slaves. Ironically, the huge social gap between the gentry

6. Walking on Two Legs

at the top and the peasants at the bottom was bridgeable, other than through imperial examinations (the esteemed and the respectable way), by accumulation of land surplus, or by being a merchant (the non-respectable and despicable way). The Chinese often address the merchants with a prefix, thus the "cunning", "sly" or "dishonest" merchant as a prototype. There is a satirical dialogue known to many Chinese: "Who has the darkest heart? The cunning merchant." A "dark" heart is a merciless heart.

Among the 71 Chinese migrants to Montreal in 1900 who had their occupations officially registered, there were 28 merchants originally from the Sunning county of China, thus making an important job category; only one third of them were labourers, with druggist, store keeper, clerk and

TABLE 6.3
Major Occupations of Chinese Males in Canada, 1931

Occupation	British Columbia %	Ontario %	Quebec %	Canada %
Personal service				
i. cooks, waiters and restaurant keepers	16.3	45.4	30.4	30.6
ii. others	6.0 25.6	4.3 91.5	4.9 89.1	5.5
Laundering				
i. laundry owners and managers	0.5	6.0	10.6	2.2
ii. laundry workers	2.8	35.8	43.2	13.6
Labourers and unskilled workers[a]	35.7	2.0	1.4	21.5
Agriculture	18.2	1.8	0.6	11.8
Trade	8.1	2.6	6.1	6.7
Others	12.4	2.1	2.8	8.0
Total percentage	100.0	100.0	100.0	100.0
N	(23,032)	(6,001)	(2,363)	(40,004)

a: not agricultural, mining, or logging.
Source: *Census of Canada*, 1931, Vol. VII, Table 49, in Laura Pao-Mercier, p. 15.

student comprising another group.[21] Proportionally, Montreal had a much larger share of Chinese stating their intended occupations as merchants at times of official registration than any other Canadian cities. Not esteemed back home as an occupation, the two dozen or so Chinese merchants in Montreal were quickly becoming the elite of the Chinese community and remained so till the present. In being the gentry of the overseas Chinese community, they exerted their political and economic influence in shaping the superstructure of the community. As early as 1888, a merchant called J. Frank Rupert began at 162 St. James Street a business selling silks and other articles brought in from Hong Kong, Shanghai and Yokohama 横濱. These Oriental goods and oddities were quickly gaining popularity and there was a considerable demand in French Canada. Also in 1888, Wong Jiao and Huang Ji started their Oriental goods store at 1801 Notre Dame, selling teas, silks, porcelains and Chinese and Japanese foodstuffs. King Tze Cheong, a Chinese general store, operated as an import firm, a retail store, and a "bank" for the Chinese immigrants. Huang Ji, having made a profit from their Oriental goods, also began to lend money to the Chinese immigrants (often at high interest rates) to set up laundries, a business adventure that eventually led to a virtual monopoly of products required by the Chinese immigrants.[22]

The success of the Chinese goods import business in Montreal began to pull in merchants of the West and the United States, as well as the better-off Chinese launderers. Businesses were later consolidated through the establishment of several companies under joint partnership. Li Sam was one of these new companies comprised of three partners, and it was formed in 1904. Subsequently, one saw the launching of Wing Sing Lung in 1906 and the three Ye brothers in 1909. The ascendancy of the merchant class, thus, began to give shape to an evolving Chinese community comprised of such dichotomies as owners–employees, merchants–poor manual labourers, the merchant gentry–working class mass. The tensions and stresses inherent in these occupational groupings and socio-economic dichotomies later became the breeding ground of conflicts within the Chinese community in Montreal for generations to come. Ironically, it was these same conflicts that gave the Chinese community in Montreal a structure and process the community has always been quite familiar with.

Historically, the press often went to great length in publicizing sensationalized accounts of illicit and "immoral" activities among the Chinese, as well as internal disputes within the Chinatown area. For a century, the term Chinatown conjured up a maze of stereotypical, and largely derogatory, images underlined by a strange blending of reactions and emotions ranging from curiosity, fear and paranoia, to hatred, prejudice and outright racism. These images are similar to those typically associated with ghettos and urban slums: dark alleys, prostitutes, gambling rings, drugs, organized crime, over-crowding, high rates of physical and mental disorders and a wide diversity of "ethnic vices".[23] The Chinese oldtimers often tell jokes among themselves of non-Chinese parents warning their children that they will be "shipped to Chinatown" and "get cut up into pieces" there if they keep rebelling and challenging parental orders.[24] Quebec in 1921 and 1923 had more drug traffic convictions than any other province except British Columbia. References were often made in the Immigration Archives to illegal drug traffic in Montreal and deportees for drug offenses in the 1920s and 1930s. The press in Montreal carried reports of "tang wars" and police night raids on laundries in the 1930s.[25] These reports, while clearly sensationalized, suggest, among other things, that some Chinese were engaging in illicit and illegal "underground" activities to make a living. On balance, gambling activities, not drugs, seemed to concern the Chinese more than the non-Chinese. The gambling trade, along with the varied job opportunities created, could have been a major means of life support for a segment of the Chinese population.

These gambling houses, run by Chinese and frequented by both Chinese and non-Chinese patrons, were located both inside the Chinatown area and the white immigrant residential areas. Those inside Chinatown were patronized mainly by the Chinese themselves. Gambling activities blossomed and were conducted very much in the public eye, at a time, since the 1920s, when the social climate sanctioned, if not outrightly encouraged such activities. The Chinese recalled gambling houses giving bribery money to the police department so that advance warnings were served before occasional, routine raids. Police arrests very rarely resulted in jail term other than fines.[26] The Chinese laundrymen saw gambling as an age-old practice transplanted from Southeastern old China into North America, a thrill, an emotional release from work drudgery, a pastime in the absence of a family life. Others saw it as a way to make some quick money, to expedite his return to China. Ironically, this dream was realized by only a limited few; many never returned to China because of "over-night losses" at the gambling table. In the short run, gambling served as a means of redistributing wealth in the Chinese community. The Chinese attributed the "wiping out" of the "urban ethnic vices", gambling, prostitution and corruption included, to the ascendancy of Mayor Drapeau's administration.[27]

By 1950, the Chinese community in Montreal was highly stratified. This overseas Chinese community saw a hierarchy with the merchants, importers, restauranters, owners of grocery and fruit stores, and several successful laundries at the top, followed by a handful of small entrepreneurs selling their services as herbalists, photographers, printers, tobacco store owners, tailors or barbers in the middle stratum. At the bottom of this social ladder was this mass of employees of laundries and restaurants who made up more than half of the Chinese population. There were the occasional door-to-door peddlers who carried vegetables, fruits and an assortment of sundries in two baskets suspended on a bamboo pole jouncing over the shoulder. The privileged persons within this mass were invariably those who worked as cooks in the Chinese restaurants and brought home wages comparable to an average factory worker, though they put in almost double their hours. Somewhere in this working mass were the rare Chinese immigrants who worked as servants, live-in cooks, or gardeners in white families. More rare were those who worked as professionals for white employers or firms. In 1951, there were less than ten of these, among whom were two salaried engineers.

Shut out totally from the work world for more than half a century, the Chinese Cantonese men "walked on two legs" (兩條腳走路), a popu-lar, yet grim, saying known within the Chinese community as a metaphor for their reliance on laundries and restaurants as the two sole means of making a living.[28] In Montreal, the Chinese males found themselves blocked from access to all job opportunities in the mainstream labour market. They were first coerced into, and then confined for decades in, the personal service sector, or more precisely, in the "ethnic enclave sub-economy". The "cultural division of labour"[29] among different immigrant groupings was well "completed" by the 1930s and 1940s: immigrants of Jewish and British origin in managerial, administrative and professional occupations, those of Italians in construction, and the Chinese in laundries and restaurants.

Notes

1. Thomas W. Chinn, H. Mark Lai, and Philip P. Choy, (eds.), *A History of the Chinese*

in California: *A Syllabus* (San Francisco: The Chinese Historical Society of America, 1969), p. 63.
2. Ibid., p. 63.
3. Ibid., p. 63.
4. Ibid., p. 63.
5. Ibid., p. 63.
6. H.H. Bancroft, "Mongolianism in America," in *Essays and Miscellaneous* (edited by H.H. Bancroft, San Francisco: History Co., 1890), p. 348.
7. Chin, Lai and Choy (eds.), p. 63.
8. Denise Helly, *Les Chinois à Montréal 1877–1951* (Quebec: Institut québécois de recherche sur la culture, 1987), p. 23.
9. Ibid., p. 37.
10. Ibid., p. 43.
11. Paul C.P. Siu, *The Chinese Laundryman: A Study of Social Isolation*. (Ph.D. Dissertation, Department of Sociology, University of Chicago, Chicago, Illinois, United States of America, August 1953), pp. 112–13.
12. Denise Helly, pp. 74–85.
13. Paul-Andre Linteau, "The Origins of Ethnic and Cultural Diversity in Quebec," in *Forces*, 73 (1986), p. 14.
14. Patricia Roy, "Educating the 'East': British Columbia and the Oriental Question in the Interwar Years," in *BC Studies*, No. 18 (Summer 1973), pp. 50–69.
15. Denise Helly, p. 24.
16. *Census Canada*, 1881, Vol. 1, Table 1, pp. 52–53.
17. Denise Helly, p. 28.
18. Laura Pao-Mercier, "Immigration, Ethnicity and the Labour Market: The Chinese in Montreal" (M.A. Thesis, Department of Sociology, McGill University, Montreal, Quebec, Canada, November 1981), p. 14.
19. Ibid., p. 15.
20. Kwok B. Chan, *Oral History of the Montreal Chinese Community* Montreal Studies Program, oral history interview with Mrs. Cai, 1983.
21. Rebecca Aiken, *Montreal Chinese Property Ownership and Occupational Change 1881–1981* (Ph.D. Thesis, Department of Anthropology, McGill University, Montreal, Quebec, Canada, September 1984), pp. 55–56.
22. Denise Helly, p. 28.
23. Kwok B. Chan, "Ethnic Urban Space, Urban Displacement and Forced Relocation: The Case of Chinatown in Montreal," in *Canadian Ethnic Studies* (Special issue on Ethnicity in Quebec), Vol. XVIII:2 (1986), pp. 65–78.
24. Kwok B. Chan, *Oral History of the Montreal Chinese Community*, 1983.
25. Rebecca Aiken, pp. 91–92.
26. Kwok B. Chan, *Oral History of the Montreal Chinese Community*, 1983. Oral history interview with Jack Liang by Kwok B. Chan at The Montreal Chinese Young Men's Christian Institution on 8–9 July 1983.
27. Ibid. Oral history interview with Jack Huang by Kwok B. Chan at the Chinese Freemasons, 1072 St. Laurent Boulevard Montreal, on May 5, 6, and 11, 1983.

28. Herman Hum, "Célébration de la republication et quelques mots d'expression," in *Association des restaurants Chinois de Montréal: l'annuaire 1981*, pp. 29–32. (Text in Chinese.) Published and printed by Wah Yan Printing Co. Ltd., Montreal, Quebec.
29. Laura Pao-Mercier, pp. 6–7.

7. In Lieu of Family

Under the ancestors' shadow. Photograph taken inside the Tan Guang Yu Tang on Lagauchetière Street.

Inside the Tan's Association. Members are contributing to the "woi".

Old Chinatown along Lagauchetière Street. (Date and source of photograph unknown.)

7. In Lieu of Family

AT the turn of the century, the Cantonese men from Southeastern China brought to Quebec not only a determination to realize a personal, as well as family project, but also some basic principles of social organization in old China. One such principle, transplanted into overseas Chinese immigrant communities, is the clan system based on common surnames which is at best an approximate re-creation of the lineage communities common to Southeastern China. Persons with common surnames coming from the same single-lineage community in China gathered together to form surname groupings or associations, and, thus, in the case of Montreal, the Lis, the Huangs, the Chens and the Tans. Overseas Chinese are also organized by county of origin and dialect. In overseas Chinese communities in Southeast Asia, membership in the clan associations sometimes cut across one another. A particular surname association might recruit all persons of the same name regardless of their counties of origin or their speech. Or it might take in only those with common surname, county of origin, and speech. Other social groups are created out of persons speaking the same dialect, or coming from a particular region (village, district, prefecture or province) regardless of surname.[1]

The formation of clan associations in overseas Chinese communities sometimes takes place through the grouping of people bearing surnames that are linguistically, or in pronunciation, similar to each other. Sometimes, persons bearing different surnames join together to form one clan association either because of the sheer lack of number when by themselves, or because of historical reasons. An example of the latter case is the Four Brothers Association, the Liu, Guan, Zhang and Zhao clans 劉、關、張、趙, whose members claim historical alliance and loyalty to each other under sworn brotherhood to save the Han Dynasty (206 B.C.–A.D. 220).

Among the first Chinese settlers in Montreal were Chinese merchants from British Columbia and the United States, and the first clans were formed around their stores in what is now known as Chinatown. These stores quickly became the natural gathering places for the bulk of other Cantonese immigrants, a social arena to exchange news from villages back home, a semi-business set up to send remittances to families in China or to obtain short-term loans from the merchants. For the mass of Cantonese workers, the stores and their owners, the merchants, thus, became the only social and communication link between old China and Montreal. It was also precisely these same historical circumstances that marked the ascendancy, and subsequent reinforcement, of the privileged social position of the

Cantonese merchants in terms of their virtual domination of the communal lives of the early Chinese settlers in Montreal.

The overseas Cantonese merchants occupied a unique social position formerly open only to the intellectual elite and landlords in traditional Chinese society. This "new" gentry of the Chinese immigrant communities quickly took on leadership positions in the beginning of the formation of communal or associational lives of the Cantonese. Because surname associations began and grew out of commercial stores, this gave the merchants direct, and almost guaranteed, access to authority and power in the Chinese community. The associations relied on several major sources of revenue, among which were profits from real estate transactions using public funds for investment, periodic contributions and donations from association members, fees charged on the transfer of funds to China, interest from short-term business loans, and, not at all uncommonly, the profits from gambling halls within the premises of the associations. With the accumulation of these monies over time, the clan associations were able eventually to move their headquarters out of the merchants' stores to rented premises. As members of the new gentry, the merchants, often the associations' "headmen", presidents or chairmen, put their Confucian principles and values into practice. Their moral obligations were discharged by the redistribution of wealth among association members through loans or other forms of financial assistance. Funds of the associations were also used to pay for judicial costs on behalf of those who had initiated lawsuits against the non-Chinese. The associations often assumed the cost of funerals for those who could not afford it. Sometimes, at the request of the members, bodies were cremated in Montreal and shipped back to China for burial through funerals set up in Hong Kong.

The new gentry of merchants overseas also oversaw the continued practice of filial piety and respect to the ancestors' spirit. Altars of ancestors were set up in the headquarters of these associations for members to pay respect to during festive celebrations. One such notable celebration ritual in Montreal was during the Qing Ming festival towards the end of March of every year which is commonly called by the Cantonese the "sweeping of the tombs". Trips were organized by the clan associations for offspring to clean and repair tombs, make offerings, recite eulogies, praise the virtues of the dead, burn incense, candles, paper clothes and money for use in the other world. These rituals made it possible for the Cantonese men, thousands of miles away from their native villages, to discharge their filial

7. In Lieu of Family

obligations, as well as to ask in return for the blessing and protection of the living by the deceased. During the 1920s through the 1930s and 1940s, trips to the Mount Royal cemeteries in Montreal for the "sweeping of the tombs" were major community events. Clan associations arranged for buses to transport just about every Chinese gathered in the Chinatown area to the cemeteries for a one-day outing, or "picnic", as leaders of the Chinese community called it. Free soft drinks were offered through special arrangements with the beverage companies. Loudspeakers were set up on site for community leaders to deliver public lectures on the importance of the Chinese being bone fide citizens in the city, of internal solidarity and unity of the Chinese, of the virtues of filial piety and respect for the ancestors.[2]

The headquarters of Li's Association at the corner of St. Urbain and Lagauchetière streets still maintains today a hall on the top floor of the building with altars, floats, an assortment of ceremonial utensils and other objects for various ritualistic occasions. A live-in maintenance man was hired for a long while to upkeep the hall's furnishings. When a Cantonese man left his native village in Southeastern China, he could, to a certain extent, take comfort in members of his clan back home discharging his filial duties on his behalf. On arrival in Montreal, he was almost instantaneously recruited into a particular clan association which saw to it that the migrants did not relax their moral behaviour. The overseas clan associations, or more precisely, their elders, quickly became the young male migrants' "substitute parents" who never seemed too hesitant or slow in building up and maintaining the moral fabric of the immigrant communities. A Cantonese might have left physically the age-old social structure while heading overseas. Nevertheless, he, invariably, entered himself into another, albeit an adapted, version of the one he knew back home.

The formation of the first surname and clan associations in Canada took place as early as 1884 (Qing Dynasty) in Victoria.[3] Without a formalized structure during their formative stage, these associations typically assembled their members on the occasion of arbitrating internal disputes, or during the annual celebration of the birthday of associations' ancestors. On other occasions, assemblies were held to deliberate decisions pertaining to contributions to the social and economic development of native villages back home in China (e.g., building schools, renovating ancestors' temples, road repairs, relief campaigns for drought, heavy rainfall, and so on). With the increase of membership and the growing complexity of association affairs, these associations began to take on formal shape. Branches quickly sprang up in major cities and towns across Canada.

Each clan association, and, therefore, all its branch chapters spread out in other Canadian cities, worships one specific ancestor, typically someone from the old gentry class of traditional Chinese society: a member of the governmental bureaucracy (e.g., a high-ranked official) or of an intellectual elite (e.g., a celebrated scholar, preferably someone who excelled in an imperial examination). The Huangs would worship Huang Xiang 黃香(文疆), a top-ranked government official of the Han Dynasty; the Lis, Lao Zi 老子(李耳), the Taoist philosopher; the Wus, Wu Zixu 伍子胥, the cabinet minister; and the Zhous, Zhou Dunyi 周敦頤 (1017–1073), a Confucianist of the Song Dynasty (960–1279). The Lung Kuang Association 龍崗公所 would have an altar in its headquarters to commemorate the Three Brothers (Liu, Kuang and Zhang) and Zhao Yun 趙雲.[4]

In the 1900s, due to changing leadership, as well as the ebb and flow of membership over time, these associations went through a basic reconstitution and reorganization. The Li Lung Xi Tang 李隴西堂 became the Li's Association. The Zhou Oi Lin Association 周愛蓮公所 was subsumed under the San Da Tang 三德堂, while the Ming Yi Tang 名義堂 was expanded and renamed the Lung Kuang Association. Several smaller tongs belonging to the Zhus, Tans, Yangs, Dongs and the Fungs were phased out in the interim. By 1967, one saw not only the eventual completion of transfer of headquarters of the bulk of these associations from Victoria to Vancouver, but the setting up of association chapters in Toronto, Calgary, Montreal and Winnipeg. Among these associations, the Huang Jiang Xia Tang and the Li Si Gong Suo (or, the Li's Association 李氏公所) had the most members. The Huang Jiang Xia Tang had by then set up seventeen chapters or branch offices across Canada while the Li's Association counted fifteen.[5] The head office of the Li's Association in Vancouver published the Li's Monthly, a means of networking, and set up "San Yi Woi" 三益會 in eastern Canada for the provision of financial aid. The Huang Jiang Xia Tang in Vancouver ran the "Man Keung School" to provide children of the Huangs an education in Chinese literature and language.

All clan associations were originally set up to protect, to provide mutual aid, as well as to look after the social well-being of their members. They also played a key role in the furthering of welfare of kinsmen and family back home in the native villages. Their contribution often took the form of charity drives to provide emergency relief on occasions of dire need or natural disasters in China. The 1949 revolution in China put an abrupt end to all this, which, ironically, left the associations with little choice other than concentrating on implementing programs beneficial to those members in Canada. The beginning of the 1950s, thus, saw the proliferation of a wide diversity of such social-recreational activities and events as scholarship drives, athletic meets and sports clubs, picnics and outings, theatrical and musical groups, major banquets on festive occasions, as well as numerous other social gatherings "to respect the elderly and to nurture the young". This turn of events was, in actual fact, a "shot in the arm" as far as the furthering and strengthening of community affairs and welfare is concerned.

The first Chinese Consolidated Benevolent Association in Canada was established in Victoria, British Columbia, in 1884, with executive direction and technical assistance from the Chinese Consul-General in San Francisco. In February 1884, a Chinese delegation from San Francisco arrived in Victoria to aid in the establishment of the Association. In June, the Association registered with the British embassy office in San Francisco, and, on 9 August, with the government of British Columbia as a charitable organization. Li Youqin 李祐芹 became the first president of the Association who led a board of directors primarily made up of the Lis and the Huangs: Huang Yanhao 黃彥豪, Li Tianpei 李天沛 and Li Yida 李奕德, among others.[6]

The early Chinese migrants in Canada never enjoyed protection of any kind from the Chinese government. Racism against the Cantonese workers in British Columbia made it necessary to set up voluntary associations such as the Chinese Consolidated Benevolent Association for self-protection and defence against racially based discrimination. In a letter sent to the Chinese Consul-General Huang Zunxian 黃遵憲 (1848–1905) in June 1884, which was allegedly written by the Association's first president Li Youqin, it can be seen that the primary goals and objectives of the Association were to counter the hostility of the white society by challenging and trying to repeal discriminatory legislation and laws; to solve problems and afflictions within the Chinese community by beginning with the prohibition of Chinese prostitution; to create internal channels of communication; and to create a permanent consulate in Canada to facilitate transactions and negotiations with the white society.[7]

The Chinese Consolidated Benevolent Association in Victoria was the only representative body for the Chinese in Canada before the setting up of the Chinese Consulate in Ottawa in 1908.[8] The erection of a building for the Association was made possible through compulsory contributions from every Chinese in the province:

> ... a notice was put up to appeal for contributions for, first, the establishment of a Chinese Association and, second, the campaign against discriminatory laws and taxes. The notice stated that a contribution of $2 per Chinese must reach Victoria before 3 October 1884, and that if any miser failed to make this contribution, he would have to pay $10 to the Association before being permitted to return to China. If anyone contributed more than $3, his name and native place would be recorded on a notice board to be displayed in the Association. Contributions to the Association were therefore compulsory rather than voluntary. A fund of nearly $30,000 was finally raised for the construction of the Association building and a hospital. The excavation of the site began on 27 May 1885, and the building was completed in July. It was a three-storey building erected on the former site of an old joss house at 558 Fisgard Street. The ground floor of the building was let, the first floor was used as the Association's office, and the second floor as a temple and a school. In 1909, the Association's office was moved to the present location at 636 Fisgard Street.[9]

While the Association pioneered in raising money among its members to pay for the homeward passage fare for those Chinese over 60 years of age and those who were unemployed or too poor to make it home on their own, the Association, being the only representation for the Chinese population in Canada, combined into one single institution the functions of an arbitrator, a protector and a benefactor.[10] It also arbitrated and maintained peace and order in Chinatowns across Canada, invariably holding arbitration hearings to deal with offenses and disputes among the Chinese before reporting them to the police. It also served as a witness in business transactions, including the selling and redeeming of young Chinese women. Complaints brought forward by the Chinese about assaults, injuries and murders by the Westerners were often forwarded to the local judicial authority. Other main types of functions and activities of the Association included protests against discriminatory laws and taxes, and fund-raising campaigns for their abolition in court.

The Association, for example, has records about their protests against the prohibiting of employment of white women workers by Chinese. A Statue of Saskatchewan in 1912, for instance, prohibited the employment of white women in any restaurant, laundry or other place of business or amusement which was kept, owned or managed by a Chinese, Japanese or other Oriental person. It was amended in 1913 by deleting the words

"Japanese or other Oriental person", leaving it applicable to Chinese alone. By November 1914, the Association had raised a total amount of $1,175 and remitted it to the Chinese in Regina to petition the Attorney-General for the abolition of the law. Finally, the law was amended in 1919, requiring a special license for the employment of any white woman or girl, without singling out Chinese by name.[11]

While the Association sent relief money to their members within, and outside, British Columbia to contest discriminatory legislations, it also came to the aid of Chinese in China and all over the world. For instance, the Association undertook a fund-raising campaign to aid the Chinese in Cuba during the Cuban's people's struggle for independence from Spain from 1870 to 1898.[12]

In organizational terms, the Association sought out representations from various local clan, surname and district associations as well as Chinese political parties, athletic and social clubs, and occupational groups to serve as "automatic" board of directors. Following a mode of operation based on democracy and annual elections, the Association in Victoria served as a primary organizational model for Chinese Consolidated Benevolent associations set up in more than twenty Canadian cities across Canada. The Association in Vancouver, established officially in 1906, quickly assumed leadership among the other twenty associations spread throughout Canada, a phenomenon mainly due to the rapid increase of Chinese population in Vancouver. In eastern Canada, one saw the birth of variously named associations in Toronto, Sudbury, Kingston, Hamilton, London, Windsor, Timmins, Quebec City, Montreal, Halifax and Fort William.[13]

Officially named The Chinese Benevolent Society, the Association in Montreal on 112 Lagauchetière West was founded between 1910 and 1920 by Lai Youtan, Jiang Tangyuan, Cao Zhenli and Weng Baoyen. The goals and objectives of the Society were meant "to provide community service to the early Chinese immigrants who had adjustment problems, and to promote fellowship; to socialize the Chinese; to coordinate the Chinese social organizations; and to help in developing better social welfare services."[14] Since the 1960s, the Society operated more as a social gathering place for the elderly than a community service centre. Subsequently, a Catholic minister, Father Thomas Du 杜寶田, and a Protestant minister, Reverend Paul Chen, took charge of the daily affairs of the Society.

Back in China, in every village, town and city, one finds a wide, often bewildering, variety of temples and shrines dedicated to the worship of many kinds of gods and spirits. In a typical village temple, one often finds the Goddess of Mercy who graces people with merciful blessings; the God of Wealth who bestows and distributes, as his name suggests, wealth and other material possessions; the Dragon God who brings rain from the Four Seas of China in times of drought; and the Earth God, the local representative from the other world. In the city, some of the gods worshipped are the God of Literature; Confucius and his seventy-two famous disciples; Goddess of Measles, Eyes and other ailments of bodily parts. The Chinese believe that great men (e.g., famous generals or officials) are reincarnations of gods, or that men with outstanding achievement become gods in their afterlives; meritorious officials, while still alive and on transfer to a distant district, are sometimes worshipped in a local district temple where they were born, allegedly to give blessing and protection to their countrymen. People who are founders or have made outstanding contributions to their trade or crafts are often worshipped by subsequent generations of colleagues as gods and deities. Lao Ban 魯班 has been worshipped for hundreds of years by carpenters. Examples of gods of this nature are numerous and there does not seem to be a limit to the number. No one seems to know how many gods are there in China; even Henri Doré's ten-volume collection, titled *Researches into Chinese Superstitions*, fails to exhaust the list of gods and divinities.[15]

While the number of gods and deities is almost limitless, an average Chinese person seldom feels obliged to worship one god, one deity or one spirit. The Chinese way in religion is one of polytheism, rather than monotheism. The Chinese man or woman strives to include, not exclude, making offerings and paying respect to all gods, or, more precisely, this god for one kind of blessing, and that god for yet another kind, and so on. In a typical Chinese household, one often finds an altar in the kitchen area for the God of the Oven who oversees that food is in plentiful supply; a porcelain statue of the God of Mercy in the living room area, a god known for her attentiveness to the woes and troubles of the mortal beings; and a set of three statues of God of Longevity, God of Wealth and God of Blessing, often displayed in a noticeable position in the household. The businessman will always have the God of Wealth looked after to ensure that their business will prosper. Then, the God of the Earth is worshipped at an altar on the floor; he ensures the household's safety and internal harmony, and is often turned to when there are accidental physical injuries to the household members. If the head of the household is a craftsman, he will make periodic offerings to

7. In Lieu of Family   185

the craft's founder. He will also worship Guan Yu 關羽 (160–219), or popularly known as Guan Gong 關公, who symbolizes the virtues of loyalty, dedication and devotion. Of course, the household's own ancestors are never forgotten. Outside the house, the mothers, wives and daughters are patrons of local village temples and shrines for blessings and protection of various kinds. Mothers pray to these local gods that their children study well in school, marry into respectable families, and pass the imperial examinations. Wives pray that their husbands prosper in their chosen trade or profession, or that their men will be protected from evil spirits while travelling and making a living in distant places, an important practice for the hundreds and thousands of gold-diggers, laundrymen and restaurant workers in America. Daughters pray to be well wed or be reunited with fathers they have not seen for decades.

> I do not know of a single city or town in China before 1949, or in Taiwan today that is without diviners or geomancy readers, physiognomists, phrenologists, mediums and all kinds of fortune-tellers. For a fee, these persons foretell the length of a person's life and his business prospects, or determine the marriageability of a boy and girl, or decide on the ritual suitability of a new house site or graveyard. They will also often undertake to arrange a meeting or communication with the gods or with one's departed ancestors. There is literally no question they do not attempt to answer, and almost no matter relating to the gods that they refuse to interpret. It is safe to say that no individual of prominence in their traditional China failed to have his fate told, not once but many times, by different professional fortune tellers.[16]

Chinese gods and deities are personified beings and embody all human attributes and characteristics, including their vulnerability to corruption, greed and receptivity to compliments and praise by humans. The gods are human to the extent that one can speak to them, tell them what one wants and desires (and does not). This communication with the gods for their blessings and protection is done by prayers; on other occasions, it is facilitated by professionals through the enactment of rituals. The gods' messages need to be read and interpreted by professionals too, often known to the Westerners as fortune tellers who are permanently attached to local temples.

The Chinese ask to be blessed and protected by as many gods as they have access to, particularly in times of personal trouble or public crises. Their loyalty is never to one god, one school of religious faith, one source of supernatural healing. The notion of one being either a Catholic, a true devout Catholic, but not a Protestant at the same time, is, in essence, foreign to the Chinese.[17] "Prayer" ceremonies to fight a cholera epidemic staged by several southwestern communities in China during the Second World War included in the altar not only images of numerous Chinese deities, but also of Jesus Christ and Muhammed. For centuries, many temples throughout villages, towns and cities in China were built together to house, simultaneously, Confucius, Buddha and Lao Zi, the founder of Taoism.[18]

To a Chinese, no gods are false or true; this is an attitude that advocates that gods are to be shared, not monopolized, to be included with others, not excluded from others. This belief in many gods is related to the other belief in the peaceful coexistence of all supernatural beings, and, thus, the relative absence of religious contentions and rivalries known in the West.

> For the American way in religion is to be more and more exclusive, so that not only is my God the only true God while all others are false, but I cannot rest until my particular view of God has prevailed over all others. The Chinese tendency is exactly the reverse. The Chinese may go to a Buddhist monastery to pray for a male heir, but he may proceed from there to a Taoist shrine where he beseeches a god to cure him of malaria. Ask any number of Chinese what their religion is, the answer of the majority will be that they have no particular religion, or that, since all religions benefit man in one way or another, they are equally good. For the Chinese way in religion is to be more and more inclusive so that my god, your god, his god and all gods, whether you or I know anything about them or not, must be equally honoured or at least not be the objects of either my contempt or of yours.[19]

Theoretically, each and every Chinese is religious in that he or she is a worshipper of deceased ancestors, whether or not the actual rituals are practiced; a Chinese is also a Confucian in heart and soul, in his ways of daily living and in the moral precepts and teachings he subscribes to. The Chinese worship their ancestors since they owe their fortune or ill-fate to their ancestors. A Chinese does well and achieves, say, becoming a prominent scholar or a high-ranking government official, not only because of his merit, but also because his ancestors have done good deeds while alive, thus blessing their offspring. Conversely, a man becomes a beggar not only because of his lazy character, but, perhaps more importantly, because of the questionable moral character of his ancestor(s).[20] A Chinese will bring shame, honour or prestige to himself as well as to his ancestors. Throughout one's entire life, one is expected to "live up to the expectations of the many preceding generations of deceased ancestors", or to "bring glory and shine to the ancestors", as the old sayings go. The Chinese also believe that the ancestors, like all living beings, have human needs. These needs must be catered to by the living offspring so that they will not become "wandering souls or fierce ghosts". In making offerings to the dead, the living burn life-sized paper models of clothing, furniture, sedan chairs, horses, donkeys, cows and servants, so that the ancestors may set up house in the other world. In the thirties, one witnessed paper rickshaws and automobiles added to the traditional variety of offerings. Of course, incense and candles, paper models of gold and silver nuggets, called *"Yuan bao"* 元寶 in Chinese, and paper money in grades of millions and billions of dollars were profusely burnt to ensure the financial well-being of the ancestors in their lives in the other world. One often measures and judges the dedication and status of the offspring by the size and, thus, cost of candles, or by the kinds of food offerings, which often include chickens, whole pigs, assorted fruits, wine and pastries. For those who do not benefit from their descendants' offerings, they must compete with each other for "left-overs" of better served spirits, or depend on handouts from charitable families. Descendants of more well-to-do families often serve charity "duplicate offerings" in public areas, such as crossroads or main roads to distant places, to ensure that their own ancestors will be able to "eat in peace". In receiving these offerings, the ancestors have an obligation to assist their descendants in this world, to cater to their wants and desires, to help ward off a major famine or flood, to help a student-scholar to excel in an imperial examination, or to ensure the business of some descendants multiply and profit.

The living Chinese, thus, live under the shadow of their ancestors. To a Chinese, the worst and most miserable plight is "while alive, to be without known parents and relatives, and when dead, to be without living descendants". In the latter eventuality, his position as a ghost will be like that of a Chinese who has no parents, no children and no relatives.[21] A Chinese man must have at least one son of his own, or he would "adopt" one by asking his son-in-law to be "his" son through adoption of his surname as well as renunciation of his original surname and consequently, his own lineage and line of ancestors. The Chinese call this practice "transfer (to another lineage than one's own) to inherit" (過繼).

The Chinese reserve their deepest devotion, attachment and ties to primary relations within the clan and the family, and the maintenance and nurturing of these relationships in terms of reciprocity and mutual dependence is fundamental to the continuation and survival of the individual, as well as of the clan and family as collective units. This principle of mutual dependence not only operates among the living, but also between the living and the dead as manifested in the Chinese view of religion and their practice of ancestral worship. The worship of ancestors may well be the embodiment of Chinese religious beliefs practiced in its most purified form. The Chinese pray, invariably, not for self-introspection, as the Westerners are supposed to do in their prayers, but to ask for "godly favours". And, in return, they strive, each in their own way according to ways that are within one's limits, to cater to the needs of the gods, deities, and departed ancestors. In that sense, the living and the deceased have a "social contract" to comply with. A Chinese will not be afraid to violate the contract, to stop serving his gods and ancestors, or even to destroy their statues, altars and temples in fury when he is convinced he has done his part while his gods have not. The relationship is put to an end just like any other human relationship.

Like other cultural values and practices, the Chinese way of religion and spiritual faith was brought into Canada both individually and in collective, organized forms. The Cantonese men came to America and Canada partly because, quite paradoxically, it was more likely and probable for them to cater to the needs of their ancestors and their gods by working overseas, by serving at a distance. It was also partly because making a living thousands of miles away from the native village would have a much better chance of ensuring the continuity of the family and clan lineage, or else they themselves, wives, children, parents, grandparents and generations of ancestors and the many gods they serve, would all perish in poverty and hunger. The Cantonese men would worship their gods and ancestors in the privacy of their homes, which were invariably the backroom of a hand laundry, or a small room in a living compound above a Chinese restaurant or grocery store, or in the headquarters of their surname or district associations, making offerings to a common ancestor as well as whatever gods the associations had chosen to pay homage to. For about a century in Canada, one of the persistent practises of these surname associations was to organize annual trips to the local cemeteries to practise the ritual of ancestral worship. Ceremonial offerings were also made in each and every festival the Chinese in Canada have chosen to celebrate. Festive celebrations provide important occasions for descendants in a distant place "to remember and commemorate one's distant ancestors", to put filial piety into practice, to affirm one's sense of continuity with the past and the origins of life. Without a family and women, the Cantonese men turned to the surname and clan associations as surrogate families.

7. In Lieu of Family

It may well be, therefore, quite misleading to classify Chinese as Taoists, Buddhists, Confucists or ancestor worshippers in the way the Westerners classify themselves as Catholics, Protestants and Jews.[22] Christianity, Judaism and Islam are monotheistic. The Chinese are, by nature, polytheists. As in other realms of their daily conduct, they, as believers, are practical and pragmatic. Subscribing to a basic moral precept of reward and punishment, the Chinese have contracted a relation with their gods in which they expect godly blessings when they provide well for their gods, do good deeds and accumulate virtues for prosperity in their afterlives. They also accept punishment and the "fury of their gods" when they are not filial, negligent in their duties, or conduct themselves as immoral mortals. Believing they "live up to their conscience", and therefore can "face their ancestors" without shame and remorse, they often allow themselves to "get even" with their gods when they feel neglected or victimized by them.

In 1885, the Chinese in Victoria built the headquarters of the first Chinese Benevolent Association in the country. In the building's ceremonial hall on the third floor called the "Palace of Saints", there is an altar on which is displayed statues of Confucius, Guan Gong, Tin Hou 天后, God of Wealth, Dr. Hua Tuo (the ancestor of Chinese herbs and medicine), and so on. This first Chinese temple in Canada looks Taoist in its overall decor, though members of the Chinese Benevolent Association would perhaps be the first to deny they were Taoists in terms of their religious faith. In a way, this polytheistic view of religion propagated by the Chinese pioneers in Canada comes close to the heart of classical Chinese philosophy, a philosophy that advocates the peaceful coexistence of all gods and deities which, in turn, allows the Chinese to worship them all, in the order and manner they choose.[23]

Father Thomas Du of the Montreal Chinese Catholic Mission was quick to point to this spiritual polytheism among the Chinese, underscoring the fact that an average Chinese of the peasantry would be, all at once, a Confucian in his moral precepts pertaining to filial piety, forgivingness and realms of interpersonal relations; a Taoist in his belief in nothingness, immaterial things and self-propagation through rituals and practices conducive to health; and a Buddhist in his ceremonial rituals while making offerings to gods, deities and ancestors.[24] For centuries in China, it could be roughly said that Confucianism tended to prevail more in the North and Taoism in the South, where the majority of the Chinese in America and Canada came from. This general geographic distribution of the two great religions in China, thus, tends to explain, to a certain extent, for instance, why most Li's Associations throughout Canada worshipped Lao Zi, the founding father of Taoism, and, in general, took on the ambiance of a Taoist temple. The Chinese in Canada, largely subconsciously, are Taoist at heart and in their daily practice in that they believe in the essence of self-propagation and self-preservation through essentially dietary practices, in the concepts of *yin yang* 陰陽, and in the existence of supernatural beings.

The fact that a Catholic priest, albeit Chinese, would include, in the anniversary publication of the Chinese Catholic Mission in 1972, an essay (in Chinese without any English text, like other articles in the publication) of his own that attempts to articulate the Chinese polytheistic view of religion deserves some attention and deep thought. One might want to hold the view, among others, that the Chinese Catholic church, at least in recent decades, has begun to recognize or even accept this religious polytheism among the overseas Chinese, and the teaching of Catholicism by the church may well need to proceed on the basis of such recognition and acceptance.

As for Protestantism, one saw among the first Chinese Presbyterian ministers in Montreal a greater degree of tolerance as well as promotion of classical Chinese ethics and philosophies of religion. Some ministers even practiced the Chinese customs and codes of conduct themselves in their private lives. During his stay in Montreal between 1894 and 1923, Chen Nanzheng, the first Chinese minister sent by the Presbyterian church to the city to set up headquarters for the Cantonese at the Knox Church in 1894, kept to such Chinese customs as, among others, the observance of the Chinese calendar and the celebration of the Chinese New Year.[25] Faithful to Confucian teachings, Chen shocked a reporter from *La Presse*, a Montreal French daily, who was present on the day of the birth of the minister's son, Paul Chen, when he said, "May your ashes rest one day in the fatherland under the care of the great Confucius."[26] A Christian baptism service did not take place until a month later. The Chinese Presbyterian Church was apparently not opposed to the Chinese holding a belief in more than one god, nor did it seem to condemn Confucianism.

In October 1961, the Chinese Young Men's Christian Insititution (YMCI), then on 84 Ontario Street West, released a publication in commemoration of its founding of fifty years. The publication[27] is filled with article after article articulating the substantive compatibility of Christianity

7. In Lieu of Family

with the classical teachings of Chinese saints and scholars, particularly those of Confucius and Mencius.

> We have all learned the spirit of Jesus Christ is grounded in three principles: First, it is self-sacrifice; second, it is friendliness to others; and third, it is love and compassion for all. The principle of self-sacrifice is similar to Fan Zhongyan's 范仲庵 (989–1052) [a celebrated Confucian-scholar] philosophy that one worries before the whole world worries, and one becomes happy and joyful only after the whole world is happy and joyful. The principle of being helpful to others is similar to the teachings of Confucius in that one who aspires to be established helps others to establish, and one aspires to achieve helps others to do so. The principle of compassion and love for all is similar to what Confucius meant by an accomplished gentleman, namely, someone who loves and is compassionate to others. These three spiritual principles are basic to human evolution, social organization and nation-building. Without them, there will be no society, no human collectivities, and no nations.[28]

The publication also records that, during the Institution's inaugural meeting on 4 October 1911, Huang Jinzhuo (also commonly known as Jack Huang, Uncle Jack), the then leader of the Chinese Freemasons, delivered a speech articulating the relationship between Christianity and Confucianism.

> Due to the small size of the hall of our own headquarters, we rented a place on 458 Lagauchetière East [formerly the Senior's Club] to celebrate the inauguration of our Institution. On 4 October at twelve noon, Chinese men and women, old and young started coming to the assembly despite the hot weather. It was 93 °F [about 33 °C] on that day. About four hundred people showed up. After the chairman Tan Lixiu 譚禮休 related the history of our Institution, Huang Jinzhuo spoke. He did a most interesting comparative analysis of the essence of Christianity and the philosophy of Confucius and Mencius. There was enthusiastic applause from the audience after his speech. Because we were scheduled to show movies, it was unfortunate that we were unable to learn more from him. It was then two o'clock. Tan led the audience in singing patriotic songs. At the end of the assembly, we showed films [in Cantonese].[29]

Back in China, the Protestant church, being better organized, more egalitarian and thus more attractive to the people, seemed to have exerted more impact and influence on the Chinese society.[30] Early Chinese immigrants actually requested Canadian Protestant churches to establish missions back home in China and, in particular, in Guangdong, their land of origin. The spread of Protestantism in Canada's Chinese community began with the Methodist church. As early as 1880, Mr. Gardiner, a retired Englishman born in China and well versed in several Chinese dialects as well as Chinese culture, was doing missionary work, while at the same time teaching English and providing interpretation services in Victoria's Chinatown.[31] In 1885, with funds raised locally from Chinese and Caucasians, Gardiner established the Chinese Methodist Church on Fisgard Street, the first Chinese Protestant church in Canada. In 1890, the church brought in a Chinese minister, Mr. Chen Shengjie 陳陞階 (a native of Guangdong's Xin Hui district) from Hong Kong. During his twelve years of service, Chen did missionary work not only in Victoria, but also as far as Westminster, Vancouver, and Nanaimo while establishing churches in these cities. When he retired in 1912, he brought in his brother Chen Yaotan 陳耀壇 to succeed him. Between 1925 and 1957, one saw the proliferation of Protestant churches throughout the west coast and, later, the country.

The Chinese Catholic church founded in Victoria outside the Chinatown area never seemed to attract the Chinese as the Protestant church did, though it enjoyed a better set up with an English primary school.[32] The church was originally run by several Chinese sisters and Caucasian priests. In its early years, the church was hardly integrated into the local Chinese community.

Father Thomas Du, at present presiding over the Montreal Chinese Catholic Mission, found an unpublished manuscript by Father Eugene Berichon of the Catholic church in which he reported there already were Chinese on the Island of Montreal before 1863. The manuscript also mentioned that there was a Catholic school named "St. Laurent" situated at the corner of Côté and Lagauchetière streets. In 1893, there were already a few Chinese registered to study English and French in this school. In 1902, Father Martin Callaghan saw to it that fifty-three Chinese were baptized.

Father Callaghan was Irish and liked to be friendly with the Chinese; he used to play his violin at the corner of St. Urbain Street for the Chinese audience. He visited Chinatown everyday with his priest brother, Luke. In those days, he indeed rendered many services to the Chinese. Fr. Callaghan also helped two young Chinese students to complete their studies in medicine. Because of his great love for those in need, he supported the weak and assisted the poor throughout his life. His residence was located near today's St. Patrick's church where many Chinese visited and sought advice of many kinds.[33] By 1904, an estimated 20% of the Chinese in Montreal were converted Catholics.[34]

Upon the retirement of Callaghan, the Chinese began to turn to the parish of "St. Infant Jesus" at St. Dominique and Laurier streets for their

7. In Lieu of Family

studies of languages. A French priest, Father Montana, who was fluent in Cantonese and had done missionary work in Guangzhou for many years, was invited by the Bishop to take up residence at the church. On 19 April 1914, three Chinese were baptized. Father Montana also succeeded in buying land in the Montreal cemetery for the burial of converted Chinese Catholics. The establishment of the Immaculate Conception Congregation about this time saw its sisters giving English and French classes to the Chinese at the basement of the Congregation. Held from one to four o'clock in the afternoon every Sunday, these classes were then known to the Chinese as "Sunday School" (主日學). There were times when as many as 150 Chinese attended Sunday School. In 1916, with assistance from sisters of the Immaculate Conception Congregation, the first Chinese Catholic elementary school in Montreal was established on Anderson Street near Chinatown. On 30 January 1922, Father Caille officially founded the Chinese Mission on Lagauchetière Street.

In June, 1957, Father Thomas Du was appointed to the mission. In August, the mission was moved into the vacant premises of an old Protestant church. In subsequent years, the mission begun adding grades one, two and three to the already existing kindergarten and language classes for adults to form an elementary school, then officially registered at the Montreal Catholic School Commission. New rulings issued by the Department of Education in 1970 that children must attend schools in their neighbourhood and that they should be sent to French schools led to the discontinuation of the elementary school. Subsequent changes at the Montreal School Commission in 1971 saw the closing of the kindergarten as well.

The old church was originally built in 1834 by the Protestants and was sold to the Catholic church in 1964. In January 1978, the Quebec government's Ministry of Cultural Affairs declared the church an historic building, thus preventing it from demolition. The Ministry also recommended that the building be reserved for religious use. In 1983, the construction of an imposing federal building, the Guy Favreau complex, which takes up the entire lot bound by Dorchester, St. Urbain, Lagauchetière and Bleury, integrated the old church into its master construction design.

Comparatively speaking, the Chinese Protestant church, led mainly by the well-to-do merchant class, seemed more intent than their Catholic counterpart in establishing and nurturing its religious links with traditional Chinese cultural values, particularly the teachings of Confucius. Back in old China, the mission work of the Protestant church, advocating an ideology of egalitarianism, was typically one of extensive involvement in the daily lives of poorer people.[35] Chinese merchants in Montreal, concerned with their children learning Chinese as well as English and with following the Confucian principles, were attracted to the consistency of Protestant teachings with Chinese ethics about family and children. On the other hand, the Catholic church, unlike the Protestants, required their followers to have been already converted before their burial by the church in the Mount Royal Cemetery.[36] Expecting and demanding assimilation of the Chinese into the mainstream society, the Chinese Catholic church in Montreal proved to be less popular with the "pure stock" of well-to-do Chinese merchants than with children of mixed marriages.[37] As such, the Catholic church seemed to have played a considerably greater role in breaking down racial barriers and promoting integration into the larger Francophone society. While the family and clan associations did their share in shielding the Cantonese men from white racism and, consequently, isolating them from the mainstream society, the Catholic church in Quebec exhibited a more tolerant attitude toward the Chinese. Actually, on several occasions, they came to the defence of the Chinese at the crest of hostility of British Columbians in regard to the "Chinese question" in the West coast.

In the early pioneering years of the Chinese community, the Christian churches were quick to provide for the Cantonese men's needs for social aid and services. Both the Catholics and the Protestants were involved in service areas pertinent to an emerging immigrant community: material aid, teaching English and French, medical help, education, liaison with government departments and ministries dealing in immigration and citizenship matters, and the dissemination of news from Chinese villages. Their first area of involvement was in education: the assimilation of Chinese children into the local school system, and teaching English and French to adults.

> It also meant if they were to stay in this country, and most of them did so, that the way would be open for them and under pleasant circumstances learn English and so help themselves more quickly to fit into the Canadian work-a-day life. It was these Christian contacts, in turn, that led to the setting up of Sunday school classes for them in our churches, and in various parts of the city. There, of course, they not only learned English, but more importantly, our Christian way of life, for in every case the Bible became the textbook.[38]

These Sunday School classes offered by the Christian churches to learn the two local languages quickly became an important point of linguistic and social entry into the host society for many Cantonese adult immigrants. Mostly illiterate in foreign languages, the laundry workers, housemaids or servants working in white men's homes, restaurant kitchen helpers and waiters, would attend the "Sunday school" to learn a rudimentary level of foreign languages which, in the long run, proved to be one of the most important skills ever acquired during their stay in Quebec. When the Catholic church began to teach Chinese to the children by founding a Chinese school on Anderson Street in 1916, learning to write and read Chinese after a full day's schooling became a significant and vivid part of growing up for many a Chinese kid in Quebec.

The involvement of the Catholic church in the Chinese community was particularly significant and conspicuous in the area of health care, reaching its dramatic apex in the establishment of the Montreal Chinese Hospital. In October 1918, an influenza epidemic broke out in Montreal during which 16,405 cases were reported and 2,768 people died.[39]

> Movies, dance halls, schools and libraries were closed, church services discontinued, public meetings were prohibited, stores had to close earlier, and worst of all, the existing hospitals were overcrowded with patients while many of their doctors, nurses and orderlies were also affected by the disease. Thus numerous patients were turned away by the hospitals, and private doctors found it impossible to cope with the situation. Such a disaster aroused the concern of the public authorities and the public-spirited citizens, and by the end of the month, more hospitals were opened. Many religious orders offered their buildings and were ready to nurse the sick. Women volunteers were organized and private care was mustered. The public reacted naturally in the face of a disaster of such magnitude.[40]

Among the first patients were the Chinese launderers. The Missionary Sisters of Immaculate Conception, who had been working with the Chinese since 1913, began visiting Chinese homes and offering care. They then set up a temporary shelter for the treatment of influenza on 66 Clark Street. One sister went to hotels, cafes and restaurants to seek out Chinese patients and another worked as a nurse. The municipal administration, the Brothers of Les Cherced St. Visteur and the Mother House of the Mission contributed to the furnishing and maintenance of the shelter. The Chinese themselves financed the shelter entirely. They paid the bills for rent, heat, lighting, food and the service of a cook. The shelter was officially opened on 18 October 1918, and continued to operate till the summer of 1919 when the epidemic came to a halt. The ending of the epidemic marked the beginning of a strong need among the Chinese community to provide health care in the form of a permanent Chinese hospital. With funds solicited from the Chinese themselves, a synagogue building on 112 Lagauchetière Street was purchased to house the hospital. This ten-bed set up was opened on 17 January 1920. By March 1921, the hospital offered the services of two doctors (a surgeon and a physician) and four nursing Sisters from the Mission of Immaculate Conception.

Between 1922 and 1945, the hospital was financed entirely by the Chinese through donations and various fund-raising campaigns within the Chinese community.

> For the first twenty years, the president and the treasurer travelled all over Canada to solicit funds from the Chinese communities. They met with various degrees of support. During the same period, every Chinese leaving Montreal for China was required to donate $10 to the Hospital, and every Chinese in Montreal had a responsibility to contribute $2 to the Hospital every year. This tithe was possible because of the cohesion of the community, and generally about 80% of them would give. Other methods were also used, such as donations during the happy occasions of weddings and birthday parties of the elders, or from visiting Chinese or Chinese operas.[41]

The year of 1945 saw the gradual weakening of community support and the lessening of Chinese donations: the hospital began to turn to public sources for funding. In 1962, the public health authorities declared the century-old building unfit and dangerous. The physical conditions were reported to be appalling: cockroaches, rats, bad ventilation and lighting, old furniture, overcrowding, and so on. On 12 July 1963, a corporation consisting of three former Chinese board members was formed. The day after, a site at 7500 St. Denis Street, a deserted foundation of the church and of the Holy Family, was bought for the construction of the new hospital. Completed in June 1965, this 55-bed Chinese institution began in the same month to take in patients from the old hospital in Chinatown.[42] As of January 1973, the hospital was classified by the provincial Ministry of Social Affairs as a "hospital centre for prolonged care of long term patients".

The evolution of the hospital had its share of conflicts between different religious and political groups in the Chinese community. When the hospital went to the community for donations in 1963, they faced resistance from all major power groups. The Nationalist League felt excluded for twenty years by an old hospital board dominated by members of the Freemasons. The Presbytarian Church complained the hospital was overly

7. In Lieu of Family

controlled and managed by the Catholics. The Chinese Association of Montreal felt slighted for not being consulted by the old hospital board on important matters.[43] The site for the new hospital also remained an issue of contention. The critics were quick to point out that the site was too far from Chinatown, and, therefore, would not be convenient for the Chinese from the Chinatown area.[44] Miles away from Chinatown, the hub of Chinese activity, the hospital had effectively distanced and alienated itself from the community's organizational infrastructure. The hospital never seems to have regained the same degree of community support it once enjoyed during its inception stage.

According to a recent Chinese census, there are at present 75 million Chinese in mainland China bearing the surname of Li, and the Lis are the most numerous among all Chinese surnames. About 8% of the Han race (who account for 90% of the entire Chinese population) in China are Lis. And there are altogether about 10 billion and 40 million Chinese in China. The Huangs come second, followed by the Zhangs.

The bulk of the early Chinese immigrants in Montreal were the Lis 李, the Huangs 黃, and the Tans 譚, often called Montreal's "Three Big Names" (三大姓). While Huang and Li have always been the most popular and numerous surnames in China, Tan is not.

The Huangs in Montreal have two clan associations: the Huang Jiang Xia Tang and the Huang Yun Shan Gongxi 黃雲山公所. Founded in 1906, among others, by Huang Liangchi, Huang Lianghui, Huang Gongsan and Huang Gongpei, the Huang Jiang Xia Tang was to "promote fellowship and cooperation among the Huang brothers and to assist in charitable, social welfare services". The Tang charged a membership fee of $3 a year, an amount that is still being charged of its 150 largely inactive and non-participatory members. Unlike the other clan associations of the Huangs, the Huang Jiang Xia Tang was set up to embrace the Huangs from all over China regardless of district origin and dialects spoken, a possible reason for the relative lack of internal cohesion among its members. Now, the Tang in Montreal is, in actual fact, a defunct institution; "it's now gone, finished, with nothing left other than the old sign of the Tang." The Huang Yun Shan Gongxi claimed Huang Juzheng 黃居正 as its first ancestor, a native of Fujian who moved to the Xin Hui district of Si Yi, Guangdong, in search of political stability and social rest in Southeast China during the transition into the Nan Song Dynasty 南宋 (1149–1279). Being second generation in Fukien, Huang Juzheng became first generation in Si Yi, and his offspring's foremost ancestor. During the eighth year of the reign of the second monarch of the Nan Song Dynasty, Huang placed first in the imperial examination and was crowned "Zhuang Yuan" 狀元, the highest possible honour conferred by the Imperial Kingdom on an intellectual-scholar. Four years later, his son, Huang Yunshan, also did well in the imperial examination. In 1921, the Gongxi in Montreal held the 750th anniversary of Huang Juanchan's foundation of his Clan of Huangs in the Xin Hui district, thus dating the origin of the clan to 815 years ago.

In 1976, the Huang Yun Shan Gongxi in Montreal celebrated its 88th anniversary, thus dating its inauguration to 1888. First started in rented premises, the Gongxi was later moved into a building on 76 Lagauchetière, bought through revenues from membership dues, members' donations and from running credit associations called "*woi*". In actual fact, the Huang Yun Shan Gongxi, like other clan associations, extracted for much of its revenue from its Huang brothers while discharging its protective and quasi-judicial functions. Members of the Huang clan would come to the Gongxi for arbitration over mainly money-related disputes. For those who made their living by running gambling rings, opium dens and prostitution joints, the Gongxi was a natural place to turn to for protection from the interference of the Lis and the Tans. In many Chinatowns at the turn of the century where Chinese preferred to settle their disputes or to seek protection of their business interests among themselves, justice was dished out by the community's elders, particularly those who sat as members of various Tangs' arbitration committees and panels. The Tangs would be rewarded with a fee for the services they delivered. Their other source of revenue was from running credit associations. A Tang or Gongxi would be the head of the *woi*s it administered, thus sharing with other members of the *woi* the interest and profit generated.

While the city police never explicitly sanctioned illicit activities among the Chinese, they supported, or even promoted, "underground enterprise" by benefitting from the collection of "black money" from the enterprisers. Owners of whorehouses, opium dens and gambling rings would regularly distribute protection money among Tangs of their clan and the police, as a safeguard against harassment from other clans and the city authorities. As the Chinese put it, the police would "see, but not see", or "keep one eye open and the other eye closed". It was this interplay of internal, as well as external, arrangements that granted the "underground enterprise" the kind of autonomy and immunity the business badly needed. The three big clans of Huang, Lis

7. In Lieu of Family

and Tans, thus, strived to manage for several decades a clear-cut territorial and ecological separation from each other, an important structural and special arrangement for the best possible minimization of inter-clan rivalry and disputes.

This territorial division to maintain "the separation of the river from the well" was, however, periodically broken up by fights between clans. The Tans were allegedly the most numerous, the most aggressive and combative among all of the clans in Montreal. Oral legends held that the Tans from the district of Du Cheng 杜澄 were particularly fond of settling disputes and differences with other clans with "fists and kicks". The economically advantaged Chen clan, while among the most numerous in China, was, and still is, a numerical minority in Montreal. Oral testimonies suggest that the Chens were often at the mercy of the Tans, and, thus, found it necessary from time to time to gang up with the Huangs to fight the Tans. Fights between the Tans and others often involved the use of such weapons as metal rings over the fingers, baseball bats and axes. The Cantonese fighters would gather in an empty lot close to a tobacco company in east end Montreal Sunday afternoons when the launderers and restaurant workers were off work. Sometimes, the victims, invariably the Huangs, would take the case to the police and, eventually, the court, only to find themselves as failed suitors, a few hundred dollars lost over legal fees.

When a Tan left Montreal for his return trip to China via Vancouver, the Huang clan in Montreal would inform their brothers in British Columbia such and such a person named Tan would be getting off such and such Greyhound bus at a certain time on a certain day. A Huang's clansman would receive the Tan at the bus terminal. He would ask the passenger fresh off the bus, "Are you uncle Tan?", who, thinking his own clansman in Vancouver was kind enough to greet him, would nod his head. The Huang man would quickly start hitting the Tan, knifing and "pushing him down into the gutter". While the attack continued, the Huang man would reprimand the Tan, yelling, "You and your Tan Clan were so combative and belligerent for all these years. I am here on behalf of all the Huangs in Montreal to teach you and your brothers a lesson. I will treat you to a big meal, all the way to China." "Treating you to a big meal" means really beating you up in Cantonese.[45]

While the Lis and Huangs have in the past century always topped the list of most Chinese represented by surnames, both in mainland China and the overseas immigrant community in Canada, the Tans are not by any means the most numerous, except in Montreal and Quebec. In 1923, several members of the merchant class of the Tan clan founded the Tan Guang Yu Tang Society. Legend held that each of the then three to four hundred Tans in Montreal was literally forced into membership by paying an annual membership fee of $3 (same rate in 1987) and a fee of $17 toward the purchase of an old building as the society's headquarters on the south side of 90 Lagauchetière Street between St. Urbain and Clark Streets. Someone, preferably from a different district or village in China to avoid unnecessary friction, would go after the father for the $20 when the son failed to contribute.[46] Tan Zhuangxi, a merchant, contributed $1,200 toward renovating the building. Lack of regular income other than membership dues almost forced the Society into bankruptcy. Tan Yuzhuang made a donation of $3,000 to enable the Society to pay its tax bills and other outstanding bills. Rents collected from two other Tan clan associations, Zhao Lun Gongxi 昭倫公所 and Tan Yuan Yuan Tang 譚源源堂, then located on the ground floor of the building, yielded only a combined revenue of about $200 a month. From late 1940s onward, the Tan Guang Yu Tang, like other clan associations in the community, began running "*San Yi Woi*" or, more precisely, "Three Benefits *Woi*s", meaning credit associations that are to the benefit of all three parties involved: the creditors, the debtors and the "*Gong*" —, typically the clan association running the *woi*. These *wois* have remained for decades the principal source of revenue for the Tan Guang Yu Tang.

On 20 June 1956, the Zhao Lun Gongxi, bringing together Chinese of five surnames, Tan, Tan, Xu, Xie and Yuan譚、談、許、謝、阮celebrated its inauguration in Montreal. The two Tans are, in fact, two different surnames and are two different ideographs in the Chinese language. The first Tan was, and still is, the surname for the large majority of the Tans in Montreal, while the other Tan, meaning "to speak or to converse", is a minority surname both in China and in Montreal. The union of the five surnames was to withstand external aggression and hostility, and to promote internal harmony and mutual aid.[47] However, unlike what happened in Toronto when the five former surname associations were disbanded and then consolidated into a *gongxi*, the Zhao Lian Gongxi in Montreal continued to exist side by side with four other clan associations created by the Tans: the Tan Yuan Yuan Tang, the Du Cheng Country Club 杜澄同鄉會, the Tan Guang Yu Tang, and the Montreal Bai Shui Tan's Gongxi 白水譚氏公所.

On the day of the inauguration of the Zhao Lun Gongxi, heads of the five surname groups paid ceremonial tribute to their common ancestor Jiang Dagong 姜太公, whose statue, a gift donation from the Gongxi's headquarters in San Francisco, was unveiled. The ceremony was quite well represented by local Chinese church groups, political parties and clan associations, along with representatives of the Zhao Lun Gongxi in Toronto and Vancouver. Speeches were delivered to amplify the importance of brotherhood, mutual aid, unity and cohesion among the five surname brothers. Chinese poems published in volume seven of the Tan Clan's Association Periodical 譚氏宗親會會刊 (5 October 1955) dwelt on such themes.[48]

The Zhao Lun Gongxi in Montreal was created about fifteen years after the Chinese in Toronto (1940) and eleven years after the Chinese in Vancouver (1944) created theirs. On 20 November 1955, an all-Canada Zhao Lun Gongxi was inaugurated in Vancouver, sharing premises then occupied by the local Zhao Lun Gongxi. The Tan's Clan Association in Hong Kong sent a gold-plated horizontal engraving in Chinese calligraphy carrying the message "Be close to the family and treat all citizens kindly." The Tans in Montreal, during subsequent decades, continued to maintain their ties with their kin in Hong Kong by contributing financial donations, and publishing news of the activities of the Tans' clan associations in Tan's Clan Association Periodical in Hong Kong. On 21 April 1957, the Tan Guang Yu Tang in Montreal called a meeting to raise funds toward the construction of a five-storey building in Hong Kong to house the Tan's Clan Association.[49] About $20,000 in total was raised in that meeting. The Tan Guang Yu Tang led with $3,000, followed by donations from individuals. On the same day, the Montreal Bai Shui Tan's Gongxi contributed about $8,000. Several Tans from Montreal remained as honorary counsellors or permanent members of the Hong Kong Tan's Clan Association.[50]

The origin of the Tan surname can be traced back two thousand six hundred and seventy-five years, to the first clan ancestor Tan Gong 譚公 who reigned as monarch over the county of Tan, now Shandong province.[51] In political and official terms, the word "*gong*" in Chinese connotes a title designation of respect, royalty and authority. In kin and family terms, it stands for the foremost head and origin of the clan lineage, thus, for example, Tan Gong. Over the years, the Tans spread themselves throughout China, with notable concentration in the provinces of Guangdong and Yunnan. The bulk of the overseas Tans were from Guangdong's four main districts: Kai Ping, Xin Hui, Tai Shan and Nan Hai 南海, in that order. The

Tans in Montreal were mainly from Kai Ping's Du Cheng and Tai Sun's Bai Shui. In actual fact, the Tans, over the span of some two thousand years, covering many a dynasty, were originally migrants from northern China before migrating overseas in the past century.[52]

Cantonese immigrants arriving in Montreal between 1890 and 1920 carried a wide variety of surnames: Luo, Wu, Tan, Xing, Fang, Ye, Hu, Yi, Mo, Lin, Chen and Liang, among others. The Chens, Luos and the Xings were among the nine most numerous surnames represented among overseas Cantonese in Canada, but not in Montreal. They all needed to wait till their numbers were large enough to form associations of any sort. The Xings and the Chens, who were related according to mythology, joined to form a society in 1916. It disbanded two years later, perhaps due to lack of numbers. In 1930, the Chens formed their own society, the Chen Ying Chuan Tang 陳潁川堂, also on the south side of Lagauchetière Street, a few doors down from the Huang Yun Shan Gongxi and the Tan Guang Yu Tang.[53] In 1932, members of the Zhou, Zai, Weng, Wu and Cao clans, then active in the grocery and restaurant business, joined to form the San De Tang on 82 Lagauchetière Street. In 1934, the families of Lei, Fang and Kuang 雷、方、鄺 set up the Su Yuan Tang 遡源堂 at 108 Lagauchetière Street.

The first group of Chinese landed and settled in Canada as early as 1858, with much of their activity confined to the city of Victoria. Among those in Victoria, the Lis were the earliest settlers and also perhaps the most numerous.[54] In 1910, there were about three thousand Chinese in Victoria, one-sixth of whom were brothers of the Li Clan. Almost all of them were young bachelors, married or not. On the basis of historical archives, it was estimated that the first Li's association, the Li Long Xi Tang, was established in as early as 1880 in Victoria, arguably the most prosperous Canadian port along the Pacific coast north of San Francisco and west of Chicago. Companies like Kuang On Lung, Tai Yuen, Po Yuen and Hung Yuen set up by the Li Clan had been enjoying a great deal of prosperity in Victoria for years. In the same year, Li Tian Pei and brothers set up the Luen Cheong Company to bring in ten thousand Cantonese immigrants from China for the construction of the Canadian Pacific Railway. In 1883, the Chinese Benevolent Association was actively being planned and formally inaugurated a year later. The Association's first ever chairman was Kwong On Lung's owner, Li Youjian; Luen Cheong's Li Tianbao and Tai Yuen's Li Youda were its Vice-Chairmen. When the three-storey building housing the Chi-

7. In Lieu of Family

nese Benevolent Association was officially inaugurated in 1885, the Li Long Si Tang donated to the Association a horizontal sign in Chinese calligraphy, a set of classical style Chinese furniture, and a ritual utensil for the altar, all of which have become a permanent part of the decor and furnishings of the Association's ceremonial hall, the "Palace of Respective Saints and Sages", on the third floor. All of these were good indicators of the economic and numerical superiority of the Li clan in Victoria.

About thirty years later, the Li Long Xi Tang in Victoria renamed itself the Li Long Xi Head Tang. With membership contributions and donations, a three-storey building on Fisgard Street was built to house the headquarters. In 1931, the Li clan called its first cross-Canada national assembly in Vancouver during which a motion was passed to abolish all Li Long Xi Tangs and Li Long Xi Head Tang, and replace them with one conglomerate association called the Li's Association. Its headquarters, named the Li's Benevolent Association of Canada, also found its site in Vancouver, which quickly surpassed the city of Victoria in total Chinese population. It was not until 1963 that the Association held their second national assembly for the purpose of the construction of the Association's building. In the summer of 1984, fifty-three years after its founding, the Association was housed in the present location of 313 East Pender Street in Vancouver.

A publication to commemorate the third national assembly of the Li Clan in Calgary estimates there are about thirteen thousand Lis in Canada, 6,760 originally from Tai Shan (52%), 2,080 from Xin Hui (16%), 1,410 from Zhong Shan 中山 (11%), and 910 from Kai Ping (7%).[55] Among these thirteen thousand Lis, 4,200 are now concentrated in Vancouver, 3,600 in Toronto, 1,250 in Montreal, 980 in Calgary and 670 in Victoria which, shortly before the turn of the century, had the most Lis, only to lose its prominence to Vancouver in the subsequent decades.[56]

The beginning of the Li clan gatherings in Montreal seemed to have all begun at the back of several grocery stores and merchant shops on the west side of St. Urbain Street between Lagauchetière and Viger streets, where Cantonese laundrymen would assemble on Sundays to catch up with news about home, or to play for a few hours various Chinese games of chance.[57] We are told that conflicts and fights between members of the Li, Tan and Huang clans for territorial, as well as economic, rights gave birth to a desire among the Lis to establish an association of their own. Presumably, a member of the Lis would complain to his brother or an uncle he was not fairly treated at the gambling rings by those of the clan rivals. Or he would grumble about the Huangs and the Tans who, having sold him a laundry shop, would try to regain their "territorial prerogative" by using the same amount of money from the sales transaction to start another laundry shop only a few doors away. He felt his territorial rights were invaded. The Li clan must, therefore, intervene, preferably in a collective, organized fashion. As the old Chinese sayings go, "Large surnames will oppress the small surnames", or "The majority will bully the minority". The tilting of the balance of power between the clans of Li, Tan and Huang, both in economic and numerical terms, was, thus, the breeding ground of conflicts and rivalries. Conflict was at one time so ritualized that physical fights between clan members would follow a certain organized course with an attendent set of rules and regulations. They would make arrangements for these fights to take place in an empty lot behind the present location of the Li's Association on Lagauchetière Street, often on Sunday afternoons, when laundry workers had a rare half-day off from work. These fights among the Cantonese men occasionally necessitated the intervention of the police, lawyers and the courts. Legend held that the Li's Association in Montreal was born overnight, frustrated by reports of bullyings, beatings and territorial invasions of other clans. Riding the crest of pent-up emotions, appeals were made by the better-off merchants and owners of grocery stores and laundry shops, to the Li Clan to contribute shares toward the launching of the construction of the Association building.

Specific people, typically the heads of "*Fangkou*" 房口 (collective households, often based on locality or surname ties), were designated to collect shares of $10, $50, $100 and as much as $500 toward the eventual building construction fund. While this contribution was not explicitly obligatory, it was estimated "just about each and every Li" then residing in Montreal had contributed some amount to this fund. A sum of $10 was the minimum a head, an impressive amount in itself given the meagre wages of the bulk of Cantonese men in those days. In 1898, the Lis in Montreal founded the Li Long Xi Tang, taking the name of an association in Victoria. In 1905, it had a membership of 100 and was under the presidency of Li Zhu, or Johnson Li to the non-Chinese, an import merchant by trade and a part-time official interpreter for the municipal court, a much respected and admired profession in the early Chinese communities in Canada.

On 27 October 1959, the Li Long Xi Tang in Montreal, following the lead in Vancouver, officially changed the association's name into Li Si Gong Suo 李氏公所, or Li's Association, signifying "the association of the

Li clan". The five main actors at the time were all of the merchant class: Li Yixin (restaurant storekeeper), Li Binyan (merchant), John T. Li (merchant), Li Daozu (laundry operator), and Henry Y. Li (bank clerk). In the letter patent incorporating the Li's Association of Montreal and signed by these five founders, the following association functions were recorded:

1. To promote the interests of the Li clan and to preserve and perpetuate the association and Chinese traditions of the said clan;
2. To promote, support and protect the status and interests of the Li clan, and the general well-being and welfare of the members therefore;
3. To establish, undertake, superintend, administer or contribute to any charitable or benevolent fund from which may be made donations or advances to needy and deserving persons;
4. To collect money by way of donations and dues, or otherwise, and to hold and expand the same in furtherance of the objects of the corporation;
5. To purchase, take or lease, hire, take by gift, devise, bequest, donation or otherwise acquire and hold real or personal property or any interest therein for the purpose of creating facilities with its usual and necessary adjuncts for the furtherance of its object, but for no other purposes, and to sell, mortgage, lease or otherwise dispose of any real or personal property;
6. To do such other things as are incidental or conducive to the obtainment of the above objects or any one of them;
7. The powers granted do not permit gambling practices of any nature, and in particular do not permit the conducting or playing of any game of chance or any mixed game of chance and skill.

The Li's Associations throughout Canada worship Bo Yang Gong 伯陽公, also known as Li Er 李耳 (Lao Zi 老子), the founder of Taoism in China, as their premier ancestor. On the third floor of the Li's Association on 94 Lagauchetière Street West is located the Association's ceremonial hall that is prominently occupied at one end by an altar, behind which is a copy of a full-colour portrait of Bo Yang Gong, seated in a saintly pose, and fanned by two children standing in front as attendants. Also on the altar was displayed a sign indicating dates on which Bo Yang Gong was born (15 February), achieved "sainthood" (1 July), and "went to heaven" (15 December). These were also dates on which ceremonies were routinely held by the Association to commemorate its ancestor. In the 1 July 1986 edition of the Li's Quarterly Magazine,[58] there was a vivid description of such ceremonial celebration on the occasion of the birthday of Bai Yang Gong:

> On March 23 (Sunday) in the afternoon, members of the Li clan and friends assembled in the ceremonial hall to celebrate the holy birthday of their Premier Ancestor. The hall was for a moment decorated as new. The flames of red candles on the altar were shining high and wide. Smokes from incense were forming circles, along with bouquets of flowers, fruits, wine and three different animal sacrifices.
>
> At five o'clock, the master of ceremony Ying Jie 英傑 announced the proceedings. It began with the chairman Zhi Rong 植榮 presiding over the sacrificial ceremony, reading teachings of the Premier Ancestor. Chong Hui 崇慧 and Qi Shan 祁珊 were assisting in the ceremony. It was then followed by Jin Rong chanting loud lyrics of blessing. Then chairman Zhi Rong spoke, encouraging members of the clan to work closely together on worthwhile tasks as well as to promote and propagate the well-being of the Li clan. At the conclusion of the ceremony, brothers and sisters were served tea and snacks. The gathering expressed itself in the close intimacy of kin feeling and bondage, celebrating a moment of peace and prosperity. On the next day (the 24th) at half-past six, a banquet in celebration of the spring season was held in the Kam Fung Restaurant. In that evening, chairman Zhi Rong began with a welcoming speech, and then proceeded to introduce representatives of the municipal government as well as known personalities of the community to the audience. A municipal government representative then rose to give blessing. Shen Yan 燊炎 thanked the government on behalf of the Association. Chong Hui then read out names of winners of the lucky draw. It was a banquet of more than thirty tables. The evening ended in the enthusiasm and applause of brothers, sisters, uncles and aunts. A video machine was awarded as the evening's grand prize.
>
> The association would like to thank those donors of prizes for the lucky draw, whose names are to be listed as follows ...

Another description of a similar occasion appeared in the 2 April 1982 edition of the Li's Monthly Magazine:[59]

> The Li's Association here, on the occasion of the return of spring to the great earth and the rejuvenation of all things, happily gathered in the Association's ceremonial hall to attend the celebration of the holy birthday of their Premier Ancestor. The proceedings were simple but solemn ...

The Li's Association, like those of the Tan's and the Huang's, has continued to stress, since its inception, its protective, paternalistic and mutual aid functions. Above all, these clans associations were there to protect their respective members from racism and hostility meted out by the white society, as well as to intervene in conflicts between various clans within the confine of the Chinese community, or, more precisely, within Chinatown. It is said that some of these clan groupings, like the Li's Association, were indeed born out of inter-clan rivalry and conflict, thus underscoring the primacy of the need to protect and to advocate on the part of the clan associations. The loyalty of a Cantonese man was first and foremost to his clan. In that, he hardly had any choice, when he felt shafted by members of the other clan invading and challenging his territorial rights, when he felt cheated or treated unfairly in the games of chance over the gambling tables, when the whites threw stones at the windows of his laundry shop, dumped garbage at the front door of his shop, soiled his clean linens, or grabbed his pig-tail chanting, "Ching, Ching, wash my pants for a dime." The Cantonese merchants who first pioneered California and later British Columbia told their relatives back home in China exaggerated tales of gold nuggets paving the streets of the "Brave New World".[60] These same merchants formed the first clans in their stores which in time became the focal point around which Chinese social life evolved. As members of a new gentry class in the immigrant communities overseas, they probably felt the moral obligation to defend the rights of their less fortunate clansmen, and to give aid to the downtrodden, the miserable, the penniless and the hapless. The new gentry, thus, began investing time, energy and money in shaping the formation of their clan and family associations, often taking on strategic leadership roles. Their service to the clan was not without personal vested interests, which were often pursued in the form of safeguarding and propagating the business interests of their own and their family lineage. In the early Chinese community, the merchants and shop owners were clearly the community elite, while workers in Chinese restaurants, grocery stores, and hand laundry shops filled the bulk of clan membership and were the backbone of the rank and file. While the merchant elite functioned to meet their clansmen's needs for jobs, accommodation, protection and mediation, they also asked for their loyalty, deference and subordination in all realms of social-economic life. Inter-clan conflicts, as well as racially based hostility on the part of white society, provided the socio-political arena in which the merchant-leaders went about the business of insulating and isolating the Chinese community from the mainstream society. In arbitrating conflicts between clans and keeping them within the confine of Chinatown, the clan associations, ironically, nurtured the dependency needs of the clansmen, and, thus, their psychological and structural isolation. The merchant-elite, in the meantime, continued to profit from this dependency. Fights were known to break out between villages and clans in old China. It was invariably the family villages' elders who stepped in as mediators and arbitrators.[61] It was also the elders who made up the governing class in the overseas immigrant communities:

> Just as the family village is governed by elders, the control of the family association is left in the hands of the older generation. Elections are held to choose officers to perform the routine work of running the organization with candidates chosen from the rank and file. However, the important affairs involving the welfare of the family are entrusted to the elders. To them falls the responsibility of protecting the honor of the family name, answering complaints lodged by other groups, and meeting some of the social and economic problems of the members.[62]

The setting up of clan associations around the merchants' stores, among other things, often resulted in the family as well as clan monopolies over certain trades.[63] These clan monopolies were often the breeding ground of violent fights between clans, more popularly known as "tang wars" in New York and San Francisco. In Quebec, the relative absence of family monopoly in the three main areas of business activity for the Cantonese, namely grocery and import, laundry and restaurant businesses, resulted in the relative infrequency of violent disputes and fights between clans and clan members[64] compared to the enormous notoriety that so mystified many an average white citizen in the United States. Bloodshed, gunfights, murders, and *tong* wars were never part of the folk mythology nor reality in the history of the Chinese in Quebec. Individual clan members would have disputes between themselves over matters of money, women and business territory. They would fight, often in a highly ritualized and regulated manner. The elders would arbitrate and intervene. Every now and then, the Chinese elders, when arbitration failed, would take the case to the municipal authorities under the tutelage of white lawyers. One clan would win a court case this time. Another clan would win several cases later. The lack of clan monopoly, the resultant "balance of power" between the clans, and the occasional creation of temporary alliances between two or three clans in opposition to a stronger, more numerous and powerful clan, resulted in the relatively calm, peaceful coexistence the Chinese in Quebec have known.

For the Cantonese immigrants in Canada, as well as in Montreal, politics, political loyalties and participation, at least up to the early eighties, centered around politics back home in China. For more than a century, this gravity toward home politics contrasted rather dramatically with the virtual absence of their political participation in the host society. In Montreal Chinatown, political activities of the Cantonese men were largely organized and structured around three political parties: the Reform Party, the purpose of which was to protect and maintain the Qing Emperor in China; the Zhigongtang, now known throughout Canada as the Chinese Freemasons, which was set up as early as 1862 in the gold mining town, Bakerville, British Columbia and whose purpose was to "oppose the Qing Dynasty, restore the Ming Dynasty"[65]; and the Guomintang, or the Chinese Nationalist League, founded by perhaps the most legendary political figure in modern Chinese history, Dr. Sun Yat Sen.

The historical affiliation of the Zhigongtang with powerful underground secret societies aimed at overthrowing the Qing Dynasty, had many consequences; one of these was the perception on the part of mystified outsiders of it as a political party advocating violence and occasionally supplementing their revenues by means of extortion and blackmail. Banned in most countries of Southeast Asia and Hong Kong, Zhigongtang members were often looked upon by the local governments as agitators largely responsible for the bulk of social unrest and other evils. The press in the United States was particularly keen on monitoring and reporting their illicit activities and the occasional eruptions of physical violence, "the *tong* wars", that they caused.[66]

The conflict and rivalry between the Guomintang and the Zhigongtang endemic in almost all Chinese immigrant communities throughout Canada was an historical and ideological irony since both political parties were grounded in a similar revolutionary philosophy and reactionary theory. It was quite well-known in Chinese communities in Canada that father and son, husband and wife, or brothers might belong to different parties, a fact accentuating the two party's commonality. In an article outlining the history of "Hong Men" 洪門, the predecessor of the Chinese Freemasons, the following judgement regarding the historical and ideological relationship between the two political parties was argued:

> It was neither the Guomintang nor the Communist party that had overthrown the Qing Dynasty and built the Republic of China. During the period when there were resistance efforts to oppose the Qing Dynasty and to restore the reign of the Han people, our country did not see the existence of the Guomintang and the Communist Party. This opposition against the Qing Dynasty thus fell on the shoulders of

brothers of the Hong Men overseas. This spectacular achievement shines as brightly as the sun and moon, and deserves the admiration and respect of thousands of generations to come.[67]

In Montreal, the conflict and power struggle between the parties saw ups and downs for a good fifty years, though largely regulated and contained within the community by a select group of leadership elite. The rivalry for power was played out during the formative years of the Montreal Chinese Hospital, a rivalry paralleling the Catholic-Protestant conflict. A bloody confrontation broke out in 1933 right in a Chinese restaurant in Chinatown. About ten to fifteen men were injured and maimed.[68] Details of the confrontation were reported to a journalist of *La Presse* by a Chinese man called San Li of the Guomintang. He alleged that the confrontation was largely a dispute between gamblers, not parties. A similar incident occurred several months earlier. The Montreal Chinese Association vowed to the city authorities that there would be no more quarrels of the same sort in Chinatown.[69] Interestingly, these two confrontations remain as the only two major, large-scale "events of fights and disputes" remembered and reported by the Chinese oldtimers some fifty years later.

Notes

1. Stanford M. Lyman, *Chinatown and Little Tokyo: Power, Conflict and Community Among Chinese and Japanese Immigrants in America* (New York: Associated Faculty Press, 1986), p. 117.
2. Kwok B. Chan, *Oral History of the Montreal Chinese Community*, and history interview with Jack Huang (Jinzhuo), 5, 6, and 11 May 1983, at the Chinese Freemasons, 1072 St. Laurent Boulevard, Montreal, Quebec.
3. David T.H. Lee 李東海, *Jianada Huaqiao shi* 加拿大華僑史 (A History of Chinese in Canada) (British Columbia: Ziyou chubanshe 自由出版社, 1967), p. 206. (text in Chinese.)
4. Ibid., p. 206.
5. Ibid., p. 208.
6. Ibid., p. 176.
7. Ibid., pp. 178–79.
8. David Lai, "The Chinese Consolidated Benevolent Association in Victoria: Its Origins and Functions," in *BC Studies*, No. 15 (Autumn 1972), pp. 53–67.
9. Ibid., p. 53.
10. Ibid., p. 58.
11. Ibid., pp. 58–59.

7. In Lieu of Family

12. Ibid., p. 60.
13. David T.H. Lee, pp. 198–202.
14. Untitled and undated document (47 pages) listing Chinese organizations and associations in Montreal, author unidentified, p. 22.
15. Francis L.K. Hsü, *Americans and Chinese: Passage to Differences*, (third edition) (Honolulu: The University Press of Hawaii, 1981), p. 245.
16. Ibid., p. 244.
17. Ibid., p. 254.
18. Ibid., p. 255.
19. Ibid., p. 255.
20. Ibid., p. 249.
21. Ibid., p. 252.
22. Ibid., p. 254.
23. Father Thomas Du, "Religion Among Chinese in Canada," in *Special Publication to Commemorate the 50th Anniversary of the Montreal Chinese Catholic Mission* (Text mainly in Chinese with partial English and French translations), August, 1972, p. 15.
24. Ibid., p. 15.
25. Denise Helly, *Les Chinois à Montréal 1877–1951* (Quebec: Institut québécois de recherche sur la culture, 1987), p. 9.
26. Ibid., p. 10.
27. *Chinese Young Men's Christian Institution in Montreal Special Publication to Commemorate its Golden Anniversary, 1961* (84 Ontario Street West, Montreal). (Text in Chinese.) Translation by author. 25 pages.
28. Author unidentified, "The Importance of 'Christian Chinese School'," p. 10.
29. Ibid., p. 4.
30. Denise Helly, p. 9.
31. David T.H. Lee, pp. 215–16.
32. Ibid., p. 217.
33. Father Thomas Du, "A Brief of the History of the Chinese Mission and Its School," in *Special Publication to Commemorate the 50th Anniversary of the Montreal Chinese Catholic Mission*, p. 25.
34. Ibid., p. 25.
35. Denise Helly, p. 1.
36. Ibid., p. 10.
37. Ibid., p. 10.
38. Reverend Paul S. Chen, *A Short History of the Chinese Presbyterian Church and Community Centre in Montreal*, undated document, p. 6.
39. *The Gazette*, 1 November 1918.
40. Stephen Chi-kin Law, "Service Functions of the Montreal Chinese Hospital—Role of Community Participation" (M.A. research report, School of Social Work, McGill University, Montreal, Quebec, Canada, October 1967), p. 23.
41. Ibid., p. 32.
42. Ibid., p. 34.

43. Ibid., p. 48.
44. Ibid., p. 39.
45. This part of the chapter on the Huangs in Montreal is based on an oral history interview with Huang Guozhen, 26 April 1987.
46. This part of the chapter on the Tans in Montreal is based on oral history interviews with Henry Tan (11 May 1987) and Tan Yexin (12 May 1987).
47. *Hong Kong Tan Clan's Association Periodical*, Vol. 9 (1 November 1957), p. 77.
48. Ibid., Vol. 7 (5 October 1955).
49. Ibid., Vol. 9, p. 75.
50. Ibid., Vol. 9, p. 15.
51. Ibid., Vol. 8 (1956), p. 159.
52. Ibid., Vol. 8 (1956), p. 160.
53. Denise Helly, p. 3.
54. David T.H. Lee, p. 47.
55. *Special Publication to Commemorate Third General Assembly of the Li's Clan in Canada*, August 1986, p. 66.
56. Ibid., p. 64.
57. This part of the chapter on the Lis in Montreal is based on oral history interviews on 21 and 24 May 1987 with Jack Li, Li Yan-san, Li Kam-wing, Arthur Li, Li Kwok-san and Li Yit-kit.
58. *Li's Quarterly Magazine*, Vol. 25, No. 3 (1 July 1986), p. 9.
59. *Li's Monthly Magazine* (313 East Penser Street, Vancouver, B.C., Canada, V6A 1V1), 2 April 1982, p. 5.
60. Stanford M. Lyman, p. 112.
61. Ibid., p. 114.
62. Ibid., p. 114.
63. Ibid., p. 116.
64. Denise Helly, p. 7.
65. David T.H. Lee, p. 230.
66. Ibid., p. 235.
67. Kin-ping Kam, "A Brief History of the 'Hong Men'," in *Proceedings of 23rd Assembly of the Chinese Freemasons in Canada*, held in Toronto (14 September 1985), p. 28.
68. Oral history interview with Tan Yu-xing, 12 May 1987.
69. Denise Helly, p. 1.

8. After the War

The young and the old.

The Chinese Family Service of Greater Montreal on Lagauchetière Street before it was moved to Côté Street. It is one of the three social service centres serving the Chinese community in Montreal.

8. After the War

THE 1923 Chinese Immigration Act, or, more correctly, the Chinese Exclusion Act, put an abrupt halt to the flow of Chinese immigrants into Canada. Between 1923 and 1947, the year when the Act was repealed, only seven Chinese immigrants were admitted into Canada, six of whom were men.[1] The Chinese were virtually shut off from Canadian entry ports for quarter of a century. The bulk of the Cantonese married men came to Canada at the turn of the century without their women and children. There were some fortunate few who went back and forth between China and Canada in the interim years to get married, to father children, or to purchase land, property and houses in their native villages, destined to leave their family behind.[2] For these Chinese men and women, marital life was brief. The overseas immigrant communities in Canada became male bachelor societies, while the emigrant village communities back home in China were to make do without husbands, fathers, sons and sons-in-law. Head taxes and passage money proved too prohibitive for women and children to come along. It was also the duty of men to provide for the family, to make good, to set his eyes beyond the native village and to set his sights far away. More importantly, the Cantonese men in Canada quickly came to face, in real life, daily news then circulating back home in China about the racist treatment of members of the Oriental race. They did not feel right in exposing their wives and children to racist humiliation and abuse.[3] It was his moral duty to protect them from the resentment and hostility of the aliens. Women and children had a much better chance of surviving and prospering if they stayed home, no matter how unfavourable conditions there were. When men in Canada prospered, women back home would also prosper. Only interested in adult male immigrant labour to meet the needs of a quickly industrialized capitalist society, the Canadian government forbade the admission of Chinese women and children into the country. The Chinese themselves, for economic and emotional reasons, did not want to be accompanied by their family either.

Between 1906 and 1924, the pre-war Chinese community in Canada was characterized by a high disproportion of males over females. The number of Chinese men per 100 women was 2,790 in 1911, 1,533 in 1921, 1,241 in 1931, and 785 in 1941. Between 1906 and 1924, out of the 43,470 Chinese immigrants admitted to Canada, there were 3,578 men per 100 women.[4] The census of 1941 reported that over 80% of the males in Canada were married. Racist hostility had actually prevented many Chinese men from identifying with Canada as their home. A Chinese witness presented the following testimony to the 1885 Royal Commission:[5]

> Chinese immigrants coming to this country are denied all the rights and privileges extended to others in the way of citizenship; the laws compel them to remain aliens. I know a great many Chinese will be glad to remain here permanently with their families, if they are allowed to be naturalized and can enjoy privileges and rights.

With no women and children around, there was no family, thus no Canada-born second generation until decades later. A significant number of Chinese second generation did not come about until the beginning of 1950s; until 1947, the second generation accounted for less than 20% of the Chinese population.[6] As late as 1971, after more than a century in Canada, over 60% of the Chinese were foreign-born. Handicapped by racially motivated federal legislation, which culminated in the 1923 Chinese Exclusion Act, several years after the United States passed theirs, the Chinese community in Canada quietly, but distressingly, went through a subsequent quarter-century of demographic stagnation. The period of 1923 to 1947 became the Chinese "Dark Age". The *Sunday Express* in 1983 published a story titled, "Vice Era is Over" which began with this nostalgic line: "It used to be said that where there was Chinatown, there was vice–backroom gambling, opium rooms and prostitution."[7]

The absence of a conjugal family life also meant, among other things, the development and proliferation of vice industries among Chinatowns across Canada. The Cantonese were notorious for their fondness of gambling. There was a Cantonese joke that when two Cantonese get together, they gamble. During social gatherings, family dinners or banquets to celebrate festivities, gambling is often a popular form of entertainment and an integral part of the responsibility of the host. Gambling within the Chinese community of Canada originated from the Fan Tan Alley 番攤巷 of Victoria, British Columbia, an alley known to the Chinese as the "bank street", after Wall Street in New York. About two hundred yards long and only wide enough to allow for two persons to walk through side by side, the alley featured restaurants, about a dozen of gambling houses of different sizes, food stands, peddlers and singers. The seating capacity of these gambling houses ranged from a couple of dozen to over a hundred persons. For a while, wherever there were major Chinese concentrations, one saw the setting up of gambling houses similar in structure to Fan Tan Alley.[8]

A Chinese man in Timmins, Ontario, a mining town born out of

8. After the War

discovery of gold and an assortment of minerals in 1901, made this comment on the Chinese involvement in gambling:

> We are humans but we lived in a subhuman way. We did not have a family with us here and we had no family life. We were hated by the whites and they did not want to have anything to do with us because we are Chinese. Among ourselves we just played some games as our recreational outlets. You know, we were not allowed to do this or that. Chinese should be blamed and not the whites. They did not like us and they made the excuses. Yes, we gambled but, surely, we were not hurting others. We had no alternatives and we had no family life here. True, at first, we did not have enough money to bring our family here. But, when we did, we were not allowed. What was more insulting was that when we took a trip back to China to see our family, or to get married, they said that we were spending their money in China instead of in Canada. Now, you go and ask how many Chinese in Timmins spend their time after work in the games. I bet many of them will say, "No time, there is a family to look after." So, who should be blamed?[9]

Chinese laundries and restaurants were labour intensive businesses which, in the Canadian context, relied very heavily on the uninterrupted supply of cheap labour, preferably recruits from native villages in China, in order to survive and compete. The superimposition of kin relations on employer-employee relations often enabled the employers who were invariably older, and better established business owners, to better monitor and control the work habits of their new recruits as well as to ensure the latter's life-long loyalty and obligation to "a kinsman's business". The new recruit often needed to work for five to ten years in a laundry or restaurant owned by his kinsman not only to "morally pay back", by showing his gratefulness to his kinsman for having given him a "new life" in Canada, but also to pay back debts incurred. The 1923 Chinese Immigration Act cut off this supply of Chinese kinsmen labour, thus effectively eliminating one competitive edge the Chinese had enjoyed over the whites: cheap, reliable, untroublesome, steady and loyal labour.

The take off of the Chinese restaurant business in Montreal in the early 1920s, and the brief boom Chinese restaurants subsequently experienced, suffered its first setback with the 1923 Act. The 1929 catastrophic crash in the stock market dealt another blow to the Chinese restaurant business. The Pagoda on St. Catherine Street between Mountain and Drummond streets, the largest Chinese cabaret-style restaurant in Montreal, was the first one of its kind to go bankrupt, subsequently followed by the folding of a string of similar Chinese restaurants as well as scores of Chinese hand laundries. Many converted their restaurants into cafes serving essentially Canadian cuisine and offering live entertainment on weekends. Others staggered on and barely managed to survive till the end of the war. Without Chinese newcomers from the native villages, owners of Chinese restaurants were not able to recruit labour. When the Chinese immigrants in Montreal were anxious to return to China right after the War, restaurants were sold to non-Chinese restauranters, thus ending an era of the Chinese restaurant business in the city.[10]

China and Canada were allies during the War. China emerged after the War as a victor over Japan and began to assert itself as a new political force in the arena of international politics. It was a political embarrassment for Canada to discriminate against a racial group of an allied country. The United States repealed its Chinese Exclusion Act in 1943 and set the annual admission quota for the Chinese at 105.[11]

During the 1939 Sino-Japanese war, Chinese immigrants in Canada were drafted into the Canadian army: about twenty in the air force, over ten in the navy, and the rest in the infantry. Many of them were sent to the battle line in England, India, Australia, New Zealand and New Guinea. In every Victory Loan Drive, Chinese across Canada were reported to be over-subscribing the quota.[12] The Chinese in Montreal set up a Security Council or, as the Chinese called it, the "*Bow-On*" brigade 保安隊 : "*Bow*" means "to protect" and "*On*" means "to keep safe". The Montreal chapter became a member of the National Security Council and dealt mainly in matters of security, protection of persons and property (for both Chinese and non-Chinese) on the occasion of eruption of a war in the city. Jack Huang, the leader of the Council, made arrangements for a war shelter and the setting up of the Council headquarters at the Sun Ya restaurant on Lagauchetière Street. Huang led a group of some fifty people, young and old, and involved them in military drills, "gun testing", and training in first-aid over weekends on Ontario and Amherst streets.[13]

> Again it was a war—The Second World War—that changed the hearts of many Canadians. In every Loan Drive, the Chinese Canadian community oversubscribed the quota. They engaged in countless war efforts and services. The duty and contributions of Chinese Canadians both at home and abroad towards the War challenged the attitudes of many citizens. The recruitment of Chinese Canadians in the armed forces and their enthusiastic support for war loan drives touched off a public campaign for their franchise. The active endorsement by the Cooperative Commonwealth Federation in this cause was helpful. With reluctance, newspapers began to support Chinese Canadians in their demands for the right to vote.[14]

8. After the War

A Chinese old-timer in Timmins, Ontario, attributed the positive change in media portrayal of the Chinese to China's participation in the War with Canada as an ally, thus marking the beginning of increasing tolerance of the Chinese on the part of the white society:

> Before the Second World War, the Whites thought and believed that we Chinese were parasites contributing nothing to society. They thought that we just want to make money and did not care. But when China fought against the Japanese who were also Canada's enemies, the Whites in Timmins came to their senses. They knew that we were not what they thought we were. When we had the fund-raising parties for the war, they came too. They began to respect us. It was sad to say that it took a war for them to turn around and consider us Chinese truly human beings.[15]

In 1945, the British Columbia government granted Oriental soldiers in the Canadian armed forces the right to vote, and the Chinese civilians, two years later, were granted the same right. The repeal of the 1947 Act did not entirely liberate the Chinese from government-imposed isolation and restriction: still only wives and unmarried children of Canadian citizens under 18 years of age were allowed to land in the country. This restrictive measure against the Chinese took effect when Canada was increasing its admission of immigrants from Europe and the United States to meet a labour shortage created by an industrial boom in the post-war years.[16] It was not until 1962 that Chinese could apply as independent immigrants. The continued liberalization of federal immigration policy in subsequent years resulted in the adoption of a universal point system applicable to all racial groups, which, for the first time in the history of the Chinese-Canadians, put them on more or less equal footing with other racial groups as far as immigration matters are concerned.

Since the Second World War, the Chinese community in Canada has experienced some fundamental changes in sex ratio, age structure, size of population, and distribution and mobility of occupations. As shown in Table 8.1, between 1947 and 1962, a total of 21,877 Chinese were admitted into Canada, many of whom were sponsored immediate family members or relatives of Chinese-Canadians, the only category of immigration allowable to the Chinese until 1962. In the 1950s, many who came to Canada were wives and children, a large segment of the former not having seen their husbands since marriage in China, and a lot of the latter not having spent the early part of their childhood with their fathers.[17] The amendment of immigration policy in 1952 extended sponsorship to spouse, unmarried children under 21 years of age, fathers over 65 years old and mothers over 60 years old. In 1955, Chinese were allowed to sponsor their fiancée to come to Canada to marry. Between 1945 and 1963, more than a third of Chinese admitted into Canada were sponsored by their husbands or fiancées. Spouses, children and parents outnumbered those intended to join the labour force. A sex ratio of 3,578 (number of males per 100 females) during the 1906 to 1924 period was reduced to 98 in 1947–1962, as well as in 1968–1976.[18] The balancing of the sex ratio and the re-unification of the family after decades of exclusion, restriction, and government imposed, and government enforced, isolation began injecting a vital source of demographic, social and economic vitality the Chinese community in Canada has never experienced before. Table 8.2 indicates that it was only in 1971 that the Chinese community in Canada achieved an equitable and balanced sex ratio: 112 males per 100 females.

In Quebec, while Chinese women did not begin entering the province to a significant degree until 1946 to 1950, a balanced sex ratio was not achieved until the beginning of the 1970s.

TABLE 8.1
Number and Sex Ratio of Chinese Immigrants Admitted to Canada, and Major Immigration Legislation Affecting Chinese Immigration, 1906–1976

Period	Total Number of Chinese Immigrants Admitted to Canada	Males per 100 Females	Major Immigration Legislation	Impact on Chinese Immigrants
1906–24	43,470	3,578	Chinese Immigration Act, 1903	Head tax raised to $500
1924–46	7	—	Chinese Immigration Act, 1923	Exclusion of Chinese
1947–62	21,877	98	Repeal of 1923 Act, 1947 Immigration Act, 1952	Repeal of Exclusion, limited sponsored immigrants permitted
1963–67	18,716	72	Immigration Act, 1962	Independent and sponsored immigrants permitted
1968–76	91,490	98	Immigration Act, 1967	Universal point system applied

Source: B. Singh Bolaria and Peter S. Li (eds.), *Racial Oppression in Canada* (Toronto: Garamond Press, 1985), p. 92.

8. After the War

Out of the total of 123,406 immigrants of Chinese origin admitted into Canada from 1946 to 1975, 38.1% went to Ontario, 32% to British Columbia, 10.6% to Alberta, 9.4% to Quebec, and the rest to other provinces.[19] In contrast to the fact that all pre-war Chinese immigrants were men destined to the labour force, a large majority of those who came in the post-war period were spouses, children and elderly parents. Among those in the work force, one saw a gradual decline in the service sector, a dramatic increase in professionals, a gradual influx of immigrants in the manufacturing industry, and a rise of the level of clerical workers.[20]

TABLE 8.2
Number, Sex and Nativity of Chinese in Canada, 1881–1971

Year	Total Number of Chinese in Canada	Males per 100 Females	Percent Native Born	Chinese as Percent of Total Population in Canada
1881	4,383	—	0	.10
1891	9,129	—	0	.19
1901	17,312	—	—	.32
1911	27,831	2,790	3	.39
1921	39,587	1,533	7	.45
1931	46,519	1,241	12	.45
1941		785	20	.30
1951	32,528	374	31	.23
1961	58,197	163	40	.32
1971	118,815	112	38	.55

Source: B. Singh Bolaria and Peter S. Li (eds.), *Racial Oppression in Canada* (Toronto: Garamond Press, 1985), p. 93.

Table 8.3 shows data on the Chinese population born in foreign countries and residing in Quebec in 1981 according to sex and immigration period. The unbalanced sex ratio within the Chinese population in Quebec began before the turn of the century and persisted through the subsequent decades till early fifties. From 1931 to 1945, 90% of Chinese were males. Chinese women of any significant numbers only began coming to Quebec with the repeal of the 1923 Chinese Immigration Act, mainly in the fifties, thus narrowing the sex ratio gap quite dramatically through the sixties until

TABLE 8.3
Chinese Born in Foreign Countries and Residing in Quebec in 1981 According to Sex and Immigration Period

Sex	Total – period of immigration #	%	Up to 1931 #	%	1931–1945 #	%	1946–1950 #	%	1951–1955 #	%	1956–1960 #	%	1961–1965 #	%	1966–1970 #	%	1971–1975 #	%	1976–1981 #	%
Male	7240	51	175	74	45	90	175	66	580	66	385	49	410	39	1155	47	1380	52	2935	50
Female	7005	49	60	26	5	10	90	34	300	34	400	41	630	61	1305	53	1290	48	2930	50
Total:	14,250		235		50		265		888		785		1040		2465		2665		5865	

Source: Research Division, Ministry of Cultural Communities and Immigration, Quebec. Canada Census 1981, Special Tabulation, Table 7: Population Born in Foreign Countries and Resided in Quebec in 1981 according to Ethnic Origin, Sex and Immigration Period.

the period of 1966 to 1970 during which, for the first time ever, there were slightly more foreign-born Chinese women than men (53% versus 47%). The balancing of sex ratio was finally achieved in 1976–1981 with an almost equal number of Chinese males and females. The 4,015 Chinese females who came to Montreal between 1946 and 1975 were mainly wives and daughters left behind at home in China or Hong Kong by men who went overseas earlier.

One important feature of the changing occupational structure among the Chinese in the post-war period concerns the opening up of more and varied job opportunities as a result of the gradual evolvement and consolidation of the dual economies, and, thus, the dual job markets: the ethnic sub-economy and the mainstream economy. The Chinese are no longer confined to making a living in one or two occupational niches. They now have the freedom to make their entry into the general job market, particularly for those newcomers who were urban dwellers prior to emigration and had the educational credentials, as well as the necessary job qualifications and experience, to compete. The entry process was partly facilitated by the growth of white-collar professional sectors in the Canadian labour force in post-war years.[21]

Important changes were also taking place within the Chinese business sector too. One saw an ethnic business sector moving slowly away from a fixation on the laundry and restaurant businesses. In Montreal, within the decade of 1971 to 1981, there was a gradual increase in the number of Chinese professionals offering medical services along with an increase in the number of restaurants and food services. As of 1981, Chinese began to involve themselves to a considerable degree in a wide diversity of areas such as travel agencies, real estate, life and auto insurance, restaurant equipment retail, food container manufacturing, civil engineering, building and construction, medicine, dentistry, flower selling, fish retail, meat retail and wholesale, hair styling, printing, photography, accounting and taxation, and immigration and investment counselling. While the Chinese were diversifying their ethnic business, they have also begun locating their businesses outside of Chinatown, thus setting in motion the crucial strategies of occupational diversification and dispersion.

The introduction of a point system in 1967 created three classes of immigrants: sponsored family members, refugees and independent immigrants. The sponsored immigrants do not need to abide by the point system and many of them are not destined for the labour force. The independent immigrants are admitted solely on the basis of employability, marketable skills, education, language ability and age. Their admissibility thus hinges on their economic adaptability as well as their demonstrated ability to meet the requirements of Canadian labour force and economy given the prevailing conditions. In the case of the Chinese in Montreal, those came as sponsored or nominated immigrants, thus, under the aid of kinship ties and informal social network, were more likely than the other three immigrant categories to join the Chinese business market.[22] At most fair in English ability and with at best an elementary school education, these workers used mainly Chinese at work. A survey of a sample of 201 Chinese respondents conducted in 1977 in Montreal established that about 35% of them worked in the ethnic labour market, and 65%, in the general labour market.[23]

Those who found themselves in the general labour market came to Montreal as independent immigrants, found and held a professional or technical job through independent search, had some university education, and spoke mainly English at work.[24] Though the Chinese labour market began to diversify since post-war years, the continued domination of the restaurant and other related businesses made it impossible for the ethnic labour market to absorb its professionals and trained white collar workers. As a matter of fact, one saw the continued outflow of such skilled manpower from the Chinese community into the general labour market.

A comparison of the vertical mobility of workers in the ethnic and general markets suggests the emergence of two very distinct patterns. In comparison to Chinese workers in the general labour market, those working in the Chinese business sector were more likely to be dislocated from their former social position upon arrival in Montreal, less likely to have fulfilled their job aspirations, and were less successful in moving out of the first jobs they took up in Canada. They were engulfed in an "ethnic mobility trap".[25] A career in the ethnic labour market is like a branch stretching outward and away from the tree trunk, from all serious opportunities of job training, promotion and mobility. A waiter in a Chinese restaurant may well one day become a manager or even an owner himself since the ceiling is low and, thus, takes less time to reach. Yet the ceiling tops it all and that is often all what a waiter hopes for. For the vast majority of restaurant waiters, kitchen helpers, cooks, and so on, the trap is a real one and the upward climb is often more illusionary than real. Chances are this waiter needs the kinship ties to come to Canada, and, thus, feels obliged to repay his kin by working in his "kinsman's store", an obligation that often paves one's path to the trap of exploitation and life-long career confinement.[26] Within the Chinese

8. After the War

labour market, the kin network and the family "turn inward, pool their resources together, and exploit themselves with the most abundant source at hand: cheap labour".[27] Hundreds of these manual workers were trapped in "dead-end" jobs that are traditionally low in pay, unchanging and immobile, and are unprotected by unions with job security and benefits.[28] These same job characteristics further reinforce the isolation of the Chinese workers from the mainstream Montreal community.

As for those in the general labour market, one saw structural obstacles and barriers hidden beneath the increasing popularity of careers in data-processing, computer and accounting among the second-generation Chinese. The 1971 census indicates that the average annual income for the Chinese in the Canadian work force was about $1,000 less than the national average.[29] This income differential persisted into 1985, suggesting the continued existence of racially based obstacles in the general labour market for the Chinese.[30]

Up to 1955, the People's Republic of China and Taiwan remained as the two principal sources of Chinese immigrants in Quebec. In 1956 to 1960, 130 immigrants from Hong Kong landed in Quebec, compared to 290 from China and 325 from Taiwan. For the subsequent two decades between 1961 and 1981, Hong Kong contributed a fair share of immigrants in Quebec, along with China and Taiwan. In actual fact, from 1971 to 1975, more immigrants in Quebec came from Hong Kong (780) than any other source country. The political upheaval in Southeast Asia since 1975 was responsible for a sudden influx of ethnic Chinese in Montreal. Between 1976 and 1981, 280 ethnic Chinese in Montreal came from Cambodia, 95 from Laos, and 1,275 from Vietnam, giving a total of 1,650 ethnic Chinese arriving in Montreal from Indochina as refugees or as their sponsored relatives.

According to the 1981 Canadian Census, out of the 19,260 Chinese in the province of Quebec, 3,550 were from the Republic of China (Taiwan), 3,145 from People's Republic of China, 2,410 from Hong Kong, 2000 from Vietnam, 695 from Mauritius, 390 from Cambodia, 340 from Madagascar, 295 from Trinidad and Tobago, and 210 from Laos. Taiwan, China, Hong Kong and Southeast Asia (Vietnam, Cambodia and Laos) thus accounted for more than half (about 58%) of the total Chinese population in Quebec, while the Quebec-born Chinese only accounted for about a quarter (24%) with 360, or no more than 2%, born elsewhere in Canada. The net result is that about three quarters of the Chinese community of Montreal in 1981

TABLE 8.4
Total Chinese Population (By Ethnic Origin) in Quebec in 1981
According to Place of Birth

Numerical Rank	Place of Birth	Number	Percent
1	Quebec	4,650	24.1
2	Taiwan	3,550	18.4
3	China	3,145	16.3
4	Hong Kong	2,410	12.5
5	Vietnam	2,000	10.4
6	Mauritius	695	3.6
7	Cambodia	390	2.0
8	Canada (outside Quebec)	360	1.9
9	Madagascar	340	1.8
10	Trinidad and Tobago	295	1.5
11	Laos	210	1.1
12	Malaysia	170	0.9
13	United Kingdom	120	0.6
14	Jamaica	115	0.5
14	Indonesia	115	0.5
16	Philippines	80	0.4
17	United States	60	0.3
18	West Germany	40	0.2
18	India	40	0.2
20	Singapore	35	0.2
21	Thailand	30	0.1
21	France	30	0.1
23	Japan	20	0.1
23	Morocco	20	0.1
23	Brunei	20	0.1
23	Burma	20	0.1
	All others	235	1.2
	Total	19,260	100.0

Source: Research Division, Ministry of Cultural Communities and Immigration, Quebec. Canada Census 1981, Special Tabulation, Table 5: Total Quebec Population in 1981, according to Detailed Place of Birth, Sex and Ethnic Origin.

were foreign-born, primarily Asian, immigrants who emigrated into the French–Canadian metropolis.

Between 1980 and 1982, 5,500 business immigrants were admitted to Canada, bringing an estimated $1.5 billion into the country and having created about 10,000 new jobs.[31] The socio-economic and occupational

8. After the War

profile of the Chinese community in Quebec took a sudden "upward" swing in 1983 when the federal government began actively implementing a policy of attracting immigrant investors to Canada. This federal policy proved particularly attractive to Chinese investors from Hong Kong who were fearful of the political and economic future of the British Colony, whose sovereignty will be returned to the People's Republic of China in 1997. Although Hong Kong is "guaranteed" by the Chinese government minimum political intervention as well as maximum economic autonomy for fifty years following 1997, an increasing number of Chinese businessmen find Canada to be an attractive place for their investment. Hong Kong is the world's third largest financial centre, after New York and London, and also the third largest container port.

On 24 October 1983, John Roberts, then federal Minister of Employment and Immigration, announced a new program to promote the admission of entrepreneurs as immigrants, effective 1 January 1984. Under the amended immigration regulation, "an entrepreneur must intend and be able to establish or purchase or make a substantial investment in the ownership of a business or commercial venture in Canada whereby employment opportunities will be created or continued for one or more Canadian citizen or permanent residents." The entrepreneur or business class will be given priority in the processing of their application for immigration, second to the family class members and refugees. While intended to include a higher processing priority for entrepreneurial applicants, the program set forth the posting of specially trained officers in key source countries (West Germany, Hong Kong, France, the United States and the Netherlands), as well as a two-year provisional admission for well qualified applicants who have not yet fully developed their business ventures. The primary intent of the program is to create jobs and this reflects the political and economic realities in Canada.

In February 1984, less than four months after the public announcement of the federal program, Gerald Godin, then Quebec Minister of Cultural Communities and Immigration, went on his "millionaire mission" to Hong Kong to "sell his wares"[32] and to "woo the well-off businessmen there". In his sales pitch, Godin promised cheap and spacious land, cheap rents and cheap hydro-power for Quebec, while extolling the virtues of Montreal as a cosmopolitan metropolitan, "bilingual city open to two cultures at the same time, English and French speaking".[33] Another important agenda on his Hong Kong mission was to personally counter what he called a "disgusting" anti-Quebec campaign by other provinces; Ontario, Alberta and Manitoba were alleged to "have been bad-mouthing Quebec over there, in the competition for investment money flowing from the British colony before it returns to Chinese rule in 1997".[34] Godin also alleged that these provinces described Quebec as a place of "separatism, political uncertainty, very severe language laws".[35] Godin singled out Hong Kong trips made by then Ontario Premier Bill Davis and then Alberta Premier Peter Lougheed to "blacken" the image of Quebec.[36] In an attempt to maintain a competitive edge, it was proposed to the provincial cabinet by Godin that a team of trade, intergovernmental affairs and tourism officials be added to the existing immigration office to create a Maison Quebec in Hong Kong.

The number of applications for immigration made by immigrant investors grew nearly 10% from 1983 to 1984, mainly due to the number of applications from Hong Kong which increased by 93.5% over one year. The three countries from which Quebec received the largest number of applications from immigrant investors in 1984 were, in order of importance, Hong Kong, France and Switzerland. These countries accounted for 55% of all applications accepted by Quebec, and 56% of the capital, $300 million in total.

Table 8.5 shows that Quebec received a total of 314 cases of immigrant investor applications (38%) from Hong Kong out of a total of 818 cases from 66 different countries. Compared to the total capital of $533,469,000 supplied by all 66 countries in 1984, Hong Kong investors brought in $244,303,000, averaging $778,000 per case which is considerably higher than the average capital of $652,000 for all 66 countries. In terms of distribution of immigrant investor applicants by sector of activity in 1984, those 314 cases from Hong Kong were concentrated, in order of concentration and importance, in wholesale (69 cases); finance, real estate (39 cases); retail (33 cases); clothing and textiles (32 cases); and hotel and restaurants (31 cases). While wholesale, finance and real estate, and clothing and textiles brought in the most capital dollars, the average capital per case was highest in furniture, followed by paper; metal, machinery, transport, electricals; watches, jewelry, toys and other; construction; and services. Like investors from the other 65 countries, Hong Kong businessmen tended to concentrate in the secondary and tertiary sectors in terms of distribution of cases of applications, total capital brought in, and average capital per case. Over the two years in 1983 and 1984, one saw the relative decrease in importance of French and other romance languages (Italian, Spanish, Por-

TABLE 8.5
Immigrant Investor Applicants from Hong Kong by Sector of Activity in 1984

	Number of cases in 1984	Total capital in 1984 ($)	Average capital per case in 1984 ($)
Primary sector	3	2,180,000	726,000
Secondary sector			
Food and agriculture	3	478,000	159,000
Plastics	9	6,791,000	754,000
Leather	11	6,817,000	619,000
Clothing and Textiles	32	26,479,000	827,000
Furniture	1	3,470,000	3,420,000
Paper	4	5,887,000	1,471,000
Printing and publishing	4	1,312,000	328,000
Metal, machinery, transport, electricals	10	13,193,000	1,319,000
Watches, jewelry, toys and other	18	21,103,000	1,172,000
Tertiary sector			
Construction	17	19,567,000	1,151,000
Transport, communications	5	2,257,000	451,000
Wholesale	69	45,218,000	655,000
Retail	33	17,060,000	516,000
Finance, real estate	39	35,012,000	897,000
Services	11	10,406,000	946,000
Hotels, restaurants	31	16,729,000	539,000
Other	14	10,394,000	742,000
Total	314	244,303,000	778,000

Source: Ministry of Cultural Communities and Immigration, Quebec, 1985.

tuguese) to the benefit of English, a development principally due to the increase of Hong Kong investors in 1984.

To step up Canadian overseas exploitation of the "gold mine", particularly in the Far East, Ottawa in 1986 created an "investor" category designed to bring to Canada people having a personal, net worth of at least $500,000, at least half of which is to be invested in new or existing Canadian businesses over a three-year period. Unlike the previous "entrepreneur immigrant" category, the investor is required to make only a "passive" investment in furthering Canada's economic development: he or she need not be directly involved in the day-to-day management of the business.

Reacting to this new federal program, the Quebec government promptly published in late 1986 a brochure titled "Choosing to Live and Invest in Quebec"[37] as part of an information and publicity campaign to lure "immigrant investors" to Quebec. In the brochure's subsection titled, "Why they chose to live in Quebec", the province was described as "a gateway to North America", a "meeting point between Europe and North America", noting Montreal's physical adjacency to New York City and Boston. Other Quebec characteristics and advantages stressed in the brochure include the province's ready access to "one of the widest markets in the world at competitive costs"; a six and a half million population made up of peoples from 80 different source countries; a democratic government promising "stability and continuity" as well as a guarantee of individual rights; quality education at all levels; "a world-famous quality of life"; and Montreal having the lowest housing costs of all the major North American cities.

Out of six "successful" immigrant investors profiled in the beginning of the brochure, two are of Chinese descent: One was a former Parisian restaurateur originally from Hong Kong, and the other, a hotel owner from Singapore. In October 1986, Louise Robic, Quebec Minister of Cultural Communities and Immigration, went to Hong Kong on the occasion of the opening of a new stock exchange there. She admitted that Quebec is "in competition with the United States and with Australia and with other countries and with other provinces of Canada who have a similar program to try to attract investors who have money and could come in and invest here and help us develop our business base and also create jobs."[38] The businesses in question are small- and medium-size companies with assets worth less than $25 million and net worth less than $10 million, a sector the Quebec economy depends on. By promoting these investments in a "diver-

8. After the War

sified portfolio" and businesses that are currently in expansion, the program will take care of the concern of some investors wanting to invest in excess of $250,000, and thus "taking over" an existing business in Quebec. This "shot-in-the-arm" is estimated to bring into Quebec about "100 business immigrants with a combined $25 million of capital during its first year."[39] In what the Montreal media described as a "sales trip" to Hong Kong, Robic was to stress to the prospective investors the following:

> Montreal being an international city, it is an interesting place to come and live. And we are just beside the biggest markets in the world—the United States, and being able to offer the new Quebecer the possibility of keeping his language and his culture. We are mosaic here.[40]

In spite of these sales pitch trips, "millionaire hunts", and counter-image campaigns by two Quebec immigration ministers, businessmen immigrants continued to be concerned with the province's Parti Québécois separatist movement and its French language law that restricts access to English primary and secondary schools to children whose parents received their primary education in Quebec in English. Totally foreign to people in Hong Kong, the French language will be more a major obstacle than the separatist movement.[41] In 1983, Canada was able to admit 7000 business class immigrants from Hong Kong. Quebec managed to attract only 10% of the total with Toronto and Vancouver proving more attractive to the bulk of the Hong Kong businessmen.[42]

Notes

1. Peter S. Li, "Chinese" (p. 92), in *Racial Oppression in Canada*, edited by B. Singh Bolaria and Peter S. Li (Toronto: Garamond Press, 1985), pp. 81–104.
2. Oral history interview with Mr. Arthur Li, at Wing's Noodles, Montreal, Quebec, 20 August 1986.
3. Ibid.
4. Peter S. Li, p. 91.
5. Ibid., p. 93.
6. Ibid., p. 95.
7. Dan Burke, "Vice Era is Over," in *Sunday Express*, 21 August 1983.
8. David T.H. Lee 李東海 . *Jianada Huaqiao shi* 加拿大華僑史 (A History of Chinese in Canada) (British Columbia: Ziyou chubanshe 自由出版社 , 1967), p. 104. (text in Chinese.)
9. Kwok B. Chan and Lawrence Lam, "Chinese in Timmins, Canada, 1915–1950: A

Study of Ethnic Stereotypes in the Press", in *Asian Profile*, Vol. 14:6 December 1986, pp. 569–83.
10. Wing-wah Ing, "Letters to the Editor", in *The Chinese Press*, Montreal, Quebec, 28 March 1987.
11. Peter S. Li, p. 91.
12. Wai-man Lee (ed.), *Portraits of a Challenge: An Illustrated History of the Chinese Canadians* (Toronto: Council of Chinese Canadians in Ontario, 1984), p. 169.
13. Kwok B. Chan, Oral history interview with Mr. Jack Huang, at the Chinese Freemasons, 1072 St. Laurent Boulevard, Montreal, Quebec (5, 6 and 11 May 1983), p. 27.
14. Wai-man Lee, p. 169.
15. Chan and Lam, p. 579.
16. Peter S. Li, p. 97.
17. Oral history interview with William Dere, at 234 Westminster, Montreal, Quebec, January 1987.
18. Peter S. Li, p. 92.
19. Laura Yuen-Ha Pao-Mercier, *Immigration, Ethnicity and the Labour Market: The Chinese in Montreal* (M.A. thesis, Department of Sociology, McGill University, Montreal, Quebec, Canada, November 1981), p. 21.
20. Ibid., p. 21.
21. Peter S. Li, p. 100.
22. Laura Yuen-Ha Pao-Mercier, p. 58.
23. Ibid., p. 40.
24. Ibid., p. 60.
25. Norbert F. Wiley, "The Ethnic Mobility Trap and Stratification Theory," in *Social Problems, 15*, pp. 147–59.
26. Peter S. Li, "Occupational Achievement and Kinship Assistance Among Chinese Immigrants in Chicago," in *Sociological Quarterly*, 18 (Autumn 1977), pp. 478–89.
27. Rebecca Aiken, "Montreal Chinese Property Ownership and Occupational Change 1881–1981" (Ph.D. Thesis, Department of Anthropology, McGill University, Montreal, Quebec, Canada, 1984), p. 265.
28. Ibid., p. 264.
29. Peter S. Li, "Income Achievement and Adaptive Capacity: An Empirical Comparison of Chinese and Japanese in Canada," in *Visible Minorities and Multiculturalism: Asians in Canada* (Scarborough, Ontario: Butterworths and Co., 1980), pp. 363–78.
30. Peter S. Li, "Chinese," in *Racial Oppression in Canada* (Toronto: Garamond Press, 1985), p. 104.
31. "Entrepreneurs Sought as Immigrants," in *Contrast*, 11 November 1983, p. 5.
32. Greta Chambers, "Let the Welcome be Real," in *The Gazette*, 25 February 1984, p. B3.
33. "Godin Tries to Lure Hong Kong Investors," in *The Gazette*, 21 February 1984, p. A3.
34. "Tell It in Hong Kong," in *The Gazette* (Editorial), 14 February 1984, p. B2.

8. After the War 233

35. Ibid., p. B2
36. Montreal CBMT 23:50 News, 12 February 1984.
37. *Choosing to Live and Invest in Quebec* (Montreal: Direction des communications and Direction des services aux investisseurs du Ministere des Communautés Culturelles et de l'Immigration, 1986).
38. Montreal CJAD 18:10 News, 16 September 1986.
39. "Quebec Eases Rules to Attract Wealthy Immigrants," in *The Gazette*, 17 September 1986, p. C1. (Source: Canadian Press.)
40. Montreal CBM 7:24 Daybreak, 10 February 1986.
41. Shirley Won, "Quebec Hustling to Win Business from Hong Kong," in *The Gazette*, 12 May 1984, p. C1.
42. John Procter, "Hong Kong Money-men Wary of 'Operation Millionaire'," in *The Gazette*, 25 February 1984, p. B5.

9. Will You Provide for Me When I Am Old?[1]

A widow. Photograph taken on 1011 Clark Street, Montreal Chinatown.

Will you provide for me when I am old? Photograph taken at the entrance of a Chinese restaurant at the corner of Clark and Lagauchetière streets.

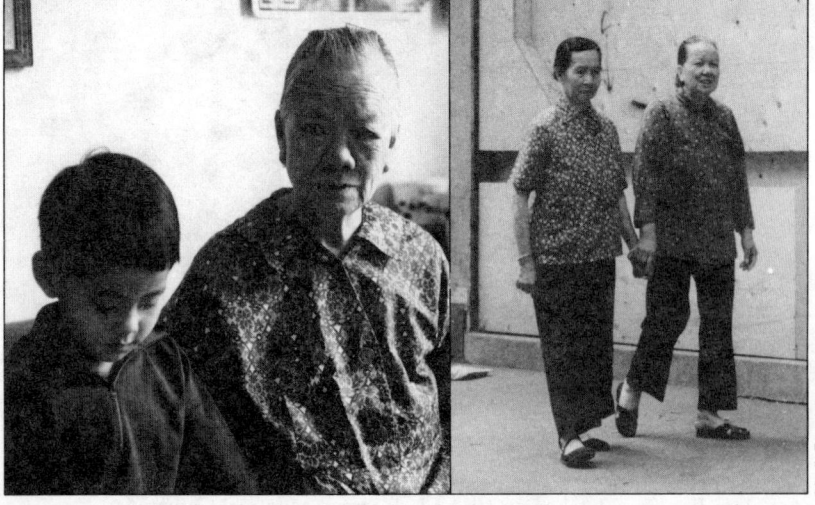

Grandma.

Sometimes.

DURING the fifties and the sixties, after the repeal of the Chinese Immigration Act in 1947, wives and daughters were sent for by the Cantonese men for a reunion with them in Canada. This was after a separation of twenty to thirty years for some, and much longer for many. Between the time the couples were married in China and their reunion in Canada, only a few women managed to see their husbands while the latter paid short visits to China, often making sojourns of one to three years.

For married male "bachelors", prolonged deprivation of a family life and marital separation had several adverse social, psychological and economic consequences. Among other things, one saw lack of initiative in owning property and making economic investment in Canada; improper balance of work and leisure; residential segregation and socio-cultural isolation within the Chinese "ghetto"; loneliness and alienation; alcoholism and heavy smoking; poor physical and mental health; and pursuit of such illicit activities as gambling, prostitution and opium use. Indeed, one of the pressing reasons that prompted husbands to send for their wives and children was that they realized they were approaching old age, had serious infirmities, and were very fearful of the prospect of aging and dying alone in a foreign land. Many of the elderly Chinese women were literally brought to Canada to nurse their ailing husbands, who then passed away within years after the family reunion in Canada.

Husbands periodically sent money back to China to support families left behind. However, life in the poverty-stricken Chinese village was difficult, and women often worked long hours as farmers or labourers to help support the family. Upon arrival in Canada, these women were often shocked by the reality of a poor, ill, aging and dependent husband. Many, in fact, continued to work to support their husbands and children, mainly as dishwashers or manual labourers in Chinese restaurants and food processing companies until they were eligible for federal and provincial old-age pensions.

These women had a history of hard work and devotion to their husbands and children. This might have engendered within them a sense of psychological hardiness, which, in turn, might have buffered them from the direct onslaught of the storm and stress of life. Strong and self-sufficient, these women played an integral and indispensable role in holding the family together, both in China and in Canada.

With the old age pension, the average monthly income of these women amounted to about $500. Since the cost of room rental and other daily expenses and necessities were low, rarely exceeding $200 per month, these women were, in general, satisfied with their present standard of living. They very rarely ran into serious financial difficulties. As a matter of fact, they saw retirement at the age of 65 as a relief from hard, menial and low-pay work.

> My husband and I worked very hard throughout our lives. I think I worked even harder and longer hours in Canada than in China. I often put in 16 hours a day and 7 days a week in the Chinese restaurant across the street. Now I can depend on the government for the rest of my life—we call the government "the good old man". The Canadian government is very nice to us and we feel very, very grateful. Every woman I know looks forward to turning 65 when she will get the old age pension. I have more than enough to live by—I do not spend very much. Throughout my life, I never spend more than is necessary.[2]

Daily, these women went through a number of routine activities: shopping for groceries and daily necessities; doing physical exercise; watching Chinese television; reading Chinese newspapers and magazines; and listening to tape-recorded Chinese music. Activities undertaken at least once a week included receiving and entertaining friends or relatives at home; visiting friends and relatives in Chinatown; watching movies shown at Chinese cinemas; attending events organized by community organizations or agencies in Chinatown; and going to church. Activities rarely pursued were: reading non-Chinese newspapers, magazines or books; watching movies at non-Chinese cinemas; going to city museums; and going out for dinners or luncheons.

The following excerpt from fieldwork notes illustrates what a typical day is like for these elderly women:

> I usually wake up at about half-past six in the morning. I would start my day preparing for myself a simple breakfast—usually a bit of Chinese rice soup or a bowl of rice with leftovers from supper the night before. I would take about an hour to finish the breakfast. I eat quite slowly. Then I sit around, clean up the kitchen, sit around again, chat with my neighbours, listen to the Chinese music tapes and what not. Then I start preparing my lunch around noon or slightly earlier. Real simple food: a bowl of rice with vegetables and some meat. Then I clean up the kitchen, and sit around chatting. Sometimes I go back to my room, turn on the radio and do some knitting or sewing. I make all my clothes myself. If it is a nice, sunny day, I would leave my room around three o'clock, walk a few blocks, sometimes alone, sometimes accompanied by a few women who also live on this level. We often go grocery shopping at supermarkets on St. Laurent (outside Chinatown) together. It is better to go outside Chinatown once in a while with someone. We often sit inside the Complexe Desjardins (an air-conditioned provincial building within a short walking distance from Chinatown) for the entire afternoon. We just sit and watch

people passing by. On a hot summer day, I would rather sit there than stay inside this stuffy and smelly room of mine. Then we would walk back to our rooms around five or six o'clock. By then, it is time to cook again. My diet is a very simple one, always very simple—I would add one or two extra dishes when my folks (a son and two grandchildren) come to visit me and stay for dinner. Then I clean up the kitchen for the use of others. The other twelve women on this floor usually start preparing their dinners around this time. We talk a lot while cooking in the common kitchen. At about nine o'clock in the evening, I would go back to my own room; I might read the newspaper, or turn on the television or radio, or, if I am tired, I would go straight to bed. During the winter, I sometimes stay inside the building for more than two weeks. It is too cold out there. I always have enough food to last for a month. When it snows, the roads become very slippery and very dangerous. I fell once and was taken to the hospital. The streets of Chinatown are narrow and I do not want to fight with the cars and delivery trucks which pass by Chinatown very often. There are a lot of things I do not do during the winter.

The total social space, as perceived by these women, was clearly divided into four compartments: the room, the public space on one floor of the rooming house (common kitchen and corridor), Chinatown (stores, churches, community organizations, streets, and so on) and the environs (stores, public buildings within two or three blocks from Chinatown). These four physical compartments constituted the total ecological context of their daily activities. While cognitive unfamiliarity with non-Chinese culture and customs, inability to communicate in French and English, and a diffuse sense of anxiety and fear about the physical environment acted as barriers, it was such factors as weather, perception of physical hazards in the urban context possibly caused by a combination of heavy automobile traffic, narrow streets and pedestrian walks, and fear of victimization by crime, that determined which activity was done where, when, and for how long.

While the women seemed to have been engaged in a number of social activities regularly and intensively, a large number of other activities such as attending non-Chinese community events or going to museums and public libraries were very rarely, if ever, pursued at all. Activities engaged in as a routine include those that are culture-bound, things that can be done on their own within the room or the premises. The women themselves decided and chose what activities to undertake with others outside their rooms or the premises. Their participation in the social milieu outside Chinatown was almost non-existent. Their own social milieu was, therefore, a well-defined and self-enclosed one, circumscribed by unfamiliarity with, and lack of interest, in the larger community and the mainstream culture.

They viewed movement within this self-delimited social space as familiar, manageable, physically safe and relatively free from victimization by crime. For these women, the average length of residence within Chinatown was seven years; six have lived there for more than twelve years and another four have been Chinatown residents for sixteen years or longer. All claimed they have lived in the district long enough to know everybody else within the building and the majority of the residents in the district. The high degree of social familiarity seemed to serve as an effective crime-detection and protection device, and helped to engender in the residents a sense of personal security.

On a typical day, the elderly women spent a substantial amount of social time among themselves. The two most popular places on a specific floor within the building were the kitchen and the corridor. Food preparation during meal times of the day in the common kitchen was a conspicuous activity of high interpersonal density. After meal times, the women often sat around in the corridor chatting. Information about self, others, and recent happenings within the community was often exchanged and discussed. The significance of these social occasions in the public place seemed to lie, therefore, not only in acquiring information through exchange, but also in engendering in the women a collective feeling of in-group cohesiveness and security. The individual felt that she belonged to the group and the neighbourhood; she felt secure as part of a larger unit. The availability of social occasions to acquire and share information about life and living was of strategic importance in view of the fact that almost none of these women ever used public, non-Chinese media.

> I should say people who live on this floor are quite close to each other. The younger and more healthy women look out for and try to take care of the older ones. We lend each other chairs and tables when one of us suddenly has a lot of visitors. We all have our own cooking utensils though—these are things we do not lend out as readily. When problems, such as medical emergency, arise, we all help to call up a Chinese doctor. We often approach each other for suggestions or help on things we cannot do or manage on our own. I will not go as far as saying that we are a family here, but neither do we turn our back on those who need immediate help. I often ask my neighbours if there is a sale in the nearby supermarkets, or where one can go for a free television or movie show, and things like that. It is always nice to know what is happening around here. If there is a theft or robbery in the neighbourhood, everybody would know the next day. We will then be a little more careful and watchful.

Densely crammed into the small Chinatown district are a multitude of family and clan associations, medical and dental clinics, churches, the headquarters of the Chinese Nationalist and Communist parties, cultural and socio-recreational associations and a social service agency. In general, the women seemed to have a good knowledge of what Chinese organization was situated where, offering what kinds of services. Mainly because of their accessibility, services available in Chinatown were often utilized. Identification of these women with the service agencies was strong. It was through the mediation of these agencies that these women were able to make contact with governmental bodies and to obtain assistance in filling out applications for federal and provincial subsidies. Having little knowledge of services and resources available at institutions and agencies outside the Chinese community, these elderly women rarely went outside Chinatown for help.

After the Second World War, with the demise of the traditional Chinese clan associations coupled with the fact that the few social agencies in the area have confined themselves to delivering such basic services as interpretation, information and referral as a result of inadequate governmental funding and lack of community support, Montreal Chinatown has transformed itself into essentially a commercial and tourist district with much of its physical space taken up by restaurants, grocery stores and art and craft businesses. The area is extremely low in community resources and services. As a community, it lacks a comprehensive social service support system and is very far from being institutionally complete. Chinatown does not have a single cultural and recreational centre. In the past five years, parks and patches of green space were expropriated to make room for urban growth and expansion, thus depriving the area of the only remaining public space for leisurely gatherings. There is, thus, a serious need for a public open space for residents in the area, especially the elderly. The provision of such services and public amenities as a club or centre for the elderly and for women, an amusement park, a Chinese cultural and recreational centre, a sports complex, and so on, was generally seen by residents of the area as most necessary and lacking.

One community worker from a nearby social service agency made the following observation:

> These elderly women spend a lot of their time and do most of their own things inside their own room or building. This is especially true during winter time when it is slippery and dangerous outside. I think the weather condition of the day affects directly whether they are staying indoors or not. There is no place in Chinatown for them to go to. There is a club for the elderly not too far from where they live, but it is

all gambling, mainly mah-jong. Some of my clients do not go there because they either do not know how to play mah-jong or they hate the game. I always have this idea of finding a room in Chinatown and install a video television monitor in it. We can help organizing these elderly women such that they will work out among themselves a schedule to show Chinese movies or television variety shows routinely and regularly. I am sure that these women are healthy and enthusiastic enough to initiate, develop and implement their own social programs. All they need is a bit of support and guidance from us. It is very important that they know there is a place nearby they can go and feel at home. A place to sit and chat, and meet their peers. An elderly club or centre like the one I just described will certainly give a bit of spice and variety to their daily routine. They need a place to go to when they feel like it, a place organized by and for themselves. Besides, this will give them a potent source of social stimulation, which, I think, will be eventually conducive to their mental health and psychological well-being.

Almost all of the rooming-house apartments in the Chinatown area are owned by the Chinese. Very few of these apartments have undergone any major renovations or electrical and plumbing repairs in the past fifteen years. Most of the rooms are small. On a particular floor, the women share one common kitchen, thus necessitating almost daily adjustment during food preparation times; they also share among themselves one or two washrooms depending on the number of rooms on a particular floor. Most windows in individual rooms are sealed during winter time to prevent heat loss. The women residents are concerned with the possibility of injuries and death caused by fire; the rooms being too small and restricting; too much or too little heat due to heating problems; and poor air ventilation.

The women expressed a keen interest and a sense of urgency in applying for admission into either new or renovated housing units for the elderly. All would like this housing unit to be built within the Chinatown area, preferably within one or two blocks from where they presently live. Low, rather than high-rise, apartment buildings were preferred, reflecting a basic need of the elderly persons for security and accessibility to the ground. Also expressed was an interest in moving into the housing unit together with their present neighbours, preferably taking up apartments on the same floor or at least as close to each other as possible. It seems that the stress of relocation can be considerably alleviated by ensuring the minimum disruption of the former social fabric.

Many of these women had lived with their children and grandchildren within, or outside, the Montreal metropolitan area prior to moving into Chinatown. For them, the death of their husbands seemed to have intensified their desire to move out on their own, preferably in areas with a substantial Chinese population. There were several reasons for their decision to maintain a separate residence from their family.

First, there were problems of intergenerational value conflicts and differences in lifestyles. As parents, these elderly women seemed very much aware of differences and conflicts between themselves and their married children and their sons-in-law and daughters-in-law in such family decision-making matters as child rearing, family control and authority, family expenditures, leisure and entertainment. The elderly women, despite years of residence in Canada, were still practising the traditional values of familism and morality characteristic of the working-class peasantry of the past generations in a tradition-bound, static Chinese society. Their children, having spent their prime years in Canada, were more Westernized and assimilated into the core values of Canadian society. The intensity of value differences seemed to be a lot more apparent and acute between the first and the third generations.

The emergence of fierce and intense conflicts between mothers and their daughters-in-law has been a long-standing phenomenon in traditional Chinese families. These conflicts often revolve around issues regarding how, and according to what set of values, the grandchildren are to be raised, who has more access to whose affection and attention, the distribution of control and authority in the family, and the desirability of adhering to such Chinese "virtues" as respect for, and support of, the elderly. While mothers feel that tradition dictates that they have legitimate and rightful access to their own son's affection and respect, the daughters-in-law believe that their husband's loyalty and obligations are first and foremost to them and their children.

The Chinese-Canadians of the second generation have long realized the need to work hard and achieve both for themselves and for their children in a society where such structural and institutional forces as prejudice and discrimination against members of a visible minority are still very much at work. Educational achievement, hard work, frugality and occupational success have very quickly become the core of a child-rearing philosophy passed onto their Canadian-born children. Sons of elderly women, like their fathers, had a long history of hard work and suffering in a wide range of menial and low-paid jobs in the service and food industries. Many worked long hours, foregoing weekends and holidays, to accumulate savings for future investment in business or in their children's education. As a result, they have very little time and energy to spend with their elderly mothers and family.

> I and my husband had lived with our son and his family in Lasalle for twelve years. Then four years ago, my husband passed away. All these years, my son often felt sorry that he had to spend a lot of time working in the restaurant [he co-owned it with three other partners] and was not able to spend time with me. There were times I had not seen him for days or even weeks. He worked very hard, like his father, to save for his children's education. He worked very hard for his family. I felt sorry for him, and more so, for myself. I did not get along very well with my daughter-in-law; she did not like the way I fed and raised her kids. I always wonder where she got the right to be jealous of my own son being nice to me. My grandchildren were still very young and were afraid of their mother. They behaved to me in a strange way. Once in a while, they forgot that I am their grandmother. It became worse when half of the time they were speaking English or French with me.

Isolation in the suburban homes became a severe problem for these elderly women, especially when communication with members of the household was often difficult and occasionally confrontational. In times of increasing family tension, many elderly women felt the need to get out of the home for a walk in the neighbourhood or a long trip to somewhere, but were handicapped by lack of means of transportation and unfamiliarity with the environment. One woman remembered those years of living with her children as waiting weeks and months before she was taken to Chinatown to shop for groceries or visit friends who lived there. While going to Chinatown to spend time sociably with friends and relatives was an experience remembered with fond memories, it also reinforced in the elderly women her acute sense of isolation.

Any cursory look at the elderly women's history of living with their children and families in the suburb reveals a complexity of "push" and "pull" factors associated with their decision to move into the rooming houses in Chinatown. One might want to argue that such factors as intergenerational and familial conflicts, and isolation and alienation in the suburb due to language and cultural barriers "pushed the women away" from their former residence. Other factors such as co-residence with, and accessibility to, peers, familiarity with the ecology of the neighbourhood, a sense of belonging to an ethnic community and its institutions, availability of community resources and services, and freedom of movement, were strong "pull" forces to make living in Chinatown an attractive alternative.

The women were not hesitant in citing "convenience to shop" as the foremost advantage of living in Chinatown. Other advantages included: convenience and safety to walk around; ease of communication with other residents; meeting people of same culture and background; proximity to many Chinese friends and neighbours; cheap rent; and proximity to church, community and social services.

> It is safe here. I am not afraid to walk around anymore. I have a lot of friends who live within a few blocks from each other. I do not have to ask anybody to give me a ride to shop or to see a friend or relative. My family used to think I am blind, deaf and dumb—we did not talk much to each other. We all speak the same language here; we talk among each other a lot. Am I really that deaf and dumb?

The elderly women were on old-age pension, about $500 a month. They were also often given some pocket money by their children every once in a while, particularly during such Chinese festivals or holidays as the Chinese New Year and the Autumn Moon Festival. Some had inherited a modest sum of money from their dead husbands. In view of their frugal living, careful management of finances, and low rents, many of these women reported that their lives were adequate and comfortable. Some even managed to send $300 to $400 a year to close and distant relatives in China. Others still considered it a familial and moral obligation on their part to aid their families in Canada when special circumstances necessitated it, or to buy them food stuffs and gifts when they were paying their periodic suburban visits. One woman revealed that she recently loaned her son a sum of four thousand dollars to aid in his faltering restaurant business.

Frugal living, half a century of self-care, hard work and saving, and a steady income from government allowance have combined to give these women a sense of financial and psychological independence, a sense of control over their own lives. That they are still able to render financial assistance to "members of the family" in China and Canada may have engendered in them a strong sense of personal control, thus continuing to fulfil their moral and familial obligations as the elder kin members. It is also through playing the role of a helping matriarch in the larger extended family that these women manage their self-identity and safeguard their sense of continuity with the family and kin. For these women, dignity and self-identity are managed by striving for independence, and by continuing within their own means to fulfil the duties and obligations of a family benefactor, rendering help where it is most needed.

The move away from children and grandchildren and the decision to join other peers in the Chinatown rooming houses is indeed a courageous one. Such a move utterly shatters her own fantasy of three generations of the family living under the same roof with the elder members being cared for, loved and respected by the younger ones. By making this decision to move into Chinatown, she is admitting to herself and to everybody else that things are not working out very well in her family, that she herself might be partially to blame for this "family failure", and, finally, that the traditional virtue of filial piety is a virtue, but a far cry from reality. However, she can then persuade herself that separate dwellings as an alternative mode of accommodation will give her the autonomy and freedom she needs. It is also an arrangement whereby intergenerational friction and power struggles are avoided. Interpersonal cordiality and intimacy are thus maintained when family members realize, acknowledge and accept the stresses and strains of living together, but still strive to help each other when needed.

A community worker commented on a woman client he had worked with:

> This client of mine is quite bitter about the way she was treated by her family when she was living with them. She moved into Chinatown three years ago. Now she is happy with her neighbours and housemates. Twice a week she calls her son and grandchildren in St. Laurent. They call her a lot, too. Sometimes they talk for more than an hour on the phone. She always spends Christmas and New Year with her family. Her son comes to Chinatown every Monday afternoon to do grocery shopping, and he will go up to see her. Monday is his day off. Sometimes, during the weekends, he will bring his children and wife to visit grandma. The two kids stay overnight with their grandma every now and then, and their father will come back the next morning to pick them up. The two kids seem to like their grandma a whole lot more now than before. I think it is kind of nice.

Canadian society holds two contradictory views about the elderly Chinese. First, they, like other members of ethnic minorities, suffer from "triple jeopardy" (being Chinese, old and female)[3] and, therefore, are much worse off than other Canadian counterparts. Second, they are protected by filial piety, a much-admired Chinese virtue. There is a long-held myth that the Chinese elderly are well respected and cared for in a three-generational family structure, a view labelled as the "Chinese veto".[4] Unfortunately, for the bulk of the elderly Chinese women in Montreal, the likely answer to the question (asked by many Chinese parents in North America now) "Will my children provide for me when I am old?" is negative. Such a reality is indeed considerably different from the all-familiar idyllic accounts of the Chinese family. In managing familial conflicts, the women opt for independence to safeguard their sense of self-identity.

At the turn of the century, these women were left behind by their husbands who had to go abroad to work to feed themselves and everybody else in the family. In the subsequent half-century, the men went back to China two or three times to see their women and their children, whom they hardly knew. When the family was reunited in Canada, some forty or fifty years later, the Cantonese man was sick, tired and worn out. In the meantime, the women continued toiling, often taking on four jobs simultaneously: in a sewing factory during the day, in the hand laundry after six o'clock in the evening, and as a wife and a mother in the household. Then, the men, one after the other, died, in foreign soil, something they were always fearful of. The widows stayed behind, choosing to live a life separate and independent from their children and grandchildren. They would sit in their small, crammed room in Chinatown, waiting for their children to visit, always eager to spend a few precious hours with them. While all this is happening, these elderly women strive to live on, in a community of widows, forgotten and often neglected. History never seems to stop playing tricks on them.

Notes

1. The data reported in this chapter were collected by a combination of qualitative and quantitative methods. A structured, close-ended Chinese questionnaire was administered to twenty-six elderly Chinese women by a community worker from a Chinatown social agency over a three-month period in 1982. It included questions on demographic and socio-economic characteristics, migration patterns, housing needs and level of satisfaction with current living arrangements, pattern of utilization of services and resources inside and outside the Chinese community, nature and frequency of social participation, and social and cultural needs as residents of the neighbourhood and members of an ethnic community.

    Following the administration of the questionnaire, I conducted intensive, unstructured interviews with ten of the twenty-six women to collect their personal oral histories, focussing on their histories of work, relationships with spouse, children, grandchildren, sons-in-law and daughters-in-law, and feelings about living in Chinatown. Both the administration of the questionnaires and the oral history in- terviews were conducted in Chinese in the homes of the respondents. The oral history interviews were all tape-recorded, translated into English, and transcribed verbatim.

    Personal, unstructured interviews were also conducted with three community workers from three different social agencies of the Chinese community, and with two Chinese physicians practicing in Chinatown, whose clientele consisted of a large proportion of elderly Chinatown residents. Through four years of involvement in community development work in Chinatown, I have had access to a variety of "naturalistic" and "spontaneous" situations and occasions to act as a participant-observer.

The objectives of this field-work were to probe the social world of Chinese elderly women and their pattern of living in coping with the exigencies and problems of life in old age. Five study areas were identified for this field-work: (1) the history of Chinese immigration to Canada and work histories of Chinese women; (2) time, space and ethnic dimensions of the women's social participation; (3) patterns of utilization of services and needs of the elderly; (4) factors associated with inter-generational conflicts in the Chinese family; and (5) the management and negotiation of self-identity by the elderly women as parents and grandparents. These Chinese women were aged between fifty-six and eighty-eight who, at the time of the study, had all lost their husbands three to ten years earlier and were living in rooming houses above restaurants or stores in Montreal Chinatown.

A version of this chapter was presented at the Twelfth Annual Conference of the Canadian Council for Southeast Asian Studies (November 1982), Lakehead University, Thunder Bay, Ontario. It was later published under the title, "Coping with Aging and Managing Self-Identity: The Social World of the Elderly Chinese Women," in *Canadian Ethnic Studies*, Vol. XV:3 (1983), pp. 36–50.
2. Unless specified, this excerpt, like others, is taken from transcripts of intensive, personal interviews with ten of the twenty-six elderly Chinese women.
3. James J. Dowd and Vern L. Bengston, "Aging in Minority Populations, An Examination of the Double Jeopardy Hypothesis," in *Journal of Gerontology*, Vol. 33:3 (1978), pp. 427–36.
4. Charlotte Ikels, "The Coming of Age in Chinese Society: Traditional Patterns and Contemporary Hong Kong." Paper presented at the annual meeting of the American Anthropological Association, Los Angeles (November 1978).

10. Remembering the Mekong River[1]

Refugees putting up temporary living quarters in Pulau Bidong, Malaysia.

One view of a refugee camp in Priary Cheras, Thailand.

Mother and child. Inside a refugee camp in Pulau Bidong, Malaysia.

Children queueing up for food in Nongkai Camp, Thailand.

THERE were no more than one thousand Indo-Chinese immigrants in Canada before 1976, most of whom were students or trained professionals living in Quebec. With the fall of the Thieu regime in 1975, about 6,000 Indo-Chinese refugees came to Canada via refugee transition camps in Hong Kong, Guam and the United States. Most of these newcomers to Canada were formerly middle class people engaged in government work, the military or the professions in Vietnam. About half were relatives of former students already here in Canada. The bulk of the Vietnamese went to Quebec and Ontario.[2] Between 1975 and 1978, Canada took in 9,060 Indo-Chinese refugees through the Special Vietnamese and Cambodian Program. From 1979 to 1980, through the Indo-Chinese Refugee Program, a total of 60,049 refugees from Vietnam, Cambodia and Laos were resettled in Canada.[3] These Indo-Chinese groups are, thus, Canada's newest ethno-cultural population, totalling over 120,000 now. The Canada census of 1981 recorded (by place of birth) 11,345 Vietnamese, 3,370 Cambodians and 2,445 Laotians in Quebec, giving a total of 17,160 Indo-Chinese in the province.[4] It was estimated that about 25% of these 17,160 Indo-Chinese were Chinese by ethnic origin. The 1981 census counted 2,000 Chinese from Vietnam, 390 from Cambodia and 210 from Laos, or about 15% of the total Chinese population in Quebec. Leaders of the local Sino-Indochinese communities maintained there were less than 100 Chinese from Indo-China in Montreal before 1975, many of whom were university students.

Central to the refugee experience is the sense of loss and grief similar to that suffered by bereaved persons over a spouse or an immediate family member, an emotional state well delineated and characterized in literature about widowhood and natural disasters. For numerous Indo-Chinese refugees, a chronic feeling of anxiety about the loss or lack of knowledge of the whereabouts of close family members seems to constitute the essence of the refugee experience. Further compounding this feeling of loss and bereavement is a sense of uprootedness from a socio-cultural milieu within which one was born and reared, an awareness of forced dislocation from a social network comprising kin, neighbours, friends and acquaintances. Like a bereaved widow, the refugee is mourning over beloved lost objects. The management of grief is undertaken by mourning, by crying and pining, by "finding" and "searching for" objects and experiences that once provided pleasure and gratification.

Studies on the mental health implications and consequences of uprootedness and forced migrations caused by natural disasters and wars have long identified a persistently recurring behavioural syndrome of the victims: an obsessive fixation with past experiences and events, an excessive preoccupation with, and idealization of, the "good old days" prior to the mishap. Such a mental set is captured by Zwingmann's concept of "nostalgic illusion",[5] defined as "a symbolic return to, or psychological reinstitution of, those events of the personal (real) past, and/or an impersonal (abstract, imagined, suggested) past which affords optimal gratification". In an operative sense, the past is systematically and, sometimes, unconsciously, idealized, humanized and glorified, while the present is ignored and overlooked, and the future devalued. A nostalgic illusion of this kind has protective utility in that it serves to help maintain affective continuity and psychological equilibrium while the victim of mishaps is experiencing the crisis of loss and adaptation to deprivation and uprooting. While temporary and short-term nostalgic illusion serves compensatory and protective functions for the uprooted, clinical attention and monitoring is warranted in cases of "nostalgic fixation",[6] "where the duration, frequency and intensity of nostalgic episodes exceed the norm, where critical and self-critical judgement of the present and progression toward a future is blocked, and where the inflicted person starts exhibiting aggressive and antisocial behaviour to the social milieu." The victims begin to impose upon themselves self-withdrawal and isolation that, in turn, generate feelings of isolation, loneliness and marginality in regard to the social environment. Self-isolation and nostalgic reaction to the stress of adaptation to a new life in a new country constitute the two major forms of uprooted behaviour.[7]

Through two distinctly different channels, Canada accepted a large number of Indo-Chinese refugees. Through the first channel, refugees came under government sponsorship. Between 1 January 1979 and 31 December 1980, some 25,000 refugees were brought in by the federal government through this channel. Typically, a government worker met the refugees at the airport, provided them with rent and living expenses at the welfare rate for one year or until they found employment. For their search for work, accommodation and language training, they were assisted by the Canada Manpower Centre, Quebec government's Ministry of Cultural Communities and Immigration, and a host of voluntary social agencies.

Under the second channel, that of private sponsorship, sponsors were held legally responsible for providing the refugees with accommodation, food, clothing and other daily amenities for a maximum of one year or until the refugees became self-sufficient. The sponsors were also ultimately responsible for helping the refugees in their search for work and language training. Some 35,000 Indo-Chinese refugees were brought into Canada through this channel.[8]

In general, refugees in Montreal rated their relations with their sponsors and with the government workers as satisfactory and pleasant, though church and private sponsors were perceived as somewhat better and more caring than government workers. There were indications that church and private sponsors (in comparison with the government workers) were seen to have maintained closer interpersonal ties with those sponsored, and were more active in ensuring that their immediate socio-economic and physical needs were met. More specifically, those sponsored by church and private groups reported that they were relatively well provided for as far as the provision of accommodation, household furnishings and clothing was concerned. In addition, they were more often given assistance in seeking employment and in coping with various job-related problems. There were obviously also more frequent mutual visits between the private sponsors and the refugees on special and festive occasions.

A sense of indebtedness and appreciation was emphatically expressed by the refugees. Many added that they were looking forward to future times when they would be in a better and more settled position to repay the debt they owed to Canada and to Canadians. Others stated that they would be readily prepared, if economically feasible, to sponsor other refugees the country might admit in the future.

In spite of significant, sometimes frustrating, communication difficulties in sponsor-refugee relationships (largely due to a lack of verbal proficiency in English or French on the part of the refugees), the refugees believed that a minimally adequate level of mutual understanding existed. They thought their needs were properly understood and, on most occasions, met by their sponsors. Nevertheless, over a period of time spanning eight to twelve months, a general decrease in frequency and intensity of sponsor-refugee interaction was detected. It was claimed by the refugees that the number of phone calls and mutual home visits by sponsors was reduced toward the last six months of sponsorship.

While both sponsors and the sponsored would not readily admit it, their relationship was essentially a patron-client relationship in which one party (the sponsor) provided and the other party (the refugee) was provided for. Especially in the early phases of resettlement, refugees were, of necessity, put into a situation of complete dependency with respect to the provision of such immediate needs as housing, clothing, food, employment and children's education. While there was a positive affective reciprocal bond between the sponsor and the refugee, there was nevertheless an economic and status difference, as well as a cognitive gap in terms of differences in perceiving and interpreting social realities, which the affective connection cannot bridge. The disparity between the affective bond and the cognitive status difference, which was inherent in the sponsor-refugee relationship, was a real source of discomfort.

There were indeed many sources of internal strain and tension in the sponsor-refugee relationship as perceived by the refugees. Both sponsors and refugees entered into the relationship as total strangers, and existing personality and temperament differences between them were often accentuated by a virtual lack of mutual understanding of the ethnic and cultural background of each other. The Chinese from Indo-China had acquired only a rudimentary knowledge of the political system, ideology, geography, climate and social etiquette of Canada—knowledge obtained chiefly through reading books and information pamphlets distributed by Canadian Embassy personnel visiting refugee camps outside Indo-China. What the average sponsor initially knew about Indo-China must have come primarily from stereotyped mass media presentations of the region and its peoples.

Compounding the fact that sponsors and refugees entered into a relationship as strangers in the interpersonal and cultural sense, the relationship was also typified by ambiguity as to goals and objectives, and the rules governing interpersonal dynamics. Lacking easily available literature on the art of building good sponsor-refugee relations, most sponsors seemed to have relied on common sense and good will.

Refugees often found it difficult to bring their daily physical and economic needs to the attention of their sponsors, and they would seek their help only when such needs became urgent. Generally, the refugees felt satisfied with how they were provided for and found it hard to justify claims for more assistance. To them, gratefulness to, and appreciation of, their sponsors often was shown by quietly making the most of what was provided and by reducing to a minimum any intrusion into the privacy of their sponsors.

An added source of tension in the sponsor-sponsored relationships has to do with the Chinese culture emphasizing the superior status of benefactors and givers over that of dependents and receivers. To many, being cast in a situation of utter dependency was more than just a novel situation. It was also a discomforting, humiliating and degrading experience. A deep

10. Remembering the Mekong River

sense of personal and ethnic pride consequently propelled some sponsored refugees to struggle hard for autonomy and independence. Often this seemed to have been interpreted by sponsors as rejection and lack of appreciation of their earnestness and good will.

Some refugees did not fully grasp the ideology and motivations behind the matter of sponsorship. Many of them suspected that the money the sponsors spent on them would have been paid out in taxes to the government anyway, and, therefore, asked whether they should feel "genuinely" and "earnestly" indebted to their sponsors. Others ventured to say that there might be ulterior motives behind Canadian citizens wanting to be sponsors. This diffuse sense of suspicion perhaps brought considerable distrust to the sponsor-sponsored relationship.

Evidently also, refugees seemed to have continually made comparisons among themselves as to what they were being provided for, and how they were treated by their sponsors. Inevitably, this led to a nagging feeling that other families seemed to have had a better deal.

Dreams are indicative of one's subjective reality and, more specifically, of the feelings and impulses, concerns and preoccupations, hopes and fears, that constitute the essential elements of the socio-psychological state of the dreamer. Dream analysis extends our comprehension of people's inner life, and reveal what would otherwise be difficult to learn except by methods used in the treatment of disturbed people in psychoanalysis, clinical psychology and psychotherapy.[9] One may want to see dreams as a representation of the fulfilment or attempted fulfilment of wishes; dreams reveal the dreamer's conflicts and internal struggles, which, in turn, give birth to fears and anxieties in the conscious mind.

One group of refugees were non-specific about their dream content. They vaguely remembered seeing non-specific, but known, faces of distant family members, friends, relatives and neighbours, and doing things with them, the details and particulars of which were beyond recall. In spite of the fact that many of these refugees had been in Quebec for quite some time, they rarely had dreams that took place in settings outside of the familiar environments of Indo-China. These same refugees managed to come to Canada with their immediate (and, in some cases, three-generational) family intact. The fact that they had not left a significant family member behind in Indo-China or lost one during the journey between Indo-China and Canada perhaps explains why the dream contents as related were non-particularistic in nature. The sense of loss was a diffuse and blunt one, a typical emotion normally felt by people going through a major crisis of transition.

Then, there were those who, by choice and arrangement or by force of circumstances, left one or more immediate family members behind either in Indo-China or in refugee camps in Asia; in contrast to the first group, they reported that their dream contents were recurring and repetitive. They remembered exactly the characters in their dreams, the kinds of activities they were engaged in, and the dominant emotion(s) that prevailed in those dream episodes. For instance, one woman recalled repeatedly seeing herself do things with her parents and older brother. The settings were either in Vietnam or in Canada, and the physical landscape in the background was a large, expansive plain with an aeroplane, suggesting the possibility of a long distance journey and a determined and well-planned departure from Vietnam. The dominant emotion associated with this dream was one of expectant bliss associated with the hope of liberty soon to be gained for good.

One young male respondent, who was confined to months of imprisonment in hard-labour camps in Vietnam as a result of an unsuccessful attempt to flee the country, reported that he persistently dreamed of "barbed wire", of images of dark, long unending tunnels, and of fear of persecution associated with dismal environments of forced and seemingly eternal confinement. Another young man dreamed many times of swimming in extreme desperation and fear in torrential storms, and of being chased by pirates and military men in motor-driven boats and ships. Both men reported waking up violently with immeasurable fear and apprehension in the middle of those nightmares. Still another young man, who had been beaten up many times by local police officers in the presence of his parents during his early sojourn in a Hong Kong refugee camp, dreamed of being subjected to repeated physical threats and brutality.

It seems the dreams of refugees reveal an overwhelming preoccupation with the past, whether the past refers to life in general in Indo-China before or after the 1975 fall, or to the boat journey and the sojourn in refugee camps. This preoccupation with the past is revealed by the relative scarcity of dreams within Canadian, as opposed to Indo-Chinese, settings.

Those with their family relatively intact in Canada tended to report that the characters they saw in their dreams were familiar acquaintances with whom they engaged in pleasant, routine, day-to-day activities. They recalled "having a good time" with those relatives in their dreams. While a sense of loss might have been there, it was at most a diffuse one lacking specific content and focus.

Specific, recurring dreams were often had by those who had undergone traumatic experiences prior to coming to Canada. Dreamers of this type seemed obsessed with their inability to come to terms with an experience so tumultuous and psychologically degrading that images of these past experiences were making repeated appearances in the unconscious mind. One might want to speculate that the degree of specificity of dream contents among our respondents seems to be a direct consequence of the level of stressfulness of past experiences encountered and the nature of personal meaning attached to them.

The wish for family reunion emerges as a dominant theme which provides "a dramatic idea" according to which the settings, characters, events and emotions of dreams are plotted by the dreamers. This is especially true for those who have left one or more significant family members behind in Indo-China or in refugee camps. To a refugee, his or her foremost concern is with the physical and psychological well-being of the rest of his family. The overwhelming wish is for family reunion in Canada which, for many, can only be fulfiled in dreams.

A Chinese epigram says: "What one ponders during the day is what one dreams about at night." (日有所思，夜有所夢) Several refugees recalled seeing faces of relatives and friends in their dreams on the day they received letters from Indo-China, or when they heard news of their whereabouts from the new refugee arrivals in Montreal, or from using the mass media. Others reported having dreams in which they actually talked or did things with their relatives after having heard nothing from Indo-China for weeks or months. One woman dreamed of travelling alone to Vietnam to bring her brother a parcel containing food and other household utensils which were requested in a letter she had received the day before. As the dream proceeded, she suddenly became terrified by the fact she was in Vietnam with her brother. At that point, she awakened and was relieved to see that she was sleeping in her Montreal apartment.

The more occupied they were with work or study in language classes, the less often they had dreams. They reported a much higher frequency of dreams of various contents during the first three months of arrival in Canada; some attributed this fact to their disturbed sense of time orientation, cold weather and an acute sense of culture shock.

Two refugees recalled having a series of traumatic dreams weeks before the May Referendum in Quebec, 1980, the specific contents of which were forgotten. While reporting these dreams, they added that they were extremely apprehensive about the possibility of yet another political independence movement in Quebec, which might mean that they could well become refugees for the second time within a span of some twelve months. The fear of political instability, persecution and imprisonment by the party in power in the Quebec government was widespread among many refugees who arrived in the province since 1979. One might want to hypothesize that the refugees' excessive mental preoccupation with the past (before or after the political transition in 1975 in Vietnam) would in one way or another interfere with their socio-psychological and economic adaptation to the present social milieu of Quebec society. Some refugees were so preoccupied with the "eternal and omnipresent" past in Vietnam that it became an obstacle to full adaptation to their immediate situation.

One woman, who apologetically reported that she might have learned only six to seven French words after having been to language classes for five months, lamented about the amount of money and energy spent on her and many others in similar circumstances by the government. She attributed her poor performance in language to the fact that she simply could not restrain her mind from inevitably wandering back to the past in Vietnam. Another woman, who once worked as a sewing machine operator in a hat manufacturing factory months after arrival in Montreal and later became part owner of a beauty salon in Chinatown, reported a persistent split between her body (while engaging in manual labour in Canada) and her mind (that was wrought with random and directionless thoughts about past events and experiences). Still another male refugee said that on Sunday afternoons when the streets were quiet and the neighbours stayed home, he spent hours sitting alone in his apartment rehearsing series of episodes of past events in Vietnam, during the boat journey and in the two refugee camps he had been to. There were moments when his mind went so far back into the past that he was convinced that he was actually anywhere other than in Canada. The distinction between present and past, here and there, was so blurred that he thought he was hallucinating.

There were significant age differences in the nature and degree of preoccupation with the past among the refugees. The older the refugee was, the more time he or she seemed to have spent on pondering past events, usually as a result of an obsessive, but painful, lamentation about what was left behind in Vietnam. The important question was: "What was lost, and what meaning was attached to what was lost by the sufferer?" First and foremost, it was a loss of, and a forced departure from, a familiar milieu within which one was born and raised, and from which one developed and consolidated a sense of personal and ethnic identity, and an adequate sense of competence. It was a sense of loss of being an active and functional participant in a universe within which one's place and role was given meaning, significance and confirmation.

Secondly, it was loss in material and social status terms: loss of property and position accumulated through many years of hard toil, suffering, thriftiness and saving. Many ethnic Chinese refugees were once well-established and self-sufficient persons of middle-class background who had started out on their own at an early age as street hawkers, transportation workers, or self-employed family businessmen. They felt they had just begun to find life comfortable and enjoyable. The sudden loss of status and personal belongings remains a nightmare, and many still found it difficult to come to terms with it. It was a loss of self-pride, personal glory and sense of achievement.

The most acute loss was of a closely knit and cohesive social network comprising kin, neighbours, friends and acquaintances. A Chinese from Vietnam is such an integral and inseparable part of a larger social network of family, kin and community that the disintegration of this social network has immediate repercussions on the individual. Since the social context contributes so much to the individual's sense of self, the individual suffers a severe loss of personal coherence when his or her social context is fractured and destroyed.[10] This sense of loss and social dislocation is perhaps most acutely felt by those who do not have their immediate family intact in Canada, and is definitely a consequence of more than just physical and social separation; it is also the result of an awareness that things can never be the same again.

For the older people, the sense of loss was multi-faceted, and was sometimes all-encompassing. Though they were all born in China, they spent their early childhood in Indo-China and, therefore, went through their primary and secondary socialization there. Their emotional and psychological identification with the community within which they were raised, educated and socialized was strong and deep. As Chinese, they may not have developed civic allegiance to the political regime in Vietnam nor to the sentiments and ideology underlying it; however, they had carved out a coherent universe for themselves within the ethnic Chinese community. It was within this more limited universe they had come to know their position, status, role, obligations and duties.

On arrival in Canada, the basis on which our older refugees traditionally built their sense of personal competence and self-esteem had been largely destroyed. The consequence was often a feeling of personal powerlessness and hopelessness. This anxiety was compounded by the loss of property and well-established businesses that were often the end-product of a lifetime of toil and thriftiness.

One phenomenon that many older refugees did not anticipate upon their departure from Indo-China was that, for the first time in their lives since childhood, they found themselves in a state of economic and sociopsychological dependency upon younger members of their families. This created a situation in which the younger family members were required by circumstances to become independent and self-sufficient, as well as responsible for the daily functioning of the family. As a result, much tension and conflict was generated in the family with which none of the family members knew exactly how to cope. In late 1979, a 72-year-old navy man acted as the chief pilot of a boat that had about two hundred refugee passengers. He steered the boat through many mishaps and perils, and brought the entire crew and passengers to safety in Indonesia. Upon arrival in Canada, he developed a range of psychosomatic diseases. He could not walk or talk. His 22-year-old son, the only other male in the family in Montreal, suddenly took on the role of an economic provider, nurse, decision-maker, and head of the family.

The recent economic downturn in Canada has generated a national public concern with unemployment and its psychosocial and economic costs. The sudden influx of thousands of Indo-Chinese refugees in Canada coincided with the economic recession and, among other things, has spurred a number of studies of the various facets of their adaptation during resettlement in the host country. Several of these studies focus on the economic adaptation of the refugees,[11] believing that successful economic adaptation is vital to overall adjustment and central to attainment of self-sufficiency and autonomy.

A national longitudinal survey[12] found the unemployment rate among Indo-Chinese refugees in March 1982 was 10.4% while the Canadian unemployment rate was 8.5%. By 1982 to 1983, the worsening economic situation in Canada not only has continued to push up its overall unemployment rate, but has also caused a sharp increase in the refugee unemployment rate. For example, the unemployment rate among Indo-Chinese respondents of a recent Quebec study[13] grew from 18% in 1981 to 32% in 1982. Half of the refugees in this survey had been unemployed at some point between June 1981 and June 1982. Unemployment is clearly going to be a key Indo-Chinese problem for a long time.

In coping with unemployment and a drastic and abrupt reduction of family income, as well as with a sense of shame and psychological resentment with continued dependency on unemployment insurance and other kinds of government financial assistance, the refugees have dug deeply into their personal, psychological, cultural and social resources. Many years of war, political and economic persecution, poverty and famines in Southeast Asia, coupled with a daily existence in refugee transition camps characterized by anxiety, frustration and helplessness have, so to speak, "seasoned and weathered" the refugees. These cumulative experiences have engendered in the refugees a firm sense of resilience and invulnerability, making them realistic and pragmatic.

An underlying philosophy of pragmatic realism enables the Indo-Chinese refugees to accept readily stresses and strains stemming from life changes. Unemployment and the transition from autonomy to dependency are only but a few of the many life changes characteristic of a life victimized by wars and uprootedness. These refugees, through historical and political circumstances, have developed within themselves a vast reservoir of "internal resistance resources".[14] It is perhaps precisely due to the availability of these psychological resources that the refugees have not become easy prey to personal disorganization and pathology.

Lay thinking on the social effects of unemployment often stresses unemployed persons as particularly vulnerable to social withdrawal and isolation which, in turn, are believed to lead to demoralization and personal disorganization. To a large extent, this view does not seem to hold true with the Indo-Chinese refugees. While a view has often been held by the public that unemployment usually has severe deleterious consequences for the family, in the case of the refugees, unemployment actually intensifies family relations, demands the pulling together of all resources and, consequently, contributes to family cohesiveness. Unemployment demands re-definition and re-organization of family roles and statuses which are tasks undertaken by the refugee families with considerable cooperation from all members.

Lesser family income means one has to cut back on many family outing items, such as going to movies or having meals in restaurants, in order to conserve and save. On the other hand, it also means the family is more ready to play together to fulfil each other's socio-emotional and recreational needs.

The refugee families have developed among themselves a low-budget way of family entertainment: a set of interlocking families bounded by friendship, kin relations, or geographic proximity have a series of dinner parties on a family rotation basis. In difficult economic times when a majority of the refugees are without work, these rotating dinner parties not only keep entertainment expenses low, but also, perhaps more importantly, keep individuals and families together. One even might venture to suggest that these parties also function to add strength to their personal ethnic identity.

While unemployment does not seem to result in personal and family pathology, the opposite seems to be taking place. To the extent that unemployment of the father (or the mother) is defined and viewed as a family, rather than personal issue, coping with new realities created by unemployment has become a family task. Unemployment contributes to, and strengthens, family cohesiveness while family members cope and adapt together and, as a consequence, keep the unemployed individual in the company of significant others. Operating in these terms, the family copes and plays together.

Participation in social networks comprising friends and kin not only serves expressive-emotional functions, but also is of much instrumental practical utility. Refugees not only actually obtained employment through utilization of the personal, social networks, but also preferred to do so.

> The social circle of the refugees has been restricted to a few relatives and friends. Friends are often asked to keep a sharp eye for possible openings in their work place as most jobs are found that way. A worker on the site would know immediately when additional workers are needed and what type of personnel would be appropriate to meet the demand. This peer-referral system is deemed most effective both by refugees seeking work and by the employers themselves.[15]

Having all been refugees serves to lessen status differences amongst the Indo-Chinese. Being unemployed further augments this process of status equalization. By withdrawing into a network of interlocking unemployed families, the jobless person knows the stigma of unemployment is considerably reduced. He or she can count on the social support of "the similar others". From an instrumental and functional point of view, the unemployed person's accessibility to such a support system is often an invaluable linkage to the job market out there. The social network, with its supportive resources, thus serves its expressive and instrumental functions. Unemployment initiates a series of life changes and demands constant adjustment and re-adjustment. Unemployment remains stressful and the unemployed person is not without difficulties and dilemmas. However, he or she knows that one is not alone.

That the refugees have so far been essentially adaptive in coping with unemployment does not disguise some emerging symptoms of psychological strain and emotional distress stemming from unemployment and from family role change and re-socialization. What is disturbing is the growing sense of pessimism among the refugees regarding their future job prospects and their employability. The important question to ask is: How much longer will it take before the personal resistance energies and the resources of the social networks are depleted to such an extent that the next straw will break the camel's back?

Notes

1. Versions of this chapter were presented at the annual meetings of the Canadian Sociology and Anthropology Association (May 1981), Dalhousie University, Halifax, Nova Scotia, and at the Asian Canadian Symposium V of the Canadian Asian Studies Association (May 1981), Mount Saint Vincent University, Halifax, Nova Scotia. Parts of the chapter were published in *Canadian Ethnic Studies* (XV:1, 1983) under the title, "Resettlement of Vietnamese Chinese Refugees in Montreal, Canada: Some Socio-psychological Problems and Dilemmas", and also in *Uprooting, Loss and Adaptation: The Resettlement of Indo-Chinese Refugees in Canada*, edited by Kwok B. Chan and Doreen Indra (Ottawa: The Canadian Public Health Association, 1987). The latter was under the title, "Psychological Problems of the Resettlement of Chinese Vietnamese Refugees in Quebec."

    This chapter is based on interview data collected during phase three of a longitudinal study of patterns of psychological and socio-economic adaptation of Indo-Chinese refugees in Montreal, Canada, carried out between 1975 and 1984. Phase one of the study examined the structure and values of Chinese families in Vietnam before 1975. Phase two analyzed the demographic and socio-economic characteristics of the total Indo-Chinese refugee population (Cambodian, Laotian, Vietnamese) in Quebec until 1981. Phase four, the last phase of the study, focused on the occupational and social adjustment of the Indo-Chinese refugees while settling in Montreal. The Mekong River, with its origin in China, runs through Vietnam, Cambodia and Laos, and gives the three countries a common geographic identity and cultural heritage.
2. Doreen Indra, "Social Science Research on Indo-Chinese Refugees in Canada," in *Uprooting, Loss and Adaptation: The Resettlement of Indo-Chinese Refugees in Canada*, 1987.
3. *Indo-Chinese Refugees: The Canadian Response, 1979 and 1980*. Employment and Immigration Canada (Ottawa: Ministry of Supply and Services, 1982), p. 32.

4. Census of Canada 1981, Special Tabulation: Population of Quebec by Place of Birth.
5. Charles Zwingmann, "The Nostalgic Phenomenon and its Exploitation," in *Uprooting and After*, edited by Charles Zwingmann and Maria Pfister-Ammende (New York: Springer-Verlag, 1973), pp. 19–47.
6. Charles Zwingmann (ed.), *Uprooting and Related Phenomena: A Descriptive Bibliography* (World Health Organization, 1977), pp. 10–16.
7. E. Kraepelin, "About Uprooting," in Zeitschr. J. D. *Ges. Neurol. U. Psychiat*, 63 (1921), 1–8, also abstracted in *Uprooting and Related Phenomena: A Descriptive Bibliography*, pp. 3–4.
8. Yuen-fong Woon, "The Mode of Refugee Sponsorship and the Socio-economic Adaptation of Vietnamese in Victoria; A Three Year Perspective," in *Uprooting, Loss and Adaptation: The Resettlement of Indo-Chinese Refugees in Canada*.
9. Calvin S. Hall, *The Meaning of Dreams* (New York: McGraw-Hill, 1963).
10. A. Antonovsky, "Conceptual and Methodological Problems in the Study of Resistance Resources and Stressful Life Events" (Paper presented at Conference on Stressful Life Events: Their Nature and Effects, June 1973 at City University of New York); Kwok B. Chan, "Individual Differences in Reactions to Stress and Their Personality and Situational Determinants: Some Implications for Community Mental Health," in *Social Science and Medicine*, Vol. 11 (1979), pp. 89–103.
11. Lawrence Lam, "Vietnamese-Chinese Refugees in Montreal" (Doctoral Dissertation, Department of Sociology, York University, Downsview, Ontario, Canada, 1983); Gertrude Neuwirth, "The Socio-economic Adjustment of Southeast Asian Refugees in Canada: One Year Later" (Paper presented at the CSAS Annual Meetings, Dalhousie University, Halifax, 1981); T.J. Samuel, "Economic Adaptation of Indo-Chinese Refugees in Canada," in *Uprooting, Loss and Adaptation: The Resettlement of Indo-Chinese Refugees in Canada*; Gilles Deschamps, "Economic Adaptation of Indo-Chinese Refugees in Quebec," in *Uprooting, Loss and Adaptation: The Resettlement of Indo-Chinese Refugees in Canada*.
12. Employment and Immigration Canada (EIC), *Evaluation of the 1979–81 Indo-Chinese Refugee Program*, 1982.
13. Gilles Deschamps, p. 97.
14. A. Antonovsky, p. 1.
15. Like others, this excerpt is taken from family profiles prepared by research assistants for the fourth phase of our longitudinal study.

11. Boat People Getting Organized and Keeping Distance[1]

Union des Chinois du Cambodge au Canada.

Union des Chinois du Cambodge au Canada.

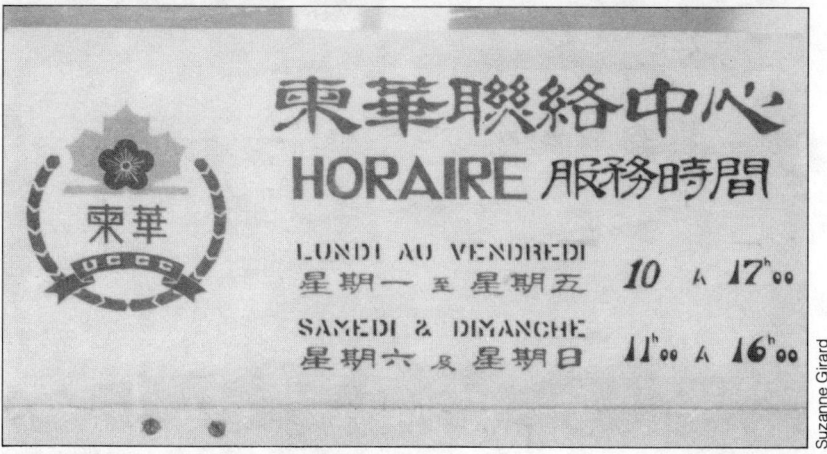

Association des Chinois du Vietnam à Montreal.

11. Boat People Getting Organized and Keeping Distance

ACCORDING to a 1979 estimate,[2] there were 15 million Chinese in various countries of Southeast Asia and about two million in the region of Indo-China. With about a million in Vietnam accounting for only 2% of the country's total population, a vast majority of the Chinese lived in Southern Vietnam, mostly in Saigon. Numbering more than 400,000 in 1970,[3] the Chinese represented 6.8% of the total population of Cambodia. They were descendants of settlers who came to Southeast Asia from the southern coastal provinces of China several centuries ago. Due to factors such as backwardness in economic and commercial development, the lack of a seaboard, and the inconvenience of internal communications, Laos had the smallest population of Chinese, which was estimated at 30,000 in 1958.[4]

The two million Chinese in Vietnam, Cambodia and Laos were ethnic minority groups in numerical terms, a demographic fact that contrasted with their dominant economic position in the region. For centuries, the Chinese in Indo-China occupied a middleman position, specializing in commerce and trade between manufactured goods and local agricultural produce.[5] The basis of Chinese trade was rice, spices, retailing and import-export. For example, field research done from 1962 to 1963 in Cambodia[6] found that eight out of the ten big import-export companies were Chinese-owned, and some 95% of the internal trade was in Chinese hands. Furthermore, 99% of the 3,500 privately owned industrial firms were Chinese representing about 90% of total private capital investment. The Chinese had, thus, developed a strong leaning towards a culture of commerce and a mentality that marked them as distinct from the indigenous Indo-Chinese populations. It was once said that every Chinese in Indo-China aspired to own a trade, and many did.

Quite paradoxically, the economic predominance of the Chinese in Indo-China contrasted dramatically with their virtual exclusion from political power, which, thus, put them in a precarious position, highly vulnerable to both political and economic persecution.

The fact that the Chinese in Indo-China were more often Confucians than Buddhists, whereas much of the region of Southeast Asia, except Vietnam, had adopted the Indian religions of Hinduism and Buddhism, has contributed considerably to the socio-cultural separation of the Chinese from the host countries. Escaping from famines, poverty and socio-political unrest in the southern provinces of China during the colonial period (1800–1945) and after the Second World War, the Chinese came to Nanyang 南洋 (the Chinese term for Southeast Asia, meaning "South Sea") to make money they could take or send back to China. A system of complex and interlocking Chinese voluntary organizations built on the basis of common locality or surname quickly proliferated to make self-protection and mutual aid possible among the Chinese sojourners.[7] These networks of organizations quickly became the cornerstones of largely self-sufficient, self-governing and autonomous Chinese communities throughout Southeast Asia, thus further reinforcing their separation from the host societies of the region.

In Montreal, a small group of Chinese students from Vietnam then attending the city's French-speaking and English-speaking universities responded to the graphic portrayal by the media of the Hai Hong episode and met at the Wing's Noodles[8] to set up the "Group of Sino-Vietnamese Volunteers". The group consisted of fifteen people, mostly university students or recent graduates; its objective was to aid the city's newly arrived Sino-Vietnamese refugees in their resettlement and adaptation in the host society.

Without a former organizational structure of its own and lacking understanding of the social service delivery system in the city, the group turned to the three then newly established community service agencies in the Chinese community for consultation, resources and leadership. Several members of the group very shortly joined the board of directors of one of the agencies, The Chinese Family Service of Greater Montreal (滿城華人服務中心), located in the heart of Montreal's Chinatown, and, consequently, spearheaded a series of front-line, first-aid refugee resettlement programs, which included receiving incoming refugees at the Mirabel International Airport, directly sponsoring refugee families then sojourning in refugee camps in Asia, and escorting, translation and interpretation. In the winter of 1981, the group, pulling together its own financial and human resources, published its first *Annuaire des sino-vietnamiens au Québéc, Canada.* Relying on personal referrals and a snowballing technique, the group was able to compile listings of people of Chinese origin from Indo-China (mostly from North and South Vietnam). As stated in the directory's first edition in 1981, its objective was to facilitate the speedy reunion of family members, relatives, friends and acquaintances scattered and dispersed by the sudden massive flight from Indo-China. The directory has been updated and published annually and is now into its fourth edition and the number of listings has been increased from 200 in its 1981 edition to 770 in 1984. Along with other circumstantial reasons, the entry of these three Sino-

Vietnamese university graduates into the board of the Chinese Family Service has to a considerable extent helped define the agency's working priorities. The immediate availability of federal and provincial funds for resettlement and adaptation of Indo-Chinese refugees has shifted the agency's priorities from the socially disadvantaged persons (e.g., the aged) of the local Chinese community to the Indo-Chinese refugees, particularly those of Chinese origin. Also, as a result of this active involvement in the resettlement of Indo-Chinese refugees, the agency, with special extra funding from the governments, has actually increased its staff; extended its contacts with other pertinent constituencies within the mainstream social service system; enhanced its organizational visibility and credibility; and, perhaps most importantly, the agency has a clear direction and identity which the agency's board of directors has been searching for since its inauguration.

By 1983, all three social service agencies (Chinese Family Service, Chinese Neighbourhood Society 華協會 and Chinese Volunteers Association 華人互助社) in the Chinese community of Montreal had been very much involved in delivering refugee resettlement and adaptation services. With a major grant from Employment and Immigration Canada, three board members of the Chinese Family Service (one of whom being the pioneering member of the "Group of Sino-Vietnamese Volunteers") worked jointly with leaders of Montreal's Vietnamese, Laotian and Cambodian communities to create Service des interprètes auprès des réfugiés indochinois (SIARI, 東南亞難民傳譯中心) to meet the ever-increasing demand for frontline refugee settlement services. With a board of directors consisting of representatives from the four Indo-Chinese communities in Montreal and a staff proficient in the various native languages of the Indo-Chinese and Canada's two official languages, SIARI played the role of relieving the workload pressure of existing voluntary agencies in both the indigenous immigrant communities and the city's social service system.

Among the Sino-Vietnamese refugees in Montreal were a class of elderly persons, formerly merchant elite and leaders of the Chinese community in Saigon, who began from 1980 to congregate periodically at banquets in Chinese restaurants in Chinatown to reunite with lost friends and relatives, to meet new friends, and to recreate the sentiment of a lost community and neighbourliness. At their peak, such banquet gatherings attracted a thousand people in one single evening, which seemed to pave the way toward furnishing the organizational skeleton of a collectivity underlined by a strong desire to re-create a once lost Sino-Vietnamese community by transplanting it from Saigon to Montreal. The original "Group of Sino-Vietnamese Volunteers", while continuing their refugee relief work, contributed much to the solidification of the emerging community's organizational structure by working jointly with this class of elderly merchant elite. Between 1980 and 1983, a number of community-oriented, folkloric activities were sponsored as a result of this joint effort. There were major annual celebrations of the Chinese New Year and the Autumn Moon Festival, in addition to other sporadic events such as outings to cities outside the province, picnics and cultural evenings. The accent of these organized activities seemed to be more on preservation and perpetuation of a cultural heritage, a way of life, a commonly shared sentiment, and the experience of having been politically and economically persecuted and subsequently forced to leave behind the Chinese community in Saigon.

There were at least two models of community development at work. One model was favoured by the original "Group of Sino-Vietnamese Volunteers" which advocated a more temporary organizational structure created to respond to a particular need or crisis and be disbanded when the need had been met or the crisis had been resolved. The other model, favoured by the elderly, formerly merchant class, promoted the establishment and nurturing of a permanent organizational structure capable of adapting and responding to the emerging needs of the Sino-Vietnamese community in Montreal and Quebec. The conflict and tension between the two organizational models was underlined by two very different ideologies. The temporary model, favoured by the young, focussed on organizational adaptability, flexibility, and freedom from bureaucratic constraints typical of permanent organizations, a model underpinned first by a dislike of duplicating services currently or potentially provided by the existing social service agencies in the Chinese community; and, second, by the desire for integrating the Sino-Vietnamese, and eventually, all Indo-Chinese of Chinese descent, into the city's Chinese community. The permanent model promoted by the elderly merchant class opted for complete organizational autonomy and freedom from existing Chinese organizations, a pre-requisite condition, they believed, for safeguarding a separate, distinct identity and heritage.

In February 1983, the elderly merchant class seemed to have won out after a series of meetings, and the outcome was the official disbanding of the voluntary youth group and the creation of the Sino-Vietnamese Sports and Recreation Centre headquartered in Chinatown and led by representations from both the youth and the elderly. In March, a public forum was organized in the Centre to examine the need for furthering the organization of Sino-Vietnamese in Montreal, resulting in the creation of a preparatory twenty-person task force charged with the responsibility of drafting a constitution for the organization and recruiting potential candidates for a general election. Within three months, a forty-member board of directors with ten alternates was elected. On 13 June in that same year, the Centre was officially registered with the Government of Quebec as the Association des chinois du Vietnam à Montréal (ACVM, 滿地可越南華僑聯誼會).

There were several ways in which the organizational structure of the Association was modelled on those of the Chinese community in Saigon. One was the distinction between the thirty-one board members in direct, executive roles and those nine in monitoring and supervisory roles; the other was the division of organizational activities and events into five categories: welfare, sports, recreation, public relations and general affairs.

An analysis of functions and activities sponsored by the Association since its official creation in 1983 indicates a pre-occupation with catering to the different socio-emotional and cultural needs of the two different generations: table tennis, soccer, basketball, dance and disco parties and folklore performances for the younger generation, chess and card games, mah-jong, picnics, outings and Chinese dinner gatherings for the elderly. In terms of actual functions and activities carried out, the Association operated no differently in essence from its predecessor, the Centre. While it was their original desire to self-organize so that that they would be in a stronger position to continue to offer social and community services to meet the emerging and changing needs of the Sino-Vietnamese community, as well as to maintain and nurture ties with their tradition and cultural heritage, the relative scarcity of functions and events towards these ends seemed to reflect a set of both internal and external problems besetting the Association.

The Group of Sino-Vietnamese Volunteers that was at the forefront in assisting the resettlement of refugees in 1980 was made up of young university students, recent university graduates and professionals. They had been in Quebec before 1975 and the "boat people" phenomenon; they were, as individuals, proficient in Canada's two official languages; and had at their command some basic skills in organizing and interacting with governments and the social service system in the mainstream society. In essence, they seemed to favour a mode of operation so that the group could be disbanded upon the resolution of the refugee resettlement crisis. This group was later in contact with the arrival of a class of relatively older Chinese men, most of whom were former merchants and businessmen commanding strategic and influential positions in both the business and the Chinese communities in Saigon back in Vietnam before 1975. Among these former merchants, there was a strong need to rebuild in Montreal their once lost community, and one important step in this direction was to establish a long-standing organization with a structure that is, ideally speaking, autonomous and relatively free from external constraints. The inherent conflict and tension between these two qualitatively incompatible models of community organization underlined the relationship between the two generations.

In the Chinese community of Saigon, successful business entrepreneurs were often expected by the community to contribute to the well-being of the Chinese people by taking on either actual executive, or honorary, positions in key community organizations.[9] Oftentimes this community expectation was translated into an ethical issue in that there was a moral obligation on the part of the entrepreneurs to repay the community from their economic gains; any refusal was often looked upon as an act of moral selfishness and moral depravity. The entrepreneurs were usually more than happy to oblige. It was also a customary practice within the Chinese community in Saigon that those who had contributed the most financially usually occupied the most influential positions in the community's major organizations. In other words, the president or chairman of a community organization was expected to, and usually did, make a larger amount of financial donation irrespective of other abilities and resources.

Within the Association, perhaps more due to circumstances than choice, an interesting division of labour was emerging in that the older generation concentrated on raising funds by soliciting donations from among the few rapidly increasing number of owners of grocery, arts and craft stores, restaurants and other professionals, while the younger generation, because of their education and language skills, interacted with the governments and constituencies external to the community. Handicapped by a deficiency in language skills, the older people, in spite of their strategic fund-raising roles, found themselves cast into a position of dependency on the younger folks, often with feelings of resentment and hostility. These feelings were also inevitably compounded by their lamentation about the demise of the traditional practice back in Vietnam that respected the wisdom of the elderly and recognized financial power as the sole determining attribute of community leadership. On the other hand, according to the young people in the organization, leadership status should be allotted to those with skills and resources crucial to managing transactions between organizations and between communities. In the North American context, these are often "cultural and political brokering skills", among which education and language competence are pre-requisites. As a consequence of this different emphasis between the two generations about leadership abilities and attributes, a younger or older person(s) who occupies a leadership position in the organization is, by definition, viewed as less than legitimate and desirable by the other generation.

The young and old generations also did not seem to have reached a consensus on the current, as well as the future, needs of the Sino-Vietnamese community either. The pre-occupation of the Association with undertaking in the past year a series of sports and recreational activities upon the initiative of some younger members of the executive has been criticized by the older ones as superficial, narrow-visioned, and disrespectful of the psychological and emotional needs of the elderly. Their preference was for the organization to develop into a full-fledged community-based social agency offering a comprehensive range of cultural, social and legal services, a goal that seems unrealistic at the moment given the limited financial strength of the organization.

It is very explicitly stated in the constitution of the Association that it is non-political and non-religious in nature; in actual behaviour terms, the organization's interaction with, and participation in, federal, provincial and municipal politics has hitherto been virtually non-existent. However, the non-participatory stand of the organization seems to have more to do with the relative instability and immaturity of the organization in terms of its development as well as a lack of understanding of Canadian politics and the country's decision-making process and machinery, than with a sense of political apathy or indifference as it was traditionally the case among the Chinese in Southeast Asia. As a matter of fact, there has been considerable explicit public expression by both the younger and older members of the Association concerning the importance of the Chinese as members of a minority to make entry into the host country's political and public office.

Lacking a permanent, professionally trained staff to respond on their own to the needs of the community for various social and community services, the organization continues to make referrals to the three social service agencies within the Chinese community, particularly to the Chinese Family Service because of its geographic proximity. Because of, and consistent with, its commitment to non-partisan, political neutrality, the organization has been particularly cautious in its stance towards the traditional political duality of pro-Communist and pro-Nationalist affiliations within the local Chinese community. On the other hand, given the fact that the large majority of Sino-Vietnamese in Quebec were refugees having been subjected to political and/or economic persecution by the communist regime of the Vietnamese government, there seems to be, especially among the older generation, an implicit, but strong, sentiment of anti-communism, as well as a leaning towards the Nationalist government of Taiwan. Comparatively speaking, such political sentiments and leanings are less clear-cut and are perhaps more ambivalent in nature among the younger generation.

While the Association had only minimal and superficial transactions with other organizations within the local Chinese community, it also had very little to do with those in the city's Vietnamese, Cambodian and Laotian communities either. Selected executive members of the Association occasionally attended their festive events, and there have been reports that a handful of elderly Sino-Vietnamese have been regularly participating in gatherings organized by the elderly club of the Vietnamese community. Emotionally, they do not differentiate between the Vietnamese in Quebec and the Vietnamese communist government that persecuted them and made them into refugees, which might explain the continuation of a social distance between the Vietnamese and the Sino-Vietnamese communities on both individual and organizational levels.

In 1979, like the Group of Sino-Vietnamese Volunteers, about twenty students of Chinese descent from Cambodia then studying in universities in Montreal banded together as a temporary group to aid in the resettlement of incoming Chinese refugees from Cambodia in a general attempt to facilitate the social and cultural adaptation of the refugees to the host society. The accent of the group's work was on introducing the refugees to Canadian and Québécois lifestyles. By late 1980 and early 1981, this group of university student volunteers was joined by a representation of about twenty older refugees who were mostly former merchants, restaurant owners, teachers, school administrators and small business men with considerable experience and expertise in community service within the Chinese community in

11. Boat People Getting Organized and Keeping Distance 275

Cambodia and, therefore, sensitive to the cultural and psychological needs of the ethnic minorities, be it in Cambodia or in Quebec.

Three years after surviving the initial shock of resettlement in a new, culturally different milieu, the need to reunite globally scattered relatives, friends, acquaintances and neighbours became paramount and urgent. This ever-expanding core group of university students and refugee volunteers responded by creating the Union des Chinois du Cambodge au Canada (UCCC, 東華聯絡中心) in early 1981, and compiling and publishing in December of the same year the first edition of a *repertoire*, a directory of listings of about 400 persons resettling inside and outside Canada.

With sporadic donations from the Chinese refugees from Cambodia themselves and a major financial contribution from a second-generation Chinese grocery store owner from mainland China, the UCCC opened its office in Chinatown in 1982, and subsequently moved to St. Denis (corner of Jean Talon). In late 1983, with small, short-term grants from the federal government's job creation program, and continued private donations, the UCCC began to hire two full-time workers versed in Canada's two official languages and various Chinese dialects to provide a range of community services geared toward refugee resettlement and adaptation. The grants were subsequently terminated due to the phasing out of the Canada Work job creation program, thus hampering considerably the organization's ability to continue providing services.

Initially begun as a group of young university student volunteers to respond to the refugee resettlement crisis in 1979, the UCCC's subsequent commitment in the following years to providing community services was severely curtailed by the termination of governmental funding. Without a full-time staff, the organization, between 1983 and 1985, consciously took on an explicit social and cultural orientation, focusing on such activities as Chinese language classes, sports and recreation events, cultural and musical evenings, and celebration of a few major Chinese festivals. Since 1983, with free access to classroom space during weekends in the Chinese Catholic church in Chinatown, teachers working as volunteers have been teaching Mandarin classes to about 200 children and adolescents from the Chinese refugee families from Cambodia. Following a model of structure typical of most community service organizations in the Chinese communities in Southeast Asia, the UCCC's board of directors undertakes functions organized into five distinct categories: welfare, sports, recreation, public relations and general affairs.

It has been estimated that a large majority of the Chinese from Cambodia, unlike those from Vietnam (many of whom were from Saigon), were originally from rural villages and small provincial towns, whereas those from Phnom Penh, the capital city, invariably from the upper, wealthy class, and more educated and skilled, had either been "slaughtered" in Cambodia or resettled in France or other European countries. In comparing themselves to the Sino-Vietnamese in Montreal, the Chinese from Cambodia (contrary to the dramatized portrayal of the Vietnamese "boat people" phenomenon by international media) believe they have suffered and lost more economically and psychologically than the Vietnamese.

It is believed that the communist regime of Cambodia since 1975 has been instrumental in obliterating much of the society's economic and intellectual elite, a policy of severe consequence for the Chinese in Cambodia. The virtual absence of an intellectual elite and the merchant class both in Quebec and in Canada seems to have serious implications for the future development and growth of the Chinese Cambodian community. Out of the twenty directors of the board of the UCCC, only five have an elementary command of the English and French languages and none seems to have the necessary experience and resources to effectively serve the cultural and political brokering functions for the organization as well as the community.

Between 1982 and 1985, the UCCC has published three consecutive annual editions of the *Repertoire*, with a listing increased from 400 to 700 names of people from North America and Europe. To a considerable extent, the effort and energy exerted in the compilation and publication of the *Repertoire* reflects a continuing need among the Chinese from Cambodia for reunification with the familiar and significant others, a need the board of directors of the UCCC has felt obliged and proud to meet. It cannot be overemphasized that this need for reunification has long-term implications and consequences in terms of the rebuilding of the scattered and lost sense of belongingness to a community in an international and global context. From an organizational standpoint, such measures signal a first step towards the development of immigrant communities in the host societies.

The UCCC, being, thus far, the only formal organization among the Chinese from Cambodia in Montreal as well as in Quebec, has been maintaining a low profile, non-participatory and inward-looking stance as far as relationships and transactions with other community agencies and organizations within and outside the local Chinese community are concerned. Without a full-time staff to deliver direct community services to its

11. Boat People Getting Organized and Keeping Distance

own people, the UCCC, often not without reluctance, continues to refer its own clients to the three service agencies in the Chinese community, and the nature of its transactions with these organizations remains as such. The UCCC's inactive and cautious transactions with the politics of Chinatown and with the Chinese community's many clan and family associations continue to allow them to maintain considerable social distance from the institutional infrastructure of the Chinese community in Montreal. Such purposive and voluntary non-involvement and isolation may well be integral to developing and nurturing a distinct organizational identity.

In the city of Montreal, there are several organizations run by and for native Cambodians, which have undertaken various social and cultural activities and events since their establishment in 1979. Like their Sino-Vietnamese counterparts, the few members on the board of the UCCC have at best maintained a casual, superficial and minimally functional relationship with them: they respond to each other's invitations to such public functions as banquets, festive celebrations, and annual organizational assemblies.

While continuing to identify themselves as ethnic Chinese both in Cambodia and in Quebec and Canada, the Chinese from Cambodia, as victims of political and economic persecution by the Cambodian communist regime, often harbour some subtle and covert feelings of resentment and distrust towards native Cambodian refugees overseas. These feelings often stem from a reluctance to differentiate and separate the communist regime in Cambodia from the native Cambodian people in general: the latter are seen by the Chinese as perpetrators by association with the former because of their national origin.

Unlike their counterparts from Vietnam and Cambodia who have finally been able to set up offices for their associations within years of their arrival in Montreal, the small group of four to five active organizers from Laos, then known as Association des Chinois du Laos à Montréal (ACLM, 寮華聯絡中心), have been rotating their business meetings since 1981 in their own homes, a decision forced on them largely due to lack of funds. Though not officially registered yet as an association, continuous attempts have been made by this group of volunteers to assemble, by telephone, Chinese compatriots from various parts of Quebec and as far away as Ottawa and Toronto over such social, recreational and sports functions as picnics, dinners, dancing parties and basketball games. Major Chinese festive occasions such as the New Year and the Autumn Moon Festival have provided them with the culturally appropriate occasions to gather together and share with each other a sentiment of commonality and kindred spirit.

Since 1982, with an intent to publish their first directory, the ACLM has been collecting names, addresses and telephone numbers of Chinese from Laos who are in Quebec, the rest of Canada, the United States and other European countries. Much of the organizational initiative and energy seemed to have come continuously from the older generation, which, in turn, was responded to with enthusiasm by the young. As a result, one, thus, did not witness the same kind and degree of intergenerational conflict and rivalry as found among the Sino-Vietnamese leaders and activists.

Like the Chinese from Vietnam and Cambodia, the ACLM has a clear preference for setting up its office within Chinatown, underscoring the relevance of geographic proximity to the Chinese community in general and to the district's institutional network in particular, for enacting the Association's community service functions. A keen sense of awareness that agencies within the Chinese community should not duplicate each other's functions and services has led the Association to decide not to run their own Chinese language classes for their children, who, in turn, have been for years sent to a weekend Chinese language school run by Chinese teachers from Taiwan and Hong Kong.

In general, the few executive members of the ACLM seem to have only limited knowledge and understanding of the history, organizational structure, and operational dynamics of the institutional infrastructure of the Chinese community in Montreal, and, as a result, have been essentially uninvolved and non-participatory in its affairs. Their transaction with the one community service agency in Chinatown, the Chinese Family Serivce, remains one of making referrals of Chinese clients from Laos. From time to time, the elderly members of the Chinese community from Laos participate in functions organized by the elderly club of the native Laotians in Montreal, and the ACLM, citing reasons of cultural and temperamental incompatibility and distrust, would only infrequently attend formal public functions undertaken by the organizations in the Laotian community in Montreal. In that sense, the degree of institutional interaction between the ACLM and the Laotian community has never been close. Neither has the ACLM been actively involved in public affairs and activities outside the local Chinese community and the larger Montreal community proper, and it seems that the ACLM, at least in the foreseeable future, is content to maintain its transactions with the external milieu as such. In comparing themselves to their Sino-Vietnamese counterpart, the ACLM is quite aware of the smaller size of their own community, as well as its relative deficiency in financial and leadership resources. However, as an organization, it seems to be sufficiently contented with the rate at which it has been organizing their community: slow, but evolving and progressing, solidly and with a clear sense of conviction.

On the other hand, the lack of political and cultural brokering skills on the part of this group of pioneering organizers will continue to limit their access to governmental funding for delivery of community and social services, which would, in turn, hamper the future growth of the financial health of the Association. Their lack of understanding of the social service system in the mainstream society makes it unlikely for the Association to make client referrals, thus limiting their transactions to making referrals to the already overloaded social agencies within the Chinese community. The unavailability of a fund of knowledge of the emerging and changing needs of the Chinese people from Laos perhaps, to a considerable extent, explains the absence of both short-term and long-term planning on the part of the Association.

Like the Chinese in Cambodia and, to a lesser extent, in Vietnam, the elite of the Chinese community in Laos was made up of mainly merchants and businessmen, as well as a small representation of school teachers and newspapermen. What was conspicuously absent from such an elite was skilled technical people and middle-class professionals because of long-standing governmental policies limiting entry of the Chinese into the few then existing professional training programs, and consequently, into the professions. This resulted in a Chinese elite class of merchants dominating the affairs and politics of the Chinese community in Laos.

Once uprooted from Laos and transplanted into Canada, these surviving Chinese businessmen and merchants, not speaking English or French, knowing very little of the workings of the public and governmental institutional networks of the host society, and lacking skills and resources in mediating the transactions between their own community and the surrounding milieu, have very quickly found themselves in an acutely weak position to contribute to the growth and development of their own organization and community. As a matter of fact, only one executive member of the ACLM has a rudimentary command of the English and French languages, and none seems to know how the city's social service system is organized and structured; neither do they seem to know what governmental programs to approach to meet specific needs of segments of their own community.

For decades, the Chinese in Indo-China have been identifying themselves, as well as being identified by both the governments and the indigenous native peoples there, as Chinese, Chinese Nationals or ethnic Chinese sojourning in a host society to make a living, thus also distinguishing themselves from the offspring of Chinese parents having intermarried with the indigenous peoples of Southeast Asia. Known as Sino-Cambodians, or Sino-Khmer or Métis in Cambodia, the bulk of them have been assimilated into the Khmer society, rarely speaking any of the Chinese dialects nor participating in the institutions of the local Chinese communities.

The Chinese in Indo-China have also organized themselves into five communities called "*bangs*" 幫, in accordance with their dialect and/or province of origin: Teochiu, Cantonese, Hainanese, Hakka, Hokkien or Fujianese. Called "congregation" in French to designate and identify a body of Chinese embraced by a language or speech group from a specific province of origin, the term "*bang*" owed its origin to the Vietnamese government as far back as 1802 ordering the Chinese to create "*bangs*" to govern themselves, mediate internal disputes, as well as to assist the government in implementing laws and statutes, and collect taxes. In the past forty years, the Chinese in Vietnam, with little financial contribution from the government, created and self-financed, within the five *bangs* or speech groups, their own family and clan associations, mutual aid societies, sports clubs, professional groups, schools and hospitals. It was customary for members of the Chinese merchant elite to occupy strategic positions in these voluntary associations. Under the overall organizing principle of Chineseness or being Chinese in a host society, these *bangs*, together, constituted the larger ethnic entity known to the non-Chinese as the Chinese community. It was also the overall predominance of being Chinese as a basis of ethnic identification that contributed to the continued solidarity among, and mutual cooperation between, the five *bangs* on the one hand, as well as mediated and inter-*bang* rivalry and disputes on the other.

The term "*bang*" also corresponds to a different, but identically pronounced Chinese word which is used by the Chinese in Indo-China to identify among themselves their secondary country of origin other than China. Thus, within Indo-China, the Chinese differentiate themselves into three *bangs* on the basis of whether one is from Vietnam, Cambodia or Laos. It is, therefore, on the basis of at least three different sources of ethnic identification (whether or not being offspring of inter-marriages; language or dialect, province of origin; and country of origin other than China) that an overseas Chinese is first and foremost a Chinese (not a Métis), comes from one of the three countries of Indo-China, is a member of the local Chinese community, and belongs to, and strongly identifies with, one of the five *bangs* within the larger Chinese community. In a broad sociological sense, Chinese in Indo-China are far from being a homogeneous group.

While the experience of being a refugee has indeed served to sublimate, at least temporarily, much of the economic, cultural, provincial and linguistic differences among the Chinese from the three countries of Indo-China by casting each and every person into the status of an Indo-Chinese refugee, it seems to have little effect on how they identify and organize themselves. Chinese from different parts of Indo-China continue to perceive and underscore the need for the establishment of their own organizations and immigrant communities. Consequently, within less than five years of arrival in Montreal, the Chinese have created the ACVM, the UCCC and the ACLM with their own bases of operation, and have been working relatively separately and independently from each other to cater to the needs of their own communities. By attending each other's public gatherings such as annual meetings, banquets, and festive celebrations, the nature of relationships between the three associations remains at best polite, superficial, infrequent and distanced.

Within the ACVM, though to a considerably lesser extent in the UCCC, rivalry for leadership between older members of the Teochiu and the Cantonese *bangs* was indeed rather intense, which marked the beginnings of the dynamics during the early phase of the development of ACVM. The focus of rivalry was on whether those belonging to one *bang* or another have more organizational skills, capabilities and financial resources, and, therefore, contribute more to the Association's leadership and financial well-being. In the UCCC, the board has actually found it necessary and crucial to re-affirm to both themselves and their members the importance of their common origin from China and Cambodia over and above allegiance to and affiliations with the five *bangs* or language groups. Incidentally, there does not seem to be evidence of similar conflicts or rivalry among those from Laos. Quite paradoxically, the ACVM, while marked by intense organizational tension since their pioneering years due to inter-generational and inter-*bang* conflicts, appears to be the most developed and organized in terms of organizational inertia and maturity. As a formal organization, the

ACVM, compared to the other two associations, has, in the younger members of their board, more abilities and resources that are integral to organizing within the community of Chinese from Vietnam as well as interacting with constituencies external to the community. While the ACVM has already begun its participation in the past three years in the institutional infrastructure of the Chinese community, the UCCC seems to manifest considerable difficulty in managing the internal workings of the association due to financial and human resources constraints. In a pure, absolute sense, the ACLM, without a constitution, an office as a base of operation, and a publicly recognized board and staff, is not an association yet, and the lack of financial and human resources will continue to constrain its organizational development in years to come.

From the standpoint of the Québécois as well as members of the local Chinese community, the Chinese from the three countries of Indo-China are firstly refugees or boat people, and secondly, Indo-Chinese in terms of their ethnicity. The label Indo-Chinese refugees, constructed from outside the refugees themselves, has the consequence of casting members subsumed under it a common destiny and a mutually shared status and life chance. Such a label, among other things, thus serves to bestow a sense of sameness among all Chinese from Indo-China, and it is within this framework and standpoint that their relations with both the local Chinese community and the larger Québécois society are constructed and managed. It is in this sense that the Chinese from Indo-China are thrown into the same ethnic pot by outsiders, whether or not to their liking.

From the point of view of the Chinese from Vietnam, Cambodia and Laos, it is quite safe to argue that they share more cultural, tempermental, geographic, ecological and historical affinity with each other than with those of the local Chinese community in Montreal. One might want to suggest that there is a greater social distance perceived and kept between the Chinese from Indo-China and the local Chinese in Montreal, than between and among themselves.

The common feeling of being Chinese and having been refugees, as a result of uprootedness from Indo-China, may well serve to unify them in the long run in spite of speech, provincial and territorial differences that have divided them for more than a century. There are factors other than a common sentiment and a mutually shared fate that may well pave the way toward integration and solidarity.

The Chinese have two sayings that describe literally their situation very well: "Help each other while in the same boat" 同舟共濟 and "Be together while in the same crisis" (患難相扶持). Underlying the two sayings is a strong moral message advocating sharing, reciprocity, mutual aid, common bondage and sentiment as means of coping with crisis. In the past three years, during discussions in regular board meetings within all three associations, there have been indications of a desire to look into the possibility of an amalgamation or union of the three associations. At least two meetings between the ACVM and the UCCC were expressly held towards this end.[10] It is quite obvious that these discussions were guided by a clear recognition of the mutual benefits of a union, such as increased political and bargaining strength during transactions with external constituencies for status and funding; avoidance of duplication of services and functions; reduction of organization overhead and other administrative costs; and possibly eventual improvement in organizational effectiveness and financial well-being as a result of putting resources together. Nevertheless, the pathway to union is not without its obstacles. The ACVM, being a more visible, better-developed and more mature organization serving a considerably larger community of clients, has been quite hesitant to share its existing skills and resources with the other two developing and emerging associations, particularly the ACLM. This reluctance of the ACVM to join forces parallels an equally strong sense of ambivalence on the part of the UCCC and ACLM, to whom such a collective union would possibly mean their initial subordination to the ACVM, and their eventual loss of autonomy and control over their own working priorities. In a union of such a nature, the strong party is fearful of having to share its resources with the weak ones, and one way to cope with this is to ensure that it has a major eventual share of power and authority in the union. Merging with the strong party in a deficient position, the weak party is also equally fearful of instant loss of autonomy, and, therefore, often pitches itself against the strong party in an intense struggle for power. One would then like to argue that it is precisely these unsettling feelings and emotions on the part of all three associations that have prevented them from furthering their efforts towards unification beyond the exploratory, talking stage. It is quite obvious that "being in the same boat facing the same crisis" in itself is not enough to merge the three associations and the three peoples.

Within fifteen years of their first arrival in Montreal, the Chinese from Vietnam, Cambodia and Laos have each established, within their own communities, a voluntary association dedicated to reunification of scattered familial and social relationships, to building community belongingness and solidarity, to provision of community services to aid in refugee resettlement and adaptation, and to preservation of cultural heritage and ethnic identity. The development of these three associations has continued since the outset to be handicapped by factors directly associated with the refugee status of their people. The virtual obliteration of the Chinese merchant elite class in Indo-China since 1979 as a result of either political and economic persecution by the communist regimes or sudden economic loss, so to speak, "scrapped the cream of the crop" of the overseas Chinese refugee communities. This historical incident has, thus, resulted in a real leadership vacuum, a problem persisting in the three communities of Chinese from Indo-China for more than a decade. Among those Chinese refugees admitted into, and resettled in, the host society, few seem to possess the physical and emotional resources to devote to ethnic group development. Invariably, they are preoccupied with locating and reuniting with lost family members, and with saving to send support to family or relatives in refugee transit camps or at home, while deeply immersed in economic and social adaptation to the host country. The continued economic marginality and dependency of the Chinese refugees themselves many years later is, therefore, closely intertwined with the lack of financial well-being of all three associations in the Sino-Indo-Chinese communities. As far as the associations are concerned, this state of economic precariousness will probably not go away within the next decade.

Other characteristics associated with refugee status that have hampered the development of the three Sino-Indo-Chinese communities include deficiency in facility with both official languages of Canada and lack of pertinent brokering skills and resources among the communities' few emerging leaders, which have immediate and long-term consequences in terms of minimising the extent of their interfacing with the governmental bureaucracy and the social service system in the mainstream society. This lack of skills in making transactions with the milieu is an important factor underlying the considerable social distance between the three Sino-Indo-Chinese communities and the host society.

Specifically, within the Sino-Vietnamese community, the issue of leadership and its role in organizational and community development has taken the form of ideological conflicts and rivalry for power between the older and younger generations. Cast in the beginning phase of community development, the Chinese from Vietnam are now facing the challenge to resolve conflicts between tradition and change, and between two contrasting modes of ethnic organizations: an "old" traditional model indigenous to, and imported from the Chinese community in Saigon that stresses organizational and community separation, autonomy, preservation of the cultural heritage, and a leadership premised on age-related seniority and respect for tradition and the elderly, and a "modernist" model that stresses integration, extensive social and political participation, and a leadership based on competencies in interfacing with governmental and public institutions of the mainstream society.

The three Chinese associations have not only maintained considerable social distance from the public institutions in the mainstream society, from the local Chinese community and from the three indigenous Indo-Chinese communities, their transactions between themselves have remained infrequent, superficial and minimal. This attempt at the maintenance of social separation may well be partly due to deficiency in organizational resources (an involuntary factor) and partly due to an inherent need on the part of the leaders of the three associations to maximize organizational autonomy as well as to minimize organizational compromise and external interference (a voluntary preference). Seen in this light, the obvious rational benefits of an "association of associations" do not seem attractive enough to overwhelm a basic need "to be able to do own things in one's own ways".

Underlying the sentiment of "an association of associations" is the expression of an ideal on the part of the leaders of all three associations that all Chinese in Montreal and, eventually, in Canada, be united and organized with a common front and a common voice. This sentiment of ethnic solidarity is consistent with all three associations preferring to set up offices in Chinatown, and with having a considerably higher rate of participation in the local Chinese community than in the mainstream society. The Chinese from the three countries of the Indo-China region have primordially identified with Chinatown and with the local Chinese community. However, this does not seem to mask their voluntary separation from the local Chinese community in Montreal, nor from each other. The history of development of the three Sino-Indo-Chinese refugee communities in Montreal, thus, points to the importance of weighing and balancing subjective and objective factors, voluntary and involuntary forces, ideals and realities in our search for understanding the development of ethnic groups, ethnicity and ethnic identification.

Like other immigrants who have been there earlier, the leaders of these three Sino-Indo-Chinese refugee communities are not without some deep feelings of ambivalence in facing both personal and organizational dilemmas that underlie tradition and change, separation and integration, cultural autonomy and assimilation. While still in the early stage of development, the three associations, handicapped by financial and personnel resources, have chosen to nurture the need of belongingness and attachment to a community. The accent has been clearly on family reunification, on "bringing people together", and on rebuilding a once lost sense of community.

Chinese from Hong Kong, Taiwan, China and elsewhere, are by no means united either. These groups of Chinese, while setting themselves apart from the Indo-Chinese, are divided by linguistic, economic, demographic, generational and historical differences. The "native and local Chinese community" is largely made up of early Taishanese speaking settlers and their descendents, who form the backbone of the institutional and commercial infrastructure of the so-called old Chinatown. By and large, these same people, largely of the merchant class operating various ethnic businesses, are at the centre of Chinese community politics, taking upon themselves the responsibility of eventually "uniting" the Montreal Chinese under The Montreal Chinese Community United Center (MCCUC, 滿地可華人聯合總會), as well as representing the Chinese community in external transactions with the wider society. The very core of power in such institutional structure has rarely been accessible to the outsiders, namely, those from Hong Kong, Taiwan, China and Southeast Asia. The three levels of Canadian government have largely looked upon the MCCUC as the community's leader-spokesperson, thus further frustrating and alienating other Chinese groups.

Other than the Indo-Chinese refugees, Chinese from Hong Kong and Taiwan, many of whom belong to the class of "economic immigrants", represent the more recent massive additions to the Chinese community in Montreal, and are by and large non-participatory as far as local community politics is concerned. In 1987, there were talks among the Cantonese-speaking Hong Kong professionals (accountants, real estate agents, newspaper publishers, and so on) to set up their own socio-recreational clubs or professional associations to look after their own interests and needs. All these are intended to add another layer of institutional structure to the local Chinese community. The Montreal Chinese Family Service, the Chinese Neighbourhood Society, and the Chinese Volunteers' Association, the three better organized community service agencies in the Montreal Chinese community, are run by Hong Kong social workers trained in Canada. More often than not, they run into conflict with the MCCUC for governmental funding and community leadership.

In the meantime, the Mandarin speaking Chinese from Taiwan evolve into a community of their own, which is primarily a loose conglomeration of a few hundred families. Social visits and mutual aid are maintained among these close-knit family units. They organize their own banquets, out-of-town trips, and cultural-recreational variety shows; they even celebrate on their own many festive occasions such as the Chinese New Year in rented sports halls from local schools.

It is perhaps more accurate to speak of several Chinese communities in Montreal, than one united, solidified Chinese community. Each and every Chinese group has been intent on consolidating internal community dynamics. An "association of associations" remains at best an ideal which, sometimes unfortunately, backfires and divides. The Montreal Chinese community should perhaps be best seen as a loosely structured system with as much inter-organizational conflict as internal solidarity and cohesiveness. The concept of the Chinese community is, thus, more an artefact, meaningful and useful to those from the outside looking in.

Notes

1. This chapter is based on a study conducted in 1986, funded by the Ministry of Cultural Communities and Immigration of the Quebec government. It was the intent of this study to trace and reconstruct the history of establishment and maintenance of voluntary associations among the Chinese from Vietnam, Cambodia and Laos, focussing on historical as well as structural factors associated with attempts by leaders of the three communities to organize their own people to meet their collective needs. The study also attempted to examine how the three communities went about constructing and maintaining ethnic boundaries while making transactions among themselves, with the local Chinese community, and the external milieu.

   The primary source of data of the study, collected in 1985, were based on in-depth individual and group interviews with twenty male adults who were past or current directors of the boards of three voluntary associations established by the Chinese from Vietnam, Cambodia and Laos. This data was supplemented by additional interviews with six informants, two from each of the three communities. Lasting about three hours, all except two interviews were conducted in Cantonese, a dialect either spoken or understood by most Chinese from Indo-China.

This chapter is an updated version of chapter 7, titled, "The Chinese from Indo-China in Montreal: A Study in Ethnic Voluntary Associations, Community Organization, and Ethnic Boundaries," in *Ten Years Later: Indo-Chinese Communities in Canada*, edited by Louis-Jacques Dorais, Kwok B. Chan and Doreen M. Indra (Montreal: Canadian Asian Studies Association), 1988.
2. William E. Willmott, "The Chinese in Indo-China" (pp. 69–80). In *Southeast Asian Exodus: From Tradition to Resettlement*, edited by Elliott L. Tepper. (Ottawa: Canadian Asian Studies Association, 1980); *The Chinese in Cambodia* (Vancouver: Publications Centre, University of British Columbia, 1967).
3. William J. Duiker, "Kampuchea," in *The Encyclopedia Americana*, International Edition (Danbury, Connecticut: Grolier Incorporated, Vol. 18, 1983), p. 275.
4. Victor Purcell, *The Chinese in Southeast Asia* (Oxford in Asia Paperbacks, second edition, 1980), p. 170.
5. William E. Willmott, p. 71.
6. Ibid.
7. Kwok B. Chan and Lawrence Lam, "Structure and Values of the Chinese Family in Vietnam", in *The Southeast Asian Environment*, edited by Douglas R. Webster (Ottawa: University of Ottawa Press, 1983), pp. 206–20.
8. A Chinese noodle factory located at the corner of Cote and Lagauchetière streets.
9. L.F. Chan 陳烈甫 , *Dongnanyazhou Di Huaqiao, Huaren Yu Huayi* 東南亞洲的華僑，華人與華裔(Taipei: Zheng Zhong Shu Ju 正中書局, 2nd edition, 1983. Text in Chinese).
10. During a group interview with five board members of the UCCC, I brought up their once expressed fervent hope that one day all Chinese in Quebec, irrespective of their birth place, country of origin, religious and political affiliations, and language, would eventually unite into one community with one voice; subsumed under this great expectation was the desire that all Chinese from Indo-China would unite, perhaps starting with the union of the three associations. However, almost in the same breath, while comparing themselves to the ACVM, they indicated their awareness that they were from a smaller and less powerful country than Vietnam, had a smaller community in Montreal, had less organizational resources and skills, and were less developed and advanced as an organization. Because of all these issues, they were quite ambivalent about the idea of joining forces with the ACVM while they were in a relatively weak position. Their preference at the moment was that they would run their association in the way they had in the past years while finding for themselves a niche in the larger Chinese community, bearing in mind the importance of working toward the long-term goal of uniting the three associations and their communities. It is important to point out that this apparent resistance to immediately uniting with the ACVM on the part of the UCCC has to do with some unpleasant early experiences of being slighted, ignored and rejected while interacting with organizations in the Chinese community when the UCCC was first established. As far as the ACLM was concerned, to unite with the other two associations was at best a distant organizational goal; it was then more preoccupied with getting their own association off the ground. However, all five members of the ACLM

11. Boat People Getting Organized and Keeping Distance 289

unanimously expressed during the group interview their ideological endorsement of being Chinese being the all-important, overall governing principle.

The incumbent president of the ACVM, an active younger force in the Association, suggested in the interview that he supported the idea of "association of associations" in principle and in spirit, but did not seem to disguise the unwillingness of the old members of the Association to share their resources with the weaker parties of such a union. Rather poetically, he volunteered that a possible model for such a united organization be named "Association of Chinese from Meikong's three countries", and explained that the Meikong River, with its origin from China, runs through Vietnam, Cambodia and Laos, and gives the three countries a common geographic identity and cultural heritage. He also suggested that a possible organizational model for the union is that the three associations continue to sponsor their cultural, social and recreational programs and activities separately for their own people but present themselves as a united body in the delivery of social and community services, thus anticipating a separation between the cultural and service functions of the union.

12. A Sore on the Mouse's Tail[1]

St. Urbain Street. Chinese as onlookers of urban "renewal".

Gilbert Duclos

Aerial view of Montreal Chinatown during the construction of the Place Guy Favreau (bottom right corner). Houses and shops were demolished, and land was cleared to make way for the colossal federal building.

St. Urbain Street being widened to ease traffic as a result of the construction of Quebec Government's Convention Centre. This public works project in effect delimited the western boundary of Chinatown.

12. A Sore on the Mouse's Tail

URBAN displacement and its deleterious effects has recently attracted considerable attention of the popular press,[2] the academics[3] and the city planners and architects.[4] Most studies of the displacement process agree, firstly, that a highly disproportionate number of the displacees are elderly, low-income and non-white; and, secondly, that the psycho-social effects of forced uprooting and relocation on them are particularly severe partly because they are most likely to be long-term residents dependent on the neighbourhood's institutions and locally-based social network, and partly because they are low in resources and, therefore, would be more likely to experience forced relocation and uprootedness as a crisis. While the exact impact of forced relocation on the displacees is not known yet, at least two studies[5] have found that dislocated families often move more than once since their first dislocation. These displacees are often merely powerless and helpless onlookers of massive urban displacement, experiencing victimization by "market forces" beyond their control.[6]

It has been pointed out by an observer of urban displacement[7] that "Often government has acted in the interests of profit maximizers via its functions as builders of freeways, commercial and civil projects. In the 1950s and 1960s, government agencies were immediate displacers; in the 1970s, the profit maximizers have been acting directly." The United States Department of Housing and Urban Development (HUD), in its 1979 Interim Displacement Report,[8] points out that about one-fifth of all displacement in the United States was directly caused by government programs and highway projects sponsored by local and federal authorities.

Lang, in his observation of the dynamics of the renewal-displacement process, provides the following description:

> By simply casting their covetous eye on a particular neighbourhood, the rich home buyers will immediately produce a surge in house prices and rents that will eventually preclude market participation by the poor. In addition, this effect will be most pronounced in the dense inner city where any physical improvements are quickly noted by local residents, speculators, and neighbourhood handicappers bent on making windfall profits.[9]

In the past five years, journalists in Montreal took the leadership in graphically portraying the economic and psychological effects of urban displacement in Montreal as a result of expropriation by the government or conversion of old residential units into condominiums by developers. These journalistic writings were dramatized by such headlines as "Renovation Craze Puts Squeeze on Low-income Roomers—Roomers Pushed out by

Gentrification",[10] "Expropriation Steamer is very Tough to Stop"[11] and "Renovation Blitz Forcing Low-income Groups from Inner City".[12]

A comparative study of the impact of forced relocation on those relocated in Montreal with those in other North American cities documents the massive destruction of the neighbourhoods of the poor during the early years of municipal reform in Montreal from 1958 to 1968 to combat organized crime.[13] During these ten years, a period often known as the "Golden Decade" in Montreal, major public investments in street widening (e.g., Metropolitain, Decarie, Bonaventure), the Metro subway, and Expo '67 were made to stimulate private investment and tourism. The expropriation of low-rent districts in the city forced their inhabitants to relocate to areas hostile to their housing and economic needs. The authors of this study are particularly concerned with "the deep sense of loss by dozens of elderly, long-time residents of the neighbourhood from which they were evicted" and "the effects of psychological trauma which must surely have hurt a number of the weakest and most vulnerable of the relocatees". The study concludes that the impact of forced relocation on relocatees in Montreal is the same as in other North American cities: higher rents, less living space and loss of neighbourhood identity.

In his book *Lost Montreal*, Luc d'Iberville-Moreau,[14] lamenting the destruction of heritage, linkage with the past, and of neighbourhoods inhabited by immigrants, makes the following observation:

> Commerce, speculation and foreign investment in real estate—often dictated from abroad without any respect for or understanding of the soul of the city—can do work against the needs and wishes of citizens by disregarding the origins, the habitants, the functions and the architecture of a district in which property is coveted.

One recent example of victims of urban displacement by governments and by "commerce, speculation and foreign investment in real estate" is the Chinatown in Montreal, which has attracted considerable journalistic and editorial coverage headlined by such titles as "City Tearing Us Apart, Brick by Brick, say Montreal's Chinese",[15] "Chinatown Won't Last Ten Years",[16] "The Changing Face of Chinatown",[17] "Chinatown Shafted (Again)"[18] and "Listen to Chinatown".[19]

Situated in the eastern part of the downtown core and bound by Dorchester in the North, Viger in the South, Bleury in the West and Sanguinet in the east,[20] Montreal's Chinatown, like most Chinatowns throughout North America, is strategically located, an important geographical factor underlying the fact that the few city blocks making up Chinatown have become attractive prey to the "covetous eyes" of developers and speculators. Within its three-mile radius, one finds within walking distance such major public utilities and amenities as hotels (e.g., Bonaventure, Grand Hotel, Hotel Champlain and Meridian), tourist attractions (e.g., St. Denis Street, Old Montreal and City Hall), and theatres, cinemas and concert halls (e.g., Place des Arts). Well served by public transport (four metro stations of two different lines within a radius of a 10 minutes walk), Chinatown is in a more or less central position, easily accessible by all districts in Montreal.[21] This factor of accessibility to downtown amenities and geographic centrality alone has rendered Chinatown particularly vulnerable to the process of renewal-displacement.

For more than a century, the term Chinatown conjures up a multiplicity of stereotypical and largely negative and derogatory images underlined by a strange blending of reactions and emotions ranging from curiosity, fear and paranoia, to hatred, prejudice and discrimination.[22] These images are similar to those normally associated with ethnic ghettos and urban slums: dark alleys, prostitution and gambling rings, drugs, organized crime, overcrowding, high rates of physical and mental disorders, and a diversity of "ethnic vices". More recently, Chinatowns are also known to maintain and support a marginal population: the elderly and the poor, handicapped by linguistic, cultural and psychological barriers.

According to a recent survey,[23] there are altogether 441 residents in Chinatown, 271 of whom are Chinese by ethnic origin. Among the 271 Chinese, about 60% (162) are 60 years of age or above. About 57% of the Chinese population in Chinatown are female, whereas almost half (46.8%) of the area's total population are widowed.

Historically, Chinatown has also been the hub of Chinese business and entrepreneurial activities, with an economy separate and distinct in functions, but also dependent on the larger economy. The display of Chinese signs, goods and commodities in Chinese bookstores, restaurants, arts and crafts and grocery stores; the inundation of Chinese folk music and the aroma of exotic Chinese cuisines; and the domination of traditional Chinese symbols portrayed in the contrasts of hugh patches of reds and yellows, provide Chinatown as an urban space with an unmistakably Chinese flavour and character. In Chinatown, one often hears the Chinese old-timers and new immigrants from various parts of Asia conversing with each other in a mix of Chinese dialects; the sheer physical visibility of the Chinese

FIGURE 12.1
Montreal's Chinatown

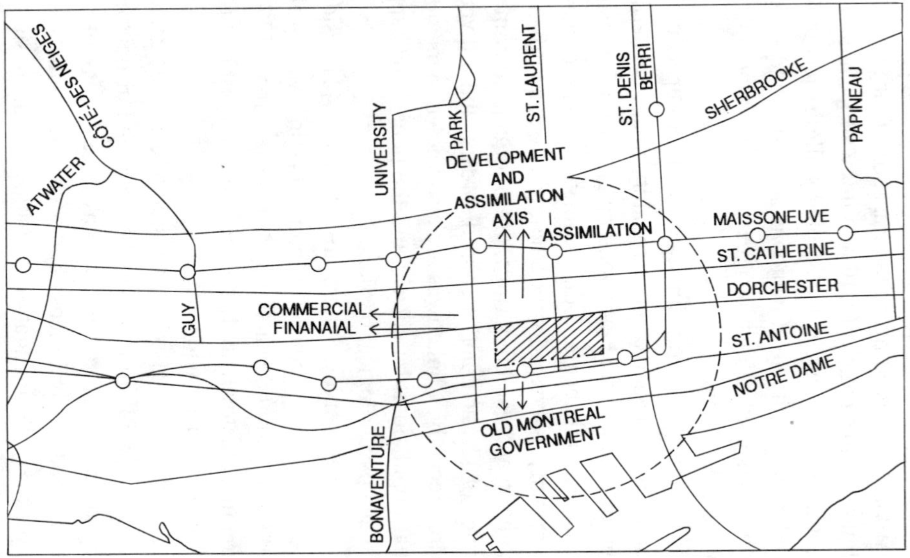

Source: Wu Menzheng, "Montreal Chinatown: A Study of Its Changing Functions." Thesis submitted to School of Urban Planning, McGill University, Montreal, Quebec.

Legend
- 10-minute walking distance
- Chinatown
- metro station

Scale 1:31000

people gives the district a distinct Chinese personality. In terms of the anthropology of language and culture, Chinatown as an ethnic neighbourhood looks, smells, sounds and feels Chinese.

From an ecological and territorial standpoint, Chinatown, to both the Chinese people and, to a certain extent, the outsiders, has well-delimited boundaries. A recent survey based on interviews with leaders of the Chinese community of the city of Montreal indicates that there is a consensus amongst them as to which city streets constitute the boundaries of Chinatown.[24] It is also their firm belief that those few city blocks belong to them and they should have the right to decide what happens in the area.

More than a century of institutional and structural discrimination created a circumscribed world for the Chinese. As stigmatized persons, they began to develop and perpetuate a self-image and self-concept based on their interpretations of how others saw, felt about and acted towards them. They were forced to lead a sheltered existence and associated themselves only with others of their own kind as a means of defence. In an attempt to cope with ethnic insults, in inter-ethnic transactions, the Chinese have chosen to accommodate by self-withdrawal and self-isolation.

Discrimination against the Chinese has left them socially and legally vulnerable and unprotected, which, in turn, creates the need to establish their own ethnic institutions in Chinatowns throughout Canada to protect and safeguard their civil, social and legal rights in their transactions with the outside society. Homeless and without a family, the Chinese in Montreal looked upon the many family and clan associations as "surrogate families and parents". A close scrutiny of functions traditionally served by the Chinatown organizations indicates a gradual loss of the protective, defensive, legal and paternalistic functions. The gradual emergence in the past few years of several community and neighbourhood-based social service organizations staffed by Canadian-trained Chinese community workers and funded by federal and provincial grants has actually rendered most of these functions obsolete and redundant. However, when the Chinese community leaders were articulating the functional significance and salience of Chinatown to the Chinese community of Montreal,[25] they pointed to two strategic functions. First, Chinatown provides a territory, a Chinese urban space, where the Chinese can perpetuate and nurture a sense of ethnic-cultural identification and pride, which, in turn, enables the Chinese as members of a visible minority to cope with external, discriminatory treatment. Second, the institutional infrastructure of Chinatown functions to safeguard the continuity of Chinese values, beliefs and symbols and to transmit them with dignity and pride to the new generations.

The construction of two large-scale provincial government buildings, Hydro Quebec in 1962 and Complexe Desjardins in 1976, take up altogether two city blocks along Dorchester Boulevard. Situated on the north side of the Montreal Chinatown, these buildings ecologically and physically delimited and "defined" its northern boundary. Another federal office building, the Guy Favreau complex, one of the largest of its kind in Canada, necessitated the clearing of six acres of Montreal downtown land bounded by Dorchester, St. Urbain, Lagauchetière and Jeanne Mance, and demolition of nine buildings outside this area to allow for the widening of Jeanne Mance and St. Urbain streets. In the process of this massive demolition and land expropriation by the federal government, two Chinese churches, a school, several Chinese grocery and arts and crafts stores, a Chinese food processing plant and about 20 dwellings were demolished and relocated outside Chinatown. The Chinese Pentecostal church on Chenneville Street just south of Dorchester Boulevard was expropriated in the fall of 1972 almost immediately after $100,000 had been spent for an additional floor and other renovation work. Between 1960 and 1980, it is estimated that more than 200 structures had been demolished for various governmental projects. This is equivalent to losing nearly 400 housing units. The widening of St. Urbain Street to make way for traffic created by major public buildings threatened to demolish a building housing the Li's Association. This move was retracted only because of strong protest from the Chinese community.

Place Guy Favreau was conceived to bring more than 10,000 federal civil servants under one roof, thus asserting the physical as well as symbolic presence of the federal government in the city and the province. The project is dubbed the manifestation of a typical "edifice complex" in Quebec:

> There is an affliction, which Jean-Claude Marsan[26] dubbed an "edifice complex," which is especially severe in Quebec. When a population contracts this disease, it develops an irrational compulsion to build large buildings. It looks to the construction of large physical structures to solve social problems. The federal government wants to strengthen its image, so what is it going to do? Build an expensive new building (Place Guy Favreau).[27]

One of the consequences of the succession of grandiose projects in the past twenty years is the creation of an artificially inflated construction industry oriented almost exclusively to large projects:

> ...The existence of this oversized labour force is being used to justify projects like

Place Guy Favreau and the Convention Centre since they will provide construction jobs. Does this mean that every year we will have to come up with yet another $200 million blockbuster building? No. We must decide that we as a society cannot afford this extravagance.[28]

When a scaled mock-up of Place Guy Favreau was revealed to the media in 1975, reaction was uniformly negative, typified by such comments as "glass-faced behemoth", "a modern horror, completely unrelated to the street", "walls of solar-resistant glass make the building impenetrable to the eye so that it is both physically and visually isolated".[29] The federal government responded to these criticisms by rationalizing emphatically the desirability of co-ordinating and centralizing federal government service to the community.[30] Yet, almost in the same breath, they (the Department of Public Works and Ministry of Supply and Services officials) admitted that the federal government itself at the time did not seem to have an urgent need for office space.[31] The government actually owned several unused, vacant buildings in the city.

The August 1977 edition of *SOS Montreal*, published by Save Montreal and sponsored by Heritage Montreal, identified ten reasons why Place Guy Favreau should not be built,[32] among which were the destruction of Chinatown, the over-centralization of government functions, the creation of major traffic congestion and the secrecy of the planning process. The last reason for objection, secretive planning on the part of the federal government, remained the most emotional and controversial, and caused the most frustration among the project's critics:

> If the project is not to do irreparable harm, it must take realities in Montreal into account. Recognition of these realities is impossible without input from the community. Input from the community is impossible if the Government keeps the plans shrouded in secrecy.[33]

It did not take long for merchants, social workers and leaders of the Chinese community to join Save Montreal and Heritage Montreal in their collective protests against the Place Guy Favreau project. Responding to pressure by Save Montreal, a $100,000 Consultative Committee was quickly created late in 1977 by the federal Department of Public Works, which the government billed as Montreal's first experiment in public participation in a major development project.[34] The Montreal Chinese Community Service Centre, now the Chinese Family Service of Greater Montreal located in the heart of Chinatown, quickly submitted to the Committee a request for allocation of space in Place Guy Favreau for a social service centre, a medical clinic, recreation facilities (a gymnasium and a swimming pool), an auditorium-theatre, a library-reading room and a day care centre, all for the use of the Chinese community. The Montreal Chinese Community United Centre, then a group established to act as an umbrella organization for the entire Chinese community in Montreal, submitted to the Consultative Committee a similar request, while stressing the pressing housing needs of the community, as well as the importance of community consultation and public input. The Montreal Chinese Professional and Business Men's Association suggested that the project might be able to "redeem" itself by catering to the need of the Chinese community for a cultural and community centre.

In an attempt to keep up the public pressure, conservationists and representatives of the Chinese community continued to meet and make written submission to the Consultative Committee. The Committee continued to hear and to receive briefs and presentations. The Place Guy Favreau project continued to demolish more buildings, expropriated more land, seemingly oblivious to external input, including that of the Consultative Committee. Political and bureaucratic promises, made as concessions to public criticism, were never delivered. Place Guy Favreau, contrary to promises made earlier, never housed the low-income and elderly Chinese residents who were displaced, saying such a move would discriminate against non-Chinese applicants. Neither did the complex grant the wishes of the Chinese community for a cultural centre and various other amenities within its premises. The old Chinese Catholic Mission Church and the school building attached to it were integrated into the complex with the understanding that both properties would be returned to the Chinese community. The church building was declared earlier by the provincial Ministry of Cultural Affairs as an historic building, and was thus protected from demolition or usage for purposes other than religious. Neither buildings have undergone renovation of any scale since the complex itself was officially inaugurated in 1983. Contrary to the wishes of the Chinese community, the south side of the complex west of St. Urbain Street never became an aesthetic, functional part of Chinatown. As a net result, a good portion of the north side of Lagauchetière Street, formerly an integral part of Chinatown, was permanently lost. Chinatown has lost an arm. The Chinese presence thus comes to an abrupt end at the corner of Côté and Lagauchetière streets, beyond which lie the ever-imposing convention centre in the south, scores of stores on the ground level of Place Guy Favreau in the north that have very little to complement the Chinese character of the

12. A Sore on the Mouse's Tail

street, and the Catholic church at the far end of Lagauchetière Street, old, dilapidated, vacant and impoverished. In a way, the church, the sole survivor of federal demolition and expropriation (only because of its historical value as declared by the provincial government), remains the only reminder of the fact that this plot of land once was within the boundary of the Chinese district.

The completion of this federal building in 1983 successfully delimited the western boundary of Chinatown. With monthly rental rates for residential units inside Place Guy Favreau between $460 and $565 for one-bedroom apartments, between $640 and $840 for two-bedroom apartments, and between $760 and $880 for three-bedroom apartments, the building can hardly be affordable for those relocatees whose dwellings were expropriated and demolished. Instead, the building, with its downtown location, has proved attractive to middle-class families of professionals and businessmen, and was filled to capacity within less than two years of its completion. As a final edition of governmental encroachment on ethnic urban space, a $580 million provincial government convention centre, taking up yet another city block, was built in 1983 and successfully delimited the south-western boundary of Montreal Chinatown. Again, like other large-scale public building projects, the provincial Convention Centre came under public criticism:

> Why should Save Montreal be drawn into the debate on the location of the (Convention) Centre when the basic issue is whether there is any need for such a facility? To my knowledge, there is not a single convention centre which is profitable. Public pressure in Toronto helped to defeat a proposed centre which the hotel lobby (no pun intended) tried to push through.... Who will be using the convention centre?[35]

Gigantic, large-scale, ultra-modern federal and provincial government buildings hover over and encroach upon the low-lying buildings of Chinatown like tombstones, seemingly reminding the Chinese people that the days of their urban space are numbered.

Displacement of ethnic urban space and encroachment by the pioneering efforts of governments have generated a number of chain effects, one of which being the gradual infusion of the interest of land speculators and developers into Chinatown. Also in 1983, a twenty million dollar condominium-office building called Place du Quartier, with a price tag between $74,000 and $118,000 for a condominium-apartment aimed at upper-middle class professionals and businessmen, was built inside Chinatown at the corner of St. Urbain and Dorchester, which further solidifies the area's northern boundary. The city sold the land on which the building was erected (which for years was the site of a city works yard) to a non-Chinese corporation called 111747 Canada Ltd. at half the price of $50 a square foot (at which the city evaluated adjoining sites when it bought them in early 1982). The selling price of $1.225 million for the land was considerably lower than the then market value given its location. Filled to capacity in less than three years since 1983, the building, aimed at upper-middle income families, has very little to complement the cultural and socio-economic reality of Chinatown. Architecturally and functionally speaking, it seems to be more in line with Place Guy Favreau and the Convention Centre. As put by one, then opposition, city councillor of the Montreal Citizen's Movement Party, now the incumbent party at City Hall, "The project will fit in well with the new Guy Favreau complexe, across St. Urbain Street, but is likely to 'destroy the Chinese community'."[36] The Chinese community condemned this transaction as one of the many yet-to-come tactics of the city to sell city-owned land to non-Chinese developers and speculators, which eventually will "shut out" Chinatown.[37] Like the Guy Favreau complexe, this condominium-office building marks the beginnings of a general trend of the middle-class people taking residence in the downtown area. In this case, they work jointly with the governments and the developers to slowly "gentrify" Chinatown.

While the former provincial Liberal government of Quebec opposed the construction of Place Guy Favreau throughout its planning and implementation stages, the municipal government of Montreal supported the project through silent acquiescence and non-interventionist blessing. Within less than a decade, Montreal Chinatown was literally smothered and hemmed in. A federal government building rose from the ground; the provincial and municipal governments did not intervene. Then in the same year, a provincial convention centre was erected; the federal and municipal governments did not intervene. In the midst of this "construction boom", St. Urbain Street was widened to expedite traffic created. Chinatown lost a couple more buildings, their only park and a Chinese pagoda donated by a local Chinese businessman to the city to commemorate Expo '67. Less than a year later, the Chinese community learned from reading the newspapers that the City Council approved in 1982 a re-zoning bylaw to permit construction by a non-Chinese developer of two six-storey towers containing 96 apartments atop three storeys of stores and offices.

12. A Sore on the Mouse's Tail

While the three levels of government collaboratively plotted the boxing and hemming in of an ethnic district, Chinatown was quickly gentrified. And in this case, governments, not developers nor speculators, took the leadership. Then the latest (certainly not last by any means) blow to the Chinese community took the form of the Chinese learning again from the media, not City Hall officials, that the City Council in October 1984 passed a zoning bylaw (No. 6513) to restrict development in the area south of Sherbrooke Street between Bleury and Sanguinet streets to residential or "special" purposes. Chinatown occupies about 30% of this area. The prohibition of commercial development along Lagauchetière Street east of St. Laurent Boulevard would cut Chinatown's growth in the one and only direction left—eastward.

This zoning bylaw almost immediately touched off intense media and public reactions calling for its repeal or modification. *The Gazette*, Montreal's only English language daily, ran a series of editorials, letters to the editor, and news reports bearing titles such as "Calling Mr. Drapeau's bluff",[38] "City should survey Chinese about Chinatown: Councillor",[39] "Drapeau wants to kill off Chinatown",[40] "Chinatown expansion good for city",[41] "Listen to Chinatown",[42] "Chinatown vents its anger against city zoning bylaw",[43] "Undo the strait jacket",[44] "More gulf for Chinatown",[45] and "Chinese push for change to bylaw that chokes development".[46] On 1 May 1985, the *Gazette* published a large-scale satirical cartoon by noted cartoonist Aislin with Mr. Drapeau, then Montreal's mayor, holding a "Save Chinatown" placard.

In a collective attempt to protest the bylaw, the Chinese community quickly gathered petitions, published bulletins and newsletters, and called press conferences. Save Montreal, the urban conservation group that contested the construction of the Place Guy Favreau a decade ago, joined in this public protest along with presentations from urbanists from Concordia University and McGill University. Calling the bylaw "racist" since the bulk of the businessmen to be affected in the designated area are Chinese, the Chinese were disturbed by Chinatown being inhibited from "natural growth and expansion".

When the city in June, 1986 called an "economic summit" to elicit public input into the future development of the downtown area, a Chinese group, the Montreal Chinese Community United Centre, among other requests, again called for a modification of the bylaw, expansion of Chinatown beyond the existing boundaries, and public consultation. The Chinese community was as upset by the socio-economic impact of the bylaw on Chinatown, as by a secretive, non-consulting municipal government that strives to impose an external view on a district regarding its development. The Chinese Professionals and Business Men's Association, the group that spearheaded and engineered the public protest, was so frustrated it threatened to adopt a boycott tactic: to divert potential Hong Kong economic entrepreneurs from investing in Montreal. A Chinese businessman, Kenneth Zhuang 張錦輝, told a reporter of *The Citizen* on 30 March 1985 that a Hong Kong-based hotel chain had decided to build a $12 million three-star hotel in Toronto rather than near Montreal's Chinatown because of the restrictive bylaw. Zhuang added that when told by the city to do business on St. Catherine Street, not Chinatown, the Chinese would go further—down Highway 401, en route to Toronto.[47] Ironically, all this was happening at a time when the Quebec government had just sent their officials and immigration ministers to Hong Kong investors to Quebec.

On 10 March 1985, the Chinese community staged what was billed the first street protest in the history of the Chinese in Quebec. About 100 Chinese representing 15 Chinese groups gathered in a vacant parking lot on Lagauchetière Street and wound their way through St. Laurent Boulevard, chanting, "Protect Chinatown" and "Save Chinatown" slogans before finishing at City Hall. White banners protesting the 6513 bylaw were strapped across Lagauchetière Street and St. Laurent Boulevard. Just before disbanding the demonstration, the crowd sang "O Canada" and tried a chorus of "Gens du Pays" to signify their identification with Canada and Quebec as well as to demand equal treatment.

Partly due to the availability of low-rental rooming houses and a spectrum of community services provided by ethnic organizations and agencies, and partly because of their strategic location in the downtown area, Chinatowns throughout Canada were historically attractive to low-income Chinese families and the elderly. A recent survey[48] has found a steady, but significant, internal migration of the Chinese-elderly from the suburbs into Chinatown. Many of these are Chinese widows with a history of co-residence with their children and grandchildren within or outside the Montreal metropolitan area prior to moving into Chinatown. Chinatown has gradually become a retirement community for the Chinese elderly.

While about 200 Chinese elderly women and men now live as retirees in rooming houses above the Chinese restaurants and stores, it was estimated that Montreal's Chinatown once supported a Chinese population of 3,000. The chain effects of urban displacement in terms of abrupt increase in land and property values, and increase in taxes, have continued to force both the local landlords and tenants out.

A recent report put out by the Montreal Chinese Professional and Businessmen's Association[49] points out that "the market for retail commercial space in Chinatown is so tight that a tenant who holds a commercial lease for a small store with only two years left (on it) can sell the lease with the store empty for $30,000." There is also evidence from real estate offices indicating that some commercial spaces on the ground level in Chinatown that are suitable for use as restaurants or grocery stores have increased five-fold in rental value within a period of four years.

Also to be victimized by urban displacement are the many family and clan associations and community-based organizations and agencies. In spite of the fact that these institutions have been part of the ecology of Chinatown for half a century, some of them will have to be closed down or relocated outside Chinatown. With its institutional and cultural infrastructure removed, Chinatown in Montreal as an ethnic neighbourhood will be uprooted from its history and heritage, and will become nothing but a commercial and tourist district catering only to the needs of consumers.

Closely following the footsteps of the local Chinese residents and the community-based associations are the small businessmen who, with increases in taxes and rentals, will suddenly discover that the pressure of business competition is too intense. With the departure of small Chinese businesses and the gradual entry of large-scale entrepreneurial businesses from outside the area into Chinatown, one can foresee a drastic reduction of the heterogeneity and diversity of the commercial facets of Chinatown.

In the case of Montreal Chinatown, urban displacement can be understood in terms of: (a) the governments spearheading and making "pioneering efforts" in using their political resources in artificially fortifying the external boundaries of Chinatown by expropriating land inside, and neighbouring, the area, and constructing large-scale, modern governmental buildings which pay little respect to the area they are encroaching upon; and (b) the gradual infusion of Chinese or non-Chinese upper-middle class interests made possible by real-estate speculators, thus pushing out the original residents, ethnic associations and family-run small businesses.

Chinatown was created by a unique set of historical, political and economic forces emanating from intergroup transactions. It existed because of an historical fact: overt structural discrimination. It has continued to exist because it serves a variety of functions, both for the Chinese and the larger society. The Chinese insist that they have historical and territorial claims over Chinatown, that the residents, the ethnic associations, the businesses as well as the traditional character of Chinatown be protected, and that they have rights to an urban space that once was theirs.

Urban displacement by several levels of governments have transformed Chinatown in the past two decades, and will continue to force out those who cannot afford to stay in the area. With its institutional infrastructure eroded and undermined, Montreal Chinatown and the larger Chinese population of the province are undergoing a transitional crisis. The crisis is worsened by government authorities who have chosen to resolve the conflict between commercial development and the rights of the people by siding with the former. City Hall is only a stone's throw away from Chinatown. The majestic white-top and bronzed buildings of City Hall are quite visible from any vantage point of Chinatown. Yet the gulf between City Hall and Chinatown has never been wider. And deep in the layers of this gulf lie decades of mutual distrust, non-confidence and, sometimes, outright hostility. A decade of federal and provincial encroachment on Chinatown was subsequently followed by an arbitrary municipal bylaw that dictates what, how and when development in Chinatown should be. In response, the Chinese tried different tactics and experimented with different approaches. They created allies with the local French and English media. They ran press conferences. They asked local radio stations to run phone-in talk shows. They asked heritage preservation groups to join them in a united front. They asked both Chinese and non-Chinese sympathizers to sign petitions, to launch the community's first ever demonstration march. They used a top-notch Jewish constitutional lawyer. They published bulletins and a report of results of public hearings, as well as compiled news clippings. They approached the Quebec Human Rights Commission for intervention. Simultaneously, they also experimented with close-door soft-talk with city councillors and federal M.Ps. They made presentations to the City's economic summit. After all this, the City only agreed as concession to limit Lagauchetière Street east of St. Dominique Street, not St. Laurent Street as originally intended, to residential development only. This amendment in actual fact gave Chinatown no more than 200 feet on Lagauchetière Street for commerical usage. Chinatown is boxed in. Any future growth and development in Chinatown will be, as vividly put by the Chinese, "like a sore on the mouse's tail", which is not much anyway.

When big-city development threatened Chinatowns in Toronto and Vancouver, the Chinese community fought City Hall. City Hall listened and the Chinese won.[50] In the 1960s, the Chinese marched on the streets when Vancouver planned to put a highway through Chinatown and build a firehall there. The Chinese stopped the plans. The provincial government of British Columbia declared Vancouver Chinatown an historical area—strict rules have been enforced to prevent developers from bulldozing historical buildings. About 20 years ago, 400 Chinese residents marched to City Hall and occupied Council Chambers when the City of Toronto, after expropriating half of Chinatown to build its city hall, made plans to demolish the rest of Chinatown. Public sympathy brought in a more sensible municipal planning process. Metropolitan Toronto now has four Chinatowns, not one. In the meantime, the Chinese in Montreal are worried about their own ethnic space, now reduced to a few city blocks. The shrinkage of Montreal Chinatown has by no means stopped, not by any measure.

Notes

1. This chapter is a revised and updated version of a paper titled, "Ethnic Urban Space, Urban Displacement and Forced Relocation: The Case of Chinatown in Montreal," in *Canadian Ethnic Studies*, XVIII:2 (1986), pp. 65–78.
2. James D. Besser, " 'Gentrifying' the Ghetto," in *Progressive* 43(1979), January, pp. 30–32; Ken Hartnett, "Tracking the Return of the Gentry: The Bad Side of Central-City Chic," in *Boston Globe*, 28 May 1977; "When City Revival Drives out the Poor," in *New York Times*, 1 July, p. A-22, 1977; Robert Reinhold, "Middle-Class Return Displaces Some Urban Poor," in *New York Times*, 5 June 1977, p. 1; Craig Unger, "The Lower East Side: There Goes the Neighbourhood," in *New Yorker*, 28 May 1984, p. 32–41.
3. Marc Fried, "Functions of the Working-Class Community in Modern Urban Society: Implications for Forced Relocation," in *Journal of the American Institution of Planners* 32:2 (1967), pp. 90–103; Michael H. Lang, *Gentrification and Urban Decline: Strategies for America's Older Cities* (Cambridge, Massachusette: Ballinger Publishing Company, 1982).
4. Chester Hartman, "Displacement: A Not So New Problem," in *Social Policy*, March/April 1979, pp. 22–27; "Comments on Neighbourhood Revitalization and Displacement: A Review of the Evidence," in *APA Journal*, 45 (October 1979), pp. 488–90; Howard J. Sumka, "Displacement in Revitalizing Neighbourhoods: A Review and Research Strategy" (Occasional Papers in Housing and Community

Affairs Vol. 2, United States Department of Housing and Urban Development, edited by Robert P. Boynton, 1978); "Neighbouring Revitalization and Displacement: A Review of the Evidence," in *APA Journal* 45 (October 1979), pp. 491–94; "The Ideology of Urban Analysis: A Response to Hartman," in *APA Journal* 45 (October 1979).

5. Franklin J. James, *Back to the City: An Appraisal of Housing Reinvestment and Population Change in Urban America* (Washington, D.C.: The Urban Institute, December, 1977); Frank Smith, *Displacement in Adams Morgan* (Testimony Before Senate Committee on Banking, Housing and Urban Affairs, 7 July 1977).
6. Chester Hartman, p. 23.
7. Ibid., p. 22.
8. United States Department of Housing and Urban Development (HUD), *Interim Displacement Report, HUD-PDR-382* (Washington, D.C.: Government Printing Office, February 1979), p. 11.
9. Michael Lang, p. 14.
10. Anne Penketh, "Renovation Craze Puts Squeeze on Low-income Roomers—The Roomers Pushed out by Gentrification," in *The Gazette*, 27 October 1981, p.1 & p. 11.
11. Frederica Wilson, "Expropriation Steamroller is a Tough One to Stop," in *The Gazette*, 19 November 1981, p. 1 & p. 10.
12. Shana Saper, "Renovation Blitz Forcing Low-income Groups from Inner City," in *The Gazette*, 25 August 1984.
13. Anshel Melamed et al, "The Effects of Forced Relocation in Montreal," in *Habitat* 27, 4 (1984), pp. 29–36
14. Luc d'Iberville-Moreau, *Lost Montreal* (Toronto: Oxford University Press, 1975).
15. Ingrid Peritz, "City Tearing Us Apart, Brick by Brick, Say Montreal's Chinese," in *The Gazette*, 18 November 1981, p. 9.
16. Toby Sanger, "Chinatown Won't Last Ten Years," in *Open City*, February/March 1984, p. 5 & p. 8.
17. Judee Ganten, "The Changing Face of Chinatown," in *Montreal Calendar Magazine*, February 1984, pp. 22–25.
18. *The Gazette* (Editorial), 29 January 1985.
19. *The Gazette* (Editorial), 27 February 1985.
20. Definition of the physical boundary of Chinatown in Montreal has never been mutually agreed upon between residents within the area and those outside it, including the government bureaucrats, planners, developers, and so on. I am presently following a definition by the planning and economic development department of the City (CIDEM). Since this definition is developed by city planners for planning purposes only, not all of the region within the boundary has the presence of Chinese activities.
21. Wu Menzheng, *Montreal Chinatown: A Study of Its Changing Functions* (Montreal, Quebec: School of Urban Planning, McGill University, 1984), p. 5.
22. Kwok B. Chan and Lawrence Lam, "Chinese in Timmins, Ontario 1915–1957: A

12. A Sore on the Mouse's Tail 309

   Study of Ethnic Stereotypes in the Press," in *Asian Profile*, Vol. 14:6 (December 1986).
23. Jean Gratton and Duy A. Kien, *La population du quartier de Montréal* (Departement de sante communautaire, Hopital Saint-Luc, January 1985).
24. Kwok B. Chan, "Problems and Needs of the Montreal Chinese Community: An Elite Viewpoint" (unpublished manuscript, 1983).
25. Ibid.
26. A noted Montreal urbanist who wrote a definitive urban historical study of the city of Montreal.
27. *SOS Montreal* (Editorial), August 1977, p. 6.
28. Ibid.
29. Edward Pitula, "Place Guy Favreau," in *SOS Montreal*, August 1977, p. 7.
30. "Buchanan Debates Details, Refuses to Promise Public Consultation" (Letter to Mr. Peter Lanken, Save Montreal), in *SOS Montreal*, October 1977, p. 11.
31. Edward Pitula, p. 7.
32. *SOS Montreal*, August 1977, p. 9.
33. Ibid.
34. Audrey Bean, Julia Gersovitz and Peter Lanken, "Guy Favreau Consultative Committee 'Hogue-tied'," in *SOS Montreal*, July 1978, p. 8.
35. Andy Melamed, "Letters to the Editor," in *SOS Montreal*, April/May 1978, p. 5.
36. Harvey Shepherd, "Chinatown Being Smothered: Fainstat," in *The Gazette*, 2 September 1982, p. A3.
37. *The Chinese Press*, 3 August 1982, p. 13.
38. *The Gazette*, 1 May 1985, p. B2.
39. *The Gazette*, 2 May 1985, p. A3.
40. *The Gazette*, 10 May 1985, p. B2.
41. *The Gazette*, 12 February 1985, p. B3.
42. *The Gazette*, 27 February 1985, p. B2.
43. *The Gazette*, 11 March 1985, p. A3.
44. *The Gazette*, 27 January 1986, p. B3.
45. *The Gazette*, 26 February 1986, p. B2.
46. *The Gazette*, 14 June 1986, p. A4.
47. *The Gazette*, 11 March 1985.
48. Kwok B. Chan, "Coping with Aging and Managing Self-identity: The Social World of the Elderly Chinese Women," in *Canadian Ethnic Studies* 15, 3 (1983), pp. 36–50.
49. Montreal Chinese Professional and Businessmen's Association, Report of the Public Hearings on the Impact of Municipal Zoning Bylaw No. 6513 upon Chinatown in Montreal, 1985.
50. Sarah Scott, "Chinatowns Flourishing in Other Cities," in *The Gazette*, 3 May 1985.

Conclusion

Chinese class at the Chinese Presbyterian Church School, 7 March 1940.

Montreal-born Chinese children in Chinese language classes.

The future generation.

Conclusion

THE first Chinese, almost exclusively male, came in 1858 from California to the mining regions of British Columbia as a result of the Gold Rush. Others joined them later, coming mainly from the province of Guangdong. When the Gold Rush subsided, they entered the workshops of the western provinces or were hired for the construction of the Canadian Pacific Railway. When the railroad was finished, most of them stayed as factory workers in British Columbia and some of them established themselves as retail workers. This marked the start of the first Chinatowns in Victoria and Vancouver. Some migrated to the eastern provinces of Ontario and Quebec, where they opened small shops in Toronto and Montreal.

The Chinese came to Canada as labour force useful for the industrialization of the nation. They contributed to the construction of one of the most important tools for national economic integration, the Canadian Pacific Railway, and worked in the manufacturing and mining industries of British Columbia. Since their first entry into Canada, the Chinese were discriminated against by white entrepreneurs and workers; were segregated into an inferior segment of the labour market; received lower wages than white labourers; were rejected by white labour unions; and were assigned to transient jobs. This inferior economic status was the direct product of capitalist expansion in Canada. Individuals in the private sector exploited and discriminated against them. Almost every segment of the civil society contributed to this collective, public rejection of Chinese immigrants. Poor white immigrants were considered as part of the provincial or national entities whereas the Chinese, as well as other Orientals (Japanese, East Indians, and so on), Amerindians and blacks were perceived as a threat to the white cultural and political hegemony. Poverty of the masses and lack of industrial development were at the roots of the white animosity toward the Orientals and Amerindians, whereas the stigma of slavery was still attached to the blacks coming to Canada from the United States. Rich white entrepreneurs looked at the Chinese as a very useful labour force and wanted them in big numbers. But native Anglo-Saxons, farmers, artisans, traders and small workshop workers saw in the Chinese misery the very fate they would endure in the industrialized economy then in gestation in British Columbia. They could foresee how they would lose their economic and social autonomy as independent workers, being progressively assigned to fill the ranks of the industrial establishments. In ideological defence, they accused the ones who were the most strange to their ideals, and also the most visible because they were also the most numerous among the newcomers. The Chinese were seen as the culprits, destroying their relatively easy-going life as independent workers. They acted violently against their entry into British Columbia and Canada and were opposed to their integration into the mainstream society. They won the first skirmish as the Chinese became victims of institutional discrimination.

This hostility of the white civil society was possible because of the legitimization of discriminatory practices against the Chinese by the state and political authorities, municipal, provincial or national. Political and civil rights of the Chinese were precluded and violated. Because of the usefulness of the Chinese labour force for the completion of the transcontinental railroad and because of the influence of white entrepreneurs, the Canadian government did not want to curtail Chinese immigration, though it was felt necessary to make concessions to white public opinion of the western provinces, especially British Columbia. Head taxes were imposed on the Chinese entering Canada. The Canadian state never opposed strongly the diverse and numerous regulations aimed at controlling the economic and political rights of the Chinese residents of the western provinces. From 1875 up to the turn of the century, Chinese were deprived of their right to vote in municipal and provincial elections in two Canadian provinces, and, subsequently, at the national level; were not included in the electoral lists; were excluded from certain occupations and could not enjoy rights granted to any other group of immigrants or residents. And, in 1923, after a rift of more than fifty years between Victoria and Ottawa about "The Chinese Question", the federal government and the legislators adopted a Chinese exclusion law, barring the entry of poor Chinese immigrants.

Trapped in economic exploitation, despised by the civil society, and denied their fundamental rights as Canadian residents, the Chinese coped with their inferior social status along two lines: avoidance and contest. Most of them receded into isolation among themselves and tried all means to avoid white society. Along with this passive process of resistance, they chose, whenever possible, to enter occupations not exposing themselves to contact or competition with white workers. This choice could not but reinforce the isolation they experienced in the labour market, though it was the only way available to them to protect their economic life from racism. The most graphic piece of data about this mode of avoidance remains the choice of the Chinese migrating to Montreal. There, they established occupational enclaves: they became launderers first, then owned or worked in restaurants, "walking on two legs", so to speak. Before, white women used to be laundresses. In

Conclusion

Quebec, laundry was not a real commercial trade until the Chinese came along. At the beginning of the century, in Montreal, about twenty enterprises using mechanical equipment were involved in the laundry trade, almost exclusively serving institutions (hospitals, steamship companies, and so on). This over-specialization maintained itself up to the 1960s when new immigrants with qualifications entered Canada. The Chinese going east found it easy to adapt to the requirements of this retail trade (meagre capital and abundant labour force through immigrants from China) though these means could also have been useful in a number of other similar service trades had they not already been in the hands of white people. As victims of racial discrimination, the Chinese laundrymen in Quebec, avoiding contact and competition with the white society, became the classic prototype of occupational isolation and personal alienation. Poor, cut off from mainstream white society, leading a married bachelor's life without women and children around, and forced to become consumers of various ethnic vices, the classic laundrymen, somewhat unwittingly, reinforced and perpetuated the same derogatory ethnic stereotypes imposed on them by the white society. Aside from these stereotypes, the Chinese continued to be perceived as both unwilling and unable to assimilate into white society. This "disinclination to assimilate" argument continued to be used by both political authorities and the civil society as a pretext for the exclusion of the Chinese.

Along with avoidance as a passive mode of resistance, the Chinese established social and cultural enclaves, building Chinatowns, funding associations and political parties related to life in China, creating a service sector for themselves and relying on their own means to adapt to their exclusion. Consequently, they could not but identify themselves with ideological and political concepts active in mainland China. Chinese coming to Canada before the 1950s were not allowed social and cultural integration.

China was a society in transformation when the poor Cantonese peasants and artisans left it between 1860 and 1923 to come to Canada. Yet they were not the "submissive miserable beings" popularly stereotyped by white ideologists. Though not every one of them was a political activist belonging to one of the secret societies trying to overthrow the imperial regime and its bureaucracy, the Chinese knew that they were victims of political privilege, corruption, exploitation and repression in their own country. Chinese immigrants were not coming from a democratic country, but they were aware of individual civil rights, of a representative parliamentary system and were not at all strangers to the concepts of justice and equality that the white people were so proud of.

The apparent passive reaction of the Chinese immigrants (avoiding white society, establishing economic and cultural enclaves, or simply leaving Canada for China for good) was not as peaceful as it looked. It was, in fact, a way of containing the violence inflicted on them by the white society and, subsequently, the violence of Chinese against white men. For example, two aims were central to the Chinese associations founded throughout Canada: to protect the immigrants against the effects of discrimination, exploitation, poverty and isolation, as well as to manage frictions between whites and Chinese. Criminality was not common among the Chinese residents. When it appeared, either against whites or between Chinese, it was politically dangerous. It amplified racism.

The apparent peaceful strategy to cope with discrimination showed its real face when active collective or individual resistance occurred. In every province where they established themselves, Chinese immigrants defended themselves against the suppression of their civil rights or against the economic exploitation they endured. Chinese immigrants fought back using white lawyers to defend their causes, organizing strikes challenging local white institutions and, when they could, using white organizations to forward their demands. But, if they succeeded in their fights against local white residents, they failed in their demand to see the political leaders of the country and the federal or provincial government put an end to the institutional discrimination they were subjected to. In 1947, the Chinese Exclusion Act was repealed and some of their civil rights restored, not because of Chinese militancy or radical ideological changes in Canadian politics, but because Canada had to yield to international pressure.

The Chinese immigrants lacked the means to win their battle against Ottawa or any provincial or municipal government because they were excluded from the political life of Canada (political parties, trade unions and lobby groups) and could not form effective and stable alliance with white organizations. When, for example, in Montreal, the white organizations, the Presbyterian and Catholic churches in these cases, forwarded the demands of the Chinese, some gains (social assistance) were obtained.

The power relations were at the roots of the failure of the Chinese immigrants, but other factors also played their role, reinforcing their inability to compete successfully within the white society. The Chinese immigrants were experiencing a process of social and ideological change because of political and economic events occurring in China, a process amplified by their social inhibition. We have seen no evidence of a perception of class conflict among Chinese themselves, though Chinese merchants and entrepreneurs exploited Chinese workers then trapped in the manual labour force. Association leaders were chosen for their economic power, not their political stand toward discrimination. The social system in China did not change drastically for the better with the installation of a republican regime in 1911; on the contrary, it aggravated the conditions of life of the peasants of the southern regions. Chinese in Canada had to maintain their families in Guangdong and did not emancipate themselves from the clanic ideology. Their social identification with Chinese concepts bound them to the welfare of their extended families, making them even more strangers to Canadian society. These various handicaps related to the status of the Chinese in Canada and in China possibly explain the failure of their attempts to counteract the discriminatory regulations against them. In that sense, the case of the Chinese living in Canada before the 1960s is significant and useful to remember when white ideologues or politicians referred, or still refer, to the disinclination or inability of certain groups of immigrants to assimilate into Canadian society.

From the point of view of the personal experiences of Chinese women, the social history of the Chinese in Quebec can be roughly divided into three periods. The first period began with their husbands leaving China for western Canada for gold digging and railroad construction while they themselves stayed behind in the native village, toiling hard in the paddy fields, and, from time to time, receiving remittances from overseas. This period is typically one of extended marital separation, a period of women without men (in China), and of men without women (in Canada). The second period began with a much-delayed re-union between husbands and wives in Canada. By then, the men would have worked as launderers for decades, some of them falling sick; the fear of a lonely death in Canada must have prompted many men to send for their women to nurse them. The Chinese women in Montreal, upon arrival, promptly found work as kitchen helpers in Chinese-owned restaurants or as manual workers in factories in the day-time, and then joined their husbands in the hand laundries in the evening while, in the meantime, preparing meals and attending to other household chores. Many women thought that life in old China was easier than that in Montreal which was often described as "life without a break". The third period saw the passing away of the Chinese men due to old age, ill health, poverty and nostalgia, once again leaving their women behind, this time in Canada. One finds these elderly widows living in senior citizen homes or rooming houses above grocery stores and restaurants in the Montreal Chinatown. For many of these widows, this kind of living arrangement was an intentional, voluntary choice. It allowed them to preserve a sense of personal identity, autonomy and control, while managing and negotiating their relations with their children and grandchildren. Many women would not hesitate to express their gratitude to Canada now that they can live comfortably on old-age pensions after lifelong misery and suffering. Ironically, these same women, half a century later, remain strangers in a foreign land, forgotten and neglected by the host society and by their offspring.

The sudden influx of Sino-Indo-Chinese into Montreal since 1979 has, simply because of their numbers, given the Chinese community in Montreal a demographic push. To a certain extent, this demographic fact has contributed to the cultural and economic revitalization of the Montreal Chinatown given the proliferation of grocery stores, restaurants and various other retail trades in the area. It is too early to delineate precisely their patterns of insertion and integration into the local Chinese community, and, subsequently, the larger Montreal society. Economic adaptation and family reunification have taken precedence, though one also witnesses active efforts of Chinese from Cambodia, Laos and Vietnam to build and consolidate their own community bases, thus setting each of them apart from each other and from the local Chinese community. More than a decade after their arrival in Montreal, the Sino-Indo-Chinese are presently negotiating their ethnic identities while maintaining their own ethnic boundaries and keeping social distance from each other.

After more than a century of institutional, as well as personal, racial discrimination toward the Chinese in Canada and Quebec, the Montreal Chinatown in the 1980s found itself in another crisis: it faced urban encroachment, displacement and gentrification by all three levels of government. The Chinese in Montreal have lost their right to self-determination and development in an urban space they feel they are entitled to for good historical reasons. Though the local media and selected urban rights lobbying groups were clearly on their side, the Chinese in Montreal found themselves fighting a losing battle against the political authorities and government bureaucrats, a fact once again attributable to their political impotence in the power relations of the larger society. The Chinese in

Montreal have long been familiar with this grim political fact.

Ironically, various federal and provincial governments in Canada in the past five years have been sending trade delegates to Hong Kong on missions to lure well-to-do economic investors and entrepreneurs to come to Canada. History has come full circle. The first batch of Cantonese came to British Columbia to work in the gold mines. Many had to pay the Canadian government hefty head taxes to get in. A century later, Canadian government officials went to Hong Kong on their "millionaires hunts" or "gold mine missions". This time, all the Chinese have to do, before being granted admission, is to promise investment in the Canadian economy. It has taken a full century for the economic attributes of the Chinese immigrants to Canada to change, "from rags to riches", so to speak. Nevertheless, these Chinese economic investors, because of their wealth, ironically, faced another form of hostility and animosity: they were accused of "buying their visas" into Canada. The Chinese in Vancouver and Toronto, while buying homes to live in or to invest in, faced accusations of creating havoc with the real estate market, thus drastically reducing chances of an average Vancouverite or Torontonian owning a comfortable home. Only a few years back, much to the displeasure of the local white residents, the Hong Kong Chinese in Scarborough (a Toronto suburb), were seen driving "Baby Mercedes" and taking up parking lots on Sundays while flooding Chinese restaurants for "*dim-sum*". Questions of the compatibility and assimilability of the new Chinese immigrants surfaced again. This time, the emotions and reasoning behind white dissatisfaction is not that they are poor, immoral, uneducated and uncultured (stereotypes imposed on the early batch of Cantonese immigrants a century ago), but that they are too aggressive, money-minded and arrogant. In a word, they are too rich to the liking of the native population. Things change. But things also never change. History has its own way of repeating itself.

This book is as much a study of the causes and costs of racism against the Chinese in Montreal, as it is an analysis of how the Chinese, at both personal and collective levels, went about coping with their conditions of life in an adopted country. The underlying theme of this study can thus be captured in the form of answering one overriding question: what did the Chinese do and not do in reacting to racism and violation of human rights, and why? The accent of such a perspective is as much on documenting what happened to the Chinese as on how the Chinese reacted to or coped with situations and incidents of racial discrimination.

This study experiments with oral history and in-depth interview materials in delineating how each of the ten elderly Chinese widows, Uncle Jack Huang, the community man, and Jack Liang, a private man, went about in their own ways coping with their life circumstances. Jack Huang's strategy was one of community involvement and participation, thus accentuating the sociological significance of a public life in moulding and consolidating one's personal and ethnic identity. In contrast, Jack Liang and, to a large extent, the dozens of elderly widows now trying to eke out their lives in the retirement community of Montreal's Chinatown, coped in their private ways, managing their self-identity in the comfort and protection of an ethnic enclave. Like the laundrymen half a century ago, these women resorted to withdrawal and isolation, a personal as well as social condition forced upon them by racism. Racism has personal and social costs, one of which is isolation and segregation. Where there is racism, there is forced, involuntary segregation; the two go hand in hand. Yet isolation and segregation breed ethnic stereotypes and further racism, thus completing the vicious circle. Nevertheless, segregation of the Chinese throughout the entire history of their experience in Canada was, and still is, seen by the larger white society as voluntary and intentional, a perception, unfortunately, lying at the core of the "unwillingness and inability to assimilate" argument. Not even the "new immigrants" from Hong Kong, the so-called economic investors or entrepreneurs, very much wanted and coaxed by the Canadian federal and provincial governments, are immune to such accusations. Seen from another perspective, one might want to conceptualize the segregation of the Chinese, forced and voluntary, as a constructive mode of personal and social adaptation to life as a stranger in a strange society. In methodological terms, the use of oral histories, archives, in-depth interviews, and parti-cipant-observation allow the social scientist a rare glimpse of how indivi-duals make the best and the most of their life circumstances in an almost heroic way. Such fieldwork experience allows the researchers access into the privacy of the emotions, psyche and preoccupations of people, of how they endure and survive under adverse circumstances. Theoretically and humanistically, it seems as interesting for the sociologists to describe what happens to people (events as stimuli, e.g., discrimination) as to document how people, as individuals and in groups, react to, cope with, or even change these events, oftentimes in their favour. In that sense, this study is a study of human survival. It is not merely a study of the stress and costs of racism; it is a study of coping, adaptation and change.

Conclusion

Lastly, this study anticipates some rethinking about the meanings of several crucial concepts in the field of ethnic relations: multiculturalism, ethnic and cultural ethnicity, pluralism, assimilation and ethnic identity. The recent experience of the Chinese in British Columbia and Ontario exposes the mythology of multiculturalism. The relevance of multiculturalism must be discovered in the process of rejecting the ideology of assimilation (i.e., to become alike) and replacing it with an explicit recognition of the reality of ethnic relations (i.e., immigrants lead a double life, nurture a dual identity). One is private, personal, ethnic, primordial, primarily expressive, oriented to traditional culture, heritage and the past, and the other is public, social, primarily instrumental, oriented to economic and political realities, and the present. One is both a Chinese and a Canadian. One is more a Chinese now than before or one was less a Chinese a minute ago than now. The doubleness of personal, as well as social, life has long been part of the sociological imagination. Assimilation upholds white supremacy and rejects ethnic sentiments; in that, it has become more than a concept, it itself is an ideology. As a concept, it is odious and fails to accurately describe the social reality of ethnic relations. Like the concept of race, it has long lost its scientific stance, becomes more prescriptive than descriptive, and, therefore, must be rethought. Sociologists would do well in focussing their theoretical and analytical attention in the future on the emergence and consolidation of ethnicity and ethnic identity while members of the ethnic minorities engage in the all-important processes of survival, adaptation, coping and social change.

Until the power relations amongst the different ethnic groups in Canada are re-arranged and re-structured, which seems unlikely in the foreseeable future, much of the economic, cultural and political resources as well as the psychic energy of members of the ethnic minorities in generations to come will be invested in experimenting with different strategies of coping and adaptation.

With the dramatic change in the demographics of a whole generation of new immigrants, one will witness more litigious or confrontational strategies being adopted. There is now some evidence of increasing political participation of the Chinese in the larger decision-making machinery. In the meantime, researchers will want to continue their watch on the sociology, anthropology and psychology of ethnic resistance.

Bibliography

Aiken, Rebecca. *Montreal Chinese Property Ownership and Occupational Change 1881–1981*. Ph. D. Thesis, Department of Anthropology, McGill University, Montreal, Qecbec, Canada, September 1984.

Antonovsky, Aaron. "Conceptual and Methodological Problems in the Study of Resistance Resources and Stressful Life Events." Paper presented at Conference on Stressful Life Events: Their Nature and Effects, June 1973, at City University of New York, U.S.A.

Bancroft, H.H. "Mongolianism in America." In *Essays and Miscellaneous* edited by Bancroft, San Francisco: History Co., 1890.

Bastid-Brugiere, Marianne. "Currents of Social Change." In *The Cambridge History of China*, edited by Dennis Twitchett and John K. Fairbank, Volume II, Late Ch'ing, 1800–1911, Part 2, p. 580. Cambridge: Cambridge University Press, 1980.

Berton, Pierre. *The National Dream: The Great Railway*. Toronto: McClelland and Stewart, 1970.

Biggerstagg, K. "The Burlingame Mission." In *The Criticism in American History*, Vol. 14 (July 1936), pp. 652–82.

Chan, Anthony B. *Gold Mountain: The Chinese in the New World*. Vancouver: New Star Books, 1983.

Chan, Kwok Bun. "Individual Differences in Reactions to Stress and Their Personality and Situational Determinants: Some Implications for Community Mental Health." In *Social Science and Medicine*, Vol. 11 (1979), pp. 89–103.

———. "Coping with Aging and Managing Self-identify: The Social World of the Elderly Chinese Women." In *Canadian Ethnic Studies* 15, 3 (1983), pp. 36–50.

———. *Oral History of the Montreal Chinese Community*. Oral History-

Montreal Studies Program, Concordia University Non-print Library, Montreal, Canada, 1983.

———. "Ethnic Urban Space, Urban Displacement and Forced Relocation: The Case of Chinatown in Montreal." In *Canadian Ethnic Studies* Vol. XVIII:2 (1986), pp. 65–78. (Special issue on Ethnicity in Quebec.)

———. "The Chinese from Indochina in Montreal: A Study in Ethnic Voluntary Associations, Community Organization, and Ethnic Boundaries." In *Ten Years Later: Indo-Chinese Communities in Canada*, edited by Louis-Jacques Dorais, Kwok B. Chan & Doreen M. Indra. Montreal: Canadian Asian Studies Association, 1988.

Chan, Kwok Bun & Denise Helly (eds.) *Coping with Racism: The Chinese Experience in Canada*. Special Issue, *Canadian Ethnic Studies*, Vol. XIX, No. 3, 1987. Calgary: Canadian Ethnic Studies Association.

Chan, Kwok Bun & Doreen M. Indra (eds.). *Uprooting, Loss and Adaptation: The Resettlement of Indo-Chinese Refugees in Canada*. Ottawa: The Canadian Public Health Association, 1987.

Chan, Kwok Bun & Lawrence Lam. "Resettlement of Vietnamese Chinese Refugees in Montreal, Canada: Some Socio-psychological Problems and Dilemmas." *Canadian Ethnic Studies*, Vol. XV:1 (1983).

———. "Structure and Values of the Chinese Family in Vietnam." In *The Southeast Asian Environment*, edited by Douglas R. Webster, pp. 206–20. Ottawa: University of Ottawa Press, 1983.

———. "Chinese in Timmins, Canada, 1915–1950: A Study of Ethnic Stereotypes in the Press." In *Asian Profile*, Vol. 14:6 (December 1986), pp. 569–83.

———. "Psychological Problems of Chinese Vietnamese Refugees Resettling in Quebec." In *Uprooting, Loss and Adaptation: The Resettlement of Indo-Chinese Refugees in Canada*, edited by Kwok B. Chan and Doreen Indra. Ottawa: The Canadian Public Health Association, 1987.

Chan, L.F. *Dongnanyazhou Di Huaqiao, Huaren Yu Huayi* 東南亞洲的華僑，華人與華裔.Taipei: Zheng Zhong Shu Ju 正中書局 (2nd edition), 1983. (Text in Chinese.)

Chinn, Thomas W., H. Mark Lai & Philip P. Choy (eds.). *A History of the Chinese in California: A Syllabus*. San Francisco: The Chinese Historical Society of America, 1969.

Deschamps, Gilles. "Economic Adaptation of Indo-Chinese Refugees in Quebec." In Kwok B. Chan & Doreen M. Indra (eds.). Ottawa: The Canadian Public Health Association, 1987.

D'Iberville-Moreau, Luc. *Lost Montreal.* Toronto: Oxford University Press, 1975.
Dorais, Louis-Jacques, Kwok B. Chan & Doreen M. Indra (eds.). *Ten Years Later: Indo-Chinese Communities in Canada.* Montreal: Canadian Asian Studies Association, 1988.
Dowd, James J. & Vern L. Bengston. "Aging in Minority Populations: An Examination of the Double Jepardy Hypothesis." In *Journal of Gerontology*, Vol. 33:3 (1978), pp. 427–36.
Duiker, William J. "Kampuchea." In *The Encyclopedia Americana*, Vol. 18 (International Edition), p. 275. Danbury, Connecticut: Grolier Incorporated, 1983.
Employment and Immigration Canada. *Indo-Chinese Refugees: The Canadian Response, 1979 and 1980.* Ottawa: Ministry of Supply and Services, 1982.
Employment and Immigration Canada. *Evaluation of the 1979–81 Indo-Chinese Refugees Program.* Ottawa, 1982.
Fried, Marc. "Functions of the Working-Class Community in Modern Urban Society: Implications for Forced Relocation." In *Journal of the American Institution of Planners*, 32:2 (1967), pp. 90–103.
Goodrich, L. Carrington & Nigel Cameron. *The Face of China as Seen by Photographers and Travellers, 1860–1912.* New York: Aperture, 1978.
Gratton, Jean & Duy A. Kian. *La population du quartier de Montréal.* Departement de santé communautaire, Hôpital Saint-Luc, January 1985.
Hall, Calvin S. *The Meaning of Dreams.* New York: McGraw-Hill, 1963.
Harney, Robert F. "Men without Women: Italian Migrants in Canada, 1885–1930." In *Canadian Ethnic Studies*, Vol. XI:1 (1979), pp. 29–47.
Hartman, Chester. "Displacement: A Not So New Problem." In *Social Policy*, March/April (1979), pp. 22–27.
———. "Comments on Neighbourhood Revitalization and Displacement: A Review of the Evidence." In *APA Journal*, 45 October (1979), pp. 488–90.
Helly, Denise. *Les Chinois à Montréal 1877–1951.* Québec: Institut québécois de recherche sur la culture, 1987.
Ho Ping-ti. "The Population of China in Ming-Ch'ing Times." In *The Making of China*, edited by Chun-shu Chang. Englewood Cliffs, New Jersey: Prentice Hall, 1985.

Hoe Ban-seng. "Folktales and Social Structure: The Case of the Chinese in Montreal." In *Canadian Folklore Canadien*, Vol. 1–2 (1979), pp. 25–35.

Hsü, Francis L.K. *Americans and Chinese: Passage to Differences*. Honolulu: The University Press of Hawaii, 1981. (3rd edition.)

Ikels, Charlotte. "The Coming of Age in Chinese Society: Traditional Patterns in Contemporary Hong Kong." Paper presented at the Annual Meetings of the American Anthropological Association, Los Angeles (November 1978).

Indra, Doreen M. "Social Science Research on Indo-Chinese Refugees in Canada." In *Uprooting, Loss and Adaptation: The Resettlement of Indo-Chinese Refugees in Canada*, edited by Kwok B. Chan & Doreen M. Indra. Ottawa: The Canadian Public Health Association, 1987.

James, Franklin J. *Back to the City: An Appraisal of Housing Reinvestment and Population Change in Urban America*. Washington, D.C.: The Urban Institute, 1977.

Kluckohn, F.R. & F.L. Strodtbeck. *Variations in Value Orientations*. Illinois: Row, Peterson and Evanston, 1961.

Kraepelin, E. "About Uprooting." In *Ges. Neurol. U. Psychiatry*, 63 (1921), 1–8, edited by J.D. Zeitschr. Also abstracted in *Uprooting and Related Phenomena: A Descriptive Bibliography*, edited by Zingmann. World Health Organization, 1977, pp. 3–4.

Krauter, Joseph F. & Morris David. *Minority Canadians: Ethnic Groups*. Toronto: Methuen, 1978.

Lai, David. "The Chinese Consolidated Benevolent Association in Victoria: Its Origins and Functions." In *BC Studies*, No. 15: Autumn (1972), pp. 53–67.

Lam, Lawrence. "Vietnamese-Chinese Refugees in Montreal." Doctoral Dissertation, Department of Sociology, York University, North York, Ontario, Canada, 1983.

Lang, Michael H. *Gentrification and Urban Decline: Strategies for America's Older Cities*. Cambridge, Massachusette: Ballinger Publishing Company, 1982.

Law, Stephen Chi-kin. "Service Functions of the Montreal Chinese Hospital—Role of Community Participation." M.A. Research Report, School of Social Work, McGill University, Montreal, Quebec, Canada, October 1967.

Lee, David T.H. *Jianada Huaqiao shi* 加拿大華僑史 (A History of Chinese in Canada). British Columbia: Ziyou Chubanshe 自由出版社, 1967. (Text in Chinese.)

Lee Wai-man (ed.). *Portraits of a Challenge: An Illustrated History of the Chinese Canadians*. Toronto: Council of Chinese Canadians in Ontario, 1984.

Li, Peter S. "Occupational Achievement and Kinship Assistance Among Chinese Immigrants in Chicago." In *Sociological Quarterly*, 18 (Autumn 1977), pp. 478–89.

———. "Income Achievement and Adaptive Capacity: An Empirical Comparison of Chinese and Japanese in Canada." In *Visible Minorities and Multiculturalism: Asians in Canada*. Scarborough, Ontario: Butterworths and Co., 1980.

———. "Chinese." In *Racial Oppression in Canada*, edited by B. Singh Bolaria and Peter S. Li. Toronto: Garamond Press, 1985, pp. 81–104.

Li, Yih-yuan & Kuo-shu Yang. (eds.) *Zhongguo ren de xingge: Keji zhonghe xing de taolun* 中國人的性格：科際綜合性的討論 (The Character of the Chinese: An Interdisciplinary Approach). Taiwan: Institute of Ethnology, Academia Sinica, Monograph Series B, No. 4, 1971.

Linteau, Paul-Andre. "The Origins of Ethnic and Cultural Diversity in Quebec." *Forces*, 73 (1986).

Lyman, Stanford M. *Chinatown and Little Tokyo: Power, Conflict and Community Among Chinese and Japanese Immigrants in America*. New York: Associated Faculty Press, Inc., 1986.

Mills, C. Wright. *The Sociological Imagination*. Oxford: Oxford University Press, 1959.

Neuwirth, Gertrude. "The Socio-economic Adjustment of Southeast Asian Refugees in Canada: One Year Later." Paper presented at the CSAS Annual Meetings, Dalhousie University, Halifax, 1981.

Pao-Mercier, Laura. "Immigration, Ethnicity and the Labour Market: The Chinese in Montreal." M.A. Thesis, Department of Sociology, McGill University, Montreal, Quebec, Canada, November 1981.

Purcell, Victor. *The Chinese in Southeast Asia*. (Second edition.) Kuala Lumpur: Oxford University Press, reprinted in Oxford in Asia Paperbacks, 1980.

Roy, Patricia. "Educating the 'East': British Columbia and the Oriental Question in the Interwar Years." In *BC Studies*, No. 18 (Summer 1973), pp. 50–69.

Samuel, T.J. "Economic Adaptation of Indo-Chinese Refugees in Canada."

In Kwok B. Chan & Doreen M. Indra (eds.). Ottawa: The Canadian Public Health Association, 1987.

Siu, Paul C.P. *The Chinese Laundryman: A Study of Social Isolation*. Ph. D. Dissertation, Department of Sociology, University of Chicago, Chicago, Illinois, United States of America, August 1953.

Staunton, Sir George Thomas. *Ta Tsing Len Lee; Being the Fundamental Laws of the Penal Code of China*, London, 1810.

Sumka, Howard J. "Displacement in Revitalizing Neighbourhoods: A Review and Research Strategy." Occasional Papers in Housing and Community Affairs Vol. 2, United States Department of Housing and Urban Development, edited by Robert P. Boynton, 1978.

United States Department of Housing and Urban Development (HUD). *Interim Displacement Report, HUD-PDR-382*. Washington, D.C.: Government Printing Office, February 1979.

Wei Cheng-tung. "Chuantong Zhongguo lixiang renge de fenxi" 傳統中國理想人格的分析 (The Ideal Character of the Traditional Chinese). In *Zhongguo ren de xingge: Keji zhonghe xing de taolun* (The Character of the Chinese: An Interdisciplinary Approach), edited by Yi-yuan Li and Kuo-shu Yang. Taiwan: Institute of Ethnology, Academia Sinica, Monograph Series B, No. 4, 1971, pp. 1–36.

Wen Chung-I. "Zong jiazhi quxiang tan Zhongguo guomin xing" 從價值取向談中國國民性(Chinese National Character as Revealed in Value Orientation). In Li and Yang (eds.), 1971, pp. 47–78.

Wiley, Norbert F. "The Ethnic Mobility Trap and Stratification Theory." In *Social Problems*, 15, pp. 147–59.

Willmott, William E. *The Chinese in Cambodia*. Vancouver: Publications Centre, University of British Columbia, 1967.

———. "The Chinese in Indo-China." In *Southeast Asian Exodus: From Tradition to Resettlement*, pp. 69–80, edited by Elliott L. Tepper. Ottawa: Canadian Asian Studies Association, 1980.

Woon Yuen-fong. "The Mode of Refugee Sponsorship and the Socioeconomic Adaptation of Vietamese in Victoria: A Three Year Perspective." In Kwok B. Chan & Doreen M. Indra (eds.). Ottawa: The Canadian Public Health Association, 1987.

Yang, Martin M.C. "Zhongguo de jiating zhuyi yu guomin xingge." 中國的家庭主義與國民性格(Familism and Chinese National Character). In Li and Yang (eds.), 1971, pp. 127–62.

Zwingmann, Charles. "The Nostalgic Phenomenon and Its Exploitation."

In *Uprooting and After*. Edited by Charles Zwingmann and Maria Pfister-Ammende (eds.). Springer-Verlag, New York, 1973, pp. 19–47.
———. *Uprooting and Related Phenomena*: *A Descriptive Bibliography*, World Health Organization, 1977, pp. 10–16.

Index

absentee landlordism, 11
ACLM, Association des Chinois du Laos à Montréal, 277–79, 281
ACVM, Association des Chinois du Vietnam à Montréal, 271–72, 281–83
adaptation, obstacles, 39, 56, 58, 258
adoption, "transfer to inherit", 187
Aiken, Rebecca, 173, 232
alienation, 45, 237, 244, 315
ancestor worship, 23, 24, 186, 188
ancient values, 23
Anti-Chinese Association, 16
anti-Orientalism, 16, 17, 29, 61–77, 110, 117, 161, 182
    see also discrimination, hostility, prejudice, racism
Antonovsky, Aaron, 264
assimilation, 320, 321
associations, 91, 92, 277, 283, 285, 297
    formation, 177–79
    functions, 181–205
    organization, 183
    revenue, 178
    see also clans
authority structure, Chinese, 25, 26

Bancroft, H.H., 155, 173

Bastid-Brugiere, Marianne, 18
"bangs", 280
Bengston, Vern L., 248
Berton, Pierre, 18
Biggerstagg, K., 18
"black money", 198
Bo Yang Gong, 205
Bolaria, B. Singh, 220, 221
bonds, China, 123
"Bow-on" squads, 109, 125, 218
Boxer Uprising, 9
braids, 52
bribery, 85
Buddhism, 26, 186, 189
Burlingame Treaty, 12

Cameron, Nigel, 18
Canada Manpower Centre, 252
Canadian Pacific Railway, 16–18, 28, 85, 88, 89, 202, 313
career confinement, 225
Catholic involvement, 7, 192–95, 210
Catholic Church, Chinese, 136, 141, 190, 192, 275
Catholic Mission, Montreal Chinese, 189, 190, 275, 300
census, Canada, 197
    1825, 28, 156
    1981, 251

Chan, Anthony B., 18, 19, 35
Chan, Kwok Bun, 35, 173, 210, 232, 288, 308, 323
Chan, L.F., 288
Chinatown, 17–18, 40, 43, 48, 70, 75, 105, 241, 294, 318
   characteristics, 130–45
   development, 17
   image, 171
   renewal-displacement, 295–307
   see also urban displacement process
Chinese Benevolent Society, 41, 119, 136, 139
   community development, 141, 142, 143
   headquarters, 17
   Victoria, 17
Chinese Consolidated Benevolent Association in Canada, 181–83
Chinese Council in Canada, 162
Chinese Exclusion Act, 215–19
   see also Chinese Immigration Act
Chinese Family Service of Greater Montreal, 268–69, 274, 278, 286, 299
   financial contributions, 272
Chinese Immigration Act, 28, 162, 164, 215, 217–19, 237
   see also Chinese Exclusion Act
Chinese Nationalist League, 120, 135, 142, 143, 144, 148, 196, 209
   see also Guomintang
Chinese Professional and Business Men's Association, 300, 304, 305
Chinese Reform Party, 135–36, 142, 209
"Chinese veto", family, 246
Chinn, Thomas, W., 172, 173
Choy, Philip P., 172, 173

Clans, 177–80, 197–209, 277, 297, 315–16
   ancestors, 180
   conflicts, 199, 204, 207–9
   confrontation, 210
   monopolies, 208
   rivalry, 208, 210
   "substitute parents", 179
   surrogate families, 188
   Chen Ying Chuan Tang, 201–3
   Four Brothers Association, 177
   Huang Jiang Xia Tang, 121, 136, 141, 145, 197
   Huang Yun Shan Gongxi, 197–98
   Li Association, 91, 121, 131, 136, 141, 199
   Li Long Xi Tang, 203–5
   Li Si Gong Suo, 204
   Tan Guang Yu Tang, 136, 198–201
   Zhao Lun Gongxi, 198–201
class, conflicts, 315
   divisions, 164, 170, 172
   elite, 269
Co-operative Commonwealth Federation, 218
collectivism, spirit of, 25
communication difficulties, 58, 146
Confucianism, 13, 23–25, 26, 31, 100, 127, 140, 151, 178, 186, 189, 191
"coolies", 28
"cousin-partnerships", 158
corruption, 85
"cultural division of labour", 172
Cultural Revolution, "Gat-min", 72

"dark age", Chinese, 216
David, Morris, 18
Davis, Bill, 228
de Cosmos, Amor, 16

deficient economy, 27
demography, 10
    Chinese in Canada, 134, 161, 226, 267
    Southeast-Asia, 267
depression, economic, 164, 217
Deschamps, Gilles, 264
d'Iberville-Moreau, Luc, 308, 323
diligence, 25–27, 40, 53, 151
discrimination, racial, 17, 44, 62, 70, 85, 117–18, 129, 137, 165, 183, 218, 243, 297, 314–16, 318–19, 320–21
    see also anti-Orientalism, hostility, prejudice, racism
dislocation, 224
diversification, 223
"diversified portfolio", 231
domestic unrest, China, 5
Dorais, Louis-Jacques, 288
Dore, Henri, 184
Dowd, James J., 248
dream analysis, 255–58
"duplicate offerings", 187
dual economies, 223
Duiker, William J., 288

"economic immigrants", 166
"economic insertion", 162
economic recession, Canada, 260
"edifice complex", 298
"Educating the East", 162
education in Canada, 192–94
egalitarianism, 194
"emigrant communities", 13
emigration, costs of, 12, 27, 28, 30, 34, 42, 158
    reasons for, 12–15, 27, 111
    sources in China, 13, 14, 29, 225
"emigratory tendency", 12

"ethnic enclave sub-economy", 172, 223
ethnic migration, 30
"ethnic mobility trap", 224
ethnic solidarity, problems, 285–87, 319
ethnic vices, 171, 216, 237
exploitation of Chinese, 6, 9, 11, 14, 16, 17, 28, 312
    by Chinese, 39–40, 111, 225
exploitative labour relations, 28
expropriation, 293–94, 298–301
    see also urban displacement process

family, 11, 24–26, 31–34, 111, 151, 178, 241–46
    conflicts, 243–44
    filial piety, 24–25
    obligations, 13, 25, 177–78, 245
    mutual dependence, 187
    values, 243
"Fangkou", 204
farming in China, 5, 33, 47
feudalism, 6
First Opium War, 5–6, 147
foreign imperialism, 5–7
foreign invasion into China, 5–11
Freemasons, in Montreal, Chinese, 109, 110, 116, 121, 128, 135, 141
    community involvement, 144, 147, 191, 196, 209
    development of hospital, 133, 141
    headquarters, 146
    see also Zhigongtang
French language law, 231
Fried, Marc, 307
frugality, 26–27

gambling, 40, 85, 99, 102, 131, 143, 171, 216, 237

gentry, 168–70
    ascendancy of merchants, 170, 178, 207
gentrification, of Chinatown, 302–3, 317
"ghetto", Chinese, 237
Godin, Gerald, 227
gold mines, 14–15, 27, 315
"gong", 201
Gong Zizhen, 10
Goodrich, L. Carrington, 18
Gratton, Jean, 309
"Group of Sino-Vietnamese Volunteers", 268–74
Guomintang, 135, 207, 209
    see also Chinese Nationalist League

Hall, Calvin S., 264
Han Dynasty, 177
Harney, Robert F., 34, 35
Hartman, Chester, 307
"Hat day", 118
health care, 195
Helly, Denise, 18, 35, 173, 211, 212
Heritage Montreal, 299
Ho Ping-ti, 10, 18
Hoe Ban-seng, 35
"Hong Men", 209
    see also Freemasons
Hong Xiuquan, 7
hostility, 80, 207, 215, 312
    harassment, 48, 58, 62, 64, 92–93, 95
    see also, anti-Orientalism, discrimination, prejudice, racism
housing costs, 230
Hsu, Francis L.K., 211
Hu Men, 6

Ikels, Charlotte, 248
"immigrant economy", 111
"immigrant mentality", 110
Immigration Archives, 171
immigration legislations, 45, 67, 216, 312
    changes, 219, 227
    point system, 223
    taxes, 28, 42, 62, 73, 77, 162, 165, 215, 312
immigrants, China, 29, 161, 225, 286
    Hong Kong, 286, 318
    Taiwan, 225, 286
    illegal, 45, 46
    independent, 223, 224
    others, 225–31, 225, 276, 318
income differentials, 16, 156, 225, 311
indentured workers, 7
Indo-Chinese, 251–81, 316
    see also refugees
Indra, Doreen M., 263
industrial development in China, 5
inequality, 16, 145
integration, 194, 282, 285
    obstacles, 258, 314–16
intergenerational value conflicts, 244, 245
"investor category", 230
    encouraged, 227–31
isolation, 77, 207, 220, 225, 237, 244, 314

James, Franklin J., 308
jobs, 15–17, 93, 113, 148, 156
    depletion, 17, 29
    limitations, 85, 94, 172, 225

Kang Xi, Emperor, 12
Kian, Duy A., 309
kinship systems, 24, 30

kinsmen labour, 217, 224
Kiu Yen Association, 122
Kluckhohn, Florence, 23, 35
Kraepelin, E., 264
Krauter, Joseph F., 18

Lai, David, 210
Lai, H. Mark, 172
Lam, Lawrence, 232, 264, 288, 308
Lang, Michael H., 307, 308
laundries, 33, 40, 47, 50, 54, 91,
    112–13, 148, 155, 217
    beginnings, 148, 155–58
    competition, 163, 165
    permit fees, 162, 165
    stagnation, 161–66
Law, Stephen Chi-kin, 211
Lee, David T.H., 18, 19, 210, 211,
    212, 231, 232
Lee Wai-man, 232
leisure, 39, 40, 99
Li, Peter S., 220, 221, 231, 232
Lintau, Paul-Andre, 173
Liu Zexu, 6
loans, 27–29, 34
Lougheed, Peter, 228
Lyman, Stanford M., 210, 211

Ma Guan Treaty, 8
MacDonald, John A., 17
mahjong, 67, 104
marriage, 29, 31–33, 97, 114, 215
    inter-racial, 97, 104, 109, 124–27
    match-made, 45, 46
    separation effects, 237
MCCUC, Montreal Chinese
    Community United Centre, 286,
    299, 300, 303
McGill Students' Association, 144
mechanization, China, 6
Middle Kingdom, 13, 14

"migrant way of life", 151
migration, effects, 30–34, 251–54
    inter-regional, 11–12
Mills, C. Wright, 2
"millionaire hunts", 231
Ming Dynasty, 5, 12, 209
Minimum wage, 161
Ministry of Communicaties and
    Immigration, Quebec, 252
Ministry of Cultural Affairs, Quebec,
    193
MNA, Member of National
    Assembly, Chinatown, 120
misgovernment in China, 5–9
missionaries, 7
mobility of workers, 224
Montreal Chinese Hospital, 70, 105,
    109, 116–22, 141, 210
Montreal General Hospital, 105
multiculturism, 319

Nan Song Dynasty, 197, 198
Nanking Treaty, 6, 12
national character of the Chinese, 26
National Day, Chinese, 144
National Security Council, 123, 218
Neuwirth, Gertrude, 264
non-assimilation, 17, 110, 161–62,
    315, 320
    see also assimilation
Northern Pacific Railroad Company,
    15
"nostalgic fixation", 252
"nostalgic illusion", 252

Occupational structure changes,
    221–27
    diversification, 223
oligarchy, China, 11
Onderdonk, Andrew, 15, 16, 17
operas, Cantonese, 71, 99, 137, 144

opium, 6, 40, 101, 110, 132, 216
Opium Wars, 5, 6, 12
"oriental menace", 162
"Oriental Question", 162, 312
"outcasts", 169
overpopulation, China, 10

Pao-Mercier, Laura, 168, 169, 173, 174, 232
Parti-Quebecois, 231
Peking Treaty, 7
"philosophy of eternity", 24
pluralism, 319
point system, immigration 1967, 223
pole ordinance, 155
polytheism, 184, 189
population displacement, China, 10
poverty, 39
prejudice, 44
    see also anti-Orientalism, discrimination, hostility, racism
prostitution, 40, 85, 99, 139, 216, 237
Protestant involvement, 136, 190–94, 210
Purcell, Victor, 18, 288

Qing Dynasty, 5–8, 12, 179, 209

racism, 14, 17, 28, 29, 39–40, 85, 110, 137, 145, 151, 161–62, 171, 181, 194, 207, 215–17, 319
    see also anti-Orientalism, discrimination, hostility, prejudice, stereotyping of Chinese
railroad work camps, 156–58, 166
RCMP, Royal Canadian Mounted Police, 132
redistribution of wealth, 172, 178
refugees, 223–63
    migration effects, 251

settlement, 268–69
sponsor-refugee relations, 253–55
Cambodia, 274–77
Laos, 277–79
Vietnam, 269–74
religion, 44, 136, 140, 141, 184, 191, 267
Chinese beliefs, 184–89
religious oppression, 9
renewal-displacement process, 293, 295
    see also expropriation, urban displacement process
resettlement aid 1980's, 274
restaurants, 39, 43, 74, 127–28, 164, 217
right to vote, 219
Roberts, John, 227
Robic, Louise, 230, 231
Roy, Patricia, 173
Royal Commission 1885, 216

Samuel, T.J., 264
Saskatchewan Statute, 182
"scarcity economy", 5, 26
second generation, 197, 216, 225, 243
Second World War, 59, 109, 122, 123, 133, 144, 147, 218, 219, 241, 267
secret societies, 209
security councils, Canadian (CDC), 109, 123
Chinese, 109, 123–24, 218
    see also "Row-on" squads
segregation, 39, 85, 167, 313, 320
sex ratio, balance, 215, 219–23
Sino-Japanese War, 8, 40, 218
Sino-Vietnamese Sports and Recreation Centre, 270
Siu, Paul C.P., 173

social activities, 238, 239
   see also leisure
social contract, 188
social control, 30
social distance and separation, 285
social dislocation, 258–59
social hierarchy, 168, 172
social organization and structure, 11, 24–27, 151, 177, 179, 270
social services, 241, 267, 271–80, 284, 297
social status, 32
socio-economics, 23, 30, 32
   impact on migration, 151
sojourner argument, 110
sponsorship, 219, 223
status equalization, 262
Staunton, Sir George Thomas, 18
stereotyping of Chinese, 16, 110, 138, 171, 295, 315
   occupational, 85
   see also anti-Orientalism, racism
stock market crash, 217
Strodbeck, Fred, 23
sub-economy, 223
subordination, 28
subsistence, China, 10, 33
suicide, 85, 101, 102, 103
Sumka, Howard J., 307
Sun Yat Sen, Dr., 135, 209
"Sunday schools", 195
suspended animation of immigrants, 30
"sweeping of the tombs", 178
"synthetic", Chinese, 23

Tai Ping Rebellion, 7, 9
"target emigrant", 34
Taoism, 26, 186, 189, 205
"the trinity of following", 31
"Three Big Names", 197

Tianjin Treaty, 7, 12
"tongs", 135
   wars, 171, 208, 209
traditions, Chinese, 13, 23, 30
"triple jeopardy", of women, 246
tourism, 86

UCCC, Union des Chinois du Cambodge au Canada, 275–77, 281–83
"underground enterprise", 198
unemployment, 160, 260
   social and familial effects, 261
urban displacement process, 293, 294, 317
   see also expropriation, gentrification, renewal-displacement process
urbanization, Canada, 160, 166

V-J Day, 144, 145
vertical mobility, 224
Victoria, 202, 203
Victory Loan Drive, 218

"wash-house establishment", 155, 156
Washerwoman's Lagoon, the Marina, 155
Wei Cheng-tung, 34
Wen Chung-I, 35
Westox, S., 16
Wiley, Norbert F., 232
Willmott, William E., 288
"woi", 159, 198
   San Yi Woi (Three Benefits Woi), 200
Woo Yuen-fong, 264
work ethic, Chinese, 26, 27, 39, 151
Wu Zu, 140

Xin Chou Treaty, 9

Yang, Martin M.C., 35
YMCI (Young Men's Christian Institution), Chinese, 86, 94, 99, 190
Yong Zheng, Emperor, 12
"Yuan bao", 187

Zhigongtang, 116, 135, 209
    rivalry with Guomintang, 209
    see also Freemasons
zoning bylaw (No. 6513), 303
Zwingmann, Charles, 264